TELEVISIONARIES

INSIDE THE CHAOS AND INNOVATION
OF THE DIGITAL REVOLUTION

TELEVISIONARIES

INSIDE THE CHAOS AND INNOVATION
OF THE DIGITAL REVOLUTION

MARC TAYER

Published by MediaTech Publishing

Book Design by Monkey C Media.
MonkeyCMedia.com

Printed in the United States of America

ISBN:
978-0-9863845-0-9 (Book)
978-0-9863845-1-6 (e-book)

Library of Congress Control Number: 2014960056

AUTHOR'S NOTE

I never thought I would have the time or patience to write a book, although for many years I believed that this was a story that absolutely had to be told. However, with Netflix and YouTube now in the video limelight, it seemed like time had passed by the significance of the development of digital TV and the story was becoming lost in history. So I started writing and didn't stop.

Although I conducted many interviews to fill in knowledge and memory gaps, I admit this account is primarily from my perspective. I generally refer to my corporate employers in the third person, although when I was directly involved in a specific event or meeting, I often use the first person pronoun "we" or "I." Quotations are mostly not verbatim but are used to capture the essence of what was said.

As we celebrate the twenty-fifth year of the digital television age, it seems appropriate to ponder the underlying technology's impact on the media world and even on society at large. This story comprises four interwoven topical themes:

- Technological innovation within a large corporation, and the difficulty of sustaining such innovation over time

- The politics and intrigue involved in industry adoption of a new technology platform

- The powerful synergy between content and technology, and how the fusion of the two is driving the ongoing evolution of digital TV

- Most importantly, the critical relevance of the people and personalities involved

On this last point, I realize there are many individuals who contributed greatly to the fields of digital TV and Internet video and are not adequately discussed within the scope of my book. For that, I apologize in advance.

■ ■ ■

With all my love to
Wendy and our children—Madeleine, Melanie, and Jason

And with special gratitude and appreciation
to my parents, Joyce and Don Tayer,
for their love, guidance, and support throughout my life

ACKNOWLEDGMENTS

To my many co-workers, customers, and business partners over the years: Many of you recalled the initial years of the digital TV revolution as the most exciting period of your careers. I hope this book helps you reminisce about those good times amid all of your hard work.

I would also like to thank Karla Olson for her superb advice on all aspects of book writing and publishing; Becky Smith and Laurie Gibson for their outstanding editing skills; and the Monkey C Media team for its excellent book design.

CONTENTS

PART THREE

PART FOUR

PROLOGUE

I. The Crossroads of Today

They are the J. D. Rockefellers and Andrew Carnegies of our time, the orcas and great whites of our turbulent oceans of media. Their strategic moves over the next several years, in television and over the broadband Internet, will help determine the outcome of the most epic battle yet for control of America's video households. This time, the challenge is coming not from a new generation of media magnates or from the US government, but rather from a new place altogether: the infinitude of the Internet fused with the Silicon Valley ethos of creative destruction.

These captains of industry have perfected the art of media alchemy, brilliantly harnessing technology in order to expand their gilded empires. They deeply understand how technology and content are bound together, forming two symbiotic sides of an increasingly valuable coin.

- **John Malone**'s Liberty Global is the largest cable operator in Europe, and this former king of US cable is intent on recapturing the domestic market as well. Just as he once led the charge into the digital television age, he now envisions a future dominated by the broadband Internet and those who capitalize on its high-speed pipes.

- **Brian Roberts**, having built Comcast/NBCUniversal into the industry's giant of giants, is wholeheartedly embracing the Internet and trying to buy Time Warner Cable in order to scale up even higher.

- With sheer will and crafty deal making, **Sumner Redstone** has elevated Viacom and CBS into the rarefied heights of television content, alongside long-time rivals Time Warner and Disney.

- **Rupert Murdoch** is using 21st Century Fox to go head-to-head with ESPN in the high-stakes sports TV market, hell-bent on duplicating his success with Fox News. In Europe, he is consolidating his satellite TV assets and would like to expand his content holdings.

- Agile and unpredictable, **Charlie Ergen** continues to stockpile wireless spectrum and acquire technology assets complementing his Dish Network, whose national footprint is behind only Comcast and DirecTV in multi-channel video subscribers.

- No one should underestimate **Chuck Dolan**, a visionary and a gentleman, with his trifecta of Cablevision, AMC Networks, and The Madison Square Garden Company.

The collective net worth of these titans is $50 billion and the aggregate stock market valuation of their companies exceeds a quarter trillion. Some multiplied their pre-existing fortunes during the digital era; others were wholly reliant on digital technology to power up their kingdoms.

But the Internet is now turning everything upside down. Netflix, Amazon, and YouTube are ascending, steamrolling over the tops of cable's broadband pipes with an increasing mass of video content and disruptive business models. Technology leaders Apple, Google, Microsoft, and Sony are all positioning for living room prominence, challenging the long-standing broadband equipment strongholds of Cisco (Scientific Atlanta) and Arris (Motorola).

Will the boundless ambitions of Google, or the creative genius of Apple, without Steve Jobs, be able to topple Comcast, DirecTV, and their tightly wound bundles of content? With AT&T trying to acquire DirecTV, what moves will wireless behemoth Verizon make given the limited reach of its video network? How will consumers find and procure the content they want, anytime and anywhere, at a reasonable price?

To better understand today's complexities, we must first experience the roller-coaster journey that led us to this tipping point.

II. Living in an Analog World

We live in an analog world. The sights we see, the sounds we hear, even the odors we smell, are continuous and direct representations of our real-world experience. The computer era ushered in the trend of translating the analog realm into an intermediary digital language, a binary string of zeros and ones symbolizing the actual phenomena perceived by our brains and senses. But this digital interception of reality is inevitably converted back to the analog domain in order for us humans to exercise our eyes and our ears.

The history of television is rich with technical and creative ingenuity, despite being based on analog technology until the 1990s. Its invention fundamentally changed the world around us, allowing dissemination of visual entertainment and information to our homes and around the globe as never before. Exciting and controversial from its origin, TV resulted from the colliding aspirations of an Idaho potato farmer, a Russian immigrant engineer, and a Belarusian-born American broadcast pioneer.

Philo Farnsworth, the potato farmer, was born in an Indian Creek, Utah, log cabin in 1906, moving to Rigby, Idaho, at age eleven. While daydreaming in his family's fields as a teenager, he conceived of trapping light in a vacuum tube and then scanning it line-by-line with an electron beam. Young Farnsworth sketched out this profound vision for his high school science teacher, showing the conversion of light into electricity, and then back into light at a separate viewing location, a crude but prescient depiction of the medium now known as television.

By the 1920s, various attempts were being made to transmit television pictures by mechanical means. They were based on the 1880s work of German engineer Paul Nipkow, who invented a spinning spiral disk with perforated holes to capture images, and on the brilliant innovations of Scottish engineer John Baird in the mid-1920s. But Philo Farnsworth's original concept was to transmit moving pictures by the delivery of electrons through free space. In 1926, investors gave him $6,000, allowing him to start implementing his invention and to file patents. Moving from Salt Lake City to Los Angeles to San Francisco, Farnsworth finally landed in Philadelphia where he worked for Philco, a company making batteries and radios.

In parallel, Russian immigrant Vladimir Zworykin, a Westinghouse employee, filed a different patent for an electronic television system. His 1929 invention of the kinescope involved using cathode ray tubes to turn electricity back into light at a receiver site. Under the wing of Belarusian immigrant David Sarnoff, the legendary president of RCA, Zworykin moved from Westinghouse in Pittsburgh to the New Jersey labs of RCA.

And so the race was on to develop the first commercial television system. Ultimately, although Farnsworth was the true inventor of electronic TV, Sarnoff had the money and the power, and RCA triumphed despite accusations of stealing Farnsworth's technology.

The first public demonstration of television occurred in 1934 at the Franklin Institute in Philadelphia, based on Farnsworth's patents. In 1936, the BBC began the world's first regular television broadcasts in England. RCA licensed the Farnsworth patents in 1939, and by 1941 the Federal Communications Commission (FCC) established the National

Television System Committee (NTSC), which issued a black-and-white television standard, also named NTSC. Delayed by its immersion in World War II, the United States finally commenced regular broadcasts in 1948.

By the end of 1953, the FCC approved the addition of color to the specification, a major innovation resulting in the NTSC color television standard. For the half-century following adoption of the black-and-white television system, the medium remained one of analog radio waves. Then in the early 1990s, a decade after the onset of the personal computer revolution, television began its migration to digital. This is the story of television's remarkable transition from analog waves to digital bits, and how this sea change impacted the technology and business worlds around it.

■ ■ ■

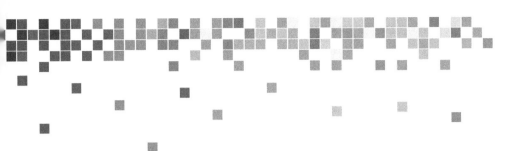

PART ONE
GLORY DAYS

1 FROM CAMBRIDGE TO CALIFORNIA

The field of digital television, as with analog television and computers, had its pioneers and innovators. In the case of digital TV, it started with a group of Massachusetts Institute of Technology (MIT) PhDs working for a mid-sized technology company in the seaside city of San Diego.

Jerry Heller was born in the Bronx and raised in Forest Hills, Queens. He and his two sisters were the offspring of a Manhattan restaurateur and a Pennsylvania coalminer's daughter. In the 1950s, New York's outer boroughs, just beyond the bridges and tunnels of Manhattan, combined an idyllic feel with a post-war optimism. It was at summer camp in the Berkshires of western Massachusetts where Heller became fascinated with ham radio, his introduction to communications technology.

The Heller family had an affinity for baseball, especially for the New York Giants before the storied team's move to San Francisco in

1957. During the 1951 season, the Giants were trailing the Brooklyn Dodgers by 13½ games in the dog days of summer when manager Leo Durocher led them to a miraculous comeback, culminating in one of sports history's most iconic moments. It happened on October 3, during the National League playoffs between the Giants and the Dodgers. Jerry Heller was in his family basement with friends watching a brand new, 12-inch, black-and-white DuMont TV when Giants' outfielder Bobby Thomson hit the "Shot Heard 'Round the World." Down four-to-two in the bottom of the ninth, Thomson's three-run homer clinched the National League pennant for the Giants, leaving an indelible impression on ten-year-old Jerry.

Four decades later, Heller would deliver his own shot heard around the world, announcing a technology breakthrough in the field of television that galvanized corporations and governments in Japan, Europe, the United States, and around the globe.

Heller displayed an exceptional aptitude for science and math from an early age. A standout electrical engineering student at Syracuse University, he received a National Science Foundation fellowship and chose MIT over Stanford University for his graduate studies. At MIT he had to work overtime to catch up with his peers, most of whom had attended the school as undergraduates. By the time he selected Professor Irwin Jacobs, future co-founder and CEO of wireless technology leader Qualcomm, as his thesis adviser, Heller was hitting his academic stride. His thesis was on a groundbreaking aspect of digital communications.[1] But before Heller received his PhD in 1967, Jacobs had already departed for the West Coast, moving to La Jolla as a University of California, San Diego (UCSD) professor.

Upon receiving his doctorate, Heller accepted a job at Jet Propulsion Laboratory (JPL) in Pasadena, a research and development facility run by the California Institute of Technology (Caltech) for the National

Aeronautics and Space Administration (NASA). These were the glory days of NASA, allowing him to work on free-ranging research into digital communications for unmanned spacecraft including the Ranger, the Pioneer, and the Voyager.

At the same time, Heller's former thesis adviser, Irwin Jacobs, at UCSD, and Dr. Andrew Viterbi, a professor at University of California, Los Angeles (UCLA), founded Linkabit Corporation to develop digital communications products for US government agencies. Their third partner in Linkabit was Dr. Leonard Kleinrock, one of the nation's most prominent computer scientists. Kleinrock was a father of computer networking, routing, and the ARPANET, which morphed into the Internet.

Andrew Viterbi received his bachelor's and master's degrees in electrical engineering from MIT. He then moved to California, where he worked at JPL and completed his PhD at the University of Southern California (USC). He left JPL in 1963 for a faculty position at UCLA. In 1967, he invented the Viterbi Algorithm for correcting errors in digital data transmissions. This technique became widely used for deep-space and satellite communications, modems, digital cell phones, and many other digital communications products and applications.

While at UCLA, Viterbi collaborated with Heller, who was still at JPL. Perhaps Heller's most important contribution to space communications as a young engineer was the discovery of the performance of coded digital transmission. He was the first person to validate the power of forward error correction using sophisticated convolutional codes decoded by the Viterbi Algorithm. Until then, the algorithm was considered only a theoretical construct in applied mathematics. But Heller validated it for use in many real-world applications. This area would become critical later in Heller's career at General Instrument, where he would apply digital communications techniques to television signals.

In 1969, Jacobs and Viterbi hired Jerry Heller as Linkabit's first full-time engineer, and Kleinrock disengaged from Linkabit, remaining as a computer science professor at UCLA. But just as Heller was about to purchase a home near UCLA and Viterbi, Jacobs decided to leave UCSD and join Linkabit full-time as well, prompting Heller to move two hours south to San Diego to be at the new company's headquarters. Viterbi later relocated to San Diego as well.

That singular twist of fate is why San Diego became a premier center for digital communications technology, with Linkabit as its fountainhead. The Linkabit engineers delivered on contracts with the Army, NASA, and the Air Force. Significantly, they developed one of the first digital modems with error correction (implemented on an early microcomputer), which was used by the Air Force for transmitting emergency action messages. Another project Heller worked on for NASA in the late 1970s, unknowingly presaging his future, was an early digital video compression system using mathematical transforms.

More than a brilliant engineer, Heller also had a keen eye for new business opportunities. In 1980 Linkabit was acquired by M/A-Com, a large East Coast microwave components company. When the San Diego M/A-Com Linkabit team found out in the early 1980s that Home Box Office (HBO) was seeking proposals for a satellite TV encryption system, Heller visited HBO in New York to find out more about their needs.

HBO had started electronic delivery of programming in the early 1970s using microwave relays, but then made television history on September 30, 1975, by broadcasting via satellite the "Thrilla in Manila," the third and final boxing match between Muhammad Ali and Joe Frazier. This event marked the beginning of the satellite television era, and HBO became the first programming service to continuously deliver its content via satellite. HBO soon became alarmed that an increasing number of homes with satellite dishes were intercepting its programming for free, and so now the company intended to secure its content delivery.

When the HBO technology and operations team of Ed Horowitz, Paul Heimbach, and Bob Zitter met Jerry Heller, they discerned something in him and his San Diego M/A-Com group that the logical choices, the existing cable TV equipment companies such as General Instrument and Scientific Atlanta, lacked: a world-class expertise in the emerging field of digital communications.

Heller also had an uncanny ability to spot and recruit top-notch technical talent. His philosophy toward hiring engineers reflected the Linkabit culture: recruit the smartest people you can find and then figure out what to do with them. On a 1978 recruiting mission to his alma mater, MIT, he met a new PhD candidate named **Woo Paik**.

A native of South Korea, Woo Paik was born to be an engineer. As a toddler he was fascinated with trucks, trains, and railroad tracks. In junior high school he built his first radio, and then moved from crystal to vacuum tube to transistor to ham radio, constantly tinkering, playing, and improving.

Paik obtained his bachelor's and master's degrees in electrical engineering from Seoul National University before applying to several PhD programs in electrical engineering. MIT responded first, with an acceptance, but Paik had recently married and Korea had an obscure law requiring a wife to wait six months before joining her husband overseas. So he enrolled in Seoul's PhD program, living with his bride at his parents' home to save money. This situation proved too difficult, however, and he moved to MIT in Cambridge, Massachusetts in September 1974, with his wife joining him there several months later.

When Heller met Paik at MIT four years later, he was impressed with the younger man's intelligence and expertise in digital communications, inviting him to San Diego to meet the Linkabit team. The New England blizzard of '78 was one for the record books, some calling it the storm of the century. Paik visited San Diego that April, greeted by its perfect climate. Combined with the opportunity to work with renowned digital communications technologists such as Irwin Jacobs, Andrew Viterbi, and Jerry Heller, the job offer was too good to pass up.

Paik's first project was a satellite modem, followed by a spacecraft modem for JPL. Just before Christmas in 1981, Heller called Paik into his office and described a new opportunity with HBO: to encrypt the pay TV company's satellite signals so the rapidly growing base of home dish owners couldn't receive its signals for free. Many other companies were already in the running, and Linkabit was known for digital communications, not television. In fact, Paik's knowledge of TV and video was so rudimentary that he purchased an introductory book on how to fix a color TV, teaching himself the basics of line scanning and signal timing information. Someone within M/A-Com had assembled a competitive analysis document, summarizing the established pay TV security systems of General Instrument, Scientific Atlanta, and others. Heller and Paik knew they had to come up with a novel idea to have a shot at HBO's business.

By the time the two men visited Paul Heimbach again at HBO in New York, Paik had crafted the idea of digitizing the audio and inserting it inside the vertical blanking interval of the video signal.[2] Heller had devised a forward error correction code to allow error-free transmission. They brought in a young M/A-Com engineer and audio expert named Kent Walker to ensure that the digital audio compression scheme resulted in good sound quality. The video was still analog, but the digital audio innovation perhaps served as a precursor to an all-digital future. HBO loved the proposal, intrigued by its digital aspects, but wanted to see some working hardware. On the spot, Heller committed Paik to the seemingly impossible delivery date of April for a working prototype, which Paik and his small team miraculously met. M/A-Com was awarded the HBO contract and found itself suddenly in the entertainment business.

Another one of Heller's exceptional recruits was **Paul Moroney**. Moroney was a gifted high school math and science student in Wenham, Massachusetts, 20 miles north of Cambridge. When he interviewed at MIT, the admissions officer warned him that he had three strikes against him: he was male, he was Caucasian, and he was local. Despite these obstacles, Moroney was accepted by MIT and matriculated in the fall of 1970.

Nine years later, when he was graduating from the school's PhD program, he was interviewed by Linkabit's Jerry Heller on the MIT campus. Impressed with the quality of the MIT alumni who had already gone to work at Linkabit, including Woo Paik, Moroney visited San Diego. He recalls Heller being dressed casually in short sleeves, relaxed and confident with a golden California tan. Heller was impressed by Moroney and offered him a job. Ironically, Moroney had a competing job offer from M/A-Com on the East Coast, but his father, also an engineer, was a M/A-Com employee. Not wanting to join his dad's company, he accepted Heller's offer at Linkabit and moved to San Diego. A month later, M/A-Com acquired Linkabit and the two Moroneys, father and son, were employed by the same company after all, although on opposite coasts.

During his first few years, Moroney worked as a development engineer on various projects including a satellite communications modem for JPL and a military modem for the armed services. Then one day in 1982, Heller called him into his office with a new assignment: to be project engineer for the company's new VideoCipher satellite television encryption contract with HBO.

2 GORILLA IN MANHATTAN

The Wharton School of the University of Pennsylvania was a hotbed of budding capitalists in the mid-1980s. The economy had recovered strongly from the deep recession of 1981–1982 after Fed Chairman Paul Volcker cranked up interest rates to 20 percent in order to halt runaway inflation. Michael Milken and Ivan Boesky reigned over Wall Street, creating financial castles out of junk bonds and arbitrage. Some Wharton graduates would take jobs at General Electric, Hewlett-Packard, and Intel; others would enter health care, consumer product marketing, and real estate. But Goldman Sachs, Morgan Stanley, and McKinsey & Company were the biggest draws, dangling six-figure bait adorned with perceived glamour to the newly minted MBAs.

I was attending Wharton, having worked in the Wall Street financial community between college and graduate school. I didn't want to go back to that world. My summer job in between years at Wharton was with a venture capital firm, and my eventual goal was to return to that area. But this was still a time when successful venture capitalists needed technology and product backgrounds, before the field was overrun with ex-bankers, and I wanted to first gain experience with a technology company developing new products and markets. During my last days at Wharton, when Rick Friedland recruited me into his corporate finance group at General Instrument Corporation, just outside Manhattan, it seemed like a good fit.

General Instrument (GI), a Fortune 500 technology conglomerate, was widely followed by Wall Street under the ticker symbol GRL. The traders and brokers affectionately referred to the company as "the gorilla," more due to the stock's erratic pricing behavior than a creative pronunciation of its trading symbol. GRL was a high beta stock, rapidly climbing up or down depending on which and how many of its seventeen separate businesses were hot or cold at any given time.

Before accepting Friedland's offer, I called a well-known stock analyst at Merrill Lynch who followed GI and asked him what he thought. His recommendation was, "Go for it; GI's an exciting company and there will be big changes, lots of asset sales and acquisitions." By the summer of 1985 I was living back in Manhattan.

There were some other MBAs already working in GI's corporate finance and treasury areas: Dave Robinson, a New Englander who had been on the ski team at Bates College before getting his MBA at Dartmouth's Tuck School; Paul Clough, a Harvard Business School graduate; and Dan Moloney, a University of Michigan engineer with an MBA from the University of Chicago. John Burke, an Ohio State alumnus, also joined the corporate office at the same time. The basic idea of Rick Friedland's program for these young, eager MBAs was for them to obtain a bird's-eye view of the company as a whole, and then in two or three years get placed at one of the operating divisions.

The three MBAs who preceded me, Robinson, Clough, and Moloney, all moved to suburban Philadelphia the next year to join the Jerrold Division, the leading broadband equipment supplier to the cable industry. Friedland got a big promotion within the corporate finance organization, and I moved into the Manhattan headquarters office for a strategic planning role, perfect for me because I had become much more interested in strategy and marketing than finance. Plus my Manhattan apartment was a mere ten-minute walk from GI's corporate headquarters on the forty-fifth floor of the GM Building, situated on the southeast corner of Central Park at Fifth Avenue and 59th Street. In 1987, Dan Sutorius, a classmate at Wharton, joined the strategic planning group as well. We helped the top corporate officers with whatever they needed, including special projects with operating divisions, and mergers, acquisitions, and divestitures.

In the dog days of summer, 1986, an intriguing new project came across my desk: GI's chairman and CEO, Frank Hickey, was proposing to buy M/A-Com's Cable Home Communications group. Hickey had wanted to team up with Frank Drendel, M/A-Com's top cable TV executive, for years. It was a perfect strategic fit, the numbers looked good, and everyone was in favor of doing the deal. When GI acquired the business for $220 million in September 1986, it suddenly felt like a much more exciting company.

Of the four business units acquired as M/A-Com Cable Home Communications Corp., the one that especially intrigued me was based in San Diego, the upstart VideoCipher Division. This business had emerged from the Linkabit Corporation of Irwin Jacobs, Andrew Viterbi, and Jerry Heller, inheriting a deep strain of its technical DNA. After HBO and Showtime adopted this division's VideoCipher pay TV satellite encryption system, many of the other leading programmers followed suit, and the business was growing by leaps and bounds.

I had only been to San Diego once before, but having grown up in the San Francisco Bay Area, I liked the idea of getting back to the West Coast. So when Ken Kinsman, the VideoCipher Division's head of operations, asked me if I could come out there and help them develop a service and repair plan for their new satellite TV descrambler boxes, a product line ramping up into high-volume manufacturing, I jumped at the opportunity. A few months later, I was offered a job transfer from New York to San Diego as manager of strategic planning.

As any current or former resident knows, there is no place quite like Manhattan, never a dull moment in "the city that never sleeps." New York City in the 1980s was the undisputed global financial center, with many corporate headquarters as well, and arts and culture rivaling that of the world's greatest cities. At night, restaurants and music venues were in abundance, and when the bars closed at 4:00 a.m., underground nightclubs opened their doors. Inside General Instrument's headquarters, high above Central Park, was a staid and formal corporate environment; outside, the sidewalks teemed with activity and the streets were filled with vehicles bobbing, weaving, and incessantly honking.

The San Diego of 1987 was the exact opposite. Still a laid-back town without traffic, the city had grown well beyond its Navy and tourism roots, becoming a mecca for communications technology and a biotech hub. Outdoors, San Diego epitomized the relaxed California lifestyle, an ever-present sun beaming down on joggers and bikers, and surfboards mounted atop cars cruising toward its seventy-mile string of beaches. But inside GI's VideoCipher Division, a few miles east of La Jolla, the pace was frenetic; employees rushed through the hallways, conversations echoed through the corridors, and meeting rooms were jam-packed.

3 A NEW LIFE IN A FAST LANE

Growing rapidly from nothing to hundreds of millions of dollars in annualized revenue presents a number of challenges, although it's certainly a nice problem to have. The VideoCipher Division was run by its president, Larry Dunham, as well as Jerry Heller (technology and strategy), Ken Kinsman (sales/marketing and operations), and another MIT PhD, Mark Medress (business development). Every department, from operations to engineering, from sales and marketing to finance and human resources, was bursting at the seams. At satellite uplink sites throughout the country, one cable programmer after another—HBO, Showtime, Disney, ESPN, Playboy, MTV, USA, Discovery—was installing the VideoCipher equipment in order to secure and encrypt their TV signals.

Turner Broadcasting was one of the last major programmers to encrypt its satellite TV signals of CNN, Headline News, and superstation

WTBS. Ted Turner and his team didn't see the benefit; in fact, they believed scrambling would reduce their viewing audience and therefore ad revenue. But John Malone, CEO of cable giant TCI, wanted all the popular channels encrypted, furious that the unencrypted cable channels, being received free of charge by satellite dish owners and commercial establishments such as bars, were undermining his business.

Malone invited TCI COO J. C. Sparkman, along with Ted Turner and GI executives Frank Drendel and Ken Kinsman, aboard his yacht off the coast of New England. Sparkman, known as one of the industry's toughest negotiators, first got Ted Turner to concede that TCI had as low of a price for carrying Turner's content as any other cable operator. Then, to make his point, Sparkman demanded free access to the content, since "free" was effectively what the satellite TV homes and bars were getting, and he wanted the same deal. The discussion went dead silent until Drendel cracked a joke to break the tension. Turner relented, agreeing to secure his content, and soon CNN and his other channels joined the others, using GI's products to encrypt and deliver their television content simultaneously to cable headends and home satellite dish owners, with GI boxes required at every site to decrypt the signals.

At the same time as I arrived in San Diego in 1987, Ken Kinsman also hired Esther Rodriguez, one of the few women executives in the company, to help develop new consumer markets. Prior to GI, Rodriguez had been a pioneer in the nascent pay-per-view (PPV) business at San Diego–based Oak Communications. That was a far cry from her origins in Cuba, which she had departed in 1964 with her husband and two-year-old daughter after the family's cattle ranch and sugar plantation were confiscated by Fidel Castro.

Like GI, Oak believed in the virtuous circle of content driving technology, and technology, in turn, driving content. Oak purchased the ONTV UHF subscription television franchises in Chicago, Dallas,

Miami, and Phoenix from Jerry Perenchio, future owner and CEO of Univision. At Oak, Rodriguez had helped deliver some major PPV events, including the 1981 "Showdown" between Sugar Ray Leonard and Thomas Hearns (with promoter Bob Aram), the Larry Holmes versus Gerry Cooney fight in 1982 (promoted by Don King), early PPV concerts by The Rolling Stones and The Who, and *Sophisticated Ladies*, the Broadway show based on Duke Ellington's music.

Kinsman, Rodriguez, and I established a new pay-per-view venture with CableData,[1] a company run by Maggie Wilderotter, and an ideal partner due to its role as the cable industry's leading billing services provider. There were already various PPV content providers serving the home dish market, including Viewer's Choice, Request TV, and TVN, selling individual movies and concerts as well as boxing and wrestling events. Our joint venture, the Satellite Video Center (SVC), was the satellite TV industry's first PPV fulfillment facility: electronically authorizing subscribers through GI's software and computer center in San Diego, automatically collecting purchase information from the subscribers' boxes, sending out bills to consumers for the content they purchased, and distributing proceeds to the program rights owners, keeping a small cut for ourselves.

Because virtually the entire domestic television content community used GI's satellite TV encryption technology, the firm had 100 percent market share of the corresponding products on the high-volume decryption side. Business was booming and profits were soaring. But GI was a widely followed public company, and there was never-ending pressure from Wall Street to show higher and higher profits, quarter after quarter. With some other units of GI experiencing cyclical downturns, the corporate finger pointed to Larry Dunham, president of the VideoCipher Division in San Diego, to offset the downturns with even higher profits. The quickest and easiest way to achieve this financial boost was by raising product prices, achievable due to the company's market control, and by reducing manufacturing costs, facilitated by the strong growth of the satellite TV market.

Boosting corporate profits by increasing consumer prices, however, not only raised the political ire of the rest of the industry but attracted the scrutiny of the US Justice Department. Its legal pursuit of Microsoft and the Windows monopoly was still a couple years in the future, and GI San Diego was a ripe target. It was unheard of for the price of a consumer electronics product to increase; TV sets and video cassette recorders (VCRs) were subject to vicious price wars and razor-thin profit margins. The Japanese electronics companies were progressively taking over the market, and the remaining American and European ones were hanging on for dear life.

As the Justice Department sifted through GI's voluminous documents, the company's most concerning potential outcome was the government declaring its conditional access and encryption security system to be an official technology standard, a "de jure" standard, as distinct from its pre-existing status as a "de facto" (market-based) standard. The VideoCipher encryption system was protecting the entertainment industry's collective television content, acting as the technical guardian of billions of dollars of annual revenue. It was GI San Diego's reason for being, the foundation of its market position. Government-administered standardization would have meant that any qualified competitor could utilize GI's specifications to enter the market, upending the company's valuable franchise and profit machine.

Surprisingly, after a prolonged investigation, the Justice Department issued its ruling: GI's VideoCipher business was a "legal monopoly." In the Justice Department's opinion, the market was working and consumers were not being damaged. The VideoCipher descrambler module, containing the core pay TV security technology, was being sold to multiple satellite receiver licensees, including EchoStar, Chaparral, Toshiba, and Uniden, and these companies were selling competitive Integrated Receiver Descramblers (IRDs) to consumers. In addition, GI had cleverly established a second source for its descrambler module at Channel Master in North Carolina. In reality, GI manufactured Channel Master's descrambler module for them, with the latter company's role limited to "seeding" the module with a unique decryption key before shipment to other IRD manufacturers.

In addition, there was a legitimate industry-wide concern, which GI stoked effectively, that if the security technology were standardized by the government, enabling multiple sources of chips and software, then no single company could be held accountable for maintaining the integrity of the system. No one would be on the hook to fix it in the event of a security breach. If the television industry's profitability were destroyed by an "open" security system, perhaps the content companies would resort to litigation against the government, having no one else to point their fingers at. Amidst this confusion and uncertainty, the Justice Department's favorable verdict allowed the GI staff to breathe a huge collective sigh of relief.

4 THE DAWN OF DIGITAL

With its dominant US position in satellite TV equipment, GI's San Diego business unit was primed for aggressive market expansion. It sought first to expand into Europe and Japan, markets which were years behind the United States in multi-channel pay TV. We were also assessing a potential new market developing in the area of high definition television (HDTV), with a wary eye on NHK, Japan's national broadcasting company, and its renowned MUSE Hi-Vision high definition television system. Technologists at Philips, Sarnoff, and MIT were also working on

HDTV technology. But in the halls and labs of GI San Diego, there was something more exciting in the air: a sense that big, unknown changes were in store for the pay television business, with its cowboyish cable entrepreneurs and giant satellite dishes.

The beginning is often the most exciting part of the process when it comes to major innovations. The motivating concept is fresh, unencumbered by the many compromises that turn an idea into a viable product. The birth of digital TV fit this description.

Jerry Heller's initial philosophy was that GI would provide the conditional access and encryption system for whichever HDTV system emerged as the winner, using the company's unique security and conditional access technology to protect the high-value content. But when he tasked Woo Paik with analyzing the various HDTV solutions under development, Paik concluded that he didn't like any of them. They all used some combination of analog video and digital audio, something GI had already done years earlier with its VideoCipher technology.

NHK's MUSE HDTV system, the front-runner, appeared to be particularly problematic for GI. NHK had been conducting research into high definition television since the early 1970s. Its MUSE system was intended for satellite broadcasting. It used analog transmission and 1125 lines of video, more than twice the vertical and horizontal resolution of the existing NTSC standard definition television system used in the United States, Japan, and elsewhere. While people marveled at the beautiful high definition pictures enabled by MUSE, GI's VideoCipher group perceived it as a significant threat to its core business, primarily because of the large bandwidth required for transmitting a MUSE signal. For satellite TV, this extensive spectrum requirement would force consumer dish sizes to grow even larger in order to receive the signals, perhaps doubling the diameter for the existing US C-band (large dish) satellite TV market. GI had recently formulated plans to reduce the C-band dish size down from three meters to two meters, presumably helping its consumer satellite business to grow. MUSE would push dish size in the opposite direction.

Heller, sensing an opportunity, sprang the following unexpected question on Paik: "Why don't we develop our own HDTV solution? Maybe we can do better." Never afraid of a big challenge, Paik didn't blink. Then Heller introduced him to a young, recently hired video engineer, merely saying: "Woo, meet **Ed Krause**, he might be able to help you."

Ed Krause's pensive, unassuming manner caused people to initially underestimate his technical ingenuity. But those who got to know him respected the way that his thoughtful and intelligent demeanor masked a fiercely competitive instinct. After Krause obtained his bachelor's degree in electrical engineering from the University of New Brunswick in Canada, one of his professors recommended that he apply to MIT for a graduate school fellowship. Arriving at MIT in the fall of 1982, one of his early tasks was getting assigned to a faculty advisor, and in the career-making happenstance of his life, he was linked to Professor Bill Schreiber, an image processing expert.

Krause soon became a research assistant for Dr. Schreiber and his small video group. But Schreiber was hatching a far more exalted plan, drawing on his previous background working for Sylvania and Technicolor in the television and movie field. Incensed that American television brands were being sold off to foreign competitors, and obsessed with countering Japan's huge lead in high definition television, Schreiber formed MIT's Center for Advanced Television Studies (CATS), raising research funding from major corporations including General Instrument. While Schreiber was not a believer in an all-digital approach, instead favoring some form of hybrid analog/digital method, his lofty goal nonetheless was to surpass Japan's HDTV technology.

Krause's PhD dissertation was on the prediction of motion within a television signal, an area that would become crucial to advanced digital video compression techniques. Upon receiving his doctorate in 1987, he was introduced to GI through Schreiber's CATS connections, accepting a job offer in San Diego. Initially Krause researched the still-esoteric area of high definition television, continuing his work from MIT in an unstructured context. Then, in early 1988, Jerry Heller, having a strong intuition that all-digital HDTV was the way to go, assigned Woo Paik to establish a new R&D group focused on advanced technology. Ed Krause was his ace in the hole.

Heller and Paik fundamentally didn't believe that the analog or hybrid analog/digital approaches were viable long-term solutions. Over the next couple years, Krause's video compression algorithms continued to show dramatic improvements in the lab, reaching a point where Heller, Paik, and Krause collectively saw the writing on the wall: the future of HDTV, and of television in general, would be digital. And it wasn't a long-term pipe dream; Krause and Paik had sufficiently advanced the state-of-the-art such that the timing appeared imminent.

Vincent Liu, another brilliant engineer with a PhD from Caltech, joined the group. The small team forged ahead, day after day, making steady and impressive progress, forming the technical core and foundation of what would become one of the most important advances in television technology history: a way to make digital HDTV a reality.

Before long, another lightbulb went off in Heller and Paik's digitally tuned brain cells, still firing from their days at MIT and Linkabit. If GI's technology could enable digital HDTV, then it could also allow multiple channels of digital NTSC, or "standard definition" television (SDTV).

Dating back to the middle of the twentieth century, the three primary television systems used throughout the world were called NTSC (North America, Japan, South Korea), PAL (Europe, China, India), and

SECAM (France, Russia), each consisting of 525 or 625 lines of video. Since an HDTV signal would require up to five times the bandwidth of an SDTV signal, it follows that for every digital HDTV channel, up to five digital SDTV channels could be carried instead. Perhaps ten or more digital signals could fit within a cable channel or satellite transponder. Digital SDTV would not have the same picture quality as HDTV, but it could dramatically alter the economics of the television business, leading to many more channels and genres, not to mention various other benefits of digitization. In fact, digital SDTV could be the near-term business opportunity, the steak to HDTV's sizzle. Consumers wouldn't even need to purchase a new TV set. New digital satellite and cable boxes would process and decode the bits, and then, using digital-to-analog conversion, translate them back to a standard NTSC signal in the home for viewing on subscribers' existing TV sets.

During 1989, I was practically commuting from San Diego to Tokyo with Lee Peterson and Vessi Smolin, establishing a joint venture with C. Itoh (Itochu) and Toshiba called Japan VideoCipher Corporation (JVCC). Our plan was to establish an operations and satellite receiver authorization center in Tokyo, similar to what we operated in San Diego on behalf of the cable programming channels, and to bring in Japanese content providers to sell pay TV services to cable headends and satellite consumers throughout Japan.

In the late summer, I returned to my San Diego office, jet-lagged from another trip to Japan, and was cornered by division president Larry Dunham and my boss at the time, the VP of Business Development, Mark Medress. Their message was: "You have a new job; we'd like you to be the core team leader for a new project. Woo Paik and Ed Krause have made tremendous progress developing digital TV technology in the lab. It's time to bring it out of the lab. We need you to define the product and market opportunity, and help turn this into a business.

We are also assigning Paul Moroney to the project. He will be the lead systems engineer."

Excited but overwhelmed, and without yet understanding the enormity of the task ahead, I knew instinctively I had just been presented with the challenge of a lifetime. At home that night I tried to explain my new role to my fiancée, Wendy, summarizing it as: "It's a start-up within the company to develop a whole new type of TV system. I don't know where it's going but it sounds like a tremendous opportunity."

From Jerry Heller's perspective, migrating the television world to digital was a no-brainer. It was so obvious and intuitive to him that when someone would ask "Why digital?" he would respond in shorthand, almost dismissively, with "There are a million reasons to go digital." Soon we were all on the same page, articulating the primary benefits of digital TV:

- Greatly expanded channel capacity for satellite and cable, with up to ten times the number of television channels relative to analog transmission

- Unlike analog television, no signal degradation with distance

- Smaller dish sizes for existing C-band satellite TV consumers

- A viable small-dish high-power direct broadcast satellite (DBS) service that could effectively compete with cable

- Better signal security since the entire picture and sound could be digitally encrypted

- Ability to store, process, and manipulate the digital signal for to-be-determined applications

- A logical path to digital HDTV

Digital video compression had already been a research area for many years at Bell Labs and a few universities. But there had been no commercial success except for a small corporate videoconferencing market in the 1980s, using products from Compression Labs (CLI) and PictureTel. However, the cost of these early videoconferencing systems was very high, the picture quality was poor, with jerky images and annoying delays, and the usage cost per hour was prohibitive.

Also, in the late 1980s, ABC News was using a simple form of video compression to transmit programming between New York and Washington over a dedicated DS3 fiber link.[1] DS3, however, used a 45 Mbps data rate, which would occupy more bandwidth than an analog television channel over either satellite or cable. As with videoconferencing, the video compression algorithms used for this application were primitive compared to what was being developed in GI's San Diego labs. Furthermore, the compression technology was symmetric, meaning very expensive equipment on both sides of the link, and therefore irrelevant to GI's ambitious goal of targeting consumer television markets.

Heller's confidence in the inevitability of digital television to the home was surely inspired by his background in digital communications theory, dating back to his trailblazing work at MIT and Linkabit. So when he saw the breakthroughs in video compression being achieved by Woo Paik's advanced technology group, Heller came to the realization that GI was perhaps the only company in the world with the in-house expertise to put it all together into an integrated end-to-end system.

5 DigiCipher

GI San Diego's tech culture was heavily oriented toward systems engineering, a mind-set quite different from organizations focused on standalone products. With a systems approach, a company can't simply develop a product in isolation. Instead, an overarching architectural design must first be conceived. Then, the actual products are derived from the system, in accordance with communications protocols and techniques specified by the system designer. If a company successfully establishes a system in the market, that company will have gained control of a new technical ecosystem, giving it an enormous competitive advantage with respect to individual products.

Along the lines of Jerry Heller's vision, there were three essential technologies for development of a complete digital television communications system:

- digital video compression

- digital transmission

- conditional access and encryption

Other key areas, such as electronic program guides, would come later. But by being the first company to develop and integrate these three critical elements into a unified system, GI could become the world leader in huge new markets.

The elusive missing piece at the time was the ability to intelligently compress a digitized video signal such that only about 1 percent of the original bits needed to be sent through a communications channel while maintaining excellent video quality. The key to digital video compression lies in two distinct areas: the statistical redundancies inherent in typical video; and the exploitation of certain properties of the human visual system (HVS), the physiological process by which images are perceived by our brains in collaboration with our eyes.

Although the retina is located in the eye, it is an integral part of our central nervous system. The retina's nerve cells create natural pixels (picture elements) from external images, which are then routed to and processed by the central visual pathways of the brain. Starting in the 1950s, Dr. David Hubel and Dr. Torsten Wiesel worked toward the discovery, primarily at Johns Hopkins University and Harvard Medical

School, that the brain's visual cortex breaks down and then reconstructs the details of an image. It does not simply repeat moving images as they are scanned by the brain. Hubel and Wiesel explored how the brain assembles images from the eye using computer-like information processing, including detection of edges, motion, depth, and color. For their groundbreaking work, the two men shared the 1981 Nobel Prize in Physiology or Medicine.[1]

A rapidly moving image, such as a TV signal, with its fifty or sixty distinct pictures per second, contains a great deal of redundant information relating to motion, color, edges, texture, and detail. In this context, "redundant" means that the human visual system doesn't really need this information in order for an equivalent sequence of pictures to be recreated. With digital video compression, the moving TV images are mathematically transformed into a digital matrix, and ultimately into a stream of bits, just like the zeros and ones of the computer world. The ultimate task for the video compression engineers is to devise sufficiently ingenious mathematical algorithms such that the vast majority of digital information, representing the moving pictures, can literally be thrown away, with minimal perceived loss in picture quality.

In order for GI's digital television application to succeed, the necessity of discarding 99 percent of the digital video bits had everything to do with the technical concept of bandwidth. Bandwidth is the difference between the lowest and highest frequencies in a chunk of communications spectrum. For example, in a cable TV system, channel 39 is defined to range from 313.25 MHz to 319.25 MHz.[2] Similarly, channel 19 in the UHF band for over-the-air television broadcasting is defined as the range of frequencies from 500 MHz to 506 MHz. Note that in both cases the bandwidth, the span from the lowest to the highest frequency, is 6 MHz. Therefore, a cable or over-the-air broadcast "channel" in the United States is defined to have 6 MHz in bandwidth.

The immense challenge for GI was to compress a digital HDTV signal to such an extent that it could fit within the limited bandwidth of a 6 MHz broadcast channel, or to fit two such digital HDTV signals in a 6 MHz cable channel.

To get an idea of how much video compression is required for this achievement, consider that a pure "uncompressed" digitized HDTV signal would take up to 50 cable channels, a total of 300 MHz of bandwidth. That is a completely impractical proposition since it amounts to a third or a half of the entire bandwidth of a cable system. Squeezing one or two digital HDTV channels into a single 6 MHz channel, while preserving stellar video quality, was a feat deemed impossible at the time.

The second essential technology for developing a complete digital TV system was digital transmission. That was in fact the expertise Jerry Heller, Woo Paik, and Paul Moroney had developed at MIT, Linkabit, and now GI. The basic challenge is to send as much data (digital information) as possible through a communications channel, such as a 6 MHz chunk of broadcast spectrum.

Claude Shannon, a University of Michigan and MIT-educated Bell Labs researcher, was one of the leading minds of the twentieth century and the founding father of the field of information theory. In the late 1940s, Shannon theorized that any kind of data, whether video, sound, or text, could be converted into digital information (strings of zeros and ones) and transmitted through space. However, there is a limit, the "Shannon Limit," to the amount of such information that can be sent through a channel.[3] The earlier work by Andrew Viterbi, Irwin Jacobs, and Jerry Heller at Linkabit, and the developments now taking place at GI by Heller, Moroney, and Paik, would all be built upon Shannon's foundational theories.

The third essential item for GI's end-to-end digital TV system was the conditional access and encryption technology. This was already a core competency of GI. In the analog satellite TV business, it was the foundation of the company's legacy VideoCipher products. This security subsystem was what allowed HBO, Showtime, and the other leading content providers to get paid for their content. All GI had to do was adapt its security technology to the new concept of an all-digital television signal.

We needed a name for our end-to-end digital television system. "VideoCipher" already had significant value and mystique as a brand, and "cipher" carried a high-tech connotation for what was still a fairly exotic security technology. So we decided to carry the brand forward into the digital realm, naming our new system "DigiCipher."

6 GETTING ORGANIZED

On the business side, we were in a hurry to devise a plan but everyone seemed to have a different idea of the path it would take. What market would we address first? Who would be our initial customer(s)? Why would they want it? How would we handle the HDTV incompatibility problem (i.e., the fact that no TV set in the country could process or display an HD signal)? What would our products be, and what features and capabilities would they have? How could we keep it under wraps, so as to not alert competitors, but still get market and customer inputs? Should we conduct consumer focus groups, since consumers had not been exposed to digital video before and no one knew how they might react?

We got a few important things right on the market opportunity side. We believed from the onset that US cable would be the biggest opportunity since there were already 50 million subscribers, growing by a couple million cable homes per year. We thought that market entry into the big dish C-band Television Receive Only (TVRO) satellite market would be easier, due to our central market position and because these subscribers were high-end video enthusiasts hungry for any and all new content. But this market only had about 2.5 million subscribers, growing by a few hundred thousand homes per year. We felt that digital technology would be the impetus to get a strong Ku-band (small dish) satellite TV business off the ground, and we were hopeful that someone would come up with the billion dollars necessary to make this happen. We characterized the HDTV market as "strategic, maybe this century, with a financial payoff next century," a shorthand way of saying it would take at least ten years for the HDTV market to take off. And we had a hunch, without much market data, that the international potential, especially in Europe and Japan, would eventually be huge.

To capture this market potential, we had to move quickly on multiple engineering fronts:

- Modifying our computer simulation to reflect the most recent inventions in our video compression technology. Ed Krause and his cohorts had recently devised some novel compression algorithms, but the computer simulations of the algorithms could only handle three to five seconds of video. While these simulations were indicative of the possible video quality, to be sure we needed longer segments of a broad variety of compressed content to be seen by many viewers, including both video experts and ordinary consumers. The problem was that it took many hours of processing time on state-of-the-art Sun Microsystems computers, programmed with the video compression algorithms, just to get one second of viewable compressed video.

- Developing a real-time hardware prototype containing the standard definition (SDTV) system (encoder and decoder). This hardware would not only allow us to view unlimited segments of compressed content, but also help convince potential customers that our technology claims were valid. Woo Paik was assigned this task with his Advanced Technology team, enabling Paul Moroney and the dozens of existing and to-be-hired engineers to start developing the real "productized" system intended for the market. Paik was given a one-year time frame, until late 1990, for completing the hardware prototype, the shortest period we deemed feasible.

- Developing an HDTV prototype. Woo Paik committed to completing this task within two years, allowing one or two HD channels per cable channel, or one HDTV channel per UHF/VHF terrestrial broadcast channel. We thought that if the HDTV prototype worked, we might consider submitting it to the FCC for the US terrestrial broadcast standard, although this was a low priority at the time. We knew the digital SDTV system was where the big financial payoff would be, at least for the next several years, so that project was the highest priority.

This challenging set of tasks required us to recruit qualified engineers as quickly as possible. Fortunately, we had some top-notch talent in house already. Paul Moroney had already embraced the critical role of lead systems engineer. He needed to understand all aspects of the system —hardware, software, encoder, decoder, chips, security, video, audio, transmission, packetization—and make sure it all worked together seamlessly. He handled this daunting role with confidence, skill, poise, and endlessly long work days. As we made progress and chipped away toward success, we felt like we were undertaking our own Manhattan Project, with Moroney as our J. Robert Oppenheimer.

Other notable engineers were selected as team leaders. Ly Tran, who had come to GI through the most circuitous and unlikely route imaginable, was selected to head the massive digital video encoder engineering activity. Fifteen years earlier, on April 30, 1975, Tran had evacuated from Vietnam on a Japanese fishing boat during the chaotic fall of Saigon. A high school math teacher from a poor Vietnamese family, he wanted to pursue the dream of a better life elsewhere, far away from the Communists who were taking over his country. When the fishing boat reached international waters, Tran and thousands of other refugees were switched to a US Navy ship. From the US military base in Subic Bay, Philippines, he was then flown to Guam and finally America, arriving at the Army camp in Fort Chaffee, Arkansas. A few months later he received a scholarship to Oklahoma State, where he received his BA in electrical engineering in 1978. After joining Texas Instruments in Houston, he moved to San Diego in 1982 where he worked for Oak Communications. Woo Paik recruited him to M/A-Com Linkabit in 1983 to work on the original HBO VideoCipher project.

Tran had a relentless work ethic and the ability to organize and lead a major engineering project. Quite simply, he did whatever it took to get a product to market. The unavoidable downside was that the engineers working under him experienced far more stress than they had bargained for. From Tran's point of view, there was a world to conquer, necessitating his "take no prisoners" approach. GI's future digital customers like PrimeStar and HBO came to value Tran's drive and character greatly.

Kent Walker, a talented radio frequency and audio systems engineer, was the same Linkabit alumnus who had helped Heller and Paik with the digital audio portion of the original VideoCipher system. He was assigned to lead the digital modem activity as well as the satellite receivers. Annie Chen was in charge of the system software. Steve Anderson had system integration and testing. And Bob Gilberg, our in-house semiconductor expert, took on the formidable challenge of developing several custom, low-cost, integrated circuits for the digital boxes. With no technical standards to work from and no merchant semiconductor companies yet providing these devices, designing our own chips was the only path toward developing a viable, cost-effective, high-volume product:

the digital set-top boxes. The design for these boxes would be passed on to Peter Polgar's manufacturing operation.

Each team leader—of systems engineering, software, encoding, decoding, chips, integration, and testing—had to come up with the additional engineers required to complete their individual parts of the DigiCipher digital TV system.

The project was expanding rapidly but we had no customer commitments. At one point, the division's head of operations, Ken Kinsman, caught me in the hall to get an update, asking: "You guys are hiring like crazy and spending tons of money; who's going to be your first customer?" Since we were nowhere near winning a customer yet, I attempted to deflect his question with a response reflecting our outsize ambitions: "We're trying to set an entire industry standard for digital TV. The customers will come." He retorted with "Go get a customer," before hustling away. He knew we would soon get hit hard by corporate for our dramatically rising spending levels if we didn't line up a customer to substantiate market demand.

As the development of the initial DigiCipher system progressed, it became clear that we had several unique video compression algorithms. Time to market was critical, but we also knew we needed to develop an intellectual property portfolio. Matt Miller, GI's corporate VP of Technology, knew how easy it was for companies to let their inventions slip away. He was instrumental in pushing us toward patent applications. Miller had been an early champion of San Diego's digital technology, even seeding it initially with a corporate R&D fund under his control. The son of a scientist who had worked on the actual Manhattan Project during World War II, Miller was armed with a bachelor's degree from Harvard and a PhD from Princeton, both in physics. He could go head-to-head technically with the MIT PhDs in San Diego. Miller remained a strong proponent of the company's digital activity over the next few years.

One of the key inventions that needed protection involved optimized methods for compressing "interlaced" television signals. Interlace technology is a type of video scanning and display technique, used since the origins of television. The odd and even lines of a TV signal are alternatively captured and displayed 60 times a second (60 Hz) in the United States and Japan, and 50 times a second (50 Hz) in Europe. In the United States, the analog NTSC standard, dating back to 1941, uses 525 horizontal lines of video to fill up a TV screen. In today's 1080i ("i" for interlace) HDTV method, there are 1080 lines of video. With interlace, the odd lines (1, 3, 5, 7, 9…) are first scanned, and then during the next sixtieth of a second, the even lines (2, 4, 6, 8, 10…) are scanned.

Another innovation involved "film mode." Movies and a large amount of TV content were originally captured by film cameras rather than video cameras. GI had devised a way to detect the presence of film material and then eliminate redundant frames. This related to a process called "3:2 pull-down," in which the 24 frame per second film image was converted, for TV delivery, to 60 fields per second.

Yet another patentable invention allowed multiple digital TV services to share a common bit stream, a technique GI called multiple channels per carrier (MCPC). One aggregate bit stream represented multiple TV channels, and then that bit stream was modulated and transmitted on a single radio frequency carrier over cable, satellite, or terrestrial broadcast media. By "statistically multiplexing" the various signals together, at any given time we could allocate more bits to the channels that had more complex pictures (e.g., lots of detail), while devoting fewer bits to the services temporarily exhibiting simple pictures (e.g., no motion).

There were many other advances: field vs. frame processing; subband coding for motion compensation; progressive refresh of superblocks; a new way of quantizing transform coefficients; an innovative "adaptive prediction mode." The ideas kept flowing, and the list of inventions kept growing. Most important, the computer-simulated compressed pictures were improving by the day.

A critical goal was to ensure that this complex array of compression algorithms would result in relatively low complexity on the decoder side, helping to keep the cost of consumer hardware as low as possible. The encoder could be very complex because it would be a low-volume product and could therefore sustain a relatively high price. But the decoder had to be as simple as possible in order to minimize the recurring manufacturing cost of the high-volume consumer digital set-top boxes. This highly asymmetric design, a complex encoder matched to a simple decoder, was an important technical achievement by itself.

Painfully aware that we were undertaking too much by ourselves, we made an early attempt to supplement our engineering resources by acquiring a digital communications company down the street from us in San Diego. Comstream was a digital modem start-up founded by former Linkabit engineers Dr. Itzhak Gurantz and Steve Blake. Gurantz had received his undergraduate and master's degrees in electrical engineering from Israel's Technion, and his PhD from U.C. Berkeley. Blake was another MIT graduate.

Jerry Heller knew Gurantz to be a world-class digital communications engineer, and Larry Dunham, our division president, completely trusted Heller's opinion, so Steve Blake and I wrote a joint business plan proposing that GI acquire Comstream for $35 million. Comstream had a growing business for digital data products with some big customers such as Reuters. We also knew that if we didn't buy Comstream, they would be discovered by future competitors in the digital TV market, and would help any such companies get to market more quickly. But mostly we wanted their expertise as well as the instant expansion of engineers relevant to our project. However, when Dunham presented the plan to Frank Hickey and the other top executives at GI's New York headquarters, they effectively vetoed the deal, and we were back to the daunting challenge of developing the entire system by ourselves.

As if the task of developing a complete digital TV system in-house wasn't sufficiently vast, there were two other strategic technologies we knew were needed: a digital video recorder, with the ability to store and retrieve the digital video signals from a disk drive; and an electronic program guide and navigation system for users to access the expanded library of content. While Jerry Heller articulated an early conception of the digital video recorder, neither of these critical technologies would be taken on by GI, creating opportunities for other companies to capitalize on them.

7 PIRACY AND CRYPTOMANIA

A dark cloud hovered ominously over General Instrument's digital aspirations. Piracy, the act of hacking the security systems protecting pay TV signals in order to get free service, had been around for many years in the cable TV business. Television pirates, the precursors of today's Internet hackers and cyber warriors, found the cable scrambling systems relatively simple to defeat. In fact, these early systems were intended more to inhibit than to prohibit tampering.

In 1986, GI introduced the VideoCipher II conditional access and encryption system, allowing content providers to secure their analog satellite TV signals. It was the latest incarnation of an ancient art. Secret writing, and its future cousins—ciphers, encryption, and cryptography—have evolved over thousands of years.[1] Of course, code breakers have been around as long as code makers. Herodotus, credited with being perhaps the world's first historian, claimed that it was secret writing in the fifth century BC that saved the independent Greek states from being conquered by the Persians. In the sixteenth century, Mary Queen of Scots was executed by her cousin, Queen Elizabeth I, after England's spymaster deciphered

Mary's secret written correspondence with her alleged co-conspirators to seize the crown. At the onset of World War II, Polish mathematician Marian Rejewski broke the code used by Nazi Germany's Enigma encryption machines. The Poles passed the secrets to their British allies, Alan Turing and his fellow cryptologists at Bletchley Park in England, facilitating their efforts to intercept strategic Nazi communications, the "Ultra" intelligence data, helping to defeat Hitler.[2]

GI all but ensured the attention of code breakers by famously, and foolishly, claiming the VideoCipher II system was unbreakable. The hacker underground took this statement as an intellectual challenge in its own right, not to mention an invitation to a big financial payoff for whoever could break the system.

VideoCipher II was indeed the most sophisticated consumer security system of its time, using the Data Encryption Standard (DES) encryption algorithm combined with a complex hierarchy of digital keys. The lowest level of these encryption keys was automatically changed several times per second. However, although the audio channels were digitized and could therefore be fully encrypted, the video was merely scrambled.

Before the pirates attacked the VideoCipher system, their hero, Captain Midnight, staged a completely new type of technical protest. Irate that HBO had scrambled its signals using GI's VideoCipher technology, Captain Midnight usurped control of HBO's main satellite transponder in 1986. He replaced HBO's signal with his own subversive message about the inherent right to receive free TV, threatening not only HBO, but also Showtime and the pay TV business at large.

The Captain Midnight stunt was just a warm-up, however. By 1988, the VideoCipher II encryption system, used by virtually all the cable programmers in the United States, had been cracked wide open. It wasn't the core encryption algorithm that was defeated, but rather the engineering implementation in the consumer box. The hackers had figured out a way to get inside GI's custom chips and implant their own software, circumventing the security integrity of the system. The pirate satellite TV dealers, generally the same mom-and-pop businesses that provided legitimate satellite TV products, were suddenly making a fortune selling "chipped" boxes.

There were two methods for using hacked chips to steal television programming. The "Three Musketeers" attack was aptly named due to its "all for one, one for all" nature. A consumer would subscribe legitimately to only one service (typically the least expensive programming package), and then the pirate software would trick the system into thinking it was authorized for all the other services too. With the "cloning" attack, a dealer would typically authorize one box legitimately for all the satellite TV channels, and then clone, or copy, the same electronic service authorization "map" into tens or hundreds of additional illegal boxes. Pirate dealers could then sell these "golden" boxes for upwards of $1,000 each.

It didn't matter that the pirates were selling these boxes for exorbitant prices. Consumers deeply resented that they suddenly had to pay for satellite TV, and were therefore willing to accept a steep price for a pirate box in order to get the free programming they felt entitled to. This mind-set dated back to the early days of satellite TV, in the mid-1970s, when HBO and the other programmers began transmitting content via satellite in order to deliver it efficiently to cable systems throughout the country. Then Taylor Howard, a Stanford University researcher and professor, designed a large satellite dish pointed up toward the sky in order to get satellite programming for free. Soon, these C-band dishes were popping up all across America. So when HBO, Showtime, and others started encrypting their signals a decade later, home dish owners were infuriated. Their TV screens went blank overnight. Their free TV had been ripped away!

GI had a high-stakes cat-and-mouse game on its hands. If it didn't figure out a way to fix the problem, it risked losing everything, and certainly had no chance with its new digital TV system. GI even had a former Israeli military engineer, Dr. Ron Katznelson, to assign to the problem. He had developed electronic countermeasures during the 1973 Yom Kippur War. Katznelson was GI's secret weapon, embedding electronic messages inside the satellite TV signals, rendering the pirate boxes brain-dead and no longer able to receive TV content. Then the pirate consumers would go back to their dealers, paying hundreds of dollars again to get their boxes "re-chipped" and reprogrammed. It made no economic sense, but their visceral need for free TV was overwhelming, with no regard for the rights of copyright holders.

While Katznelson focused on electronic countermeasures, GI also hired a former FBI agent, Terry Luddy, tasked with getting the FBI more interested in pursuing the pirate dealers. At first the FBI had no interest, ignoring the problem and feeling they had much more important things to do. But Luddy worked them relentlessly, showing them how much illegal money was involved and how much of that money was tied to the illicit drug business. Soon Luddy had FBI agents collaborating with him on raiding some of the larger pirate operations. He would then feed some of the evidence into Ron Katznelson and GI's software team, who would devise ways to "kill" dozens and sometimes hundreds of boxes with a single zap from the sky.

The piracy problem didn't immediately hurt GI financially. In fact, it increased the demand for descrambler boxes because the pirates needed GI's hardware in order to implant the pirate software. But claims from the programmers and the cable industry, that GI didn't care about the piracy problem and was not interested in solving the problem, were false. The TV programming community—HBO, CNN, ESPN, Showtime, Playboy, and others—was livid. The fact that GI's system had been breached was costing them money every day, eroding their paying subscriber base. If the pirate activity was not stopped, they would have to convert to a new encryption system from a different company, an extremely expensive proposition. GI was starting to be threatened with lawsuits from its customers, and some executives received threats from the pirate community. The entire business was under siege. At the peak of piracy, the ratio of pirates to legitimate consumers reached a level of 8 to 1, with about 2 million homes with hacked boxes getting free pay TV relative to a paying subscriber base of 250,000. At this level, GI San Diego's entire business was on the verge of implosion.

GI was also being crucified in the media, especially by its competitors who saw an opportunity to bring the company down. Yet GI had its defenders. Taylor Howard, inventor of the home satellite dish and founder of Chaparral Communications, credited VideoCipher Division president Larry Dunham for effectively managing a crisis situation, calling him "a young man holding a tiger by its tail." At a trade show lunch, I was seated at a table adjacent to attendees from ESPN and GI competitor Scientific Atlanta, and overhead one of the SA guys ridiculing us endlessly about piracy. It was encouraging to hear John Eberhard, an ESPN engineer, interrupt him and say, "They're actually very good technically and they are trying to fix the problem."

GI was fighting for its life, and was prepared to do whatever it took to rectify the situation. Paul Moroney and a few of his top systems engineers, including Steve Anderson, Allen Shumate, and Jim Esserman, were inventing some clever new tricks in GI's battle against the pirates. Joe Markee created a new security engineering department, completely dedicated to defeating the pirate community by technical means. Along with this group's system enhancements, a new, security-hardened custom chip was developed in-house by Bob Gilberg's chip design group.

One of the key innovations of GI's new security chip was a tamper-proof design incorporating battery-backed memory and a fuse, ensuring self-destruction of the chip and its internal software if probed by a would-be hacker. Another major advance was a novel cryptographic concept called "encryption key chaining," linking critical subscriber data, such as content rights, to the underlying encryption key in such a way that hackers could never get the correct key. This secure chip and its successors were highly successful, acting as silicon vaults protecting tens of billions of dollars of pay TV content to this day.

But getting this highly secure new chip into the installed base of consumers would not only take precious time but would also require flawless execution of a consumer hardware recall and replacement program. In the meantime, there were millions of existing pirate boxes in the field, with more being introduced every day.

Then, the potential death blow occurred. John Grayson and his pirate engineering company in Canada, Dectec International, figured out how to build a VideoCipher descrambler box without even using modified GI hardware. This "BlackCipher" box, built from scratch with Grayson's own components and software, could have meant the end of GI's business in San Diego.

In August 1990, Paul Moroney hired Eric Sprunk to replace Roy Griffin who, along with Steve Anderson, had led the security engineering group after Joe Markee created it. Markee had left GI to start his own company.

Sprunk's role as head of the security engineering group grew into one of the most important jobs in the company. Protection of its customers' television content was, more than anything, GI San Diego's reason for being. Sprunk was an electrical engineering graduate of UCSD in the field of communications systems. He had joined Linkabit in 1983 as a young engineer, where he worked on the digital audio hardware for the original VideoCipher I system. Importantly, his engineering foundation was at the systems level, and he also had gained some experience in military security engineering from Linkabit.

Sprunk brought to his group a mind-set essential to any good cryptographer: the necessity and ability of getting inside the heads of the pirates, to think like they thought. He understood that any security system could be compromised. From the pirates' standpoint, the issue came down to fundamental economics. Is breaking the system worth the upfront R&D investment, plus the recurring cost of supplying and maintaining an illegal supply of products? If GI locked the front door, the pirates would find a back door. If we shut the windows, they'd come through a crack in the wall. Sprunk referred to this endless cat-and-mouse game as our version of the Maginot Line, named after the French Minister of War who built tremendous fortifications and booby traps along the France-Germany border in the 1930s. Unfortunately, Hitler's blitzkrieg through Belgium in 1940 circumvented the line, causing the fall of France in six short weeks.

GI had another constraint: the recurring cost of security hardware in its decoder. If the solution was designed too expensively, with security overkill and excessive complexity, it would eat into the company's profits and hurt market growth. But if GI security engineering cut too many corners, the pirates would devour it and the entire system could crumble. One of Sprunk's critical tasks was to help the GI product team find the optimal balance: a new security solution sufficiently difficult for pirates to break, frustrating them just enough to make their investment too high. In striking this balance, Sprunk and his team of cryptographic engineers performed brilliantly.

This philosophy was one that DirecTV and Dish Network would be faced with a few years later, as they deployed smart card systems for their small-dish digital satellite TV services. The path they chose was less secure and more vulnerable to hacking than GI's technique.

Another one of Sprunk's roles was to be GI's primary interface to the National Security Agency (NSA). The NSA, authorized by President

Harry S. Truman in 1952, is the US government agency responsible for analysis and interception of foreign communications and also for protecting US government communications. Now known almost universally for much broader snooping, due to the Edward Snowden leaks, in the early 1990s the NSA was still an obscure organization shrouded in mystery. Hence the previous nickname "No Such Agency."

Given that GI's business was centered on entertainment television, it may be surprising that the NSA had such an interest in our activities. But at the time, encryption algorithms, such as those used in the VideoCipher security system, were on the US munitions list, subject to stringent export controls. Since we wanted to serve international markets, NSA approval was required. NSA personnel visited GI periodically in San Diego, gathering intelligence on what the company was doing with encryption technology, and Sprunk would visit them at their Fort Meade, Maryland, location. His impression of NSA was of an organization highly trained to be tight-lipped about its goals and objectives and very competent cryptographically, the exact type of culture one would expect from the agency tasked with gaining access to foreign intelligence secrets. Sprunk had to walk a fine line, providing just enough information to gain NSA approval for export licenses, but without disclosing the company's deepest cryptographic secrets.

By 1990, Rick Segil, head of San Diego product management, and Dick Armstrong, VP of Service and Support, were ready to implement the security upgrade plan. Endowed with GI's new battle-hardened design, the new VideoCipher II Plus Renewable Security satellite boxes started shipping to consumers early in the year. In 1991, with HBO as the industry front-runner, the programmers began transmitting their satellite TV signals with the new, secure technology. They needed to continue broadcasting the original VideoCipher II data signal, however, so that the legitimate base of VideoCipher II consumers could continue to receive programming while GI upgraded them to the new descrambler boxes over time. GI then stepped up to its industry responsibility, investing about $100 million to upgrade the legal satellite TV subscribers' boxes at no charge.

Finally, in 1993, after the legitimate installed base had been upgraded to VideoCipher II Plus receivers, each with a Renewable Security slot in the event of a future breach, the VideoCipher II data feed was turned off permanently, thereby rendering useless the remaining pirate boxes. Notwithstanding its ethical obligations, GI's $100 million upgrade cost turned out to be a very wise investment. Most of the pirate consumers became legal, buying new, secure GI descrambler products and providing the company with approximately $400 million of high-margin revenue over a short period. And more importantly, it cleared the path for GI to cleanly market its new digital TV system to the subscription television industry. The cloud had been lifted.

8 DBS, Still Just a Dream

Through its Hatboro, Pennsylvania, operation, General Instrument was the leading supplier of broadband equipment to the domestic cable industry, which had more than doubled from 18 million subscribers in 1980 to over 36 million by 1985. But GI's direct broadcast satellite (DBS) ambitions dated back to the early 1980s, several years before it acquired the VideoCipher satellite TV business from M/A-Com, and long before that San Diego business unit hatched its digital television technology.

The vision of DBS advocates was that higher-power satellites would enable TV signals to be distributed directly to homes equipped with small circular dishes, with no cable middleman. Media companies like Time Inc. and Warner Amex also realized that communications satellites would allow their programming services, HBO and MTV, to be delivered to consumers nationwide, beyond cable's footprint.

The Comsat Corporation appeared to be in the lead in the early 1980s. Its Satellite Television Corp. (STC) subsidiary, led by DBS pioneer Mickey Alpert, planned to launch high-power satellites and sell programming to consumers with 2-foot-diameter dishes. Then, in 1982, GI blindsided Comsat by investing in a new venture, United Satellite Communications Inc. USCI was championed by GI CEO Frank Hickey and Director of Business Development Hal Krisbergh. It had a drastically lower capital investment plan than Comsat's STC since USCI planned to lease transponders on a medium-power satellite rather than build and launch its own high-power bird.[1] In the same time frame, Rupert Murdoch also made an unsuccessful early attempt at the US DBS market with his Skyband venture.

Another doomed satellite TV endeavor was Crimson Satellite, a late 1980s joint venture between HBO and RCA Americom (now SES), conceived in large part by Ed Horowitz. Early in his career Horowitz had specialized in microwave engineering at TelePrompTer, once the nation's largest cable television operator. After joining HBO in 1974, he played an instrumental role in the company's long string of technological innovations, including satellite delivery starting in 1975 and encryption of the company's satellite signals in the early 1980s.

Horowitz's grand plan for Crimson Satellite was compelling. HBO would use GI's technology to migrate its current C-band satellite signals, as well as those of Viacom and other programmers, to a medium-power Ku-band satellite, and then sell this content to cable operators and small-dish satellite TV subscribers. The cable industry effectively killed the idea, however, when TCI threatened to delete HBO's signals from TCI's cable systems nationwide. HBO's parent, Time Inc., conferred with its cable subsidiary, American Television and Communications (ATC), about whether the company should succumb to TCI's demand. The answer was a resounding "yes." So Time shut down Crimson, sold the satellite to

SES in Europe, where it was renamed Astra 1B, and made Horowitz the fall guy within HBO for the failed venture.

With none of these early DBS ventures reaching fruition, the big dish C-band Television Receive Only (TVRO) market remained the only game in town if you couldn't get cable or wanted a cable alternative with many more channels of content. When the C-band satellite TV market started to blossom in the 1980s, due in large part to consumers' ability to intercept free programming intended for cable redistribution, the cable operators became increasingly alarmed. The cable industry needed to stop this runaway train, and programmers like HBO realized that by encrypting their satellite signals, they could also sell the content to the growing C-band home dish market.

Congress, pushed by its constituents accustomed to receiving free satellite TV, was considering making the scrambling of satellite TV signals illegal. But the Cable Communications Act of 1984 struck a compromise, allowing programmers to scramble their signals so long as they provided a technical and marketing mechanism to sell these signals to home dish owners. When the programmers started encrypting their content with VideoCipher II technology in the mid-1980s, the cable companies tolerated this form of pseudo-DBS. The 3-meter-diameter dishes were big and expensive, and the market was not perceived as a real threat to the growing cable business.

But with the advent of digital in the early 1990s, a reprisal of the STC/USCI/Skyband DBS drama occurred, this time with a new set of players and eventually a much different outcome. These new ventures would evolve into DirecTV and PrimeStar. Once again GI, this time fronted by its San Diego VideoCipher business unit, would vie for a piece of the DBS action.

Larry Dunham, president of GI's VideoCipher Division, had personally contacted Hughes Communications regarding his unit's new digital TV project. In January 1990, a team from Hughes visited San Diego, led by Jim Ramo, Larry Driscoll, and Jack Godwin. Ramo was in charge of marketing for Hughes's numerous communications satellites. After giving us an overview of their extensive satellite fleet, the discussion turned to Hughes's DBS plans.

Ramo explained that Hughes had a renewed interest in launching a high-power DBS service. But he had been through this exercise so many times at Hughes that he qualified his comments by saying, "We'll believe it when we see it." Ramo cited financing as the biggest hurdle, since the launch of a DBS service required up to $1 billion of risk capital. Going up against the powerful cable companies was a monumental undertaking, requiring very deep pockets and nerves of steel. The Hughes guys didn't believe access to programming would be nearly as big of an issue, reasoning that the content companies were always looking for additional conduits into homes.

Hughes characterized its general interest as "semi-serious," contemplating a late 1993 or early 1994 satellite launch for a high-power DBS bird, with twenty-seven transponders and full CONUS (continental US) coverage.[2] In addition, it was considering up to a dozen additional transponders blanketing Hawaii. Dunham and his team were intrigued by what they heard, but Hughes had downplayed its vision to such an extent that GI wasn't sure how real it was. As for the idea of using GI's digital TV technology for its DBS service, Hughes was clearly intrigued but thought it sounded like "black magic" and like it was "too good to be true."

The next month, in February 1990, two separate announcements hit the wire. First, GE Americom, the satellite operator subsidiary of GE, announced a medium-power DBS venture with nine US cable operators including TCI, Time Warner, Cox, and Comcast. This announcement of K Prime Partners, the predecessor to PrimeStar, excited the GI team in San Diego, but was frustrating at the same time.

GI's disappointment stemmed from the fact that Larry Dunham, Ken Kinsman, Mark Medress, and I had recently visited GE Americom's headquarters in Princeton, New Jersey. At this meeting we informally offered to be part of a new DBS venture with them. We would contribute unspecified funds and bring to the table our conditional access and encryption technology, as well as our satellite receiver design and manufacturing capacity. We had significant credibility with them because of our industry experience and also because of our unique national consumer authorization center, the DBS Center.

At that time, GI's DBS Center in San Diego was the only facility of its type in the world. Powerful Digital Equipment Corporation (DEC) computers were running custom software developed by GI's engineers. Its purpose was to determine which programming services any individual satellite TV subscriber was authorized to receive, allowing video to be descrambled and viewed, and audio to be decrypted. The data inputs to the facility came from the various television programmers and content packagers, consisting of subscriber information and the services they were signing up for. The system's output was a composite authorization stream for the entire country's home dish owners. This data stream was sent to every content uplink site in the country, where it was inserted within the VideoCipher satellite TV signals. When these signals reached the downlink satellite antennas at every cable headend and consumer dish site in the United States, the GI boxes would extract the data stream. The DBS Center was fault-tolerant with redundancy, and there was a ready-to-go backup facility many miles away in the event of an emergency. After all, millions of consumers around the country couldn't have their TV interrupted just because of a big earthquake in California.

There was a mystique surrounding the DBS Center, primarily due to its uniqueness at the time. We showcased it to curious visitors from all over the world, hosting major delegations from Japan, Europe, Canada, and elsewhere. A similar type of facility would be needed for any new DBS operator, such as K Prime (PrimeStar) or Hughes.

The second announcement, also in February of 1990, was for Sky Cable, the precursor to DirecTV. Sky Cable was announced as a $1 billion high-power DBS venture backed by Hughes Communications, NBC, Rupert Murdoch's News Corporation, and Chuck Dolan's Cablevision Systems.

Having lost the opportunity of being an equity partner in K Prime, with the guaranteed additional benefit of being its technology and equipment supplier, GI's efforts shifted back toward the traditional business development and sales relationship with service providers. Since K Prime intended to use an in-orbit, medium-power Ku-band satellite operated by GE Americom, it didn't need to go through the time-consuming and expensive steps of satellite construction and launch. GI knew Scientific Atlanta was its most likely competitor for K Prime's business, although there would be others, and believed it had a one-to-two-year lead in developing a digital satellite system.

Soon GI started receiving the telltale signals that it was in trouble, with phone calls and scheduled meetings slowing down dramatically. Matt Miller, GI's corporate VP of Technology, obtained some back-channel intelligence from his old Viacom contacts and relayed the bad news: "The fix is in for the other guys." Miller's inside information was correct, and in May 1990 K Prime announced it would launch its medium-power Ku-band satellite TV service with Scientific Atlanta's analog BMAC system. Scientific Atlanta had always been a formidable competitor, but GI also understood K Prime's decision to be partially a function of severely ruffled feathers. K Prime's owners, the big cable operators, resented the way GI was milking its success with VideoCipher and exerting too much market control. Furthermore, GI had burned some bridges as a result of the VideoCipher piracy problem.

By Thanksgiving, K Prime had launched service in twenty-four test markets, with seven superstations and three pay-per-view channels. Each of the nine cable partners took responsibility for marketing, equipment installation, and customer service in their respective franchise areas.[3] They were treating K Prime essentially as an extension to cable, not an exciting or ambitious business. But K Prime was indisputably up and running with a live service that allowed a much smaller dish than that required for C-band satellite TV.

Scientific Atlanta had won this skirmish. GI thought it might have another shot at K Prime's business if and when the service went digital and became more serious. However, its competitor would have the substantial advantage of being the technology incumbent.

9 A MOMENTOUS DECISION

General Instrument was largely uninvolved and disinterested in the over-the-air television broadcast market, the domain of CBS, ABC, NBC, Fox, PBS, and their affiliated stations. Its focus was on the far more dynamic cable and satellite subscription TV businesses. There were a few exceptions: The CBS Broadcasting network used GI's VideoCipher I encryption system to deliver its national signals via satellite to affiliate stations in local TV markets throughout the country; C-band satellite TV content aggregators, such as Superstar/Netlink and Primetime 24, used VideoCipher II for distributing distant network local signals to home satellite TV subscribers; and all domestic cable operators used GI's cable gear to carry local broadcast signals under the FCC's "must-carry" regulations. But that was the extent of GI's participation in the broadcast TV market.

Joe Flaherty, CBS's highly regarded senior vice president of technology, had visited GI's San Diego division headquarters in 1990 to see an early digital HDTV demonstration. Flaherty was a subcommittee chairman on Dick Wiley's FCC Advisory Committee on Advanced Television Services (ACATS). Wiley had championed the idea that the United States should have a competition, a technical shoot-out between the world's leading electronics companies, to select a new technology for the country's over-the-air TV broadcasters. The government would supervise and administer the process, but the winner would be the private company or consortium with the best technology.

This approach differed greatly from what was occurring elsewhere. In Japan, through industrial policy, the government had funded NHK's development of the analog MUSE HDTV system. In Europe, through the leadership of French President Françoise Mitterrand and German Chancellor Helmut Kohl, government bodies were heavily subsidizing the development of HD-MAC, the European Community's analog HD response to Japan's MUSE technology.

CBS's Flaherty was passionate about the US television and technology business, and he was stunned by the digital HDTV demonstration he saw in San Diego. As one of the earliest true believers in HDTV, Flaherty wanted the United States to have the best system possible. An all-digital HDTV solution from an American company, leapfrogging both Japan and Europe in one fell swoop, was a dream come true. Pondering what he had just seen, he asked Jerry Heller and Larry Dunham whether GI would consider a last-minute submission to the FCC advanced TV broadcast competition. Dunham and Heller were ambivalent, unsure how GI would benefit and wary of diverting resources from the digital SDTV project for satellite and cable. Making the decision even more difficult, one of Dunham's sources was telling him that the FCC deadline was "soft," and the company could submit its technology at a later date, after the official deadline.

In late May 1990, Woo Paik, Paul Moroney, Mark Medress, and I gathered in Jerry Heller's office for his weekly staff meeting. Heller opened the meeting in his calm, precise manner: "Well, we are about to make history." Silence enveloped the room. He explained that Larry Dunham had made the decision to enter GI's DigiCipher HDTV system into the FCC competition as the world's first all-digital HDTV solution. As satellite/cable pay TV guys, we were unsure about the implications of Heller's disclosure. The one thing we knew for sure was that our digital TV project would no longer be undercover; the rest of the world would be alerted to what we were doing.

Just before the June 1 deadline, Dunham and Heller went to Washington DC, where they were joined by GI's lobbyist, Quincy Rodgers. Together they submitted a six-figure check for admission to the FCC competition. Thus began an arduous process with many twists and turns, through corporate boardrooms, nerve-racking testing in the independent labs, and the inevitable, infuriating political machinations. The submission itself, once it hit the news wire, was a technical shot heard around the world, startling government bureaucracies and corporations throughout the United States, Japan, and Europe.

Here is a sampling of the immediate headlines:

"First All-Digital HDTV Developed by VideoCipher"

In a surprise announcement, the VideoCipher Division of General Instrument Corp. has made an 11th hour high definition TV proposal to the Federal Communications Commission, just barely squeaking in under the wire for submissions. Called DigiCipher, the stunning all-digital system fits in 6 MHz of bandwidth and is the first in the world to be proposed as a broadcast standard and the first to achieve such dramatic compression of video signals. (Gary Kim, *Multichannel News*, June 11, 1990)

"Local Firm Proposes TV Advance"

The VideoCipher Division of General Instrument Corp. sat in a big poker game late last week, when the San Diego-based unit anted up $175,000 to submit a proposal for a high definition television standard. The VideoCipher standard is one of seven systems that met a June 1 filing for such a proposal with the FCC. Other competitors include NHK from Japan, Zenith, Philips, and the Massachusetts Institute of Technology. J. Lawrence Dunham, president of the VideoCipher Division, said the company decided to file its application only last week and submitted its application on the deadline day. VideoCipher's technology—called DigiCipher—is the only one of the submissions to employ all-digital technology. This system assigns numerical digits to define and compress video information for broadcast. (Craig D. Rose, *San Diego Union-Tribune,* June 5, 1990)

Inside GI, it was clearly time to separate this project from the rest of the initiatives underway. We needed to recruit new people with somewhat different expertise and a specific focus. In this case, we needed an individual dedicated to the logistical, strategic, political, and business aspects of the FCC HDTV process. This was the first of several times the company would be confronted by digital TV–related business opportunities beyond its immediate capacity.

Bob Rast had been an RCA engineer for many years before joining ATC, a big cable operator later acquired by Time Warner. He was a rare individual who not only understood the broadcast TV business, from his RCA days, but also the cable business, from ATC. He also had a current consulting client, CableLabs, the R&D consortium representing the North American cable industry. Intelligent and articulate, Rast was an engaging public speaker and had the air of a diplomat in his interpersonal dealings. He was adept at listening to and synthesizing multiple points of view before navigating toward common ground and a compromise position. Jerry Heller knew he had found an ideal fit for the job.

Several months later, in January 1991, GI entered into a partnership with MIT for the FCC competition, forming the American Television Alliance. In addition to pooling technical resources, the idea was to differentiate GI from the group referred to as "the European consortium," comprising Philips (based in the Netherlands) and Thomson (headquartered in France), plus NBC and the David Sarnoff Research Center, two American entities.

The announcement of the GI–MIT partnership generated considerable media interest:

> "HDTV Bid Fuels Cooperation, MIT Venture More Than Money"
>
> The Massachusetts Institute of Technology's agreement to team up with a former competitor in its effort to set the standard for advanced television in the United States yesterday stunned observers of the high-stakes technological battle. As reported in yesterday's Herald, General Instrument of New York will fund MIT's high-definition television proposal, while still developing its own HDTV system. Both will be presented to the Federal Communications Commission for testing.
>
> But the agreement between MIT and General Instrument goes beyond funding: the two organizations unveiled a comprehensive agreement known as the American Television Alliance, under which they will share technology in a bid to win the FCC competition for the HDTV standards.
>
> To some, the alliance suggests the type of long-term cooperation that has enabled Japanese corporations to establish a commanding lead in areas such as consumer electronics and semiconductors. But Dr. Jerry Heller, head of General Instrument's HDTV program

in San Diego, said there was no conscious effort to mimic the Japanese approach. "We (at GI) weren't looking at HDTV as the lone gunslinger," said Heller, who earned his doctorate from MIT in 1967. "We think of words like alliance, partnership and consensus, which sound somewhat Japanese. But one of the key things is that the whole idea of digital transmission is an American idea." (Jeffrey Krasner, *Boston Herald,* January 31, 1991)

"Two Competitors in Pact on HDTV Plan"

Last June, General Instrument became the first company to propose an all-digital approach to HDTV, which promises images with film-like crispness and the full dimensions of a movie screen. Since then, all-digital approaches have been announced by two groups: a consortium formed by NBC, Thomson S.A. of France, Philips N.V. of the Netherlands, and the David Sarnoff Research Center in Princeton, N.J.; and a venture by the Zenith Electronics Corporation and the American Telephone and Telegraph Company. In the wake of the General Instrument proposal, researchers at MIT's Advanced Television Research Program became convinced they could replace their earlier proposal with an all-digital approach. (Edmund L. Andrews, *New York Times,* January 31, 1991)

Comments that came out years later put this event in a historical context:

"A Perspective on Digital TV and HDTV"

Two years and eight months into the US FCC Advisory Committee Advanced TV process, on June 1, 1990, General Instrument proposed an all-digital terrestrial HDTV system, and television was forever changed. The digital era had begun and analog television was doomed worldwide! Television was to make its most fundamental technological change since its invention and its subsequent colorization. (Address by Dr. Joe Flaherty, SVP Technology, CBS Inc., 1997)

"Chiariglione and the Birth of MPEG"

That impression was fortified by General Instrument's startling mid-1990 announcement that it had found a way to do digital HDTV in a standard broadcast environment. At the same time, since the company was the dominant player in cable set-top boxes and a pioneer in satellite downlinks, its announcement legitimized digital TV rather as IBM legitimized the PC, observes Dragos Ruiu, video strategy manager for Hewlett-Packard. (William Sweet, Senior Editor, *IEEE Spectrum*, 1997)

Entering the FCC competition with the DigiCipher HDTV system was an audacious move with unknown consequences for GI. As the project progressed down an independent path of engineering and management, it enhanced the company's credibility for the immediate endeavor of establishing a digital SDTV standard for satellite and cable TV. Because the FCC process was focused on high definition television, a sexy new category, it garnered most of the headlines and media attention. But it was an unintentional subterfuge of sorts, as GI was devoting far more resources to developing its digital SDTV system with imminent market potential.

10 TECHNOLOGY LBO: GOLD MINE OR OXYMORON?

While GI was working diligently in San Diego to develop its groundbreaking digital TV solutions, the wider business world was in turmoil. During the 1980s, leveraged buyouts had become all the rage. Elite Wall Street investment firms were using debt to buy companies, and then selling them a few years later for enormous profits.

Forstmann Little & Company and Kohlberg Kravis Roberts (KKR) were the two most renowned leveraged buyout (LBO) firms of that era. Their ultimate goals were the same, but their financing techniques stood in stark contrast. KKR loaded up its target companies with junk bonds, while Forstmann Little typically used a substantial portion of equity along with lower-interest debt. This divergence was best exemplified in the bidding war for RJR Nabisco, a company that KKR ultimately acquired in November 1988 for $30 billion. The title of the book *Barbarians at the Gate,* which tells the story of RJR Nabisco's takeover by KKR, indicates the type of campaign that was waged.

Losing RJR Nabisco to KKR sent Ted Forstmann on a tirade. He was an extremely competitive person in every regard. A hockey goalie as a Yale undergraduate, he played for-profit bridge at Columbia Law School and was a strong amateur tennis player throughout his life. He ridiculed and derided KKR for using high-yield, high-risk junk bonds to finance its acquisitions, a tactic Forstmann equated with using "funny money," or "wampum."[1]

The ideal leveraged buyout candidate generates steady, reliable cash flow and is undervalued by the stock market. The acquirer typically attempts to streamline operations without damaging growth prospects, often a tricky balancing act, thereby increasing profitability so that the company could be taken public again through an initial public offering of new shares. This LBO purchase-to-sale cycle typically occurs within a five-to-seven-year window. Forstmann Little had established a strong track record by acquiring companies that fit this bill including Dr. Pepper, The Topps Co. (baseball cards, Bazooka bubble gum), The Pullman Co. (automotive components), and Gulfstream Aerospace (corporate jets).

Although technology companies are usually poor choices for leveraged buyouts, Forstmann Little was intrigued by the upside potential from GI's digital HDTV breakthrough in San Diego, on top of the company's strong cash flows from its traditional businesses. Coincidentally, Forstmann Little was plotting its corporate takeovers just one floor below General Instrument's prominent corporate headquarters on the forty-fifth floor of the GM building in Manhattan, which had spectacular views of Central Park and the New York City skyline. Frank Hickey, GI's long-time CEO, was attracted by Forstmann's overture because he wanted to monetize the company, seeking to make his mark and step out from the persistent shadow of his predecessor, Monty Shapiro.

To that end, GI's Rick Friedland and Forstmann Little's Steve Klinsky spent weeks together in a room poring over spreadsheets, trying to make the numbers work. On Father's Day in June 1990, however, Forstmann Little walked away from the table, scared off by GI's complicated portfolio of businesses. But the allure of GI's digital HDTV technology was strong, and soon Ted Forstmann and his partners returned to finalize the negotiations. When the firm announced the $1.6 billion cash acquisition of GI in July 1990, many eyebrows were raised in the business community; an LBO of a technology company was almost unheard of.

Unlike KKR, Forstmann Little didn't use high-yielding junk bonds to purchase GI. Equity and subordinated debt made up half the price, with the remainder coming from senior bank debt. Forstmann Little's equity came primarily from pension funds of major corporations, including GE, AT&T, and Boeing, as well as from public entities such as state pension funds. The subordinated debt resembled equity in that it didn't require principal repayment for eleven years, and the senior debt was tied to short-term interest rates, which had fortuitously started a dramatic decline from the high rates of the 1980s.

Even with Forstmann Little's less aggressive financing technique, the acquisition of technology companies still was risky. The cash flows were variable and there was the likelihood of getting blindsided by some unforeseen technology breakthrough. But where traditional investors saw excessive risk, Forstmann Little smelled a potential gold mine: GI was the global leader in broadband communications systems, owning market-leading franchises in cable and satellite TV equipment. There was a major additional upside if the company's digital TV ambitions were to come to fruition.

The dealmakers were to experience a rude awakening, however, and it involved economic and political events around the world. Prior to the leveraged buyout, GI had won a major contract in the United Kingdom with British Satellite Broadcasting (BSB) for a new pay TV security system called EuroCypher. This lucrative project included the development of an "access control module" to be sold to multiple European satellite receiver manufacturers.

BSB had the exclusive license in the United Kingdom to launch the world's first high-power DBS satellite for television broadcasting, capable of delivering new sports, movie, and family channels to tiny home dishes. BSB was owned by a consortium of British media giants: Granada Television, Pearson, Virgin Group, and ITN. The service launched in March 1990 with great fanfare. British consumers were starved for new programming content beyond the limited BBC and ITV channel offerings. Business was going very well for GI's VideoCipher Division at this point, with high volumes of the new security module being shipped into Europe, the first big international win in a burgeoning global satellite TV market.

A year earlier, however, Rupert Murdoch had become frustrated by being locked out of the UK high-power DBS business. He had unilaterally launched Sky Television, a competing service, using Astra, a medium-power pan-European satellite. Sky TV had considerable momentum with its time-to-market advantage, while BSB was spending hundreds of millions of dollars on its high-power satellite construction and launch, plus marketing and original programming costs. So when Murdoch proposed a merger in November 1990, BSB's corporate shareholders could hardly resist. BSkyB was the result, controlled by Murdoch and his News Corporation. It became one of the world's most successful pay TV platforms and dominated the UK media landscape.

What was great for Murdoch was disastrous for GI and its new owner, Forstmann Little. Immediately after the BSB/Sky TV merger, the GI group in San Diego received an abrupt call from Murdoch's organization, instructing the company to immediately stop shipping the EuroCypher product across the Atlantic. Suddenly, GI San Diego had lost its biggest international customer and, to make matters worse, was stuck with a warehouse full of products, millions of dollars' worth of instantly obsolete inventory.

The bad news didn't stop with the BSkyB fiasco. Domestic cable operators were in the midst of a major cutback in capital spending, directly whipsawing GI's cable equipment business. US banking regulators had become increasingly concerned with the bank loans being made to heavily indebted corporations such as cable operators, causing them to enact stringent rules for highly leveraged transactions and crippling the cable operators' ability to borrow money to finance the purchase of equipment from GI.

GI's satellite TV venture in Japan with C. Itoh and Toshiba was not going well either. After an auspicious start, a competing consortium of leading Japanese programmers had united with Sony in a new venture called SkyPort, supported by the Japanese government's impenetrable industrial policy.

Nothing seemed to be going right for GI. Forstmann Little's new prized possession had been hit by a triple whammy within months of the acquisition. Although none of these setbacks was predictable, it was as if Forstmann Little had been set up for a fall. The conventional wisdom, that technology companies should not be subjects of leveraged buyouts, appeared to be painfully obvious. The time had come to bet the company on digital, at least from the standpoint of the VideoCipher Division in San Diego.

11 BRIGHTON'S LAST STAND

When a company is brewing a disruptive technology, it confronts the balancing act of keeping a low profile, thereby gaining time to increase its lead, while pursuing publicity, which alerts competitors and gives them the impetus to catch up. GI's cover had already been blown by its June 1990 FCC submission for DigiCipher HDTV, plus a few trade articles based on leaks regarding GI's digital SDTV solution for satellite and cable. Given the circumstances, the San Diego group decided to throw caution aside, and it chose to make its big move at a trade show in the English seaside town of Brighton.

At one point during World War II, Brighton had become a safe haven for London evacuees. In *Quadrophenia*, Pete Townsend's 1973 musical work of genius, The Who immortalized Brighton as the location of a big showdown between The Mods and The Rockers.

For the media world, Brighton's last stand was in late September of 1990. That was the year the International Broadcasting Convention (IBC) outgrew this quaint coastal resort on the English Channel before moving to bigger quarters in Amsterdam. IBC is the premier annual trade show for companies engaged in the creation and delivery of entertainment and news content.

Still naïve about the long and winding road to success, GI's VideoCipher Division rented a booth at IBC Brighton in an attempt to make some early market headway in Europe. It was the international debut of the DigiCipher technology, where the company would publicly display the world's first digital SDTV and HDTV pictures. Little did GI know the competitive juices it was about to unleash.

News of GI's breakthrough had already been publicized months earlier, due to the drama surrounding its last-minute FCC digital HDTV submission. But through some combination of doubt and denial, the reality had not yet sunk in across the Atlantic, and the European Community was still frozen inside its new analog HD-MAC initiative. Europe Inc. had erected HD-MAC to block the Japanese MUSE analog HDTV system out of Europe, spending nearly $1 billion in the process. Additional funds had been expended on HD-MAC's standard definition derivatives, DMAC and D2MAC, which were also next-generation analog television solutions. GI's public unveiling of digital television at the Brighton IBC made the threat from its western flank all too obvious.

GI had a small, unassuming booth on Brighton's beachside pavilion, in the low-rent district of the grand trade show. The first visitors wandered in haphazardly, curious and skeptical. Cable TV was still not very established in Europe, except in a few countries like Belgium and the Netherlands, and satellite TV was just getting started with Murdoch's BSkyB in the United Kingdom. Some companies knew GI from its defunct BSB relationship in the United Kingdom. But when visitors from Philips, Thomson, the BBC, Sony, and the European Union stood in the viewing areas, they couldn't believe what they were seeing. Some accused us of fabricating the demos, saying our claims were impossible, that there was simply no way such pristine digital pictures could be achieved in television channel bandwidths. But when the initial guests kept returning with additional executives, a second time, a third time, even a fourth, each with a bigger and more astonished group, we started to realize we had struck an international nerve. Suddenly, Japan didn't seem like the big, bad threat; it was this group of Americans from Southern California.

Europe wasn't about to let some American company invade its turf, home to some of the world's oldest broadcasters and largest consumer electronics companies.

We handled the commotion as well as possible, not yet fully realizing the alarm bells we had set off. These were some of the European media headlines:

"Compressing the Future"

It is a measure of the strides made in HDTV technology that over thirty companies exhibited HDTV-related products at this year's IBC...Yet while Europe was toasting the future in 1250 and 'mock' 1250-lines, US systems manufacturer General Instruments [sic], tucked away on a modest stand on the esplanade, was quietly stealing the show with a first European showing of its DigiCipher video compression technology... The system is also flexible. The degree of compression can be varied from 2:1 (HD) up to 10:1 (SD) on a satellite or cable TV system. The impact of all this for cable and satellite viewers keen to improve programming choice and visual quality could be immense... (Paul Barker, *Cable and Satellite Express,* October 5, 1990)

"DigiCipher Takes IBC90 by Storm"

If the system lives up to its specifications, it will be the most significant event in the history of television since Benjamin Franklin nearly electrocuted himself. (John McCormac, European satellite magazine [name unknown], October 1990)

As we traveled back across the Atlantic to San Diego, we were ecstatic about the attention and response, but I recall wondering whether we had tipped our hand a bit too soon. It didn't take long to get the answer. Just a few months later, in early 1991, we started hearing about the European Launch Group and its Digital Video Broadcasting (DVB) project.

Just as the MAC project had served as a barrier against Japan and MUSE, we suspected the DVB project was being orchestrated to keep us and our digital technology out of Europe.

12 A New General for the Digital Battlefield

The partners of Forstmann Little—Ted Forstmann, brother Nick Forstmann, Brian Little, and Steve Klinsky—wanted fresh leadership for their new company, General Instrument, with their own man in the top job. They found what they were looking for through Forstmann Little's influential Advisory Board. Bob Strauss, former chairman of the Democratic National Committee and US Ambassador to the Soviet Union and later Russia, was a member of that board, as was George Shultz, Secretary of State under Ronald Reagan. Strauss recruited Donald Rumsfeld, a close friend of Shultz and a well-known figure in both the public and private sectors, to the advisory board. The Forstmann Little partners trusted Shultz's recommendation that Rumsfeld could increase the value of GI and take it public again. They hired Rumsfeld in October 1990, replacing GI chairman and CEO Frank Hickey, who had run the company since 1975.

Donald Rumsfeld grew up in the northern suburbs of Chicago, the son of a feisty schoolteacher mom and a World War II veteran dad who sold real estate. After attending Princeton, he became a Navy aviator and flight instructor. At age thirty Rumsfeld was elected to his first of four terms in Congress from Illinois' 13th congressional district, departing in the middle of his fourth term to serve in President Richard Nixon's cabinet. In 1973 he became US Ambassador to NATO and then returned to Washington in the mid-1970s, becoming President Gerald Ford's Chief of Staff before serving as the nation's youngest-ever Secretary of Defense at age forty-three. When Ford lost reelection to Jimmy Carter, Rumsfeld continued a remarkable career crisscrossing between the public and private sectors. He was G.D. Searle's CEO from 1977 to 1985, credited with turning the company around during a period when NutraSweet brought the firm great success, and then sold the pharmaceutical giant to Monsanto in July 1985 for $2.7 billion.

The year after he was hired to lead General Instrument, Rumsfeld moved the company's headquarters to his town, Chicago. He shed many of the New York corporate staff while retaining key executives such as Rick Friedland and Matt Miller, Viacom's former chief technologist who had been previously hired by GI in New York. Rumsfeld hired a loyal corporate staff in Chicago, including people he had known from previous government and private sector engagements.

Named one of America's toughest bosses by *Fortune* magazine in 1980, Rumsfeld's authoritarian leadership style was intimidating, although employees felt the company was in strong hands and going places. With his legendary 3 × 5 index cards, he was the master of quotes and pithy sayings, such as "If you mess up, fess up," and valued the importance of knowing when to say "I don't know."

Rumsfeld had a big-picture perspective and initiated a multi-year process of focusing GI on its sweet spot of broadband communications. Consistent with his philosophy of continually pruning businesses, products, and activities, he sold off various unrelated businesses. With GI's operating businesses in the satellite and cable TV areas, he delegated to local division management, conducting formal, rigorous and metric-driven reviews. But when it came to the FCC HDTV standardization process, he saw the opportunity to play a direct role, a logical area and zone of confidence consistent with his knowledge of Washington and skills as a savvy Beltway insider.

Forstmann Little spared no expense with its portfolio companies, hosting extravagant events with noted luminaries. At one such event in Aspen, they invited George Shultz and George Gilder, the visionary technologist, to mix with the top executives of their portfolio companies. When Gilder asked Rumsfeld if they could spend some time together to discuss the future of media and communications technology, Rumsfeld turned to Jerry Heller as his delegate.

In early 1991, Forstmann Little remained understandably concerned about the recent downturn hitting GI's business so soon after they had defied LBO logic and practice by purchasing the company. Spending levels were ramping up quickly in San Diego, particularly on R&D and engineering manpower, well ahead of any customer commitments. To make matters worse, there was internal second-guessing about whether we should even be embarking on the development of a digital system. Former CEO Frank Hickey and his staff in the Manhattan corporate office had been very supportive, believing time was of the essence in a highly competitive world, and asking if more funding could accelerate development. While the San Diego division pulsed with excitement, some employees were skeptical, thinking more was being bitten off than could be delivered, not a completely cynical perspective given the daunting challenges ahead.

There was significant naysaying from the Hatboro, Pennsylvania, cable equipment unit. They were saying things like "Cable operators will never buy boxes that cost $300; we can't even get them to buy $150 advanced analog converters." There were also some typical not-invented-here comments, like "What you guys are doing in San Diego isn't really new; what's the big deal?"

All-in with digital, the San Diego team was far enough along in its understanding, passion, and commitment to defuse these questions. But the San Diego division had an even bigger agenda: to get the company to accelerate development of the digital cable portion. The digital cable market was projected to be GI's largest opportunity. With an already overfull plate of development and no guarantee that corporate funding would continue to flow, the San Diego group knew the corporation would not begin a substantial digital cable development process without its Hatboro division fully on board.

To resolve the impasse over how big a priority digital should be, a full-day company strategy meeting was held in Peddler's Village, Lahaska, Pennsylvania, just a half-hour north of the Hatboro cable equipment division headquarters. Jerry Heller delegated to me the task of being the main presenter, so I formalized and updated a comprehensive business plan and put together a series of overhead slides showing market size, market strategy, product development plans, the competitive landscape, and financials.

A team of us from San Diego arrived on the East Coast the night before, our confidence offset by the fear that the entire project would be jettisoned if the meeting took a wrong turn. Rick Friedland and Matt Miller came from corporate, providing continuity for Rumsfeld from the previous administration in New York. A few Forstmann Little executives also came to assess the situation, taking a pulse on what they had bought and what the future potential might be. The Hatboro division was represented in force, led by division president Hal Krisbergh and his top executives Ed Breen, Geoff Roman, Dave Robinson, and Dan Moloney. Jeff Hamilton, the first Hatboro engineer assigned to the digital cable project, was also in attendance, as was Frank Drendel, chief executive of GI's CommScope unit, based in Hickory, North Carolina.

Five years earlier, GI had acquired CommScope (and Drendel) along with the San Diego VideoCipher Division. A legend in the cable business and a strong ally of GI's San Diego unit, Drendel was famous for buying and selling the CommScope business multiple times. He originally purchased it from Superior Continental Corporation in 1976 with a group of Hickory-based investors. Drendel was a master at nurturing customer relationships, allowing CommScope to flourish as the leading provider of coaxial and fiber optic cable. Each time he completed a buy/sell cycle of his company, Drendel's personal wealth increased commensurately.

My hotel room in Lahaska was sitting on a busy two-lane highway with loud trucks roaring by through the night. I lay awake anxiously rehearsing the multiple presentations I had to make. But the next day it went reasonably well in the face of many tough questions and lively arguments. We were all on the same team after all, and the real competitors were starting to wake up to the colossal market opportunity for digital television equipment.

We had a lengthy discussion about Scientific Atlanta (SA), our nemesis in the cable and satellite TV businesses. It is hard to overestimate the visceral antagonism between the two companies in those days. The animosity was mutual and historic, stemming from the fact that the two companies were effectively a duopoly, with a winner-take-all fervor, and the cable operators and content providers pitted us against each other for every deal.

SA's initial competitive response to GI was a completely different type of digital video compression, called Vector Quantization (VQ), which it had licensed from Utah State University. VQ compression was to be combined with SA's internally owned "SEDAT" digital audio technology. SA also had an analog HDTV system under development, called HD-BMAC, resembling the European HD-MAC standard but with SA's proprietary technology.

Both companies, GI and SA, were known to favor proprietary technical solutions, locking in customers and thereby driving higher market share, product margins, and profits. For example, in the analog cable set-top box market dominated by GI and SA, gross margins exceeded 30 percent while products in the broader consumer electronics market, such as TV sets and VCRs, had razor-thin, single-digit margins. The mainstream consumer electronics companies from Japan and Europe were dying to get into the more lucrative cable equipment business, but they were effectively locked out by the specialized and proprietary video scrambling systems developed by GI and SA.

But the world was changing. Industry standards were being viewed as increasingly important for industry growth, and the cable operators were getting tired of the constant feuding between GI and SA. On the other hand, they liked the fact that the duopoly was American and that the two companies would customize equipment to their needs. However, the operators were a little wary about the San Diego VideoCipher group. We were closely tied to the cable programmers, a constituency having constant tension with the cable distributors. Further, the operators thought GI San Diego might have the audacity to team up with a cable enemy, such as Hughes, with its high-power DBS ambitions.

In Lahaska we also discussed the companies in the FCC competition for the HDTV over-the-air broadcast standard, namely the Philips/Thomson/Sarnoff/NBC consortium and the Zenith/AT&T alliance. While concerned about their larger financial resources, we felt we had a significant advantage in time-to-market as well as in the systems engineering aspects. We were already developing an end-to-end digital television communications platform, from content origination all the way to consumer viewing, with the complex cable headend infrastructure equipment in the middle.

We also discussed a new venture called SkyPix, which was working with a Silicon Valley video compression company, Compression Labs (CLI). At the time, CLI was the only other company with a credible digital compression story due to its role in the emerging videoconferencing business. But CLI wasn't directly involved in the HDTV process, didn't have a cable headend or consumer decoder product, didn't have conditional access technology, and was working with SkyPix on a Single Channel Per Carrier digital video encoder, which we deemed to be a technical non-starter in the emerging multi-channel digital satellite and cable markets.

One final competitive issue was discussed for the first time at this GI corporate strategy meeting. MPEG (pronounced "em-peg"), an emerging international digital video compression standard being embraced by the Philips/Thomson consortium in the FCC HDTV competition, would become a central topic for many years to come. In fact, given our strategy at the time—namely to establish our own proprietary compression technology in the market—MPEG, as a technology, would become the biggest competitor of all.

At the end of the meeting, as the discussions started to drift, Drendel saved the day with a diplomatic compromise. "This is fantastic technology," he declared, proposing that the San Diego division should continue its development full-speed ahead, targeting the satellite TV and content provider markets as well as ongoing participation in the FCC HDTV competition. The Hatboro division could wait a little longer to see how the market developed, allowing it to continue its focus on other near-term product development priorities. With the digital cable potential hanging in the balance, everyone seemed reasonably satisfied. Rumsfeld and Forstmann Little were given more time to make sense out of all the confusion before deciding how much more to bet on digital TV.

13 THE SPECTER OF MPEG

We first caught wind of the MPEG activity in 1990. The Moving Picture Experts Group (MPEG) falls under the umbrella of the International Standards Organization and the International Electro-Technical Commission, with a mission of developing specifications and standards for the coding of moving pictures and associated audio. MPEG's leader and convener, Leonardo Chiariglione, was well suited for his role, having blended a classical education with a technical one at both his native Polytechnic University of Turin and at the University of Tokyo, where he obtained his PhD.

The initial activity, MPEG-1, started in May 1988 and was oriented toward digital video storage applications, such as CD-ROMs for personal computers. Thus MPEG arose from a completely different direction, a world apart from GI and its television and broadband communications targets. At first I was GI's sole representative to MPEG and perhaps the only non-engineer attending the meetings. We didn't have any spare video coding engineers to send, and at that stage our goal was understanding MPEG strategically: where it was going and how quickly, who was involved, and what it meant for GI.

It was soon evident that MPEG might become a force to be reckoned with. Many of the top video research engineers in the world were already involved, representing major companies like Philips, AT&T/Bell Labs, Thomson, IBM, and Sony. It was a relatively exciting time for the mundane world of technical standardization, in large part due to a heightened sense that something important was in the air. GI had recently gone public with its digital television project, and there was a growing sentiment within the MPEG community that the emerging standard should also strive to cover the digital television application.

In December 1990 an early MPEG-2 meeting was held in Berlin, memorable for historic reasons unrelated to the technical discussions. This weeklong session occurred before the committee became focused on digital television. Nonetheless, the event's location became highly symbolic on a couple of levels. First, the Heinrich Hertz Institute was the official host of the meeting. Hertz, a nineteenth-century German physicist, built upon James Maxwell's electromagnetic theory of light, proving the existence of electromagnetic waves propagating through space and able to carry information. The scientific unit of frequency "hertz" or "Hz," defined as "cycles per second," was named in his honor. Ironically, even though the MPEG participants were not yet focused on communications applications, the meeting could not have been hosted by a more appropriately named entity. For example, satellite transponders are typically 24 MHz, 36 MHz, or 54 MHz in bandwidth (equating to frequency ranges of 24, 36, or 54 million cycles per second). Similarly, US cable and terrestrial broadcast TV channels are defined in 6 MHz chunks of communications spectrum (a frequency range of 6 million cycles per second).

The second salient point about the December 1990 Berlin MPEG meeting was that it occurred at the end of the year of the Berlin Wall's physical destruction. As a souvenir, the Heinrich Hertz Institute gave each attendee a few crumbled pieces of the original wall. The fall of the Berlin Wall not only marked the end of the Cold War but also signified the beginning of independence for certain Soviet Bloc states. Foreshadowing the Internet, satellite television was crossing borders and connecting the world, bringing news and entertainment across geographic boundaries, opening up the eyes and minds of oppressed masses that were living under authoritarian regimes.

Several months later, an important milestone marked the May 1991 MPEG meeting in Paris. At a cocktail party for the US delegation, I spotted Sid Topol, the esteemed former CEO of our archrival, Scientific Atlanta. In Paris for an unrelated reason but still involved with SA, he saw my GI badge and asked me what I was doing there. After I told him about MPEG, he asked me why no one from SA was there. I simply shrugged in response.

At the next ANSI[1] meeting in the United States, I observed Allan Ecker, SA's chief technology officer, enter the room and then later saw him salute three additional SA engineers also in attendance. SA's proprietary digital system had not gained any market momentum, and this meeting was the company's strategic turning point toward MPEG. It was fairly obvious that my chance encounter with Sid Topol in Paris had resulted in SA being pushed into the MPEG regime. Soon after, at a subsequent cable trade show, we observed SA tearing down its signage for the proprietary VQ digital compression system and putting up MPEG posters instead. Suddenly SA had more of a presence in MPEG than us, and we were about to find ourselves on the defensive.

It was an interesting moment. The initial phase of digital TV development had been filled with excitement and promise. GI had an early lead but competing activities were emerging and no one really knew how the technology or market would play out. It wasn't long before we entered the next phase, which was exhausting, filled with action, and fraught with strategic pitfalls.

■ ■ ■

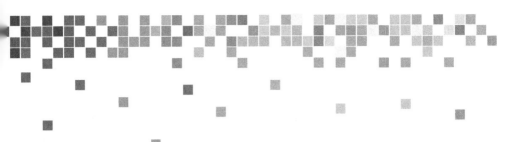

PART TWO
THE SPRINT AND
THE MARATHON

14 THE MAVERICKS OF NASSAU COUNTY

Establishing a disruptive technology in a pre-existing market is not a simple matter. Numerous unforeseen roadblocks and hurdles are imposed by competitors, customers, and government authorities. On the way to a sustainable long-term success, the innovator is also challenged by many urgent fire drills. In the case of digital TV, one such early footrace occurred between General Instrument and Cablevision Systems Corporation.

Cable industry icon Charles (Chuck) Dolan was born an entrepreneur, growing up in Cleveland during the Great Depression. His first deal was selling a Boy Scouts column to the *Cleveland Press* for two dollars a week.[1] As a young man he sold his video editing and production company to a New York firm and then moved east with his wife, creating immensely successful businesses and making a permanent impact on the media business.

In 1965, Dolan founded Sterling Manhattan Cable, the country's first urban underground cable TV system. After Time Inc. invested in his new company, Dolan hatched the idea of a subscription television channel. In the early 1970s, a skeptical Time Inc. finally approved his plan, seeding The Green Channel with $150,000 and renaming it Home Box Office in 1972. Dolan had hired a young lawyer, Jerry Levin, to help him get HBO off the ground. The pay TV concept was initially established with the movie *Sometimes a Great Notion*, starring Paul Newman and Henry Fonda, based on Ken Kesey's novel. This event was followed by an NHL hockey game featuring the New York Rangers live from Madison Square Garden.

When Chuck Dolan departed Time Inc., Jerry Levin became HBO's new leader. In 1973, Dolan formed what would become Cablevision Systems, with roots in Nassau County, Long Island, and subsequent expansion throughout the New York metropolitan area. Dolan had an innate sense of the value of owning content. On the heels of founding Cablevision, he also started a sports channel, Cablevision Sports 3, renamed Sports Channel New York in 1979. He then formed a content subsidiary, Rainbow Media, which included Bravo. Dolan also started the Playboy Channel in 1982 before selling Rainbow's interest to Playboy Enterprises in 1986. For the next few decades, Rainbow Media would remain a major force in the content world, owning American Movie Classics (AMC), the Independent Film Channel (IFC), SundanceTV, and equity interests in numerous regional sports channels throughout the country.

Cablevision was at the vanguard of many groundbreaking initiatives over the years, and the person Chuck Dolan and his son Jim relied on for all things technical was Wilt Hildenbrand. Hildenbrand developed a lifelong fascination with technology in the Air Force. He joined the Dolans at Cablevision in 1976 as chief engineer of the company's Long Island system and ultimately became executive vice president of engineering and technology for the entire company. Hildenbrand established a strong track record of implementing novel technologies, buttressing Cablevision's strategic position along the way. Fiercely independent and willing to take risks he deemed best for the company, Hildenbrand designed microwave networks for sports events, built a massive satellite uplink facility for national content delivery, and implemented fiber optic distribution to small neighborhoods of cable subscribers.

When Hildenbrand heard about General Instrument's new digital TV technology, he became interested immediately. Woo Paik's advanced technology team had finished the real-time digital SDTV hardware prototype ahead of schedule, and by August 1991, Paik, Mark Medress, and I were on-site at Cablevision's Hicksville, Long Island, headend, sweating buckets in a room filled with Cablevision executives and New York franchise authority bureaucrats. The company's valuable cable franchises were up for renewal, and competitors were salivating at the opportunity to seize the country's largest metropolitan market.

Back in San Diego, we had leased a part-time satellite transponder and rented a portable uplink truck. Rainbow, Cablevision's content subsidiary, provided us with the programming to be compressed and delivered at a 4:1 ratio—that is, four digital standard-definition TV signals within one satellite transponder, as opposed to only one TV signal using analog technology. On Long Island, Chuck Dolan was present with his top executives and board members, ready to put on a show for the New York cable franchise authority.

As Ed Krause initiated the transmission from San Diego, Paik, Medress, and I held our breath, unsure whether the first coast-to-coast digital satellite television transmission would actually work. Suddenly the TV sets in the room lit up with flawless digital pictures filling the screens. Granted, it was digital SDTV, not HDTV, but very few people had seen HD at this time anyway, and the pictures dazzled with eye-popping clarity. The possibility of digital cable TV had apparently been pitched to the franchise authorities as one of several reasons for renewing Cablevision's lucrative franchises. Behind the scenes, the local government officials had been told that this technical feat was a first, and they would be witnessing history. We were rewarded with a round of applause, and before Chuck Dolan came over to personally thank us, we overheard Hildenbrand say to him, "You have no idea how many hoops these guys had to jump through to get this done."

Flying home to San Diego, triumphant and relieved, we knew we had just taken an important step in the right direction. Anxious to get back to work, Woo Paik's team only had a few months until the next critical milestone, when the DigiCipher HDTV real-time hardware prototype had to be shipped to Washington DC for the FCC's digital broadcast testing competition.

15 SHRINKING THE DISH

The Cablevision digital SDTV demonstration would not have been possible without advances in satellite communications technology which had taken place during the previous two decades. Satellite TV was still a novelty in the 1980s. The fact that cable systems received most of their programming from satellites high up in the sky was largely unknown to the tens of millions of cable subscribers. The big 3-meter dishes in backyards across America, mostly in rural areas but increasingly in the suburbs, were something of a curiosity. But for the dish owners, it was the pinnacle of TV and an unknown precursor of the Internet.

These consumers had paid up to three thousand dollars to have Television Receive Only (TVRO) satellite systems installed at their homes. They felt righteously entitled to enjoy the fruits of their investment for no additional charge: more channels than anyone else in the world, including virtually every cable channel, raining down from more than a dozen different satellites; East and West Coast feeds of the same channel, allowing an early form of time-shifted viewing; wild feeds, unintended for household viewing, from broadcast networks and international news outlets; many foreign and ethnic channels; raw sports footage backhauled from stadiums to TV production studios in New York and LA; even a NASA channel. If you surfed the sky with your BUD,[1] you never knew what you might encounter with these early satellite TV systems.

Communications satellites for television signals utilize the geostationary orbit, in which satellites move in the same direction and at the same rate as the spin of Earth. British futurist Arthur C. Clarke, cowriter in 1968 of Stanley Kubrick's *2001: A Space Odyssey*, is credited with conceiving the geostationary orbit for communications satellites. In this orbit, 22,300 miles above the equator, a communications satellite appears fixed to a single point on Earth, such as the backyard of a home. The dish antenna in that backyard doesn't have to move in order to track an individual satellite. And with an actuator and positioner attached, the dish can track multiple satellites in the sky, their precise orbital positions stored in memory inside a consumer's satellite receiver.

The large satellite dishes popping up outside homes across America in the 1980s were called C-band dishes because of the frequency band used by the satellites from which they received their TV signals. A C-band satellite typically has twenty-four "transponders." A satellite transponder comprises the electronics capable of receiving and transmitting one analog TV channel within a fixed bandwidth. These C-band satellites use relatively low power for amplifying the TV signals. To compensate for these satellites' low power, the dishes in people's backyards needed to be large in order to receive and focus the electromagnetic energy. The 3-meter diameter dishes were ungainly. They were too large and heavy to be mounted on houses because in high winds they might literally rip off a section of the roof or porch to which they were attached. And so they sat mostly in rural and suburban yards, where homeowners had the space for them.

The Holy Grail for satellite communications companies was to enable small, unobtrusive dishes using higher power Ku-band satellites. Ku-band satellites use a much higher frequency band than that used by C-band satellites.[2] There were already medium-power Ku-band satellites circling the skies, but these were not powerful enough to meet the needs of Hughes Communications. Hughes was especially keen on using very high-power satellites in the so-called direct broadcast satellite (DBS) band. The Hughes executives felt that high power was essential in order to facilitate pizza-sized 18-inch dishes and make satellite TV a breakout consumer business. These antennas could be mounted directly on rooftops or porches in urban areas.

The FCC had authorized eight distinct DBS orbital locations covering the United States, with 9 degree spacing between them in order to avoid interference with adjacent satellites. The three most important locations, the prime real estate in the sky for high-power DBS, were at 101 degrees, 110 degrees, and 119 degrees west longitude. These destinations referred to the distance from the Greenwich Prime Meridian in London. These orbital slots were highly desirable because they hovered directly over the center of the continental United States, allowing the signals to blanket nearly the entire country. Hughes reserved twenty-seven of these DBS frequencies with the FCC at the 101 degree position.

Meanwhile, a famous Minnesota broadcasting family, the Hubbards, had licensed another five transponders at the same orbital position. In 1984, Stanley S. Hubbard had developed the industry's first satellite news gathering vehicle using Ku-band and analog video technology. He then established Conus Communications, a company whose entire foundation was based on satellite news gathering. Now, in the 1990s, Hubbard Broadcasting was dead set on getting into the DBS business, the next big wave in satellite communications. To this end, Hubbards' DBS entity, United States Satellite Broadcasting (USSB), pooled its satellite frequencies with those of Hughes, giving the two companies a combined total of thirty-two.

Using traditional analog television technology, however, the maximum number of TV channels Hughes and Hubbard could deliver to consumers was limited to thirty-two: one analog TV signal per satellite transponder. Such a constraint would hardly pose a competitive threat to cable, which already had more than twice this channel capacity in many cities and suburbs. So when GI's Larry Dunham and Mark Medress continued calling on Hughes, claiming that digital TV technology would enable a tenfold increase of up to 320 digital channels on one satellite, it was music to their ears.

16 STAR WARS

Hughes was eager to find promising new solutions in the satellite TV business because of the market difficulties it faced. The initial Sky Cable partnership between Hughes, News Corporation, Cablevision, and NBC was falling apart, a classic case of too many corporate cooks in the kitchen. On the competitive front, K Prime, the precursor to PrimeStar, was launching service with Scientific Atlanta's analog system. And another new venture, SkyPix, threatened to usurp Hughes's market position.

SkyPix, based in Seattle, was founded by two brothers, Fred and Richard Greenberg, to broadcast pay-per-view movies via satellite. In 1990, Comsat agreed to invest $100 million in the new venture, but the big satellite company pulled out later that year. Then Roy Speer and his Home Shopping Network (HSN) teamed up with SkyPix. This alliance caused the cable industry, as well as Hughes, to start feeling the heat again. Speer was a credible and larger-than-life figure who had committed an initial $30 million to get SkyPix launched. It would start as an eighty-channel medium-power Ku-band satellite service using digital video compression technology from Compression Labs. Mitsubishi agreed to finance the consumer receiver equipment.

In the spring of 1991, Hal Krisbergh, Matt Miller, and I visited Speer for an exploratory meeting at HSN headquarters in St. Petersburg, Florida. The walls of his office were lined with self-aggrandizing memorabilia ostentatiously framed. He seemed flattered that GI was knocking on his door, but at the same time he appeared suspicious of our motives. A savvy and ruthless entrepreneur, having built HSN from scratch, he knew deep down he couldn't trust the cable industry, for which GI was the proxy in this case. The cable industry was unlikely to help a would-be competitor such as SkyPix. Speer did extend an olive branch, however, by offering to let us build the satellite receivers.

For a brief period it looked like SkyPix had a shot at being the front-runner in the DBS market, a business in which the first-mover advantage could be significant, and where K Prime (PrimeStar) was constrained by its analog delivery system. But SkyPix's technology didn't work as promised and its partnerships began to unravel. By September 1991, Roy Speer and HSN pulled out of the entire arrangement, citing SkyPix's failure to meet certain unspecified milestones. SkyPix entered bankruptcy a year later.

Paul Allen, technology investor and Microsoft co-founder, was intrigued by the potential for video compression technology. He committed $150 million in a reorganization plan to take over SkyPix's assets and emerge from bankruptcy, only to withdraw his plan a few months later.

Yet another satellite TV venture had bitten the dust, and the path was clear again for Hughes.

After the dissolution of the Sky Cable partnership, Hughes decided to go it alone in the consumer satellite business, in the form of DirecTV. DirecTV issued a Request for Proposal (RFP) for its DBS content delivery system and consumer equipment in 1991. Our team at GI had already met with them a few times and had a good idea of what they wanted:

- a digital SDTV system that could meet its schedule of launching service by early 1994

- a turnkey consumer system priced at under $700 retail, including all the necessary DBS components: an Integrated Receiver Decoder (IRD), an 18-inch-diameter dish, and a Low Noise Block downconverter (LNB) with feedhorn

- a highly secure conditional access and encryption system, with the security provider having a monetary incentive to fix the system in the event of piracy

- a roadmap to HDTV in the future

- a company they could rely on, with no conflict of interest, to be their partner in success

Hughes's undertaking, encompassing the various cost, technical, business, timing, and competitive dimensions, was gargantuan.

GI San Diego thought it had a good shot at winning the DirecTV business. Our main advantages were our lead in developing a complete digital system and our experience in pay TV security. Our biggest disadvantage was lack of a retail brand name, which we attempted to cure by aligning ourselves with Sony and Toshiba in a joint proposal. GI had also previously hired Mike Meltzer and Greg Gudorf, two consumer electronics experts from Sony.

Soon it became obvious that we were very much in the running, but compatibility with the emerging MPEG-2 video compression standard arose as a major issue. If we suddenly changed to MPEG-2, it would delay product development by at least a year or two, thereby neutralizing our most important advantage—time to market. However, we were fairly certain that no competitor could get DirecTV an MPEG-2 compatible system on time, either. We were not reticent in explaining that belief to Hughes.

As the RFP process approached its conclusion, Mark Medress received a call from Hughes. They explained that they had appreciated everything GI had done, and it was a very difficult decision, but they had decided to go in a different direction. They asked whether GI would consider providing its conditional access and security technology as an independent component, but GI declined, preferring to stay focused on the complete systems approach.

Startled by the bad news, Medress asked if we could have one more shot at convincing them that GI was the only solution if DirecTV really wanted to launch on time. They agreed, and I rushed off to the San Diego airport to fly up to LA, near Hughes's El Segundo headquarters. As I waited at the gate to board my flight, I heard my name paged on the intercom (this being the pre–cell phone era). The airport employee had a landline phone waiting for me, with Medress on the other end. Hughes's Bill Butterworth had called back and said not to bother sending me to LA; their decision was final.

We were devastated by the loss of the DirecTV business, which we felt had enormous potential. But after a period of self-reflection, we realized it was a big world and we had to move on. GI San Diego president Larry Dunham tasked us with getting a post-mortem report on why we had lost. The DirecTV guys told us we were the runners-up out of several competitors, but they had decided on Thomson Consumer Electronics[1] because of the RCA consumer brand and the MPEG-2 compatibility issue. While we had brand-name retail consumer electronics partners (Sony and Toshiba), they had a major concern about GI's cable TV ties, and our pricing was higher than Thomson's. They wanted a separable conditional access and security system so they could hold the provider of that technology accountable in the event of a piracy breach. Furthermore, Hughes was a system integrator itself, and didn't like the fact that we were developing the entire digital system ourselves.

The details of the DirecTV system were announced in February 1992. Thomson received an exclusive order for one million units of a new RCA digital satellite receiver before second sources could enter the market. NDS, an Israeli company acquired by Rupert Murdoch in 1992, would provide the conditional access and encryption system, in the form of a smart card. And Compression Labs, SkyPix's former partner, would develop the MPEG encoders. DirecTV itself would perform project management, coordinating the different companies, something they were experienced with due to their background in spacecraft and satellites.

Separately, investor Ted Forstmann arranged a meeting between Rupert Murdoch and GI corporate executives Rick Friedland and Jim Faust to explore whether GI and NDS, owners of the world's two leading pay TV security systems, could do something together. Faust had recently been recruited into GI from Scientific Atlanta, where he was head of international business. The meeting was held at Murdoch's office in New York, with representatives of Allen & Company, the prestigious and secretive investment bank, present in case a potential transaction arose. Other than Ted Forstmann trying to sell Murdoch a Gulfstream corporate jet, however, not much transpired and GI and NDS remained brutal competitors for years to come.

17 ALL ROADS LEAD TO SAN DIEGO

General Instrument had gained confidence and credibility with the digital SDTV hardware prototype built by Woo Paik's advanced development team. It was capable of running our latest video compression algorithms in real time. We had also proven end-to-end capability by transmitting digital signals from San Diego over a national satellite to Cablevision Long Island. To bridge the gap before our commercial system was ready, we built a demonstration room at our 6262 Lusk Boulevard division headquarters. The San Diego headcount was growing rapidly, and we would eventually occupy six buildings in the Sorrento Mesa high-tech area of San Diego. But 6262 Lusk was "Building 1," ground zero for digital TV, and it was buzzing with activity and a heightened sense of excitement.

Larry Dunham had resigned as president of the San Diego VideoCipher Division after a dispute with GI CEO Donald Rumsfeld in Chicago. Dunham had been the strong, steady leader of a business that contributed enormous profits and cash flow to the corporation. He had also started GI firmly down the digital path with a steadfast certainty that we could hit another home run, and succeed with an even bigger second act than the original VideoCipher satellite TV encryption franchise.

As our corporate office searched for a replacement for Dunham, Jerry Heller and then Tom Dumit, GI's corporate general counsel, acted as temporary general managers of the San Diego unit, reporting to Rumsfeld. Finally, Jim Bunker, our new division president, arrived in October 1991. Bunker had been a thirty-year veteran and a top executive at M/A-Com with a background in sales and microwave electronics. From his M/A-Com career he knew some of the early VideoCipher employees as well as Frank Drendel. Drendel's CommScope business had been part of GI's 1986 acquisition of M/A-Com Cable Home Communications along with the VideoCipher Division.

Bunker, a gregarious, blue-blooded New Englander with unbounded energy, possessed an engaging interpersonal style and contagious enthusiasm. The digital TV technology was new to him, as it was to most people at that time, but he was a quick study regarding the competitive environment and knew just enough about technology to be dangerous. First and foremost, he was a salesman. He loved interacting with customers as much as with employees. He was clearly having a great deal of fun on the job, and his positive attitude permeated the organization, even with the crushing pressures of a seemingly impossible product development schedule.

Bunker was also a tireless traveler, always ready to jump on a plane to visit customers. He relished poking good-hearted fun at his employees, and we teased him for his habit of dashing through airports even when there was plenty of time to catch the flight. Another hallmark was his insistence on good, old-fashioned business rules: a firm handshake, a clear look in the eye, prompt return of phone calls, and an edict to always look presentable, even when traveling on a red-eye, because you never knew whom you might run into.

As 1991 came to a close, we were able to demonstrate four digitally compressed SDTV channels using the same 4:1 prototype hardware as for Cablevision, as well as a computer simulation of two digital HDTV channels. We also had the lab equipment to simulate a satellite link using QPSK modulation, and a cable TV link using a rudimentary form of QAM.[1] These modulation techniques are analogous to using FM or AM for sending analog TV or radio signals.

The time had come to show the television community what we had. Soon visitors were flowing in daily. At first Ed Krause ran all the demos, never complaining, but we knew he had far more important work to do as our video compression algorithm ace. Chris Higgins took over the lab and demo responsibility, freeing Krause to focus all his energy on improving and refining the HD video compression algorithms, critical for the upcoming FCC advanced television testing in Washington DC.

Before DirecTV's RFP and decision to go with RCA, executives came from Hughes Communications. Rob Hubbard and Ray Conover visited from Hubbard Communications of Saint Paul, Minnesota, explaining they might decide to team with Hughes for a common DBS business.

The HBO team of Bob Zitter and Craig Cuttner also arrived, becoming early champions of what we were doing. HBO's subscriber growth had stalled and it was searching for a new expansion path. The company had more programming than it could fit on one channel. Zitter, encountering the incredible efficiency allowed by digitally compressed television, brainstormed the idea of the pay TV "multiplex." His concept was inspired by Sumner Redstone's multiscreen movie theater business, National Amusements. Zitter's hypothesis was that if HBO could create more channels, with alternative themes, and offer them to cable subscribers for no additional fee, then subscriber growth would resume. Cuttner, Zitter's right-hand technologist, would become our most valuable source of customer inputs into a rapidly evolving product roadmap. This was especially important to us since HBO was the content industry's unofficial technology leader, the industry bellwether.

Ed Horowitz was another early visitor. He had moved from HBO to Viacom as chief technology officer in 1989, hired by CEO Frank Biondi, himself an HBO alumnus. Horowitz brought along Paul Heimbach and Doug Semon, one of Viacom's top cable engineers. At the time, Viacom was not only a content powerhouse but also still a major cable operator. Viacom had an experimental advanced cable TV system in Castro Valley, California, with 150 channels of analog TV as well as video-on-demand. Horowitz wanted the cable side of Viacom, represented by Semon, to get an early look at GI's new digital technology. Horowitz immediately knew the importance of what he saw. He asked Jerry Heller, "Would you guys consider selling a piece of this?" to which Heller replied in his calm and noncommittal manner: "I suppose so, at the right price."

The stream of visitors was continuous. Reggie Thomas, ESPN's head of Operations and Engineering, visited from Bristol, Connecticut, along with his top engineers, Chuck Pagano and John Eberhard. Mike Aloisi from Showtime and MTV Networks also came to see us. TVN's Stu Levin and Greg Pasetta drove down from LA. Vince Roberts and Bob Witkowski arrived from Disney; Jim Heyworth, Lindsay Gardner, and Mike Schlesier came from Viewer's Choice, a leading pay-per-view programmer based in New York; Marwan Fawaz, a young engineer (and future CTO of Charter) from Times Mirror Cable; Wilt Hildenbrand and Al Johnson from Cablevision Long Island; Howard Miller and Mark Richer from PBS in Alexandria, Virginia; David Fellows from Continental Cable; Gregg Burton and Jay Aldrich from Rainbow Media.

PrimeStar was pondering an upgrade to digital from SA's analog BMAC system, and David Beddow became a regular guest with his team of Gary Traver, Kim Johnson, and Thad Mazurczyk, always wanting to see the latest improvements. Jim Chiddix, future CTO of Time Warner Cable, came from ATC/Time Warner. Tom Jokerst came from CableLabs, where he was on loan from Continental Cable. Nick Hamilton-Piercy visited from Rogers Cablesystems of Toronto.

Delegations from CableLabs, Telesat Canada, and JCSAT (Japan) made the journey to San Diego. Industry statesman Chuck Hewitt, chairman of the Satellite Broadcast and Communications Association (SBCA), paid us a visit, along with Dick Johnson, who would later become a top executive at EchoStar and Dish Network. Taylor Howard, the founder of Chaparral Communications and the man who invented the home satellite dish for American backyards many years earlier, visited to see the next big thing in satellite TV.

The simple reason all these people were visiting us in San Diego? We had the world's first and only functioning digital TV hardware (SDTV), plus our digital HDTV computer simulations were knocking people's socks off. Most of these guests sensed it was the beginning of something big, although the exact timing and market implications were still fuzzy.

The visiting engineers, representing the media content companies, went back to their offices and summarized what they had seen in San Diego, and then the marketing and programming executives debated what it all meant for the future of content creation, packaging, and distribution.

The cable operators were interested in the technology but were less excited than the content community, not seeing much of a need to do anything soon. After all, they still had a virtual monopoly in their franchise areas, with no real competition in sight. Unsure what they would gain by going digital, they were skeptical of committing to an uncertain new technology.

With our initial product still several months from completion, interested parties kept coming to see our demo system into early 1992. NBA Commissioner David Stern was one of the most memorable visitors, flying in from New York with Ed Desser, president of NBA Television. They wanted to understand how digital technology might affect the future of professional basketball, which Stern would propel into a multibillion-dollar global brand over the next twenty years. In late 1994, an initial fruit of Stern's ambitions emerged when NBA Television began selling the "NBA League Pass," a package of 400 out-of-market games, to satellite TV subscribers.

But the most important visitor of all was Dr. John Malone, from TCI headquarters in Denver.

18 THE KING OF CABLE

John Malone grew up in Milford, Connecticut, the son of an engineer. At Yale he received dual undergraduate degrees, in electrical engineering and economics, foreshadowing an extraordinary career blending a deep technical understanding with incisive business acumen. Malone's career began at Bell Labs, which paid for him to attend graduate school at Johns Hopkins. After receiving his PhD in Operations Research, Malone returned to Bell Labs before joining McKinsey & Company, where he helped restructure General Electric into strategic business units. His meteoric rise within the cable industry began in the early 1970s when General Instrument, another McKinsey client, hired Malone as president of its Jerrold cable TV equipment subsidiary in Pennsylvania.[1]

Speaking at his alma mater (Yale) in 1999, Malone cited a "lifelong audacity to be different" as one of the keys to his success in the cable and media industry. "If you accept conventional wisdom, you are accepting, at best, average results. If you want superior results, you have to push boundaries. You've got to bang against the wall, challenge the common perception…and be willing to take risks as you're doing it." He also cited one of the best pieces of advice he ever received, coming early in his career from Moses (Monty) Shapiro, GI's long-time leader and the father of future Monsanto CEO Robert Shapiro. Monty Shapiro had built GI, primarily through acquisitions, until his retirement in 1975, when Frank Hickey took over. Malone said, "He [Shapiro] told me to always ask the question 'If not?' In other words, always evaluate whether your assumptions might be wrong."[2]

In a 2001 Cable Center interview, Malone recalled GI's formative position in the emerging cable business upon his arrival at GI's Jerrold cable electronics unit: "There was a point when I said that the accounts receivable at Jerrold had exceeded the whole net worth of the cable industry … I think, by a factor of two to one, because at that time Jerrold had huge market share in supplying the electronics, but also in financing (the building of) cable systems, doing turnkeys, and when I first got there we actually were the number three operator in the business. Jerrold owned a whole bunch of cable systems."

In 1972 Malone was lured to his GI customer, Tele-Communications Inc. (TCI), by founder Bob Magness. Magness was originally a cottonseed salesman and cattle rancher who became one of cable TV's early pioneers, building and buying systems in various western states including Texas, Montana, Wyoming, Colorado, and Nebraska. When Malone arrived in Denver, TCI was a bootstrapped, highly leveraged company in a precarious position, with debt of $132 million, annual revenue of only $18 million, and a market capitalization of $3 million.[3] Making use of the equipment financing facility he had established at GI Jerrold, by the early 1980s Malone expanded TCI into the country's biggest cable operator, creating enormous value in the process.

Malone was prescient in his willingness to invest in content, not only to feed his cable systems but also for the content's intrinsic value, which he was confident would compound over the years as the subscription TV market expanded. In 1980, Bob Johnson, a staff member of the National Cable Television Association, approached Malone with the idea of a cable channel aimed at the black television audience. Malone listened intently and then invested in Black Entertainment Television (BET). When John Hendricks, founder of The Discovery Channel, was running out of money in 1985 and making contingency plans to shut down, he met Malone and his TCI associate John Sie. They led an investor group that kept Discovery alive. Participants included Gene Schneider (the founder and CEO of United Cable), Newhouse (Advance Publications), and Cox Communications. Malone also took equity positions at various times in Turner Broadcasting, QVC, Starz Encore, and News Corporation.

Former Vice President Al Gore once called Malone "a monopolist bent on dominating the television marketplace." According to a 1993 *Fortune* magazine interview, Malone felt his one meeting with Gore a few years earlier had been cordial but that Gore's ire was raised when TCI and the cable programmers began scrambling their analog satellite TV signals in the mid-1980s using GI's VideoCipher technology. This situation enraged the country's C-band satellite dish owners, concentrated in rural states such as Tennessee. This is where Gore's ancestors had settled after the Revolutionary War and where as a child Gore had worked during the summers on his family's tobacco farms.[4] Malone asserted: "My attitude has always been that if we get too big, it's a legitimate role of government to say 'You're too big.' They just don't have to be so personal about it. He [Gore] called me Darth Vader and the leader of the cable Cosa Nostra." [5]

Malone also became known as an extraordinary financial engineer, creatively and aggressively consummating tax-free spin-offs to shareholders and asset exchanges with other media companies. Josh Sapan, CEO of AMC Networks (formerly Rainbow Media), contrasted his own boss, Chuck Dolan, with Malone: "Malone is certainly the smartest guy in any room he's in. In a room with him and Chuck Dolan, Chuck is the most creative business guy and Malone is the smartest."[6]

While Malone was becoming a dominant player in the cable and content industries, he always maintained his focus on the technological underpinnings, deeply understanding how technology could drive his business. When he heard about GI's advances in digital television he quickly sensed the strategic importance for his company and his industry. Upon visiting GI in San Diego, where he was able to see the digital technology with his own eyes, he decided to be proactive and get on top of the technology, not wait around to see what might happen with Hughes and others.

At another dinner meeting in San Diego, Donald Rumsfeld was introduced to Malone by GI's Frank Drendel, with Jim Faust and various other GI and TCI executives present. Rumsfeld noticed his friend Pete Rozelle, retired Commissioner of the National Football League, at a nearby table, prompting Drendel to introduce Rozelle to Malone. Drendel said: "Meet John Malone, your biggest customer; he's the guy who brings football games into millions of homes."

19 TCI Takes Charge

John Malone was the most powerful man in the cable business. Through TCI, he wanted to exploit the new digital television technology before the coming onslaught from DirecTV. But he knew he couldn't act rashly. The cable industry, along with the major programmers pumping content into cable headends, needed to explore its options before committing to a particular company or digital technology. In early 1992, TCI, Viacom, CableLabs, and PBS issued a comprehensive Request for Proposal to several technology companies for a digital television satellite and cable delivery system. After a lengthy process, General Instrument and Scientific Atlanta became the two finalists, opening up more specific and direct discussions between TCI and the two leading equipment vendors.

The point man tasked with focusing GI's digital activity to the benefit of TCI and the cable industry was Tom Elliot, TCI's VP of Engineering. A plainspoken Montana native, Elliot entered the business in the 1960s through Western Microwave, a company co-founded by Bob Magness and later merged into what became TCI. Elliot joined Malone at TCI Denver in the 1970s. Having grown up with TCI in the pre-Malone, Bob Magness days, he knew instinctively that for digital technology to work over cable, various technical hurdles had to be overcome, especially in the cable infrastructure. Elliot understood as well as anyone that many cable systems, especially the older rural systems owned by TCI, might have difficulty passing digital signals through to subscribers without thorough testing and upgrades.

Elliot also knew that GI's digital compression technology could make satellite TV competitors much more threatening to TCI's cable business. So he became an internal advocate, urging TCI to move quickly and preemptively. Like Malone, he wanted the cable industry to come together and embrace digital with a common platform, better able to withstand the likely onslaught from new DBS competitors such as Hughes. This meant he had to find a way to get GI and Scientific Atlanta to work together, a tall order for contentious rivals. He called the two companies' digital teams to Denver to see if he could broker a compromise.

As Jerry Heller and I entered TCI's conference room at the Denver Tech Center, we could feel the tension. It didn't matter that TCI was trying to bring us together, attempting to do what was best for the industry. Rivalries as deep and intense as that between GI and SA can't be suppressed, not even with the biggest customer in the room. But both sides remained calm and diplomatic on the surface.

The meeting concluded with one important breakthrough for the industry: TCI would become a proponent of one of GI's most important innovations. Our method of statistical multiplexing enabled video data from multiple sources to intelligently share bandwidth. We described our novel bit allocation technique to the assembled group. The system gave the more complex digital channels (for example, those containing lots of detail or rapid scene changes) more bits, while fewer bits would be temporarily allocated to the easier-to-compress channels. SA attempted to argue that GI's statistical multiplexing was a poor technical practice from the perspective of network management.

The discussion went around and around until Jerry Heller ended the debate with the following simple point: "Why wouldn't you [TCI] want statistical multiplexing since it means you can send ten digital movies through a single cable channel instead of six?" From that point on, statistical multiplexing became a given in the field of multi-channel digital video compression. Maximizing system capacity and bandwidth efficiency, while still allowing the best possible video quality, became critically important.

Malone and Elliot were convinced that GI had the best security and conditional access technology for protecting content, which had evolved out of GI's painfully learned lessons in the face of rampant satellite TV piracy. They also believed GI to have the most advanced video compression technology, not being impressed by recent MPEG demonstrations they had seen. Furthermore, GI had designed its compression system to allow one-quarter of the decoder memory chip requirement compared to MPEG-2, a significant cost savings for every digital set-top box.

As the momentum swelled behind the emerging MPEG-2 standard, however, Elliot was starting to see video quality improvements. He thought the MPEG community might be catching up to GI. He called Jim Bunker in San Diego and said GI needed to get up to Silicon Valley to talk to some people at semiconductor start-up C-Cube, specifically Didier LeGall, CTO, and Alex Balkanski, co-founder. C-Cube was one of the driving forces behind the MPEG standard, with LeGall chairing its video committee, and was developing the world's first MPEG-2 single-chip video encoder.

Woo Paik and I traveled up to Milpitas, near San Jose, for what was to be a confrontational meeting. GI was the biggest obstacle to MPEG's (and C-Cube's) goal of international unification behind a common video compression standard. At the end of the meeting, our approach was still at odds with C-Cube's. We parted our separate ways, certain to meet again in the future.

GI's position was becoming increasingly tenuous, however, with DirecTV selecting RCA/Thomson's MPEG solution and with TCI continuing to play off SA and others against GI. We faced the real possibility of being relegated to a niche role, a follower, in the promising new market we had jump-started.

Taking a much-needed break in March 1992, I escaped to Jackson Hole, Wyoming, for a ski trip with a couple of friends. One night, while in the Million Dollar Cowboy Bar, I ran into Frank Drendel, who was there with a group of cable industry leaders. Hearing my frustration, Drendel smiled knowingly, and said, "We got you covered; what if I told you God was here?" He motioned toward John Malone at the other side of the bar, indicating that Malone would stand by GI in the end.

That reassurance was not enough to calm GI's anxieties. In mid-1992, Don Rumsfeld hosted a corporate strategy retreat at a resort outside Phoenix, with executives from Chicago; Hatboro, Pennsylvania; and San Diego. Several of us presented updates within our areas of focus, and then Jim Bunker, Jerry Heller, and I had a separate session with Rumsfeld to discuss the MPEG-2 dilemma. TCI's Tom Elliot was clearly pushing in the direction of MPEG-2 and it felt like the situation was coming to a head. I summarized the MPEG-2 status, and then a heated debate ensued regarding whether we should continue marching forward with our own proprietary DigiCipher video compression or switch to MPEG-2. Rumsfeld was clearly concerned, as we all were, and gave the command: "We need to either get Elliot off his MPEG campaign or jump on board the MPEG-2 train; it's time to make a decision."

Later that night at the company cocktail party and dinner, I was seated at Rumsfeld's table.[1] I learned the importance of being very careful about what you say around him. I already knew from previous strategy meetings that if you were not completely prepared and organized, he would dress you down; I had seen this happen a few times to other GI executives. I was commenting, in a critical way, on how we were treating customers with respect to pricing and services in the VideoCipher market, where we had a virtual monopoly. He seemed to misinterpret my remarks as defending an arrogant corporate culture, of leveraging one's market position and customers, and proceeded to make an example of me to the group. He said, with his emphatic, authoritative tone, "No. When you have a strong position in the market, that's precisely when you need to nurture your customers, not take advantage of them." Knowing that he meant it as a leadership lesson, and that if I got defensive I would be digging myself deeper into a hole, I kept my mouth shut during the rest of the dinner.

20 THE RACE TO MARKET

The prototype DigiCipher digital SDTV system built by Woo Paik's team gave General Instrument an outstanding marketing tool and proof of concept. We were confident that we had a one-to-two-year development lead over any competitors, but the pressure was on to develop the real product as our competitors were moving fast to catch up. Scientific Atlanta was working the content providers and cable operators diligently, and Compression Labs, Philips, and Thomson were all starting to accelerate the development of their own digital systems.

In addition to being able to show functional hardware, GI had another significant advantage: its nexus with the content community due to the VideoCipher business. But no one was going to make it easy for GI, considering the high stakes, customer resentment for taking advantage of our VideoCipher market position, and lingering industry wounds from the satellite TV piracy debacle. And in early 1992, GI was still six months away from being ready for a field test.

The leading cable programmers were starting to formulate plans to use digital technology for the creation of more channels, knowing they needed to stay ahead of their competitors on the content side and attracted by the economics of being able to distribute new digital services at a fraction of the cost relative to analog delivery. The satellite operators—Hughes, GE Americom, and PanAmSat—were assessing the impact of digital compression on their businesses, and were considering new pricing models such as selling fractional satellite transponders or establishing shared transponder "condos." They were also concerned that transponder pricing would drop precipitously, hurting their profits, due to a potential capacity glut if the content providers didn't fill up the supply side with new digital services. At the time, DirecTV's launch was at least two years in the future, awaiting new satellites, finalization of the MPEG-2 standard, and the Thomson/RCA digital receivers along with Compression Labs' encoders and the NDS conditional access system.

In addition to targeting the domestic digital TV market, GI had substantial global ambitions as well, having tasted the European and Japanese markets with our analog technology. Jim Faust played a dual role as Corporate VP International. He was based in his hometown of Chicago, where he reported to Rumsfeld, while also leading the San Diego team with its international business development activities. He shuttled tirelessly between Chicago and San Diego, still "digital central" for GI at this time, and traveled the world in pursuit of deals. Faust had a strong contact list and was a schmoozer extraordinaire who was liked by just about everyone in the business.

Kris Kelkar transitioned from engineering to international sales. Bob King was hired for his strong telecom background, from previous jobs at SAIC and Motorola, to build a new business in the emerging market of private video networks. Jeff Wallin, a seasoned international business development guy with expertise in the Asian markets, also joined the company. Paul Hearty, hired to direct the company's standardization activities, was also well connected in the Canadian TV market. And Jeff Pockey, a top-notch field engineer, converted over to a sales role, combining his interpersonal skills with a deep understanding of how customers used our technology. I had been promoted to director of business development, with an initial focus on convincing the domestic content providers to purchase and deploy our digital system. We were ready to take the world by storm.

At HBO, Bob Zitter's idea was gathering steam. He had convinced other HBO executives that a multiplex of channels, unified by a single subscription price and the HBO brand, could regenerate subscriber growth. Ed Horowitz had hired Zitter over a decade earlier, in 1981, to handle HBO's operational and technology issues, including negotiating agreements with technology companies. With Horowitz now at Viacom, Zitter was in charge, and he was going to make sure HBO continued its reputation as the industry's technology leader.

Our early product definition and customer interactions with HBO paid a major initial dividend when they agreed to be our field test partner, starting in June 1992. We provided a four-channel DigiCipher SDTV encoder for HBO's satellite uplink site on Long Island along with several dozen digital satellite receivers for participating cable headend affiliates. HBO provided the content feeds and undertook primary technical responsibility for administering the field test. Through this critically important step, Zitter hoped not only to prove that the technology worked in a real-world environment but also to corroborate his theory that a multiplex of programming could juice up HBO's subscriber growth rate.

GI technical maestro Paul Moroney was orchestrating the overall systems engineering activity, ensuring that the various components all played together harmoniously. The elements of the DigiCipher SDTV system were coming together quickly in San Diego: Ly Tran's high-performance encoder, Annie Chen's complex network and control software, and Bob Gilberg's critical-path challenge of designing several low-cost integrated circuits for the high-volume decoder boxes. Without the timely success in developing these cost-effective chips, the product would not be viable in the market. Finally, the product management and engineering teams were interfacing with Peter Polgar's operations group to ensure a smooth transition from development to system integration and from test to production.

As our initial DigiCipher product reached field test readiness in mid-1992, we encountered a major roadblock. Domestic content providers, including HBO, PBS, ESPN, and others, wanted our product, but they were starting to hear that TCI and the other cable operators might go in a different direction. Given the constantly shifting dynamics and balance of power between the content providers and the cable operators, the content side didn't want to deploy a digital television system without assurance that their new digital satellite signals would be compatible with the future plans of the cable industry. So even as HBO and the US television programmers entered into contract negotiations with us, all eyes were on TCI's decision.

The international television programmers didn't feel the need to wait, or even to undergo the rigors of a field test; they wanted to take advantage of the compelling economics of digital content distribution immediately. First out of the blocks, in the summer of 1992, was Rogers Cablesystems, the leading Canadian cable and content company. Jim Faust knew Ted Rogers from Faust's Zenith days, when Zenith had built an entire analog cable set-top box factory in Toronto to supply Rogers with equipment. Now Rogers wanted to use GI's DigiCipher system for satellite distribution of various programming. Next up was Multivision, a Mexico City–based program provider owned by the prominent Vargas family, and Telefe, a media company in Argentina. Based in Hong Kong, Star TV[1] installed a GI system for its emerging pan-Asian satellite TV system. The Middle East Broadcasting Center signed up with us for delivery of Arabic-language content throughout the Middle East and Europe. We were off to a strong start overseas.

Back in the United States, Wilt Hildenbrand ordered a multi-channel digital system enabling Cablevision to deliver digital ads throughout the New York metropolitan area in one of the industry's first targeted advertisement ventures, through a Cablevision subsidiary called the New York Interconnect.

Our joint field test with HBO ran from June through November 1992. Managed expertly by HBO technologists Craig Cuttner and Elmer Musser, it was surprisingly smooth and successful. Even more important, Zitter's belief in the consumer benefits of an HBO multiplex was supported by a substantial increase in subscribers at cable systems participating in the test. We finalized our contract negotiations with HBO and also with the PBS network for digital satellite delivery to its local TV station members. But neither HBO nor PBS would sign or announce these important contracts until TCI and the cable industry weighed in. Our strategic domestic content provider agreements sat on the shelf, unsigned, awaiting the final decision of John Malone.

21 A HEALTHY COMPETITION GETS VICIOUS

GI knew it was stepping into uncharted territory, outside its comfort zone of satellite and cable TV, when it entered the Federal Communications Commission's HDTV process, in June 1990, just before the submission deadline. It was supposed to be a straightforward competition with the winning system becoming the US over-the-air digital broadcast standard, thereby garnering the lion's share of future HDTV equipment royalties. But that was not how it played out in the corridors of Washington.

The broadcasters established the Advanced Television Test Center in Alexandria, Virginia. There would be six sequential "test slots" lasting several weeks each, with each competitor's system being examined against dozens of criteria. Mark Richer, vice president of engineering at PBS, was assigned to manage and administer the testing process on behalf of Dick Wiley's FCC Advisory Committee on Advanced Television Services (ACATS).

Woo Paik and his team, having successfully developed the one-off digital SDTV hardware prototype, were able to apply their laser focus on the next emergency project: the on-time completion of the world's first all-digital HDTV hardware prototype. With militaristic discipline and a "must do" attitude, the engineers in Paik's Advanced Technology group worked around the clock, as if their lives depended on it. With GI's "Slot 3" FCC time window approaching rapidly, this small, devoted group of engineers had only a few months left to complete the digital HDTV encoder and decoder using a 1080-line interlace (1080i) HDTV system.

Paik's team was young, smart, and eager. In addition to video compression guru Ed Krause, the group included Vincent Liu, focused on encoding and decoding; Scott Lery and Adam Tom, tasked with the digital transmission subsystem; Rabee Koudmani, project management; Fernando Toro, the analog front-end; and Henry Derovanessian, motion estimation.

Philips, Thomson, Sarnoff, and NBC—the Advanced Television Research Consortium—had Slot 1 in the FCC testing process, set for the summer of 1991. The basic idea of the consortium's Advanced Compatible Television (ACTV) analog solution was compelling: it would be a "backward-compatible" system, meaning existing NTSC television sets, over two hundred million of which were installed in homes around the country, could extract a regular, standard definition NTSC signal from the new, enhanced ACTV broadcast signal. From the same aggregate signal, a newly purchased "enhanced resolution" TV set could presumably get a much better picture, although it wasn't considered true high definition technology.

This elegant idea solved a thorny chicken-and-egg problem with respect to introducing a new television standard in the United States. If the pre-existing TVs and the new, enhanced resolution TVs could each get a picture from the same signal, a smooth and seamless transition to the new standard could be achieved over time. However, as the ACTV system began its testing in the summer of 1991, a fatal problem emerged: the picture quality was deficient. While this system didn't have a chance, the same consortium had another opportunity with a digital HDTV system it was developing, slated for test Slot 5.

The second contender was NHK, Japan's state-owned broadcaster, credited with pioneering the development of analog HDTV technology. NHK's "Narrow MUSE" system had FCC test Slot 2. Narrow MUSE was a derivative of the analog MUSE HDTV system that NHK had developed for satellite delivery. It had to be "slimmed down" for the much tighter 6 MHz bandwidth constraint of the US over-the-air broadcast infrastructure. But as with the European consortium's ACTV system, the picture quality was poor.

Then came the moment the television industry, and the technology field at large, had been waiting for with great anticipation. Computer companies were especially intrigued, eager to see if the digital bits of the computer world would really translate into the moving pictures of the television business. In late November 1991, GI moved its all-digital, 1080i HDTV system into the Advanced Television Test Center's lab right on schedule. GI had only one rack of equipment for the encoder and a second rack for the decoder. With respect to video quality, this Slot 3 system performed with flying colors, with only one minor glitch that was fixed quickly by a system reset.

The buzz from the private halls of the test lab was that GI's video quality had been outstanding. This had been the first digital HDTV system ever developed or tested, and the fact that it had surpassed expectations underscored, at long last, that the future of television would indeed be digital. It was a breathtaking moment. The naysayers' days were numbered. Regardless of whether this particular system would be the ultimate winner, GI had essentially just proved there was no going back. The United States, and eventually the rest of the world, was going digital.

Riding high out of the Advanced Television Test Center labs, GI decided to make a splash and build momentum before the other digital systems had the chance to test. Rumsfeld, together with our HDTV point man, Bob Rast, and our DC lobbyist, Quincy Rodgers, arranged for a major publicity event the following week at the US Capitol Building. It was billed as the world's first-ever over-the-air digital broadcast of an HDTV program. In reality, a few weeks earlier, Woo Paik and his engineers had secretly arranged with KPBS San Diego to broadcast a digital HDTV signal from PBS's transmission tower to GI's San Diego office prior to the big event in Washington. The KPBS test had been a success, powering through the mountains and canyons of San Diego, unfriendly natural obstacles to a digital signal. But this was on a national stage, in the US Capitol Building, and Rumsfeld had told Paik and Rast in no uncertain terms that the historic broadcast absolutely had to work, with 100 percent likelihood.

Midday on March 23, 1992, and then again in the evening, GI successfully conducted a digital HDTV broadcast over the PBS Washington DC station. As the American flag fluttered across the screen, its brilliant stars and stripes ablaze with red, white, and blue, the room, which was filled with senators, congressmen, and FCC commissioners, was overcome by an overwhelming sense of patriotism and pride. An American company had achieved what no one thought was possible.

The event was described in GI's internal employee newsletter:

> Live from the nation's capital, with General Instrument chairman Donald Rumsfeld back in familiar territory, GI made

broadcasting history on March 23 with a landmark DigiCipher demonstration. At shortly past noon in a room at the US Capitol, Rumsfeld, former Secretary of Defense and White House Chief of Staff, led the event with opening remarks to a group of television industry notables before signaling to the DigiCipher team to initiate the broadcast. Woo Paik and Chris Higgins passed the word to T. J. Tanner, who was standing by eight miles away at the transmission tower of WETA, Channel 26, a Washington DC public TV station. Tanner then switched off the normal NTSC programming and rolled the tape of the HDTV program prepared especially for the occasion.[1]

GI, temporarily freed from the test lab until its Slot 6 GI/MIT system was ready, kept raising the stakes for the other contenders in the FCC competition with a series of firsts. Following the broadcast to the US Capitol, GI conducted the first digital HDTV over-the-air broadcast of live (as opposed to taped) content in April 1992. This event used UHF Channel 15 to send the signal to GI's demo suite at the Las Vegas Hilton during the National Association of Broadcasters trade show. After that, we proceeded with the first demonstration of a digital HDTV consumer VCR prototype (with Toshiba), also in April 1992; the first two-way cable transmission of digital HDTV in May 1992; and the first satellite transmission of a digital HDTV signal in August 1992.

Meanwhile, when the time had come in the spring of 1992 for Zenith and AT&T to commence their Slot 4 testing, they weren't ready. GI had set a very high bar for the Zenith/AT&T alliance. Their 720-line progressive (720P) digital HDTV system had produced poor video quality in the early testing, and it could have been over for Zenith and AT&T. But they pulled out all the political stops and requested a two-week extension, hoping their engineers could fix whatever issue was causing the video problems. Stuck in the middle of the political wrangling, Mark

Richer, the PBS executive who was managing the testing process on behalf of the broadcasters, became visibly upset at Zenith and AT&T's behavior. But he didn't have the authority to disqualify them as they lobbied for an extension of their testing. Then, almost miraculously, the political support they needed came from the most unlikely of places: the next competitor, the Slot 5 Philips/Thomson/Sarnoff/NBC consortium. Given another lease on life, the Zenith/AT&T video quality was tested again, showing a minor improvement but still a poor result overall.[2]

The Philips/Thomson consortium's rationale for supporting Zenith/AT&T's extension request soon became clear. The Philips/Thomson group wasn't ready either, so every day of additional testing by Zenith/AT&T would buy them valuable time for their upcoming Slot 5 testing. But it still wasn't enough, and the Philips/Thomson consortium still couldn't deliver its prototype on time. They requested a one-month delay, grounds for disqualification in the eyes of some observers. People were starting to wonder if this was even a real competition.

Rumsfeld, a political operative par excellence, and Rast, whose generous sense of fairness and compromise had been pushed past the breaking point, were incredulous. I remember being in a meeting with Rumsfeld and Jerry Heller during this period, and a phone call came into the office from Bob Wright, the CEO of NBC, which was part of the Philips/Thomson consortium. Wright was asking for Rumsfeld's support in accommodating their request for delay. A scornful look enveloped Rumsfeld's face, but he maintained his professionalism with a polite but firm denial.

When the Philips/Thomson consortium's Slot 5 system finally arrived, it was packaged within fourteen racks of equipment, a monstrosity relative to GI's streamlined implementation of a single rack each for the encoder and decoder. During testing, the consortium's 1080i digital HDTV system was riddled with stops and starts, equipment tweaks, and excuses. Because the Philips/Thomson consortium was so late getting started, it wasn't going to be able to finish all of its tests on time. It was an almost ludicrous situation that we thought spelled impending disaster for our competitor. But then a whole new series of political machinations ensued, with them being awarded another extension, allowing them to complete all the required tests. At the end of the test period, we heard that the video quality had looked very good.

GI was astounded. The process had been politicized and corrupted. It was spinning out of control. We had one more shot, though. GI had teamed up with MIT for the Slot 6 system, a 720P progressive digital HDTV system like that of Zenith/AT&T. If we ended up with the best 1080i interlace system, from the Slot 3 testing, and the only strongly performing progressive system in the upcoming sixth and final test slot, all the excuses and delays of our competitors during the previous several months wouldn't matter. We could still win. But the picture quality of the GI/MIT Slot 6 system, tested late in the summer of 1992, was poor, not even close to the stellar performance GI had achieved earlier in the year with its Slot 3 system.

It was anybody's guess what would happen next. GI thought its Slot 3 system had clearly won overall and that the remaining competitors had cheated. But it was far from a slam dunk, especially with the Philips/Thomson group's strong video quality performance and the ongoing political gyrations. At one point, Robert Reich, President Bill Clinton's Secretary of Labor, released a statement favoring the European-led group, reasoning that they would provide manufacturing jobs in the United States, whereas GI didn't even make TV sets.

In reality, none of the systems was ready for prime time, each having ample room for improvement, including GI's. Our system had experienced some problems on the digital transmission side due to interference from adjacent signals. There were no specific rules in place to resolve the conflict, leading to rumblings of another round of testing, along with innuendos of litigation if one competitor was selected as the sole winner. In this overheated environment, there was no way the FCC was going to cleanly pick a single winner.

Inside GI, we were trying to figure out what all this meant for our digital satellite and cable activities. We knew there would be major implications if and when the FCC made a decision, but we didn't know exactly what form the FCC rules would take or how the cable industry would respond. From the business perspective of most broadcasters, content providers, and cable operators, HDTV was a dubious proposition. It would require large capital investments and allocation of unprecedented amounts of bandwidth, with no assurance that consumers would pay higher service fees or that advertisers would pay higher rates.

GI's frustration and anger was running high but we forced ourselves to keep the FCC process in perspective. One thing was certain: we had to continue at light speed with our DigiCipher standard definition (SDTV) satellite system. Our digital cable system would soon shift into high gear as well. We had proven without doubt that digital HDTV would eventually happen. But the near-term opportunities remained in the trenches of the free market, with the imminent decisions of TCI, HBO, and other powerful forces within the media business, not in the bureaucratic hallways of the nation's capital.

22 MPEG World Tour

In July 1992, in the midst of the FCC advanced television broadcast testing, and while General Instrument was inking its first deals for the DigiCipher SDTV satellite system, the MPEG "world tour" converged in Angra dos Reis. This tropical Brazilian coastal resort, Portuguese for King's Cove, lies on a picturesque bay 100 miles south of Rio de Janeiro.

Torrential rains obscured the beautiful scenery, but it was an eventful meeting for another reason. It was at Angra dos Reis that the MPEG-2 committee decided to abandon the idea of a future MPEG-3 video standard for HDTV. Instead, the group subsumed the higher resolutions and bit rates of HDTV into MPEG-2. In one fell swoop, the MPEG-2 specification extended its charter by claiming the GI, and FCC, territory of digital HDTV.

Also notable at the Brazil meeting was that Rich Prodan, one of CableLabs' top technologists, was in attendance. CableLabs, representing the major US cable operators, was getting directly involved. I discussed GI's technology and product development activities with Prodan. He appeared curious but was clearly more interested in the recent occurrences at the MPEG meeting, favoring the idea of an open standard versus a proprietary video compression technology owned by a single company such as GI. Once back in San Diego, I emphasized to GI management that we needed to start sending some video engineers to MPEG with more active participation.

TCI's Tom Elliot was also becoming increasingly concerned about the MPEG-2 standard. Its picture quality had improved considerably, in part due to the MPEG committee adopting some of GI's video compression techniques. Elliot still thought GI had better technology, but the gap was closing and MPEG seemed to have significant momentum. The digital TV technology battle was shaping up to be GI against the world, and Elliot was unsure how long he and TCI could stand by GI.

In late September 1992, I was planning to skip the Tarrytown, New York, meeting of the US delegation to MPEG. My wife, Wendy, had just given birth to our first child, Madeleine, in San Diego, and I wanted to be part of her first week. But my phone rang at work with Rick Friedland, GI's corporate CFO, on the line, congratulating me on becoming a father. He had heard I wasn't attending the NY meeting and was calling to say I needed to go. The next day, as a bouquet of flowers arrived for Wendy from GI Chicago, I rushed off to the airport. Tom Elliot was already in Westchester County trying to assess the true status of MPEG-2. The writing was on the wall. Elliot was clearly getting on the MPEG-2 bandwagon, with or without us.

In October 1992, Elliot summoned Jim Bunker to a meeting at the Hyatt Regency Denver Tech Center, near TCI headquarters. Ed Breen, GI's head of cable sales, was also there. Elliot's message was blunt and startling: "TCI was going with Scientific Atlanta for its digital system. GI was out. TCI wanted SA's MPEG-2, not GI's DigiCipher technology. It's over. Time for you guys to go home."

But Bunker, ever the consummate salesman, was not going to give up. He retorted by climbing out on a limb, telling Elliot that GI had a stealth MPEG-2 activity also, and that Paul Moroney, GI's top systems engineer, would come to Denver the next day to elaborate. Bunker then called Moroney in San Diego saying that he needed to whip together a presentation and be in Denver the next morning to explain to TCI how GI's digital system was MPEG-2 compliant. Moroney was dumbfounded. He knew a little bit about MPEG-2, but GI's current system design was not MPEG-2, and he didn't feel he knew enough to do justice to Bunker's command. Moroney crammed and digested the details of the MPEG-2 spec overnight, crafting a story literally on the fly while heading to Denver. His presentation was brilliant and convincing, enough to sway Elliot and TCI back over to GI's side, knowing Malone still wanted GI's security and conditional access technology.

But when Elliot told Bunker that GI was back in the game with TCI, his message wasn't simply to switch from DigiCipher compression to MPEG-2. There was another twist. GI would team up with AT&T and essentially bring to the MPEG-2 committee a new proposal. We would call the new, undefined joint GI/AT&T video compression technology the MPEG-2 "Entertainment Profile," comprising the pre-existing MPEG-2 standard with certain GI/AT&T agreed-upon improvements, including the ability to enable a lower-cost consumer hardware implementation relative to the current MPEG-2 technique. While thrilled to be back alive with TCI, we were baffled by the business rationale of our sudden shotgun marriage to AT&T, our powerful rival in the FCC HDTV competition.

The two AT&T groups we were hooked up with were Bob Stanzione's networks systems business unit and a Bell Labs video compression R&D team. In 1992, Bell Labs was still in a class by itself among the world's premier technical research institutions. Its countless innovations included the transistor, the laser, the communications satellite, and even proof corroborating the Big Bang theory of the Universe. With the FCC HDTV competition taking its sharp turn toward digital, the opportunities offered by video compression technology, an area Bell Labs had been researching for years, rose to the forefront of this venerable organization. This was a period in American industrialization when basic research outfits were being pressured to consider the commercialization of technology, and Bell Labs perceived a sizable monetization opportunity.

At TCI's direction, Jim Bunker entered discussions with AT&T's Bob Stanzione, while Jerry Heller, Woo Paik, and I interacted with the Bell Labs video compression group. If GI were to stay on top with TCI and achieve its digital cable ambitions, the company had no real choice in the matter. TCI was apparently getting in bed with AT&T, and GI preferred to be in the middle of the action rather than relegated to the sidelines again. Underscoring the importance to AT&T of this opportunity, two heavyweights from Bell Labs, Dan Stanzione and Arun Netravali, were involved.[1] Heller, Paik, and Bob Rast already knew Netravali as the leader of Bell Labs' HDTV project, the unit representing AT&T in the Zenith/AT&T FCC testing process.

Soon the reason for the three-way arrangement was revealed. Seeking to expand beyond cable TV, TCI was positioning itself to get a piece of the multibillion-dollar local access telephony business with AT&T. Eight years earlier, in 1984, AT&T had been forced by the Justice Department's landmark antitrust suit to divest itself of the Regional Bell Operating Companies, known as the Baby Bells. The original Baby Bells—Ameritech, Bell Atlantic, BellSouth, NYNEX, Pacific Telesis, Southwestern Bell, and US West—were still natural monopolies in the local phone business, while AT&T's long-distance market was becoming increasingly competitive. These not-so-little offspring were eating into AT&T's profits, and a deal with TCI could reduce the bite while giving TCI an entirely new business opportunity. After all, TCI, like the Baby Bells, had wires going directly into millions of consumers' homes. In fact, TCI's wires were broadband coaxial cable wires, fat communications pipes, not narrowband twisted-pair copper like the phone lines, so TCI could actually one-up the Baby Bells and carry AT&T's future into subscribers' homes. Together, AT&T and TCI would be a formidable team. This wasn't quite the pre-divestiture AT&T, front and center in every home in America, but it was still a major force. It not only was the leading long-distance phone company but also owned the prestigious Bell Labs and the huge telecom equipment business that would later become Lucent.

TCI's Tom Elliot attended the London MPEG meeting at the end of 1992, where he met with Woo Paik and me, to make sure GI was getting on board with the emerging standard. In February 1993, the Italian delegation hosted the MPEG meeting. By this time, GI was fully engaged in MPEG-2 activities, sending a full contingent to Rome, including Woo Paik, Ed Krause, and Paul Moroney, in addition to me. The TCI/GI/AT&T proposal to impose an "entertainment profile" on MPEG, however, went over in the international standards community like a lead balloon. Other MPEG members called us the co-conspirators, accusing us of attempting an MPEG takeover. If GI and AT&T wanted to submit improvements, we had to get in line like everyone else. Each technical contribution would need to be evaluated on its own merits by MPEG's video committee, chaired by Didier LeGall, C-Cube's CTO.

This decision was disconcerting, and we needed a change of scenery. Since the video part of MPEG-2 was nearly complete, I asked Woo Paik if he wanted to take a break from the meetings, where everyone seemed to be glaring at us derisively. In the afternoon, Paik and I visited the Sistine Chapel. It was humbling to see Michelangelo's renditions of the creation of man, the sun and the planets, the division of water from earth, and of light from darkness, giving us some much-needed perspective. The following afternoon, Ed Krause and I ventured out to see the ancient ruins of the Roman Forum. As we emerged from the subway, however, we were surrounded and mugged by a large band of gypsy women. We emerged unscathed except for the damaged watch around Krause's wrist.

Rumsfeld's directive, to decide once and for all whether to continue fighting MPEG or to embrace it, was reaching its conclusion. TCI's John Malone and Tom Elliot were becoming increasingly swayed toward the open standard. DirecTV had based part of its technology decision on MPEG. And the Philips/Thomson consortium had a late but strong MPEG-based performance in the Slot 5 FCC HDTV testing. GI's adoption of MPEG-2 into its product roadmap was inevitable.

23 THE BEST WESTERN SHOW

In June 1992, Forstmann Little took General Instrument public again in an initial public offering, issuing 22 million shares at $15 each. With Donald Rumsfeld at GI's helm, the company's financial performance had improved considerably from the precipitous downturn immediately following the leveraged buyout. The VideoCipher piracy problem had been fixed, the cyclical cable business was recovering strongly, and GI was shipping its first digital SDTV systems to content providers.

There was also a growing recognition in pockets of the technology community that, with the advent of digital television, the TV and the computer would come together. GI's corporate VP of Technology, Matt Miller, was an early proponent of this "convergence," and he used Don Rumsfeld's stature to set up an introductory meeting with Bill Gates, Microsoft's co-founder and CEO, in the fall of 1992.

Gates and his chief technology officer, Nathan Myhrvold, hosted Rumsfeld, Miller, and Jim Faust at the Microsoft headquarters in Redmond, Washington. Gates was a C-band VideoCipher home dish owner and seemed to know far more about GI and the cable business than GI knew about Microsoft. Nevertheless, he appeared quite impressed with GI's market position and communications systems knowledge, spanning from digital compression to conditional access technology, and from digital transmission to set-top boxes.

Matt Miller also brought Intel into the mix. And he began separately discussing a similar initiative with Apple Computer, favored by the GI San Diego team over Microsoft. The San Diego group felt Apple had a much better software user interface and also identified more with Apple's "think different" out-of-the-box culture, even though Steve Jobs was outside Apple at the time, running NeXT Computer and Pixar. But this concept of merging the personal computer with the digital cable box, while intoxicating, was well ahead of its time.

The annual Western Cable Show in Anaheim, California, was everyone's favorite industry trade event. More informal than the national Cable Show and less techie than the Cable-Tec Expo, the Western Show had a party atmosphere. Deals were done in the day and everyone let loose at night. The fun, free-spirited ambience was partly because of the warm Southern California climate, even in December, partly attributable to the content provider community being there in force, their extravagant budgets providing a festive punch, and partly due to plain-old tradition.

Rock bands such as Little Richard and The Bangles played the parties at night, and during the daytime exhibition hall hours, superstar athletes signed pictures at ESPN's booth while celebrities greeted visitors at CNN and Lifetime. Scantily clad models adorned pedestals at Playboy and Spice, and for those with small kids, The Disney Channel invariably had an on-site artist drawing personalized sketches of Mickey Mouse or Snow White. Disney also hosted private parties at Disneyland, across the street, with a choice ride or two open for its guests. GI held a famous party at the Western Show, where food and drink flowed in a lush garden veranda setting jam-packed with guests, while wheeler-dealers like Frank Drendel, Hal Krisbergh, and Ed Breen held court with their customers.

Year after year, the Western Cable Show was business and trade show entertainment at its best. But the Western Show in early December 1992 was even better for General Instrument. This was the forum at which TCI's John Malone would articulate his 500-channel future vision for cable, using GI's pay TV security system and digital set-top boxes made by GI and AT&T. Don Rumsfeld hailed the bombshell announcement as "a decision which could well represent the launch of the Digital Age in the United States."

We felt like we had finally crossed the Rubicon, the Italian river passed by Julius Caesar in 49 BC, and a metaphor I used over the years to represent the inflection point of a new business, a point of no return. Three eventful years had passed since the company's digital television project had been unveiled, and GI had been sprinting the entire time. TCI's announcement stated that its digital cable service would commence by early 1994, barely a year away, timed to coincide with DirecTV's intended launch. But the new system, which would differ in many ways from GI's first-generation DigiCipher I system, was not even defined or specified yet.

Some thought the company had just hit a home run, but in reality we had only reached first base. The battle for digital supremacy would rage on for several more years. For the race to be the market leader in digital television communications equipment was not just a sprint, it was also a marathon. "This is just the beginning," said Malone. "This first round of products is the first of an evolution. We want to deliver a broad range of services adapted to the individual needs of the consumer."[1]

According to the *Wall Street Journal*, "Mr. Malone envisioned a cable system in which subscribers have access to scores of pay-per-view channels with movies available at a moment's notice and airing around the clock. Such a system would also have plenty of free channels for interactive and computer services, multiple versions of such networks as HBO and MTV, sports of every kind, and an endless selection of niche channels. There might even be a channel devoted to favorite shows, such as '60 Minutes,' in case viewers missed the initial telecast. Subscribers would navigate through this sea of choices with an interactive programming guide operated through a remote control."[2]

24 BEHIND THE SCENES

In the weeks preceding Malone's Western Cable Show announcement, GI's Jim Bunker and Geoff Roman had been holed up with TCI's Tom Elliot in Denver, conducting intensive negotiations. At one session, GI's Rick Friedland, visiting from Chicago, was called out of the meeting by J. C. Sparkman, TCI's chief operating officer. Like Malone, Sparkman had been a GI Jerrold employee years earlier. He was agitated because GI's Digital Cable Radio music service (later renamed Music Choice) had announced its European launch, causing the stock price of TCI's competing service, DMX, to slump. Sparkman's blunt message to Friedland was that his grandchildren's wealth was tied up in DMX equity, and they had just lost $4 million that day because of the Music Choice announcement. "Take that back into the negotiations," he said.

The basic tenets of the deal were:

- TCI would place an initial order with GI for one million digital cable set-top boxes, which would incorporate certain semiconductors manufactured by AT&T.

- GI and AT&T would jointly develop the video compression technology, preferably in line with the evolving MPEG-2 standards.

- GI would license its conditional access security chip to two additional digital cable set-top box manufacturers, such second sources to be selected by TCI.

- TCI would also receive a license for GI's conditional access technology and would operate a centralized set-top authorization center in Denver.

- TCI would purchase GI's digital TV infrastructure equipment, such as encoders and satellite modulators, for TCI's new state-of-the-art content distribution facility in Denver, to be called the Headend In The Sky (HITS). TCI would also purchase GI's digital cable headend infrastructure equipment, comprising various software and hardware elements, to control and operate its digital cable systems throughout the country.

- The content encoded at HITS would be licensed from third parties and would be packaged and distributed not only to TCI headends but also to other cable systems not owned by TCI. TCI would charge a fee for this content-aggregation service and would also charge an additional (optional) fee for authorization services (for non-TCI cable operators that didn't want to re-encrypt the content with a different conditional access system).

In a lengthy interview conducted the following month by *Satellite Business News*, Malone made some noteworthy comments regarding the competitive environment TCI was addressing through its new deal with GI and AT&T:[1]

Q: What's your overall assessment of DirecTV at this point?

A: I think they're going to do it. I think it's for real. I think they're going to be a real competitor, and I think we have to compete with them. And we're going to do everything we can to effectively compete with them and to hold our market share as much as we can and be a vigorous competitor.

Regarding TCI's willingness to be in the DBS business through its equity stake in PrimeStar:

Q: Even if it went to high power, with the capital involved in that?

A: Absolutely.

Q: So TCI will be in the DBS business?

A: Unless the government stops us, you bet. I think it's a good business.

Q: The other area that we really want to touch upon is the technology. Is it fair to say that the system that you guys announced is proprietary to GI and AT&T?

A: I hope not. Well, I guess it's a mixed answer. We think it's going to be MPEG-2, or at least be fully compatible to MPEG-2 with respect to the video compression and with respect to the transport layer. The audio is up in the air.

Q: The conditional access (security) system, will that be proprietary?

A: That will be GI proprietary.

Regarding GI and the piracy problem:

> Q: Some people have wondered why, given that you have been the loudest critic of the VideoCipher [scrambling system and piracy], you would go down the same street again with General Instrument.

> A: I guess it's a little bit like if you were going to hire a navigator for your ship, and the guy who had been the navigator for the Titanic applied, would you hire him? And the answer would be probably, because he'll never make that same mistake twice. The reason we're picking GI, quite honestly, is because we think they're the best supplier with the best equipment. And we think we understand why we got in trouble with the VideoCipher…

In San Diego, GI developed a new specification for the joint GI/AT&T system, under the working name "JointCipher." But by Christmas 1992, AT&T was suddenly no longer part of the deal. AT&T apparently couldn't get what it wanted out of TCI, and vice versa with respect to TCI's opportunity to get into the local telephone access business. Bunker was summoned again to Denver, along with Bob Stanzione from AT&T. Elliot was there with Larry Romrell and J. C. Sparkman, two of TCI's top executives. The last time Bunker had been called to Denver the message had been: "You're out, SA is in." This time, the TCI team told AT&T they were out of the deal, there was no more "JointCipher," and "GI was it, the sole system developer."

Once again GI was on its own for developing an entirely new digital television system, with guidance from TCI including the requirement to be MPEG-2 compatible. All eyes from Denver were on the two GI divisions, the VideoCipher Division in San Diego and the Jerrold Division in Hatboro, Pennsylvania. We had just over a year to deliver to TCI, by "early 1994," an end-to-end digital satellite and cable system with a dynamically shifting set of product features and specifications.

With the TCI deal presumably in the bag, Ed Breen and his cable sales team moved into high gear. Next in line was Comcast, a top five cable operator at the time. Brian Roberts, president of Comcast, stated: "We're convinced that [digital] compression technology is not only going to benefit our cable TV subscribers by making a whole new world of media services accessible to them, it will also help stimulate the future development of what we see as an important multimedia marketplace in the nation." Mark Coblitz, Comcast's vice president of strategic planning, praised DigiCable (GI's name for the cable portion of the DigiCipher system) as an "excellent foundation for a digital platform."[2]

Within a few months, GI had booked orders not only from TCI and Comcast, but also from Newhouse, Sammons Communications, Cablevision Industries, and TeleCable Corp. The next year, Century Communications, Cox Cable, Adelphia, Shaw, Jones Intercable, and Rogers Cablesystems placed purchase orders. These were all sizable independent cable operators at the time, before the upcoming waves of industry consolidation through acquisitions. The fact that they were all lining up to buy GI's digital cable boxes indicated substantial market momentum.

But some major operators, including Time Warner, Cablevision Systems, and Canada's Videotron, had not yet weighed in with their decisions. And GI's development of its second-generation system, including the digital cable headend equipment and set-top boxes, was a much bigger project than had been anticipated. The publicity felt good but the company's success was far from assured.

GI often joked in those days about the short half-life of agreements with its cable customers; a "done deal" didn't exist until after products had been shipped, installed, and made functional in the field. And the longer the time interval between order and delivery, the greater the risk of the opportunity vaporizing, either by customers moving on to other options or by aggressive competitors jumping into the fray.

25 CONTENT IS KING

John Malone was the king of cable. But the true king, the ultimate master of the subscriber, is the content. For without the content, TCI and the other cable operators would have no monthly subscription to sell, no cash annuity that, in those days, valued cable operators at several thousand dollars per subscriber, irrespective of bottom-line losses. Malone recognized the power of content early, investing in start-up programming services such as BET and Discovery Channel. Warner Communications' famous "I Want My MTV" campaign, Ted Turner's visionary concept of a twenty-four-hour news network, and America's eternal love affair with sports all highlighted that cable would have to carry what its subscribers wanted.

Perhaps no single individual embodies the phrase "content is king" to a greater extent than its originator, Viacom owner Sumner Redstone, reflecting his firm belief that, while distribution is critical, content is the place to be for enduring value. Redstone grew up poor in the West End of Boston, a tenement area in the Depression-era 1920s and 1930s, populated by Irish immigrants and European Jews. After graduating from the prestigious Boston Latin School, he enrolled at Harvard College. His degree was awarded in absentia, however, as he was serving with the US Army breaking Japanese coded messages during World War II. Upon his return to Boston he attended Harvard Law School. Exiting his legal practice as a young man, Redstone joined the Northeast Theater Corporation, the drive-in movie business owned by his father, Michael Rothstein. The two men had wisely purchased the underlying land, enabling them to later build indoor theaters and allowing National Amusements, their successor company, to become an indoor movie exhibition powerhouse. But Redstone kept returning his focus to content, knowing that to be his calling.

In 1987, Redstone made the most important move of his career, acquiring Viacom for $3.4 billion in a hostile takeover. Viacom had started life within CBS as its content syndication arm, selling programming rights after the initial series ran on the CBS broadcast network. But in 1971, the FCC prohibited TV networks from also being in the syndication business, forcing CBS to spin-off Viacom. By the time Redstone purchased Viacom, the company owned MTV, Nickelodeon, Showtime, and The Movie Channel. He recruited Frank Biondi as CEO. Biondi had been CEO of Coca-Cola Television, owner at the time of Columbia Pictures, and before that he served as chairman and CEO of HBO. In 1989, Biondi hired Ed Horowitz from HBO to be Viacom's chief technologist.

Paramount Pictures came into the Viacom fold in 1993 when Redstone won a bidding war against Barry Diller and John Malone. To pay for this $10 billion jewel, Redstone sold Madison Square Garden to Chuck Dolan's Cablevision, unloaded Viacom's cable systems to a Malone-led cable consortium, and later sold the Simon & Schuster publishing business to Pearson of the United Kingdom.

Crucial to General Instrument's digital television market strategy was convincing major content providers to begin using the company's system for digital satellite delivery to cable headends. GI believed that if it were successful in that endeavor, it would have a major advantage over competitors in the secondary content distribution chain from cable headends to cable subscribers.

As HBO continued its joint field test with GI in the second half of 1992, the international content community enthusiastically embraced digital television technology. Rogers Cablesystems deployed the

DigiCipher satellite delivery system to send digital feeds of Canadian Home Shopping Network, YTV (a children's channel), and Vision TV (an interfaith religious network) to cable headends. Nick Hamilton-Piercy, Rogers' vice president of engineering and technical services, stated: "There are at this point no contingency plans for alternate analog feeds."[1]

From Multivision in Mexico to Telefe and CineCanal in Argentina, and from the Middle East Broadcasting Centre in the Middle East to Star TV in Asia, GI's DigiCipher system was quickly spreading its wings around the globe. Peter Lambert of *Multichannel News* wrote: "Less than three years after General Instrument unveiled the world's first all-digital TV system, digital transmission via satellite has become a reality in four regions: North and South America, Asia, and the Middle East."[2]

After John Malone's deal for GI's digital cable system hit the wire at the December 1992 Western Cable Show, the GI San Diego team brought in a new flood of contracts for the DigiCipher satellite system. Orders rolled in from TVA in Brazil, Discovery Channel Latin America, ABS-CBN in the Philippines, PCTV in Mexico, Po Hsin in Taiwan, and CCTV in China. It was a big world and it seemed to be coming GI's way.

There was a big wrinkle, however, in all this early success. GI was shipping to these customers its first-generation system, DigiCipher I. The system performed very well both technically and operationally, but it was not compatible with the second-generation system that TCI and the other cable operators had just ordered. This discrepancy prompted GI's content customers to start negotiating upgrade clauses in their original contracts, such that when the next-generation MPEG-2 based system, DigiCipher II, became available, GI would upgrade them at a reasonable price.

GI's agreement with HBO was critical to its domestic market strategy. The GI/HBO joint field test was finalized by the end of 1992, and HBO began rolling out commercially in January 1993, becoming the first US programmer to deliver digital entertainment programming to US cable operators. HBO initially used DigiCipher I for its HBO and Cinemax multiplex services. Over time it added various other genres and categories of content, facilitated by the economics of digitally compressed satellite delivery. A December 1, 1992, press release stated: "'HBO is crossing the frontier to the next major technological milestone in television—digital transmission,' said Bob Zitter, HBO senior vice president, technology operations. 'It seems appropriate in this, our 20th anniversary year, to add another chapter to HBO's long history of technological leadership by becoming the first television network to provide full-time compressed digital television to our affiliates.'"

PBS, one of the four participants in the 1992 CableLabs Request for Proposal, also ordered a DigiCipher system to distribute new programming to its member stations around the country. In May 1993, Viewer's Choice and Request Television, the industry's leading pay-per-view content providers, announced contracts with GI, using DigiCipher to deliver multiple new channels of pay-per-view service. BBC World Service Television purchased a DigiCipher system to establish the first transatlantic digital video link.[3]

Toshiba, GI's partner in the 1989 Japanese satellite TV venture with analog VideoCipher technology, and the developer of the first prototype HD-VCR to function with GI's FCC DigiCipher HDTV system, struck a deal to package the DigiCipher technology into a digital satellite news gathering system for the Japanese market. This product concept would allow far-flung news operations to "backhaul" video footage to network headquarters, using a fractional satellite transponder. The new system expanded the availability of global news and lowered its delivery cost.

Another new business was also taking off: the private network business that Bob King had been hired to develop. Microsoft purchased a system for "Microsoft TV," providing video-based product information and training to its field sites, customers, and channel partners. Spector Entertainment Group used DigiCipher for delivering its programming to the wagering industry. Jones International selected DigiCipher to expand its "Mind Extension University: The Education Network," a pioneering distance-learning network, and to launch the Jones Computer Network as well as new health and language channels. Ford Motor Company employed GI's digital system for the "FordStar" satellite network, linking Ford and its auto dealers in a two-way data and one-way video network. And with Esther Rodriguez's connections south of the border, we landed a major deal with Red Edusat for a massive new distance-learning network throughout Mexico. Red Edusat was created by the Mexican Department of Education to reach tens of thousands of primary and secondary schools with multiple new video "classes," making it the largest distance-learning network in the world at that time.

But entertainment television content, fed by satellite to cable head-ends, was most central to GI's digital market strategy and, to this end, one of the company's most important and gratifying deals occurred in August 1993 with Sumner Redstone's Viacom. The HBO deal was of immense strategic value, but Viacom was the other pay TV giant, and having both of them on board greatly enhanced GI's ability to establish a digital television standard and the leading market position.

Ed Horowitz, Viacom's head of technology, had initially decided to go with Scientific Atlanta for digital satellite content distribution. SA was aggressively touting its MPEG-2 system, and Horowitz had become convinced of the importance of the emerging video compression standard when he was hosted by Thomson/RCA's Joe Clayton at the February 1992 Olympics in Albertville, France. Horowitz had also been one of GI's toughest critics on the piracy issue, especially painful to him since he had been among the strongest and most influential VideoCipher advocates when he headed HBO's technology group in the mid-1980s.

Moreover, Viacom had sued GI for underpayment of royalties related to VideoCipher product sales.

But we had fixed the industry's piracy problem and settled the Viacom royalty issue, so when Horowitz learned about our MPEG-2 migration plans with TCI, HBO, and others, he switched his Scientific Atlanta decision to GI, saying: "The GI digital system will likely provide a graceful transition to widespread deployment of MPEG-2." Viacom planned to use DigiCipher I as an early entry delivery vehicle for its multiplex satellite channels such as Showtime 2, Flix, and MTV Latino, and then upgrade to GI's MPEG-2 based DigiCipher II system when it became available, thereby becoming compatible with TCI.

With the various digital satellite and cable deals in hand, GI's corporate office was riding high. The company consummated a secondary public stock offering in March 1993 at $30.50 per share, more than double the initial public offering price of nine months earlier. Leveraged buyout firm Forstmann Little had invested less than $200 million in equity for its 1990 acquisition of GI, borrowing the remainder in subordinated debt and bank loans. The firm's equity stake was already worth ten times more than its investment.

Don Rumsfeld and Rick Friedland had skillfully navigated the company through its loan covenants during a difficult period, renegotiating with the banks at crucial times, with cash flow barely covering the minimum required 1.5-to-1 debt service ratio. Ted Forstmann's rantings and ravings about the destructiveness of KKR's use of junk bonds and "wampum" had come true in the case of the RJR Nabisco takeover and others. If it hadn't been for the subordinated debt used in the GI leveraged buyout, the banks could have taken the upside right out of Forstmann Little's pockets. Instead, the investment firm pulled off one of the most lucrative leveraged buyouts in history, at least until that point in time.[4]

26 FROM DIGITAL TV TO HIGH-SPEED DATA

Once General Instrument's initial digital TV solution was operational, new content and genres started coming out of the woodwork at an unprecedented pace. Fulfilling John Malone's 500-channel vision was simply a matter of time. Our feeling was that the communications spectrum would eventually fill up with traffic, a variation on the theme "If you build it, they will come" from the movie *Field of Dreams*.

To some, Bruce Springsteen's 1992 song, "57 Channels and Nothin' On," was a statement about the lack of compelling content on cable despite the capacity. Others noted that it was really a metaphor for the emptiness of life. But the critics were missing the point. The purpose was not just to provide more and more channels. The higher purpose of channel expansion was all about giving consumers more choice. In the TV world, each viewer has several favorite channels. But every individual's group of favorites is unique, and therefore more channels, including niche and special interest channels, were needed to optimize viewing options for more people, a utilitarianism of the spectrum.

Yet the fact that a digital TV system entailed the transfer of an extremely high-speed digital bit stream had started some of us thinking about an entirely new idea. In 1993, Jim Bunker dropped by my office with an intriguing question. He had been talking to Matt Miller, GI's corporate VP of Technology, who was having exploratory discussions with Intel on a "high-speed data over cable" venture. Since GI's digital television communications system incorporated a high-speed digital modem that could send data at 30 million bits per second (30 Mbps), what if general information—generic data, as opposed to digital video— were transmitted over a separate pipe in the cable system? "Would that be a good market and a product we could sell?" Bunker wanted to know.

While we had pursued the advancement of digital TV, transmission of computer data had evolved from a completely different angle. During the 1970s and 1980s, the ARPANET had continued to expand. Building on its earlier work with UCLA and University College London, the National Science Foundation had developed the Computer Science Network (CSNET), and the Internet communications protocols, TCP and IP, were developed. The ARPANET began to morph into the Internet, bringing supercomputers at various university and government research sites into the mix. It culminated with the consumer Internet phenomenon in the mid-1990s, driven by the Netscape browser, the World Wide Web, and ubiquitous e-mail.

But in 1993, Bunker's query about the market viability of moving high-speed data over cable sounded like a distraction from our digital TV activities, in which GI was completely absorbed. Moreover, we had been involved for several years in a data venture with X*Press, a partnership between McGraw Hill and TCI, which aggregated news feeds and provided stock quotes from dozens of organizations all over the world (including the Associated Press, Reuters, and Standard & Poor's). Rick Segil's product development group had developed a product called Info-Cipher, which inserted the X*Press data into CNN's satellite TV signal and was then offered to cable subscribers. A GI InfoCipher consumer box then extracted the data for presentation on the subscriber's computer. The project had limited commercial success, however, mainly because it was a one-way data broadcast and was very low speed, at only 9600 bits per second.

At the same time, preliminary notions about transferring generic digital data were being tossed around in other parts of the company. GI's Matt Miller had been discussing a joint venture with Avram Miller, Intel's VP of Business Development, and with Les Vadász, a founding employee of Intel who had overseen development of the company's first microprocessor. Their grand idea was that the two companies would provide the technology and equipment for data transfer to cable systems at no cost. In turn, the cable operators would offer a high-speed data service to their subscribers, and the GI/Intel venture would reap 20 percent of the proceeds.

So it was that we were soon starting another "skunkworks" project in San Diego, which would evolve into the cable modem broadband Internet revolution. At the December 1993 Western Cable Show, the year after Malone's digital TV announcement, Mitch Kapor, founder of Lotus Development Corporation and co-founder of the Electronic Frontier Foundation, was in a small corner of GI's booth demonstrating a cable modem with a Mosaic[1] browser developed at the University of Illinois.

The venture never materialized, and it turned out that Intel's chips were too expensive, but we continued on our own with a project called SURFboard, a double entendre reflecting the new catchphrase "surfing the Internet" as well as the prevalence of the San Diego surf culture. However, unlike digital television, where we started as the lone soldier in the wilderness, with cable modems there were a few other companies— Zenith Data Systems, LANcity, and Com21—onto the same idea at the same time. It would become a separate story in a parallel universe to what was unfolding in the digital television arena. The seeds of the broadband Internet were being planted. And perhaps someday the twin revolutions, digital television and the broadband Internet, might even intersect.

27 | THE TROJAN HORSE OF SOUND

As the digital television industry moved inexorably toward the MPEG-2 video compression standard in 1992 and 1993, a separate technology battle was brewing in the United States over which digital audio method would be used in conjunction with the TV signal. GI had selected Dolby digital stereo for its first-generation DigiCipher I system. We planned to use a new, state-of-the-art Dolby surround sound system in DigiCipher

II, called Dolby AC-3 and later rebranded as Dolby Digital, allowing six channels of audio at a very low bit rate.[1] We considered Dolby sound to be an ideal counterpart to high-quality video, believing that movie theater–like surround sound would help sell the concept of digital TV, even with standard definition video.

The MPEG-1 standard, however, had specified a digital stereo audio technology called Musicam, developed in Europe primarily by Philips of the Netherlands. When the MPEG-2 standard started taking shape, a requirement was inserted that the MPEG-2 audio system shall be "backward compatible" to MPEG-1 audio, essentially locking in an expanded version of Musicam. This backward compatibility allowed an older device to be able to extract an MPEG-1 stereo audio pair from the new MPEG-2 audio signal. The requirement raised the ire of many people who felt it was rigged and unfair, precluding the new international MPEG-2 standard from selecting the best and most efficient sound system possible.

Part of GI's rancor stemmed from its belief that Dolby was a better technology than Musicam due to its ability to compress a surround sound signal into a lower bit rate. Part of it was that Dolby was an American company, based in San Francisco, and was a long-standing icon in the music business along with its legendary founder Ray Dolby.[2] Part of it was we had appreciated working with Dolby in developing the DigiCipher I system; their licensing policy had been reasonable and their engineering support had been excellent. Part of it was that our next-generation system, DigiCipher II, already incorporated Dolby Digital. We already faced a substantial schedule delay because of switching to MPEG-2 video instead of our own video compression, and moving to a different audio technology would further burden us with another change in the midst of product development. Part of it was that in the American FCC HDTV competition, where some of the same issues were playing out, it was the European companies, Philips and Thomson, that were pushing for MPEG audio, a technology largely owned by Philips. Finally, it just didn't seem right that, although the digital television revolution had started in the United States, MPEG was trying to impose a European-owned audio solution on the rest of the world. So I took on a new personal mission: to make Dolby the US digital TV standard for audio.

Internally, I had to defend Dolby with CEO Rick Friedland and division president Hal Krisbergh. They correctly perceived MPEG audio as a path of less resistance politically. I argued that Dolby was a better technology for surround sound, using some recent test results as evidence. This wasn't a sufficient reason, however, so I made the case that switching to MPEG audio would introduce yet another schedule delay in our DigiCipher II product development. We were under incredible schedule pressure from TCI and many other customers to deliver the new system, so this rationale made business sense. However, we couldn't just decide on Dolby unilaterally; our customers demanded that we obtain the imprimatur of the international technical standards community. Dolby understood the risk to its business if the MPEG wave took over digital audio and readily agreed to work closely with us.

The next battle involved the American National Standards Institute (ANSI), the US delegate to MPEG. I lobbied some of our key DigiCipher I customers, including Bob Zitter at HBO and Jim Heyworth, CEO of Viewer's Choice, to submit letters stating they intended to continue using Dolby in the next-generation system if it were technically proven to be equal to or better than the current MPEG-2 audio standard. In parallel, and more in the context of the FCC HDTV competition, Dolby obtained similar letters from US Senators Dianne Feinstein and Barbara Boxer, as well as from Congresswoman Nancy Pelosi, addressed to the ANSI/MPEG group and stating that Dolby should be added to the international standard.

At the next ANSI meeting I arranged to get on the agenda as a speaker. I read each letter in sequence to the other members of the US body. A vote was taken, and the US delegation to MPEG agreed it would present a united position to the international MPEG group that Dolby should be added as part of the digital audio standard. Undoubtedly I had made some enemies, but Dolby was on its way. At the July 1993 MPEG meeting in New York, hosted by Columbia University, the MPEG-2 leaders begrudgingly agreed to another round of testing, to determine whether a surround sound audio system without the constraint of backward compatibility to MPEG-1 audio would perform better than the current MPEG-2 audio technique. The test results proved that "Non Backward Compatible" audio (for example, Dolby Digital) was better technically. Eventually the MPEG-2 standard added Non Backward Compatible audio.

Another significant event occurred at the July 1993 MPEG meeting. The Hughes participants, representing DirecTV, had an announcement to make. It had been a huge boost to the MPEG-2 standard when DirecTV announced it would go with the MPEG-2 RCA digital system instead of GI's proprietary DigiCipher compression technology. So it came as a substantial blow when Hughes's MPEG delegates, apologizing on behalf of DirecTV, stated they couldn't wait any longer for the MPEG-2 transport specification.[3] To get to market on time, DirecTV would have to proceed with its own technical solution for this portion of its digital satellite system and would therefore not be fully MPEG-2 compliant.

28 THE GRAND ALLIANCE

In December 1992, Don Rumsfeld hosted a meeting at GI's Chicago headquarters to determine the company's strategy relative to the FCC over-the-air broadcast HDTV process. While GI was confident its Slot 3 system had performed the best overall during the previous competition, Bob Rast's presentation to Rumsfeld conveyed his belief that the FCC advisory committee would not pick a single winner, even after another costly round of testing.

That night, Rumsfeld hosted a GI holiday party at his home, where he polled his guests on what they thought the company should do. Rast, Jim Faust, Rick Friedland, and the others offered their opinions. With Rumsfeld leading the discussion, they reached a consensus that the FCC would keep moving the goal line, continuing to avoid selecting a winner. Therefore the team agreed that the company's best course of action was to form a merger with the other proponents and to present a unified front to the FCC. Rumsfeld then enlisted Rick Friedland to get Zenith, AT&T, and the other companies on board.

Lofty and evocative, the phrase "Grand Alliance" has been used multiple times throughout history, most famously during World War II when FDR, Churchill, and Stalin united America, Great Britain, and the Soviet Union against Hitler's Nazi Germany. The term was also used to describe a political coalition formed in seventeenth-century Europe when a Grand Alliance of countries decided to end France's expansionary plans under Louis XIV; another one occurred in the Philippines in the early 1960s.

Dick Wiley, head of the FCC committee on advanced television, had apparently heard about GI's effort to form a coalition with the other digital HDTV competitors. On February 18, 1993, he issued a letter to the proponents instructing them to "explore a grand alliance," preferably before the commencement of another round of testing.[1]

Throughout much of 1993, the various participants in the FCC testing were locked in bitter and divisive discussions, the looming threat of re-testing being about the only thing driving them back together. The additional tests would be performed on the four digital HDTV systems:

the 1080i interlace and 720P progressive HDTV systems from the GI/MIT alliance; the 720P HD system from Zenith/AT&T; and the 1080i system from the consortium comprising Philips, Thomson, Sarnoff, and NBC. NHK's analog Narrow-MUSE system was officially eliminated, as was the Philips/Thomson consortium's enhanced definition solution.

Dick Wiley steered the discussions, displaying evenhandedness, diplomacy, and the view that collaboration, not competition, was best for the country, now that digital was a fait accompli. Assuming the business and technical issues could be resolved, the notion of a Grand Alliance was compelling. But reaching agreement among the three separate groups, representing eight distinct entities, each with differing perspectives and objectives, was not a simple matter.

Would the combined system use progressive or interlaced scanning? Zenith, AT&T, and MIT strongly favored the progressive method, corresponding to the Slot 4 (Zenith/AT&T) and Slot 6 (GI/MIT) systems that had been tested the prior year. They believed progressive scanning was more future-proof, the way of the computer world, while interlace was a television relic that should be permanently shelved. But the television-oriented parties—GI, Philips, and Thomson—were interlace advocates, pointing to the fact that the two interlace systems had greatly outperformed the two progressive systems in the competitive testing.

What audio system should be used? GI preferred Dolby, which it was also using in its DigiCipher SDTV systems for satellite and cable TV. The Philips/Thomson group had used Musicam (MPEG audio) for its Slot 5 HDTV system and, in fact, Philips largely owned the Musicam technology. And MIT, fronted by Professor Jae Lim, had its own proprietary audio technology.

Should the over-the-air digital transmission system employ GI's QAM modulation or Zenith's VSB modulation or something else? What type of packetization scheme should be used? The companies diverged on all of these issues, with equally competent engineers arguing passionately about the relative merits of each approach.

By May 1993, the Grand Alliance was proceeding, but with the companies' disparate agendas, coupled with mistrust from the previous testing, the whole deal could easily have disintegrated. Failure would send the FCC and the entire country back to the drawing board to figure out yet another official US broadcast standard for advanced television. Instead, through give and take, pushing and shoving, prodding and persuading, the gang of eight agreed to collaborate on a "best of the best" system. Unification seemed preferable to the alternative of enduring another round of expensive, time-consuming testing, with no certain outcome if precedent were to be the guide.

The promise of the Grand Alliance was captured on the front page of the *New York Times*:

> "Top Rivals Agree on Unified System for Advanced TV"
>
> The three top rivals for the right to develop the next generation of television technology in the United States agreed today to join forces on a single approach, hastening the biggest change in broadcasting since the advent of color.
>
> The agreement to collaborate on high-definition television, a move strongly supported by top Federal officials, eliminates the likelihood of protracted disputes and litigation, which could have delayed the introduction of the technology for years. With to-day's agreement, HDTV—offering wide-screen pictures nearly as bright and clear as movies and sound approaching the crispness of digital compact discs—could be available as early as 1995.
>
> The agreement to collaborate also represents a broad technical consensus that the next generation of television sets will be much more than boxes to amuse couch potatoes. Instead, the

industry has paved the way for television's rapid convergence with the interactive world of computers and high-speed two-way communications.

Not Just "Pretty Pictures"

The new HDTV system will be digital, meaning the signals will be transmitted in pulses that replicate the ones and zeros of computer code, instead of the traditional, less precise, technique of transmitting television signals in electromagnetic waves.

The movement to an all-digital approach began with General Instrument, a manufacturer of cable and satellite television coding devices. The company proposed a digital system in 1990, just before the F.C.C.'s deadline for submitting HDTV proposals had passed.

At first, most broadcasting experts ridiculed the proposal because they were convinced that a video image would require too much data to be translated into digital code. But by the end of that year, all of the other rivals except the Japanese broadcasting company, NHK, had replaced their original proposals with digital systems.[2]

The technical details of the system still needed to be resolved, one painstaking issue at a time. The video format debate—progressive versus interlace, computer world versus television world—was still raging with no compromise in sight, almost like a religious schism. The group accommodated this irreconcilable stumbling block by incorporating both types of scanning formats.

As for video compression and transport, the MPEG-2 standard, upon which the Philips/Thomson system had been based, was nearing completion, and the FCC Advisory Committee essentially imposed it on the new alliance.

The audio and digital transmission subsystems remained completely up in the air. The selection of a digital sound system was eventually determined through testing at Lucasfilm's Skywalker Ranch in Marin County, north of San Francisco, in favor of Dolby AC-3 (Dolby Digital). And through some additional testing, Zenith's Vestigial Sideband (VSB) method was selected over QAM as the technology for over-the-air modulation and transmission.

So the Grand Alliance came together, amid an odd mixture of relief, compromise, and lingering resentment. These were the agreed-upon standards for over-the-air digital broadcasting:

Video Formats:	720 lines Progressive (720P) and 1080 lines Interlaced (1080i), with a long-term goal of 1080 Progressive (1080P)
Video Coding:	MPEG-2 Main Profile video compression
Audio Coding:	Dolby Digital (AC-3) digital surround sound
Transport:	MPEG-2 Transport Stream packets
Transmission:	8 VSB modulation and forward error correction
System Information:	GI's DigiCipher system information tables, evolving over time to the ATSC Program and Service Information Protocol (PSIP)

With 1994 approaching, what began as a bona fide technical competition had evolved into a tense, drama-filled union of rivals. The FCC process had been under way for six years, including the four years from when GI sounded the starting gun of digital. While the result was a massive compromise, there was finally an agreed-upon set of specifications for the next generation of digital broadcast TV.

The digital standard definition (SDTV) market was already taking off around the world for satellite TV applications, and digital cable was coming next. The FCC advanced television testing process had proved one thing for certain: the future of HDTV in the United States, and ultimately in the world, would also be digital. Referring to the fact that the analog HDTV systems in Japan and Europe had been leapfrogged and rendered obsolete, Ed Markey, chairman of the US House of Representatives subcommittee on telecommunications, called the Grand Alliance's creation of the new specifications "one of the great late inning comebacks of all time."[3]

But selection of the digital HDTV technologies was one thing; still to come was a political phase, with powerful and influential new voices entering the fray; and then most important of all, the market phase. The Grand Alliance had survived a messy process and done its job. But the great compromise did not necessarily mean American households would be seeing beautiful new high-resolution TV pictures anytime soon.

The question remained, to be debated forcefully and inconclusively for years to come, of whether consumers even wanted or needed HDTV. Granted, the pictures were spectacular, with up to five times the resolution of standard definition television. But how much did consumers really care about picture quality? How much would they have to pay for new HDTV sets? What content would they be able to watch? There were plenty of opinions, but no one really knew the answers.

GI would stay involved with the FCC process to help bring it to closure. But it was time for the company to put all of its energy into the digital cable and satellite markets, where its enormous near-term business opportunities resided.

29 THE FIRST CONSUMER DIGITAL TV SERVICES

General Instrument's expanding list of digital satellite TV customers on multiple continents was impressive. But these content providers were wholesaling their digital signals to cable headends or commercial TV stations, still one big step removed from the consumer. There remained an open question of who would be first to deliver digital signals all the way to the home, the content endpoint paying everyone else's bills. And correspondingly, which technology company would mass-produce the first consumer digital boxes?

Since GI's second-generation MPEG-2 compatible system that had been ordered by TCI and the other cable operators, called DigiCipher II, was still in an early stage of development, and the FCC process for over-the-air digital broadcast signals was stalled, the immediate question was whether DirecTV (and its supplier, Thomson/RCA) would be able to claim this honor uncontested. PrimeStar was operational with Scientific Atlanta's analog BMAC system, but the fledgling service only had about 65,000 subscribers, a consumer base intentionally constrained by the cable owners' mixed objectives as well as the possibility they would have to upgrade the entire subscriber base to digital.

GI had been prodding the PrimeStar executives to get moving with digital before DirecTV stole all their thunder, but its efforts seemed to be hitting a brick wall. It wasn't that the PrimeStar executives, led by John Cusick and David Beddow, didn't fully understand that time was of the essence. Their hands were tied by the consortium of cable operators that owned PrimeStar, some being less concerned than others about the threat of DirecTV. Pursuing DBS in a meaningful way was an extremely expensive undertaking, and PrimeStar's six cable owners—TCI, Time Warner, Comcast, Cox, Continental, and Newhouse, along with satellite operator GE Americom—each had its own core business to worry about. In addition, GE's satellite was a medium-power Ku-band bird, requiring a 1-meter dish, much smaller than the 3-meter C-band dishes but significantly larger than the 18-inch pizza-sized dishes that DirecTV was readying for volume production.

Belatedly, PrimeStar issued a Request for Proposal (RFP) for a consumer-oriented digital satellite television system, followed by an exhaustive evaluation process with several hopeful competitors. GI had an advantage since it was the only company already shipping a functional digital system, DigiCipher I, although it was shipping only to commercial customers such as HBO and Viacom, not yet for consumer applications. Furthermore, GI's proposal promised a future equipment upgrade to DigiCipher II, allowing compatibility with MPEG-2 and the digital cable system we were developing for TCI and the other cable operators. In that scenario, PrimeStar's digital signals could be marketed not only to satellite TV consumers but also to cable headends for subsequent digital redistribution down the cable lines.

At the end of the RFP process, in early 1993, the three finalists were General Instrument, Scientific Atlanta, and Philips. Each contender had its own advocates within PrimeStar management and its cable-dominated board of directors. Malone's perspective at TCI was that the cable industry needed to get into the DBS business far more aggressively and that GI was the only company that could make this happen anytime soon. Time Warner Cable liked the continuity with SA, while others favored the consumer branding aspect of Philips.

Malone prevailed, and once again Jim Bunker was summoned to Denver, this time all the way from Gothenburg, Sweden, where he was attending a close family friend's wedding. Rumsfeld tracked him down, issuing the ultimatum: "Aren't you the president of GI San Diego?" Bunker skipped the wedding and rushed back to Denver, along with Jim Faust from GI Chicago, to close the PrimeStar deal. Negotiations ensued and by August 1993, GI received a $250 million initial order for consumer satellite receivers and associated digital uplink equipment. With a sudden sense of urgency, PrimeStar had to be live with digital signals before DirecTV.

Fortunately, GI had started product development in earnest before the deal was inked. But the task was enormous, involving a multitude of system-level enhancements, a new digital consumer receiver, and a long list of new encoder features. The teams of Rick Segil and Keith Kelley, GI San Diego's vice presidents of product management and engineering, respectively, had only six months to get PrimeStar on the air. Ly Tran and his world-class encoder engineering team, including Siu-Wai Wu, Mike Casteloes, Bob Nemiroff, Bob Stone, and John Shumate, had to shift from high gear into overdrive to meet PrimeStar's fastidious requirements.

They delivered, and on March 22, 1994, PrimeStar made history by launching its digital satellite service. Its digital TV signals were the first to go all the way to consumers' homes, and its consumers were the first in the world to use consumer digital TV boxes, GI's PrimeStar digital satellite receivers.

GI's digital TV equipment contract wins with the content providers, cable operators, and PrimeStar were gratifying, but all the hype was setting off alarm bells outside the company. By the end of 1993, the US Justice Department initiated an investigation into whether GI had accumulated too powerful of a market position in the nascent and burgeoning digital television business. For GI San Diego, it was a déjà vu moment. Five years earlier, we had been vindicated by the Justice Department concluding we were a legal monopoly for the VideoCipher II satellite TV encryption system. That ruling had been highly controversial, with lingering questions of whether it had been a correct or appropriate decision.

This time GI was caught in the middle of a legal battle and escalating war of words between two valued customers, Viacom's Sumner Redstone and TCI's John Malone. Viacom had filed a major antitrust suit against

TCI and various other cable operators, asserting monopolistic intent to employ GI's technology in order to dominate and control the emerging market for digital television content delivery.

The *Wall Street Journal* published the following article in March 1994:

> "Probe of General Instrument Resulted in Large Part from Viacom, TCI Feud"
>
> Among the major actions in the suit, Viacom alleged a "TCI/GI conspiracy" to "create and control...distribution" of cable television programming through the use of the equipment supplier's technology.
>
> The dispute was harsh and expressed in personal tones...Viacom accused Mr. Malone of using "bully boy tactics and strong-arming competitors." "In the American cable industry, one man has, over the last several years, seized monopoly power...That man is John C. Malone."[1]

The previous day, the *New York Times* had written:

> "Antitrust Inquiry on Cable Gear, General Instrument's Dominance at Issue"
>
> The Justice Department's antitrust division is investigating whether General Instrument Corporation, a leading supplier of equipment to the cable television industry, may have a stranglehold on the delivery of advanced video services...The inquiry could have a broad impact because General Instrument has evolved into a technology gatekeeper in the cable television industry...[2]

After scrutinizing GI's contracts with TCI, the Justice Department offered a settlement in July 1994 mandating that certain exclusivity provisions needed to be modified and requiring cable companies that also owned content to agree to sell that content to competitors, to the great benefit of DirecTV. GI had dodged another bullet. And PrimeStar ordered another million digital satellite receivers.

DirecTV's service was launched during the summer of 1994, several months later than the April date it had intended, with RCA digital receivers on the retail shelves of Sears and Circuit City stores. GI's prediction to Hughes, that DirecTV's market entry would be delayed if they insisted on MPEG-2, was correct. The service started with MPEG-1 video compression, upgrading later to MPEG-2. Furthermore, in the middle of system development, Hughes had decided DirecTV couldn't wait for the standards committee to finalize the MPEG-2 systems specification, a separate element from MPEG-2 video, and therefore DirecTV launched with its own proprietary transport and packetization system. And sure enough, just as we had warned, after DirecTV had a million units installed, their NDS security system was hacked, and the service had a serious piracy issue on its hands. GI had predicted the security breach based on the extensive piracy being suffered by Murdoch's BSkyB DBS service in the United Kingdom, which was also using NDS smart cards. But DirecTV would prevail through all of these issues, and the business originally referred to as "Deathstar" by the cable industry would gain strength through sustained subscriber growth, along with a dramatic rise in stock market capitalization, right out of cable's pockets.

In September 1994, DirecTV signed the most important programming deal in its history: the exclusive rights to out-of-market National Football League games. This sports package, branded as "NFL Sunday Ticket," would not only add fuel to the escalating cost of sports television rights, but it would greatly differentiate DirecTV from its current and future competitors, with the exception of the large-dish C-band market.

Stu Levin, founder and CEO of TVN, had first started working on a C-band deal with the NFL in 1992. In 1994, the NFL started paying TVN for access to its C-band satellite transponders. As part of the deal, the NFL also had to provide TVN with ad spots and a small share of the NFL Sunday Ticket revenue. But the real breakthrough enabling Levin to secure this deal was Rupert Murdoch's coup in December 1993, when his upstart Fox TV network blindsided CBS chairman Laurence Tisch with a $1.6 billion four-year deal to broadcast NFL games. This new TV contract with Fox provided the NFL with the flexibility to create NFL Sunday Ticket, first through Levin's TVN service for C-band satellite subscribers, and soon thereafter with DirecTV.

But the most dramatic event that had occurred in 1994 remained the world's first digital television signals being sent directly into consumer households, a half-century after the creation of the analog NTSC standard. All the content providers that had gone live in the previous year with GI's DigiCipher I system were "just as digital" in their transmissions as PrimeStar, but their signals were being digitally decoded in the headends of cable affiliates and then re-distributed down cable as good old-fashioned analog NTSC signals. Now, with PrimeStar and DirecTV, digital video content was finally being mainlined directly into consumers' homes, all the way to the GI and RCA digital boxes adjacent to their TV sets.

The digital age had truly arrived, but the DBS wars were just beginning. By the end of 1994, DirecTV had caught up and passed PrimeStar in subscriber count, although both services were growing rapidly. Clearly there was a strong pent-up demand in America for a home entertainment alternative to the cable companies. And PrimeStar, with some but not all of its cable owners on board, was crafting plans to launch high-power satellites by 1996, in order to enable use of 18-inch dishes and thereby compete more effectively against DirecTV.

30   BICOASTAL BICENTRICITY

Don Rumsfeld had been at the helm of General Instrument for nearly three years by the summer of 1993, having fulfilled his contract, and was ready to move on. With the one million shares of GI stock granted to him by Forstmann Little upon being hired, he reportedly departed with a $23 million pre-tax gain, net of $2.8 million of his own money invested.

In August, Forstmann Little brought in Dan Akerson to replace Rumsfeld as CEO, with Rumsfeld staying on as chairman for a while before leaving the company. A graduate of the United States Naval Academy, Akerson had been MCI's president and COO when Ted Forstmann recruited him, offering him not only the top job at GI but also a partnership interest in Forstmann Little. Akerson had been credited with catapulting MCI into the forefront of the telecommunications business, bringing in British Telecom for a 25 percent equity stake and enabling MCI to become a formidable competitor to AT&T in the long-distance telephony market.

Akerson's tough, no-nonsense management style was similar to Rumsfeld's, but an example of how their styles differed came to light when Ted Forstmann offered each of them a Gulfstream G3 corporate jet from one of his other companies, Gulfstream Aerospace. While Rumsfeld had refused the gesture during his tenure, citing cost-containment issues, Akerson readily accepted the perk. Like Rumsfeld before him, Akerson retained Rick Friedland as his right-hand man in Chicago. But Akerson sometimes talked in grandiose terms, saying: "My goal is to be as big as Microsoft."[1]

In 1994, GI's sales and earnings rose while long-term debt was paid down, causing the company's stock price to skyrocket. Forstmann Little had already made a killing through GI's public stock offerings, but the firm still owned a large number of shares and was not done cashing out.

One of Akerson's main tasks was to ensure that the operating divisions in San Diego and Hatboro, Pennsylvania, worked together to develop the essential next-generation product: the MPEG-2 compatible DigiCipher II content delivery system for the US cable operators. There were many necessary hardware and software components of the system, the development of which had been divvied up between the two coasts, and the entire system had to come together in order for the high-volume product, the digital cable box, to function and become the next growth engine for the company. Timely delivery was crucial for maintaining the upward momentum of the company's stock price and the resale value of Forstmann Little's remaining shares.

The West Coast and East Coast divisions of GI, the VideoCipher Division in San Diego and the Jerrold Division just north of Philadelphia, had starkly contrasting corporate cultures. While there was no dearth of smart, hard workers at either location, the DNA and work environments were radically different. The San Diego culture reflected its Linkabit heritage, favoring advanced engineering degrees and a philosophy that superior technology could drive markets. The atmosphere at Jerrold was redolent of cable's origins, a fiercely independent, sales-driven, grassroots work ethic, combining street smarts with a can-do attitude. Another big difference was in employee stability: the Hatboro employees were mostly long-timers, even "lifers," while the VideoCipher workforce was constantly turning over, either through periodic layoffs or with entrepreneurs leaving to start new companies.

"Jerrold" derived from the middle name of Milton Jerrold Shapp, an engineer who served as a World War II officer before moving to Philadelphia and founding Jerrold Electronics, a pioneer in the cable industry. He sold his company to GI in 1967, enabling him to finance his race for governor of Pennsylvania. He served in that office for eight years during the 1970s. GI's Jerrold Division had good engineering but its biggest strengths were in manufacturing and sales, making it a seemingly ideal partner for its sister division across the country, which excelled at complex systems engineering and product innovation.

Hal Krisbergh, head of GI's Jerrold Division since the mid-1980s, had an ebullient personality driven by a visionary perspective and an unshakable sense of optimism. Krisbergh proclaimed GI's digital TV contract with TCI as "the biggest deal in the history of the company," believing it would lead to GI becoming one of the few most powerful and important technology companies in the world. By sheer force of will and tenacity, he had prodded the cable industry into the analog addressable set-top converter age, convinced that the ability to communicate with interactive cable boxes in the home was the wave of the future.

Krisbergh started a GI subsidiary, Cable Video Store, one of the earliest pay-per-view movie services, as a vehicle to prove the concept of subscriber addressability and impulse purchasing to the cable industry. A consumer could click on a remote control button to instantly order a movie or boxing event, the price being automatically added to the cable bill. Krisbergh also started a home shopping service, Cable Catalog Store, allowing consumers to make impulse home shopping purchases from a wide variety of products. And he formed, along with Dave Del Beccaro, Digital Cable Radio. Later rebranded as Music Choice, it became the industry's first digital music service, piping dozens of channels of digital stereo, of every possible genre, into the home. These pioneering services were nothing less than the pre-Internet precursors of Netflix, Amazon, and Pandora.

Krisbergh was supported in Hatboro by a strong management team. Bob Cromack headed up manufacturing, responsible for the massive factory complex in Taipei and also manufacturing facilities in Mexico. GI had been the first American company to recognize the potential for high-quality, low-cost volume manufacturing in Taiwan, and this capability provided a sustainable cost advantage over its competitors.

The highly automated General Instrument Taiwan (GIT) electronics factory cranked out several million cable boxes a year, making it one of the largest consumer electronics production facilities in the world.

Ed Breen was in charge of sales. With a winning, ever-present smile and heaps of charisma, he was the kind of guy you wanted on your team. Or, rather, you wanted to be on his team. Breen ran a sales machine achieving over 60 percent market share in analog set-top converter boxes year after year. His team of loyalists—Matt Aden, Pete Wronski, Bick Remmey, and others—conducted sales the old-fashioned way, camping out at customers' sites and wining, dining, and golfing with them at great expense. They did whatever it took to get the order.

Geoff Roman's sweet spot was the junction of technology and business. He spoke the technical language of the cable CTOs but also knew how to get deals done, making him instrumental in the company's strategic direction. Tom Lynch was responsible for the Distribution Systems business unit, which developed cable infrastructure equipment such as amplifiers, switches, and taps. Outgoing and amiable, Lynch had a strong business sense and great instincts for the company's bottom line.

Dan Moloney managed the cable set-top box business, the division's pre-digital profit machine, with analytical business acumen and deep insights into the cable business. Before the TCI contract materialized, a small team worked in Moloney's group planning for the digital cable market, coordinating with San Diego and creating an early foundation. Jeff Hamilton was the initial engineer focused on digital cable, and Dan Sutorius was dedicated to product line management. Dario Santana and John Burke remained focused on the highly successful analog set-top business, with Marc Kauffman leading the systems engineering activity. Burke also had responsibility for GI's product role in the Sega Channel, another forward-looking venture offered by TCI and Time Warner Cable to their subscribers. The 1990s game machine war was between Sega and

Nintendo, before shifting to Nintendo versus Sony, and later Microsoft. But while Sega was in contention, it allowed cable subscribers the ability to download games, via a GI cable adapter, to their Sega game consoles. Chuck Dougherty, another long-time Hatboro employee, was responsible for various cable infrastructure products and also managed the telephone companies' entry into the TV business, while Mike Pulli was developing the microwave cable business before moving into a sales role.

Dave Robinson led the company's successful entry into Cableoptics, GI's fiber optic distribution business of laser transmitters and optical amplifiers, helping to enable the hybrid fiber optic and coaxial cable architecture that is still prevalent today. After leaving the company to manage AT&T's new cable group in Massachusetts, he was hired back by Krisbergh in 1995 to head up the newly formed digital cable business unit. Robinson recruited Carl McGrath from AT&T to lead the rapidly growing digital cable engineering department and also hired Denton Kanouff from RCA as vice president of marketing. Dan Sutorius, who had been engaged with the company's digital cable activity almost from the beginning, continued with product line management. Larry Vince had a critical systems engineering role, ensuring that the various complex software and hardware components worked together.

At the end of 1993, Jim Bunker left the company as president of the San Diego business unit, leading to a sustained period during which the West Coast operation was left adrift. Business remained strong, with the digital satellite TV business taking off, but the site lacked a local leader and was essentially operating under the thumb of the Hatboro cable unit.[2] The business that had been such a strong contributor to company profits with its VideoCipher franchise, and had then re-invented itself as the proud and bold innovator of the digital television revolution, had become rudderless, with low morale, high employee turnover, and deep uncertainty about its future.

In June 1994, I transferred to Hatboro from San Diego with my wife and baby daughter to lead a new technology licensing business unit revolving around GI's central position in the digital TV market. Dave Brown, an engineer who had left the company to get his MBA at UCLA, was rehired in San Diego and took over my business development role with the content providers. After landing with my family at the Philadelphia airport, a local couple sharing the van ride to our temporary living quarters had greeted us in a puzzled and sarcastic tone: "You're moving from paradise to Philadelphia?"

But when I arrived in Hatboro, the place was firing on all cylinders. Employees were scurrying around looking for available meeting rooms and engineers were being hired as quickly as they could be qualified for the jobs. There was a palpable excitement in the air, an East Coast version of what I'd experienced in San Diego the prior few years.

The initial corporate-level meeting arranged by GI's Matt Miller between Don Rumsfeld, Bill Gates, and their teams had resulted in a three-way partnership among GI, Microsoft, and Intel, code named Pandora. Its purpose was to capitalize on the technology buzzword of the year: convergence. The idea was to develop a next-generation set-top box merging GI's cable TV, video, and security expertise with Intel's microprocessor architecture and software from Microsoft. The media loved the plan, and convergence became the talk of the tech world. But it was a premature vision that didn't yet make sense as a business proposition. The chasm between the home entertainment world and the computer domain was too wide, and consumers had no interest in bridging them together. TV was fundamentally a "lean back," relaxing and enjoyable experience, while the PC world was "lean forward," tied mostly to the workplace.

It didn't take long for Pandora, the GI deal with Microsoft and Intel, to unravel. But Krisbergh carried the basic concept forward. He adopted the term "bicentricity," evoking a dual-centered technological base for cable boxes with two evolutionary paths: traditional television viewing, which would become increasingly interactive; and a separate capability riding the PC revolution with its growing set of applications. The set-top box envisioned by Krisbergh would be the intelligent maestro residing at the epicenter of the bicentric universe. Blended functions could occur sometime in the future, with the two parallel worlds ultimately coming together in an era of true convergence.

Our primary competitor, Scientific Atlanta, appeared to be on the sidelines. But in some ways SA was thinking even more strategically than GI, recognizing that ownership of more advanced set-top software, along with an applications layer on top, would become a valuable platform. Furthermore, SA recognized the critical importance of the intelligent network as an organic entity, above and beyond the digital cable box at the end of the line. Its strategy seemed to be: "Let GI play around with Microsoft; we're going to create our own 'middleware' environment and interactive network, and monetize entirely new assets."

Echoing the mantra of the computer software business, PowerTV, a start-up that later became a captive subsidiary of SA, positioned its product as an interactive TV operating system distinguished by hardware-independence and open architecture. Software developers could use the middleware to create exciting new applications. In contrast, GI ceded the middleware to third parties, especially TV Guide with its Interactive Program Guide, an essential software element allowing consumer navigation of an unprecedented number of channels and choices.

Soon after my arrival in Hatboro, in the late summer of 1994, I traveled down to Virginia with Dan Moloney for an industry event hosted by Bell Atlantic. Moloney had a new role—overall responsibility for the telephone companies' entry into the TV space—and we had just signed a massive deal with Bell Atlantic Video Enterprises, which was finally committing to getting into the video business in a big way. After a couple false starts, this time around they had decided to build Hybrid Fiber Coax (HFC) cable systems, in direct competition with TCI and others, using GI's digital system architecture. Earlier that year, in February 1994, Bell Atlantic had called off its $21 billion acquisition of TCI. Now it was going to build its own cable systems instead.

Bell Atlantic was a "common carrier" in the highly regulated telecommunications market and therefore had a sharply different, and more public, way of conducting business than the freewheeling cable operators. After social introductions, I was ushered on stage with various Bell Atlantic executives. As the auditorium doors swung open, I started to sense the extent to which I'd been unintentionally set up. Many of our competitors' employees flowed in, representing most of the leading electronics, technology, and software companies. Envious that GI had won this huge deal, they smelled blood and wanted in on the action.

The meeting started out fine, with the Bell Atlantic executives providing a business overview followed by my summary of GI's technology and licensing policy. Then the questions started. One after the other, the attendees peppered me, probing for business and technical details that even Bell Atlantic thought were out of bounds. Bell Atlantic went so far as to defend GI as its partner, but with their service rollout plans still half-baked, it was obvious the whole meeting was ill-conceived. A sense of relief washed over Moloney and me as we returned to Pennsylvania. GI continued developing a digital system for Bell Atlantic during the next several months, but it was another false alarm for telco video. They decided to hold off on the subscription TV business once again, canceling our contract and reverting back into video hibernation mode.

The telcos remained a disappointing wild card in the television arena for many years. They had impressive balance sheets and cash flow but no coherent strategy for entering the video business. In contrast, TCI was laser-focused and chomping at the bit to get into the digital game and defend its turf against DirecTV. As the dual coasts of GI worked together to develop what had become a monstrously complex digital system, TCI designated Hewlett Packard and Scientific Atlanta as the two initial second sources for the GI digital set-top boxes.

The city of New Orleans was the host site for the 1994 National Cable TV convention. The night before the show opened, I was holed up late in my hotel room negotiating final contractual details with Hewlett Packard. The pressure was on both sides to compromise and sign the deal, as a mystery press conference had been scheduled for the next day. The deadline forced closure.

At the media event Rick Friedland took the stage along with TCI's Tom Elliot and HP's Webb McKinney, while I sat in the audience with Tom Beaudreau of TCI. It was major industry news that HP, at that time one of the world's most prominent and profitable technology companies, was entering the cable business by licensing GI's digital TV technology.

HP enthusiastically pursued its new business, enticed by a 500,000-unit initial order from TCI. With a small technical support team in Hatboro and San Diego, I was doing my best to help get HP to market, directly in competition with my GI co-workers down the hall.

Scientific Atlanta was a completely different story, signing our license agreements mainly in order to appease TCI. It soon became obvious that SA was in no hurry to develop a compatible product. Licensing GI's technology for the digital future of cable, even with an initial 300,000-unit order, was too bitter of a pill for SA to swallow. They paid us our license fees and accepted our technical documentation, but that was the extent of their effort. Behind the scenes, Time Warner was formulating its own digital cable strategy, separate and apart from TCI, and was luring SA into its fold with the promise of a lead role in developing a competing digital technology platform.

A few years later, in 1997, we licensed British company Pace to make compatible digital boxes. We also licensed Panasonic and Zenith as PrimeStar second sources, but PrimeStar would meet a different fate before either company was able to convert its GI license into a digital set-top box order. HP eventually dropped out of the business, unable to get the high profit margins it wanted from TCI. Pace also exited the domestic business before coming back years later, dusting off its license to finally achieve a significant market position the next decade.

31 Doesn't "Open" Mean "Free"?

During the early 1990s, our competitors successfully argued that General Instrument's DigiCipher video compression was closed and proprietary while MPEG-2 was open and free. Those who really understood technical standards and intellectual property rights knew this claim to be specious. It was one thing for a standards body to provide a publicly available (that is, open) specification. But whether products relying on this standard violated the patent rights of one or more companies, typically triggering royalties, was a completely different and separate issue.

As with most standards bodies, MPEG requires its member companies to agree to license their patents essential to practicing the standard on a reasonable and non-discriminatory basis. But GI's competitors had spread a persuasive but misleading argument conflating the fact that MPEG-2 was open with the incorrect presumption that it was royalty-free. By the time MPEG-2 was approaching finalization, dozens of television programmers and service providers around the world had committed to its use under the erroneous assumption that it would not entail patent-related royalties. The movie studios had also decided to use the emerging video compression standard for the new DVD market. And the FCC had imposed MPEG-2 on the Grand Alliance, for the US digital HDTV broadcast standard.

Behind the scenes, there was a growing and alarming realization that MPEG-2 infringed on numerous companies' patents, and the market situation suddenly turned quite ominous, almost to a state of panic. What if DirecTV and the US cable industry launched digital TV services to millions of subscribers, only to find out they, or their equipment vendors, were being held hostage to outrageous royalties, or even an injunction against shipping or using MPEG-2 products? What about the Hollywood studios planning to use MPEG-2 to encode thousands of movies on DVDs? And what about the broadcasters and consumer electronics companies pondering the potential of HDTV? The entire market for MPEG-2 digital television could be dead on arrival. Customers started whispering that if MPEG didn't resolve the royalty issue favorably, they would just use GI's proprietary video compression instead.

The US cable industry decided it had better facilitate a solution. Baryn Futa, CableLabs' Chief Operating Officer, had an ambitious idea. He would corral the top five MPEG-2 patent holders together as a core group, persuading them to pool their patents and offer a reasonable joint license, and then get the various secondary patent holders to follow. The five founding companies in the MPEG-2 Intellectual Property Rights Group were GI, Sony, Philips, Matsushita, and Thomson. AT&T (Bell Labs) was also believed to be in the top tier but apparently had already indicated it would not participate in any such patent pool. Futa retained Ken Rubenstein of the New York law firm Meltzer Lippe (and later Proskauer Rose) to conduct a thorough analysis, reviewing 8,000 patents and ultimately correlating dozens of essential patents to the MPEG-2 standard.[1]

I was still GI's Director of Licensing, and Futa asked me to be the chairman of the newly formed MPEG-2 IPR Group. Honored by Futa's request, I accepted, but not without some trepidation as I was relatively new to the patent and licensing arena. The individuals representing the other four companies were among the leading intellectual property experts in the world: Yoshihide Nakamura of Sony; Karel van Lelyveld and Huub Beckers of Philips; Hiroaki Horia of Matsushita; and Béatrix de Russé of Thomson Consumer Electronics. They were the licensing gurus of the biggest consumer electronics companies, and I was a licensing neophyte being asked to be their chairman.

After a series of tedious, multiday meetings, we sketched out a draft joint licensing structure and had it reviewed by attorneys to ensure that it didn't run afoul of antitrust law, even obtaining a preliminary green light from the US Justice Department. Then, with great fanfare, we invited all interested companies to a March 1994 meeting in Paris. I presented the basic, high-level joint licensing proposal and answered questions, accompanied by Ken Boschwitz, GI's San Diego division counsel, there to keep me out of any legal trouble. The meeting went well, which was a tremendous relief, although the audience was pushing for more details than we were ready to provide.

Not everyone in the patent holders' group, however, was on the same page. The main issue was whether the MPEG-2 license would be the typical one-time royalty imposed at the end-product level on hardware and software companies. The European members of the group started advocating a "use fee," whereby users of the technology—studios, content providers, DBS service providers, cable operators—would pay royalties on some scale relative to their actual use of the technology. The argument was that "we" electronics companies were getting squeezed on profit margins through brutal competitive forces, while the media companies were making all the money.

But the concept of use fees was shocking and unprecedented, causing a high level of outrage to erupt in the media community. Once again, GI's proprietary DigiCipher compression was put into play by the media powers as a fallback position if MPEG didn't get its house in order. One might think GI was relishing its position, but we had finally abandoned our initial goal of establishing a proprietary video compression standard and we were completely entrenched in developing our MPEG-2 compatible system. GI just wanted to finish the digital cable product and start shipping in volume. Furthermore, the likelihood of having to indemnify our customers for video compression, now that we knew how many patents were involved from other companies, was alarming. MPEG-2, in contrast, would give us some legal cover, and we could effectively pass on the royalty, if it was reasonable, to our customers.

The use fee debate raged on for months, with Baryn Futa and me pleading with the other patent holders to give up on their dream of assessing annuities on the media companies. It all came to a head the following year, in March 1995, when we converged in Lausanne, Switzerland, to resolve the matter once and for all. The situation had become so dicey that HBO's Barbara Jaffe and Craig Cuttner insisted that they personally attend the meeting. I took them out to dinner the night before, assuring them that everything would be fine. Sure enough, the issue of use fees was cast aside the next day, with the caveat from the Europeans that "the time for use fees had arrived and it would happen 'next time.'"

The painstaking details of the licensing pool were finally worked out, and a couple years later, with MPEG-2's future finally secure, Baryn Futa arranged for a July 1997 press conference and business licensing summary in Tokyo for interested technology companies to celebrate and learn about the agreement. Futa had resigned as CableLabs COO and formed a new company, MPEG-LA, to administer the MPEG-2 licensing activities. The reception was held at the elegant Hotel Okura, with sumptuous plates of sushi and other delicacies served by demure Japanese women in exquisite kimonos.

Since many companies were already shipping MPEG-2 products, the entire industry was extremely relieved to see the licensing issue resolved. This is how *Multichannel News* reported on the agreement:

"MPEG Licensing Group Starts Road Show"

"This is a very, very important occurrence," said Tony Wasilewski, chief scientist of Scientific Atlanta's digital video systems group. "Licensees of MPEG-LA can rest assured that they are getting all of the rights needed to implement MPEG-2."

"Hopefully, this means that there's only one outfit that we need to deal with on these kinds of intellectual property issues," said Jim Chiddix, chief technical officer of Time Warner Cable. "That also stops people from getting too greedy with licensing fees."

"This is a watershed event," said Marc Tayer, vice president of business development for General Instrument, who was on site for the Tokyo stop on the MPEG-LA tour. "It's unprecedented in that there are a few dozen patents owned by several companies around the world, making it a very difficult business scenario, absent this kind of pooling effort, for a licensee. The true benefit is an orderly, comfortable market for MPEG-2."[2]

The resolution to the "open versus free" tension of MPEG-2 would set a far-reaching precedent for future digital video standards: the pooling of hundreds of patents owned by dozens of companies, licensed jointly to all comers for a reasonable fee on a nondiscriminatory basis. The same general theme would foreshadow the "network neutrality" issue more than a decade later. As discussed in Chapter 66, Netflix and the broadband Internet would take center stage, igniting a raging debate regarding the rules of the ostensibly open road and who should pay whom for what.

32 YET ANOTHER COMPETITIVE HURDLE

By the mid-1990s, several years into its digital journey, General Instrument had defeated piracy, survived two Justice Department investigations, rebounded from the devastating loss of the DirecTV business to RCA, fought against and then embraced the MPEG-2 standard, suffered a billion-dollar bait-and-switch from Bell Atlantic Video Services, and endured five years of battle with archrival Scientific Atlanta for market leadership. But GI still wasn't ready to produce and ship the digital cable products that were in such high demand by its customers. In fact, it was over a year late and still had a long way to go.

There was no way SA was going to give up. On the contrary, they dismissed GI's digital TV equipment contracts with the cable operators as nearly worthless paper. SA knew as well as GI that the cable customers could always find a way to get out of the deals until they had accepted and installed volume product, especially if a more timely or better solution were available that fit their business needs.

SA understood that GI's strategic advantage in getting the content providers on board digitally was a handicap. But with the cable operators there was an opening in GI's armor a mile wide, and not only SA but also the rest of the technology companies attempting to enter the digital TV market would do their best to exploit it. Digital Video Broadcasting (DVB), the European digital TV standards for satellite, cable, and over-the-air broadcasting, had emerged largely in reaction to GI's "stealing the show" at the 1990 International Broadcasting Convention in Brighton, England. Now DVB was a full-fledged set of digital television technical standards, incorporating not only MPEG-2 video and audio but myriad other technology elements necessary for a complete digital TV communications system.

GI had already developed equivalent techniques independently, ahead of DVB, in its rush to get to market. This was done out of necessity since there were no standards to follow in areas such as modulation, forward error correction, encryption, and carriage of critical elements such as conditional access and security messages, closed captioning, and teletext. GI was contributing its additional techniques for digital satellite and cable transmission to the standards set by the Advanced Television Systems Committee, which were evolving as part of the FCC and Grand Alliance process. Meanwhile, however, DVB was creating a separate technical cookbook showing how to design an end-to-end digital television system for various applications. The competitive market was starting to line up not only as GI versus the rest of the tech world but also as ATSC versus DVB.

In the North American market, Scientific Atlanta was at the vanguard of a growing DVB bandwagon, arguing to the cable operators and to the remaining content providers that they should skip the TCI/GI ATSC-based DigiCipher II system altogether and instead switch to DVB. There were even innuendos that the GI claim of being compliant with MPEG-2 and ATSC standards was a sham, a smokescreen for a proprietary takeover of the country's digital television future. And SA was making the same argument to TCI, knowing that this leader among cable operators was getting increasingly frustrated and upset with GI for being late on the digital cable boxes it had ordered, while DirecTV was getting bigger and stronger every day. There were also still two major cable domestic operators that had not committed to GI: Time Warner and Cablevision Systems.

TV/Com, a new San Diego company that had grown out of the defunct Oak Communications, was relying on the DVB standard for its entry into the digital television equipment market. Just like SA, TV/Com wanted to stymie GI's market position. It formed a multi-company alliance, called the North American Digital Group (NADG), focused on establishing a common set of DVB-based technical standards that would be adopted for digital TV applications in North America. More than sixty organizations and companies were represented at TV/Com's inaugural NADG meeting in Washington DC in late October 1994, including AT&T, Bell Atlantic, CableLabs, Hitachi, IBM, Panasonic, Philips, Scientific Atlanta, Thomson, Uniden, and Viacom.[1]

Other DVB-based threats kept coming out of the woodwork. A new satellite TV venture, AlphaStar, launched a medium-power DBS service based on the DVB standards, although it ultimately declared bankruptcy in May 1997.

Stu Levin, founder and CEO of TVN Entertainment, announced a deal including technology and content aggregation that would compete directly against TCI's digital Headend in the Sky. Levin was a pioneer in the satellite pay-per-view entertainment business. He had launched TVN in the late 1980s with the novel idea of putting "movie theaters in the sky," licensing hit movies from the Hollywood studios. Each movie would occupy its own satellite transponder for a sustained period, re-starting every two hours just like in a movie theater. Paramount Pictures and Universal Studios were investors in TVN. The C-band TVRO satellite subscribers loved the service, which also featured sports events and concerts. It was far more advanced than cable with respect to the choice and convenience of accessing recently released movies, foreshadowing the video-on-demand future of cable. Since the early days of digital, Levin had been planning to launch a digital cable content platform, and now he was going head-to-head against TCI, with digital technology based on the DVB standard. We were able to convince him to switch to our system, however, mainly due to our underlying security and conditional access technology.

But Time Warner Cable was a far more important competitive factor than any of the alliances being assembled by SA, the North American Digital Group, and the other DVB advocates. Almost as powerful as TCI,

Time Warner Cable was getting serious about launching an interactive digital TV service on a national basis. The cable industry appeared to be splitting into two opposite camps: Time Warner and SA were lining up against TCI and GI. With GI's tardiness in delivering digital cable boxes to TCI, the risk was increasing that TCI might even agree with SA and Time Warner to align itself with the European DVB standards, automatically knocking GI off its fragile pedestal.

33 You Go Left, I'll Go Right

If the two coasts of GI—Hatboro, Pennsylvania, and San Diego, California—had disparate corporate cultures, the divide between TCI and Time Warner, the nation's two biggest cable operators, was even more pronounced. TCI's cultural roots stemmed from its rural cable TV, western plains origins, a manifestation of grassroots America at its entrepreneurial best. Time Warner Cable was formed by the fusion of the Warner Cable and ATC cable TV franchises, residing under the blue-chip, big-city umbrella of Time Warner Inc., itself a result of the 1989 merger of Warner Communications and Time Inc.

Steve Ross, the dominant personality at Warner and then Time Warner, was born in Brooklyn as Steve Rechnitz to parents who lost everything in the Great Depression. Displaying an entrepreneurial flair as a young man, he leapfrogged from his collection of small businesses (funeral parlors, rental cars, and office cleaning) to the glamorous halls of entertainment, where he would become an archetypal old-school media mogul. The driving force behind Warner Communications in the 1970s and 1980s, he emerged as the architect of the modern media conglomerate by orchestrating Warner's 1989 merger with Time. Following the merger, Warner's Steve Ross and Time's Dick Munro were co-chairmen and co-CEOs. Upon Munro's retirement in 1990, Ross became sole chairman and co-CEO with Munro's second-in-command, Nicholas J. Nicholas Jr., who had been president of Time Inc.

Nick Nicholas had been promised the sole CEO job by 1994, but in 1992 Steve Ross, dying of cancer in Los Angeles, maneuvered Nicholas out of the job. Instead, HBO chief Jerry Levin took over as Time Warner CEO. Levin ran Time Warner for the next ten years, acquiring Turner Broadcasting System in October 1996 and arranging the $164 billion merger in 2001 with America Online (AOL), headed by co-founder and CEO Steve Case. Time Warner shareholders fared poorly in this deal, occurring as it did during the height of the Internet bubble, prompting Levin's expulsion and the ascension of Richard Parsons to CEO of AOL Time Warner in 2002. One of Parsons' early acts was changing the company name back to Time Warner.

Time Warner Cable's management carried more of a polished and sophisticated disposition than the rough-and-tumble style of their counterparts at TCI. Another stark difference was the nature of their cable systems. Time Warner's systems were primarily clustered in urban and suburban areas, serving hundreds of thousands of subscribers within the same interconnected geographic footprint. TCI owned thousands of smaller franchises dispersed across rural America, controlled from over 1,000 individual cable headends. This difference in population density made it more efficient for Time Warner to upgrade to higher capacity with fiber optics, whereas TCI's overriding strategy was to leverage its digital Headend in the Sky, built in Denver with GI's technology, as a national upgrade to digital. This method gave TCI's rural cable systems a powerful, centralized resource to add hundreds of new digital channels to its distributed subscriber base at a relatively low cost.

Time Warner Cable's technology leaders were Jim Chiddix and Mike Hayashi, as well as Michael Adams, Louis Williamson, John Callahan, and Ralph Brown. Their mind-set, along with that of Time Warner

Cable CEO Joe Collins and Time Warner's top executives at the time, Ross and Levin, was epitomized by the 1991 decision to upgrade the 77-channel Brooklyn/Queens system to 150 channels, including dozens of channels of pay-per-view movies.[1] To accomplish this massive upgrade, however, Time Warner used analog technology, not digital. They also invested in more fiber optic infrastructure, stringing optical glass fibers to neighborhood nodes, each node serving 500 to 1,000 homes, with coaxial cable carrying the signals from the fiber nodes to subscribers' homes.[2] I visited the Queens facility in 1992, meeting with general manager Barry Rosenblum and his staff, and found them enthusiastic about their analog upgrade while clearly disinterested in digital technology.

Time Warner was also far less concerned than TCI about the likelihood of losing cable subscribers to new satellite TV services such as DirecTV, perceiving its urban and suburban customer base to be less inclined to cut the cable cord in favor of installing satellite dishes. So instead of rushing to digital, as TCI was, Time Warner was in no particular hurry to get there.

Instead, Time Warner Cable conducted its now-famous test of its Full Service Network (FSN) in Orlando, Florida, the location of its second largest cable division. FSN was designed to use digital technology to explore a whole new array of interactive services, not merely to expand channel capacity. Time Warner proclaimed FSN to be the world's first digital, interactive television system. It would provide Time Warner's Orlando customers with on-demand access to a cornucopia of entertainment and informational services. In its own press release, Time Warner described FSN as "integrating the technologies from the cable, computer, and telephone industries to provide interactive television, telephony, and on-line computer services."[3]

The Orlando Full Service Network test involved 4,000 trial customers and was conducted from December 1995 through December

1997, serving as a digital learning ground for Time Warner. It offered such varied services as video-on-demand, interactive shopping, interactive games, an interactive program guide, and, famously, the ability to order pizza with a remote control, with Pizza Hut delivering to the subscriber's home. Tom Feige was president of the Full Service Network, supported by VP of Engineering Jim Ludington and Yvette Gordon (Kanouff), a talented engineering director in a male-dominated business. She would later rise to become one of cable's top technology executives, first at SeaChange, then at Cablevision Systems, and on to Cisco in 2014.

Some in the industry criticized FSN as being overly futuristic and impractical, using software and computer servers from Silicon Graphics and a multithousand-dollar-per-unit digital cable box from Scientific Atlanta, not something that could scale across Time Warner's millions of subscribers. But the Orlando experiment was visionary and forward-looking, serving as a valuable consumer market research platform for applications and services. Also, many of the software architecture concepts adopted in FSN are still used today for unicast services such as video-on-demand. Finally, the Orlando test underscored the reality that when Time Warner would eventually roll out its digital TV service nationally, a few years later, it would do so on its own timetable, in accordance with its own corporate goals.

As TCI and Time Warner maneuvered in 1996 for the future strategic direction of cable, another consequential battle erupted concurrently, centered on two competing digital cable transmission methods. The first had been designed by GI for its DigiCable solution, while the second had been created by the European DVB standards body for digital cable in Europe and potentially elsewhere. Both solutions utilized a QAM modulation technique, but they diverged when it came to the associated method of "forward error correction."

Forward error correction, or FEC, has nothing to do with video compression. It is a mathematical method of adding bits (more zeros and ones) to a digital TV signal. These extra bits do not represent the content payload (whether video or audio), but rather are appended to the actual content for the specific purpose of facilitating error-free digital transmission. In other words, these additional FEC bits ensure that the digital content received by the cable subscriber is exactly the same as what was originally sent by the content provider. Inside the digital set-top box in the consumer's home, any transmission errors caused by noise or interference in the radio frequency channel can be mathematically corrected, enabling a perfect replica of the information sent from the origin.

As the divergent market visions for harnessing digital technology were being played out within TCI and Time Warner, this "QAM/FEC" digital cable transmission aspect became the latest technical dispute between GI and Scientific Atlanta. The same battle was shaping up on a broader front between GI and Hewlett Packard, our licensee, on the one hand, and the DVB community, including SA, on the other hand. And this same schism was exacerbating the divide, by proxy, between TCI and Time Warner, threatening to further split the industry in two.

The QAM/FEC method for GI's digital cable system had been designed under the direction of Paul Moroney in San Diego. It used a highly sophisticated technique called "concatenated trellis coded modulation."[4] Its technical DNA could be traced back to GI's Linkabit roots, where digital communications experts such as Jerry Heller and Paul Moroney had cut their teeth earlier in their engineering careers. In contrast, the DVB solution had been designed by committee, resulting in a simpler, more basic method, a "Reed-Solomon block code." GI was positioning its method as technically superior to DVB, an accurate claim given its 2 decibel (2 dB) advantage in signal-to-noise ratio, a key measure of signal robustness, or strength, though a noisy channel. This substantial technical advantage, so GI's argument went, would be particularly crucial in older cable systems, where it would be difficult to push digital signals through the aging pipes to subscribers' homes in a flawless and intact manner.

SA and others in the DVB camp didn't hesitate in countering this argument in force, disputing and even trivializing it as a minor, irrelevant distinction. But apart from dramatically outnumbering GI (and HP), the "rest of the world" had a very important advantage. DVB had wisely specified its QAM/FEC digital transmission technology for both "64 QAM" and "256 QAM," while GI's solution had initially defined only a 64 QAM version. The difference between 64 QAM and 256 QAM has to do with how many total bits, and therefore how many digital TV services, could be pumped through a 6 MHz cable channel. With 64 QAM, 27 Mbps could be sent down a cable channel, equivalent to six or seven digital TV services. But with 256 QAM, the number of digital services could be increased to ten or more within a single cable channel.

It didn't matter that very few, if any, cable systems at that time were capable of handling the 256 QAM signals; GI's solution appeared to be a shortsighted dead end. SA had discovered another major vulnerability in its nemesis, and GI suddenly had yet another competitive emergency on its hands. If GI didn't invent a credible 256 QAM "extension" immediately, the company faced the very real risk that its digital system would need to be redesigned once again, precisely what SA and the rest of GI's competitors were shooting for. At this late stage, GI would become a follower rather than a leader overnight, its already-late digital box deliveries to TCI would be in jeopardy, and competitors would beat GI to market with digital cable products.

So in hopeful desperation, we turned once again to Paul Moroney, our top systems engineer in San Diego. As if he didn't have enough on his plate already, Moroney was assigned the improbable task of devising a 256 QAM extension to GI's digital cable system in two weeks, with the additional requirement that it had to provide the same 2 dB technical advantage over DVB that its 64 QAM version enjoyed.[5] To say that Moroney and his San Diego team of digital communications engineers, working with technical consultant Chris Heegard, pulled off a miracle would be an understatement. In fact, they came through not only with a superior 256 QAM extension but with an entirely novel concept of how to scale the digital capacity even farther into the future. In a matter of weeks, GI went from being on the ropes of humiliation to back in the center court, neutralizing and surpassing SA and DVB in this technically crucial area.

TCI, knowing that GI was now fighting a high-stakes battle on a global stage, beyond the controlled borders of the domestic cable sandbox, enlisted Dick Green, CableLabs' CEO, to shepherd GI's new 64/256 QAM/FEC solution into the US and international standards bodies as an open standard. GI was represented in this latest mission by Jeff Hamilton, an engineer from its Hatboro location, with the full support and political leadership of Green, a highly respected industry statesman with a strong technical pedigree in television, cable, and standards activities. After a few months of persistence, the GI solution successfully became a domestic and international open standard, side by side with DVB.[6]

But even this triumph was insufficient. GI's latest victory and leadership status was still at risk as long as the company could not ship digital cable boxes to TCI and the other customers impatiently awaiting delivery. SA and its allies continued to dispute GI's claims of technical superiority. Furthermore, echoing the previous GI vs. MPEG video compression debate, there was a growing opposition claiming the DVB transmission method was open, free, and non-proprietary, while the GI transmission standard was loaded up with GI patents, which GI might later use to stifle competition and extract royalties.

In reality, no one knew for certain whether the DVB cable transmission method was covered by patents, while we had already established a licensing policy for our equivalent technology with a $0.25 per unit royalty. Into this volatile situation stepped Broadcom, a Southern California semiconductor start-up founded by Dr. Henry Nicholas and Dr. Henry Samueli, themselves both experts in digital communications technology. SA had previously provided venture funding to Broadcom, but Broadcom desired, more than anything, to embed its chips in GI's digital boxes, the crown jewel design win for a semiconductor start-up dreaming of an IPO.

34 TWO HENRYS AND A NEW CHIP

Broadcom's co-founders, Dr. Henry T. Nicholas III and Dr. Henry Samueli, had sharply contrasting styles and personalities, often a winning combination for a tech start-up. Both men received their bachelor's, master's, and PhD degrees from UCLA in electrical engineering. They worked together at TRW before starting Broadcom in 1991 with $5,000 each of their own money.[1]

Nicholas, called "Nick" from an early age, was extroverted, hyperactive, and muscle-bound, with a penchant for pumping iron while listening to heavy metal music. He grew up in Ohio but moved to Los Angeles with his mother and sister after his parents divorced. His mother then married Robert Leach, the scriptwriter of the successful 1960s TV series *Perry Mason*, who became Nick's father figure. A brash and meticulously dressed workaholic, Nick pressured his employees to work around the clock. Wall Street analysts called him Czar Nicholas due to the way he ruled his company with an iron fist.

Samueli, five years older, exuded a composed, intellectual confidence in the vein of GI's Jerry Heller. His parents survived Nazi Germany and moved to LA, where Samueli grew up and worked in his parents' liquor store as a teenager. A prolific inventor, eventually named on more than seventy US patents, Samueli was Nicholas's thesis advisor at UCLA.

As the front-runner in the digital television equipment market, GI was the number-one target customer for Broadcom's first digital TV device, an integrated QAM/FEC chip which would serve as the guts of the digital cable transmission subsystem. Every single digital box manufactured by GI would require one of these critical chips. But Broadcom had a major marketing roadblock. GI was designing its own equivalent chip in Phoenix, for internal use, with a small group of engineers who had stayed with GI in 1989 after the spin-off of GI's microelectronics semiconductor business into a separate public company, Microchip Technology.

No company had yet developed a low-cost, highly integrated QAM/FEC chip, a necessary feat in order for GI to make a reasonable profit on its digital cable boxes. It was clear that the internal chip design group in Phoenix was not going to succeed in time, and this particular area had become an impediment to GI getting to market. So even though SA had provided some corporate funding to Broadcom, Dave Robinson's digital cable group in Hatboro started warming up to the start-up's advances.

The only other company competitive with Broadcom at this stage was ComStream, the digital modem company GI had nearly acquired five years earlier at the beginning of its digital product development activities. Just down the street from GI in San Diego's Sorrento Mesa technology business park, ComStream had expertise equivalent to Broadcom's. Its co-founder and CTO, Itzhak Gurantz, was a close former associate of Jerry Heller, Paul Moroney, and Woo Paik from their Linkabit days and was among the foremost authorities in digital transmission technology.

But ComStream had been burned before by GI and, wary of delaying its existing DVB chip product roadmap, thought GI would probably have to change to the DVB standard under market pressure.

As Broadcom's Henry Nicholas arrived in Hatboro for a May 1995 meeting with GI's Dave Robinson and Carl McGrath, he asked for an impromptu meeting with me, GI's Licensing Director. His proposal was straightforward: If I agreed to waive our $0.25 per chip patent royalty, Nicholas would have his co-founder and CTO, Henry Samueli, analyze the design to verify whether it indeed provided the technical advantage claimed by GI over the DVB standard. The quid pro quo was that if Samueli agreed with GI, Broadcom would support us publicly in the North American cable market versus DVB. Samueli, like ComStream's Gurantz, had nearly unassailable technical credibility in the engineering community, so this was clearly a valuable gesture. Since the crux of our licensing strategy hinged on our conditional access and security technology, we didn't view the $0.25 per QAM chip patent royalty as much of an issue. In addition, our market leadership role was at risk if DVB usurped GI's digital cable transmission standard. So I agreed to Nicholas's proposal.

A week or two later, Tim Lindenfelser, Broadcom's VP of Marketing, called me with good news. Samueli's technical assessment corroborated our claims, and Broadcom was already advocating GI's digital cable transmission method as technically superior to DVB by a significant margin.

But there would be one final showdown: a four-way conference call between TCI, Time Warner, GI, and SA. SA was claiming that GI's advantage, even if it were true, was a red herring and that the real issue was "open DVB" versus "proprietary GI." After our royalty-free license deal with Henry Nicholas and Broadcom, some GI executives had been whispering to both TCI and Time Warner that the company's

QAM/FEC patents would be available royalty-free to all comers, trying to take that SA/DVB argument off the table once and for all.

The four companies had their key technical people on the call. A few GI personnel, including me, were on from Hatboro, and Paul Moroney and Chris Heegard, GI's technical consultant, joined the call from California. The conversation revolved around whether GI's 2 dB advantage was legitimate and, if so, what did that really mean in the context of digital cable transmissions. The discussion went around and around, with SA claiming that DVB had some offsetting advantages and that, in the long run, cable systems would be upgraded anyway and the 2 dB differential wouldn't much matter. But then Heegard, outraged that the SA engineers were downplaying and minimizing GI's invention, stepped in, declaring loudly and clearly: "Those issues have nothing to do with it. The 2 dB difference is a fundamental, first-order advantage; everything else is in the noise." Those four words, "fundamental, first-order advantage," resounding with the force of Heegard's technical expertise, rang out in the tension of the conference call. There was no credible counterargument. Time Warner seemed to move toward GI's position, and SA effectively conceded by silence.

But there was still a related battle brewing regarding whether GI's digital transmission standard or the DVB standard should be used for the emerging market of broadband cable modems. In 1995, the World Wide Web, accessed through the Netscape browser, was becoming the rage for anyone with an Internet connection, especially for those at work with higher data speeds than the painfully slow, dial-up phone modems still prevalent in homes. An effort to design an open standard for high-speed cable modems was proceeding within the Institute of Electrical and Electronics Engineers (IEEE, pronounced "I Triple E"). This activity, called "802.14," was a precursor to the highly successful CableLabs standard, DOCSIS (pronounced "dok´ sis"). So in late 1996, a mirror image of the GI/SA debate about digital cable TV transmission was playing out regarding the technology for high-speed Internet over cable. DVB's QAM/FEC standard was gaining momentum, and GI's version was once again being portrayed as closed and proprietary.

GI had been arguing that it was beneficial for the cable modem Internet standard to use the same QAM/FEC digital transmission technology that was being adopted for digital cable TV. Our rationale was that, someday, television and the Internet would converge, and it would be more efficient for the industry, and for consumers, to have the same chip perform the dual functions of digital cable TV and broadband Internet.

With Time Warner's final decision on the method it would use for digital cable TV transmission still pending, GI decided it could solidify its position by announcing a royalty-free license for its QAM/FEC digital transmission patents. Companies don't like to give away intellectual property, a hard-earned currency of innovation, but in this case we felt that the benefits far outweighed the costs. Incorporated within GI's November 6, 1996, press release was a quote from CableLabs' Dick Green, representing the view of the North American cable industry:

> "This action is significant," stated Dick Green, president of CableLabs, "because it establishes with certainty that GI will license [its] ITU J.83B FEC technology royalty free. This contribution is a welcome step in permitting the specification of a common downstream modulation for all cable services. We hope that other companies will follow GI's lead."[2]

GI had finally neutralized the DVB threat being held over its head in the North American cable market by competitors, the penultimate step in a long string of stumbling blocks toward digital cable leadership. The company was on the last leg of the marathon with the finish line in sight.

By the end of 1996, GI's first digital cable boxes were being installed and tested in Hartford, Connecticut, TCI's chosen system for debuting the world's first commercial launch of digital cable television, preceding its national rollout. Integrated inside each GI digital box was an Electronic Program Guide called Prevue Interactive, later rebranded as TV Guide On Screen, with software developed by United Video, a subsidiary of TCI.

Nearly three years after PrimeStar became the first consumer digital television service, using satellite delivery, the age of digital cable had finally arrived.

35 SITTING IN (HDTV) LIMBO

PrimeStar and DirecTV were rapidly expanding their digital satellite TV businesses in the mid-1990s, with GI bringing its second-generation digital system to market for TCI and the other cable operators. In contrast, the FCC's HDTV process went into a prolonged period of suspended animation. The companies forming the Grand Alliance were building their respective portions of a new combined prototype digital HDTV system. But it was unclear when, or if, the FCC would declare an official standard, and an even fuzzier question was whether the marketplace would embrace HDTV.

As the Grand Alliance pushed ahead to complete its final prototype, a digital HDTV system purporting to be "the best of the best," the action shifted to the backrooms and public relations agendas of special interest groups and politicians. There were three main antagonists at this late stage:

- The broadcasters, fronted by John Abel and the National Association of Broadcasters (NAB) trade association

- The powerful computer industry, represented by Apple Computer, DEC, Microsoft, and the Grand Alliance's MIT

- FCC Chairman Reed Hundt

One should recall that the broadcasting industry was disingenuous about wanting HDTV in the first place. It had pursued this decade-long wild-goose chase in order to prevent others, namely the mobile communications industry, from gaining the valuable unused UHF spectrum. The NAB had lobbied and played along during the entire FCC process. But now that a tangible HDTV system appeared to be on the horizon, with sizable financial commitments by broadcast stations coming due, the NAB's true colors re-emerged: Why should broadcasters invest the millions of dollars required to launch an HDTV station? Shouldn't they be able to do whatever they want with "their" new spectrum? If, as the Internet demonstrated, it's all just a digital pipe, couldn't the broadcasters make more money sending data services instead of HDTV? Do consumers really need or want HDTV?

Many of the broadcasters seemed to literally turn against HDTV as if it were a four-letter word, a new enemy rather than a huge leap forward. John Abel, the most vocal of the NAB's lobbyists, stated: "Digital does not mean higher quality. Digital means flexibility. What is the public policy rationale of having the same content on two channels?"[1]

The computer industry was obsessed with a completely different issue. There was a wide cultural chasm between computer interests and consumer electronics companies. The former group, led by Apple, DEC, and Microsoft, detested the fact that the Grand Alliance system included interlace scanning, a hallmark of television technology for the previous half-century and a method that had greatly outperformed the progressive HD systems in the FCC testing. They believed interlace to be a dinosaur, like the broadcast TV business itself, and wanted to kill it once and for all. They were lobbying for progressive scanning to be mandatory in order to better display text and graphics. It was insufficient for the computer companies that the Grand Alliance had equally accommodated interlace and progressive scanning in the standard, even inserting a long-term goal of getting to 1080P progressive. They viewed the inclusion of the 1080i interlace mode as a trap, a Trojan horse, a stupid idea that would perpetuate a tired, old technology. "Long live progressive, death to interlace," was the arrogant essence of their mantra.

And then there was FCC Chairman Reed Hundt, who had replaced Alfred Sikes in 1993. He didn't seem to know what to do or how to proceed with his white-hot inheritance of HDTV, so he blustered, flip-flopped, and stalled. Especially averse to stacking the broadcast spectrum deck with HDTV, he viewed the still-unused UHF spectrum as part and parcel of the broader information superhighway. "The term HDTV was coined to describe the possibility of getting pretty pictures," said Hundt. "But what's clear to everyone now is that advanced television is not about pretty pictures anymore. It's about the digitization of television and a huge range of new services—a true watershed moment for the broadcast world."[2] When the FCC finally adopted the Grand Alliance system as the official US digital broadcast standard, Hundt would make one last quip, calling the second channel spectrum giveaway to broadcasters "the biggest single gift of public property to any industry this century."[3]

Valid points, perhaps, but Hundt seemed to be missing the entire historical perspective of HDTV, as well as its future importance, and the possibility that it might not happen at all without some government impetus. Ironically, Hundt was appointed by President Bill Clinton, a Democrat, yet was favoring a free market approach to this particular issue; his predecessor Al Sikes, Republican President George H. W. Bush's FCC Chairman, had strongly advocated government supervision and selection of an HDTV broadcast standard in the face of technological threats from Japan and Europe.

Fortunately for the HDTV proponents, two TV stations stepped up to the plate in July 1996 and began broadcasting high definition signals: Capital Broadcasting's WRAL-HD channel 32 in Raleigh, North

Carolina; and WHD-TV, the Model HDTV Station in Washington DC. No consumers had HDTV sets yet, but the stations were nevertheless showing that private industry was proceeding with HDTV. It was another small but important step forward, coming more than four years after Rumsfeld had orchestrated GI's historic HDTV broadcast to the US Capitol Building.

Margita White, president of the Association for Maximum Service Television and chairwoman of the Model HDTV Station project, said: "This adds tremendous momentum toward HDTV's real-world introduction. Its purpose is to provide a real-world station environment." Gary Shapiro, president of the Consumer Electronics Manufacturers Association, whose members stood to benefit greatly from a new generation of consumer electronics equipment, chimed in: "We are turning the switch on."[4] But these voices, representing the true believers, the isolated champions of HDTV, were pushing against the tide.

FCC Chairman Hundt delivered a position paper at a New York media conference in September 1996, providing some telling insights into his viewpoint:

> I think if the Grand Alliance of broadcasters and TV manufacturers had a favorite rock song, it would be Tired of Waiting For You by the Kinks. And if they had a favorite book, it should be Great Expectations—but they are afraid it is Remembrance of Things Past. And if they had a favorite FCC Chairman—well, let's not get into that…

> I want to open up with a summary of the answers: there should be only three basic rules for digital television. These would be (1) a rule protecting digital broadcasters against interference; (2) a rule creating spectrum caps to prevent over concentration; and (3) a rule ensuring that digital spectrum is used to provide public interest programming…

The dedicated and hard-working members of the Advisory Committee tried in good faith to produce a consensus standard. Unfortunately, they did not succeed. Important players in two huge American industries—Silicon Valley and Hollywood—object strongly to some elements of the standard…

Maybe a good way to start to resolve the standards question would be to lock all the interested parties in a room—the TV manufacturers, the broadcasters, the cinematographers, the computer software groups, maybe the digital cable and digital satellite industries, too—and keep them locked together until they hash out a de facto standard that will accommodate each of the legitimate issues raised—and that is good for consumers. Could that technique work?…

The existing rules for broadcast TV—regulating how many "channels" one can own in a market—will be outdated. With DTV, a broadcaster's "channel" will yield one HDTV program, or could be used for multicasting of six kinds of programs, as well as other uses. The Internet, too, makes these rules even more obsolete. But some spectrum cap will be necessary.[5]

Finally, in December 1996, the FCC made its move and adopted the Grand Alliance system as the US broadcast standard. There was no specific requirement for HDTV. Congress authorized an additional 6 MHz UHF channel to each of the 1,600 broadcast TV stations in America, free of charge but with the traditional public service obligations and with the additional requirement that the new spectrum should be used primarily for digital broadcasting. It could be multi-channel SDTV or HDTV, at the broadcaster's discretion, optionally supplemented by some new type of digital data service.

The Grand Alliance had developed a digital HDTV broadcast system and proved that it worked over the public airwaves. The FCC and Congress had sanctioned the system as the official US broadcast standard. Free spectrum had been allocated to the TV stations, with a somewhat vague public service commitment of getting digital signals on the air. All that remained was the market. Would broadcasters decide to deliver HDTV, multi-channel SDTV, or some digital data service with their new spectrum? Who would step up to produce expensive HDTV content? How much would HDTV sets cost? What would happen over satellite and cable, where the vast majority of Americans were getting their TV signals? Would consumers buy into HDTV to get much better pictures and sound?

36 GAMBLER HITS THE JACKPOT

Charles Ergen's curiosity about satellite communications was piqued as a young boy in Tennessee. In 1957, his father, a nuclear physicist at the Oak Ridge National Laboratory in Knoxville, took young Charlie to a nearby field to see the world's first artificial satellite, the Soviet Union's Sputnik, in orbit. This milestone triggered the Space Race segment of the Cold War and etched into Charlie Ergen's vision a lifelong interest in satellites.

After receiving his BA from the University of Tennessee, Ergen graduated from Wake Forest University with an MBA, taking an accounting job with Frito-Lay. He also played blackjack professionally, and with his friend and future business partner Jim DeFranco, descended on Las Vegas. The two men did quite well until they were kicked out of town for allegedly counting cards.[1] Ergen found blackjack mundane anyway, not even considering it gambling due to his high confidence of winning by leveraging his knowledge of probability and statistics.[2]

The gambling mecca had done him a big favor by expelling him, as he ended up making far more money in the satellite TV business than he ever could have in Vegas.

Ergen and DeFranco started EchoSphere in 1980, just when the C-band home satellite TV market was blossoming. Their company became a leading manufacturer and distributor of satellite receivers. By the late 1980s, when HBO and the other programming services began encrypting their satellite signals with General Instrument's VideoCipher technology, Ergen's thriving company became one of GI's largest customers for descrambler modules, integrated into the EchoSphere and Houston Tracker satellite receiver brands.

The consumer satellite TV hardware business had been good to Ergen, but he had much grander ambitions. In 1987 he filed an application with the FCC for a high-power DBS orbital position. When he heard about GI's digital television technology, he knew such an innovation could transform small-dish DBS from a dream to a reality, and he proceeded to learn everything he could about the technology to facilitate his new business venture, EchoStar.

In 1993, Mark Schmidt, a GI communications systems engineer in Paul Moroney's group, dropped by my office in San Diego. Schmidt was an expert in "satellite link budget" analysis. Satellite link budgets involve a highly technical skill set incorporating various parameters related to a satellite's orbital location and the power "footprint" imposed on Earth by its electronics and antenna. The goal is to determine the optimal digital communications techniques to use, such as the type of modulation and forward error correction codes, so as to enable a certain minimum dish size while leaving some margin for error due to rain fade and other interfering factors.

The always-resourceful Charlie Ergen had somehow found out that Mark Schmidt was the key GI engineer to talk to about his satellite link budgets, and Schmidt was asking me whether it was OK to talk to Ergen. I called Ergen to see if we could get more involved with his project, knowing it was a long shot due to our companies' history of rivalry. He assured me we had a chance, so I gave Mark Schmidt a green light to proceed with the caveat to not help him too much until we knew if there was a business opportunity.

The year 1995 was monumental for Ergen and EchoStar. First, the FCC allowed his company to acquire, from Directsat Corporation, twenty-one DBS transponders (frequencies) at the highly desirable 119 degree west orbital position. Then came his satellite construction and launch phases, where Ergen rolled the dice in his characteristic way. Known for his extremely frugal decision making, he had contracted with Long March, the Chinese rocket launch company, to get his first high-power satellite into orbit. This was a risky bet, a cold, probabilistic calculation reminiscent of Ergen's former life as a blackjack player. McDonnell Douglas, with its Delta rockets, and General Dynamics, with its Atlas launch vehicle, had far more successful track records. Either of these American launch companies had an 80–90 percent likelihood of getting the satellite into orbit, versus 50–60 percent for Long March. But the Chinese were hungry to get into the business and priced their satellite launch services much more cheaply than their American competitors in what became an early, fruitful endeavor to gain global share in a strategic market.

On January 25, 1995, Long March failed for the second time in less than eighteen months to get a satellite into orbit, surely shaking Ergen's confidence as his launch date approached later in the year. EchoStar completed an initial public offering in May, giving his company a new source of cash in the event its first satellite exploded before arriving at its designated position in the sky. Then, just before New Year's, EchoStar 1 was dramatically launched without a glitch.

Ergen's gamble with the low-cost Chinese space vehicle had paid off in a big way, and the Dish Network was born. As if to underscore Ergen's luck, in February 1996, Long March's poor track record resumed when an Intelsat satellite failed to reach its orbit, the third Chinese failure in seven launch attempts.[3] But Ergen's bird had slipped through the cracks, awaiting the arrival of hundreds of digital TV signals to be broadcast to small dishes across the United States.

PrimeStar and DirecTV had a two-year lead, and the cable operators were also preparing to launch digital TV services. But Ergen was committed to giving all of them a run for their money. Not wanting to pay a third-party manufacturer such as GI or Sony to make his satellite receivers, and having considerable experience himself from the C-band business, he designed the Dish Network consumer receivers internally. After procuring a smart card security system from Swiss company Nagra and purchasing digital video encoders from Divicom, a Silicon Valley start-up funded by a consortium of French companies, Ergen was ready to go.

Most analysts, and even industry insiders, discounted Dish Network's chances, believing there was insufficient room in the market for another satellite TV provider. But they were making a big mistake by underestimating the single-mindedness, craft, and luck of Charlie Ergen.

37 TROUBLE IN PARADISE

Dan Akerson resigned as General Instrument's CEO in July 1995, remaining chairman until the end of the year. Measured by return on equity, GI had been Forstmann Little's most successful acquisition, and Akerson remained with the investment firm as a general partner, in pursuit of a follow-up success to GI. Rick Friedland had been invaluable to Akerson as GI's president and COO, and Forstmann Little made him the new CEO rather than bringing in another outsider as they had done with Rumsfeld and Akerson. Friedland had been with the company for seventeen years, surviving its many permutations and climbing the corporate ladder one big rung at a time. While fundamentally a numbers and operations guy, his long tenure provided him with an innate feel for the pulse of the company, and he sensed an alarmingly deteriorating situation on the West Coast.

As the greatly expanded GI team in Hatboro scrambled on all fronts to complete development of TCI's digital cable system, there was trouble in paradise. The San Diego operation was struggling in its effort to bring its portions of the second-generation MPEG-2 compatible system (DigiCipher II) to market, a massive and highly complex development effort. Until the company's large customer base of content providers could be upgraded to DigiCipher II, it almost didn't matter that the digital cable box was lagging; its utility to the cable operators and their subscribers was wholly dependent on the front-end of the system, allowing digital content to be encoded and encrypted in a compatible format. Moreover, TCI's Headend in the Sky, a comprehensive, national content aggregation and delivery facility based in Denver, was awaiting GI San Diego's completion of the new encoders and security system.

Following Jim Bunker's departure as San Diego's division president in December 1993, a crisscrossing, dysfunctional organizational reporting structure had been instituted, with various people on either coast reporting to people on the other coast who, in turn, reported back to the first coast. The original San Diego division leadership—Larry Dunham, Jerry Heller, Ken Kinsman, and Mark Medress—had departed, as had video compression guru Ed Krause. Morale in San Diego, where the early excitement over digital had once been palpable, was at an all-time low. There was a feeling that the bottom was falling out, that the entire business was in jeopardy, a déjà vu sense of the pervasive feeling of doom during the depths of the VideoCipher piracy fiasco.

When Ed Krause resigned from GI in 1994, he moved to the Bay Area as co-founder of Imedia with his GI teammates and MIT cohorts, Adam Tom and Paul Shen. Imedia was an innovative start-up taking cable headend digital video processing to the next level and also inventing some technology foreshadowing the consumer digital video recorder (DVR). Jerry Heller was an angel investor in Imedia and also an important strategic adviser. Continuing the brain drain, Woo Paik left GI, first joining Qualcomm and then jumping to a local start-up, Tiernan Communications, founded by another GI San Diego alumnus, Jim Tiernan.

Ken Boschwitz, the San Diego division's general counsel, and Rick Segil, VP of Product Management, were doing their best to hold things together, but they lacked the authority to really take charge. Rick Friedland, from afar in Chicago, understood the dimensions of the San Diego morale and human resource problems. He also knew where the company's innovative juices in digital television had sprung from and was concerned for the overall future of the company. The digital cable project, while managed from Hatboro, was so intertwined with San Diego engineering that if the West Coast didn't deliver on its portions, the entire effort was in jeopardy, along with the value of the company.

Into this swirling corporate maelstrom, in the summer of 1996, entered a storm force of a man named Michael Bernique. A product of New England prep schools, Bernique attended college at Notre Dame and then received his master's degree from University of Chicago in international relations. He had been senior vice president of sales and service at DSC Communications, a leading telecom equipment company. At DSC, he had worked with Tom Eames and Pete Keeler, who left DSC to start Next Level Communications, a switched digital video technology company that GI acquired in November 1995. The predominant thinking at the time was that the telephone companies were going to take over the cable industry, either by acquisition or by building their own fiber networks, thereby making the cable system architecture obsolete. High-flying telco video ventures had formed, such as Tele-TV (Bell Atlantic, NYNEX, Pacific Telesis) and Americast (BellSouth, SBC, SNET, GTE, Disney).

Sensing that GI's San Diego business needed local leadership to restore its performance and morale, and valuing Bernique's telecom background and sales-oriented customer focus, Friedland hired him to be division president. The San Diego operation was an independent business once again. Hal Krisbergh had left the company as president of the combined Hatboro/San Diego operation the previous year following a power struggle with Friedland. A GI newcomer, Larry Osterwise, had subsequently been in charge of both coasts, also operating out of Hatboro for a brief period, until Ed Breen, the company's biggest rainmaker, replaced him from inside. And now Breen and Bernique would be peers, Breen in Hatboro and Bernique in San Diego, just as Krisbergh and Bunker had been counterparts a few years earlier.

I relocated back to San Diego at the same time, in June 1996, with a promotion to VP of Business Development. And Woo Paik also rejoined GI in San Diego. As Bernique arrived from Texas, there was new excitement and a fresh sense of optimism in the air. Perhaps the West Coast business unit could rise again from its state of disarray and disharmony.

Three decades earlier, a young Mike Bernique had been a Swift Boat commander in Vietnam, becoming a legend due to a singular event at a remote tributary. Ha Tien, a region in Vietnam near the Cambodian border, was used as a rest stop for American crews on missions in the Gulf of Siam, near the main island base of An Thoi. Hearing rumors that the Viet Cong were extorting money in the Giang Thanh River, north of Ha Tien and leading into Cambodia, Bernique decided to explore in contravention of American military rules. When he and his men encountered the extortion operation, a battle erupted, resulting in several Viet Cong being killed. Bernique retrieved the cache of enemy materials but, following diplomatic protests by Cambodian Prince Sihanouk, was then summoned to Saigon to justify his actions to top Navy commanders. Under the threat of being court martialed, Bernique was awarded a Silver Star by the Navy instead, and the river tributary where the event took place was named Bernique's Creek.[1]

Even lacking knowledge of this wartime history, it didn't take long for GI's San Diego employees to realize they were suddenly in the iron grip of a tough new leader, a 180 degree change from the preceding state of drift and decline. It was such a drastic shift that it was impossible to fathom the outcome, with renewed hope colliding with the fear of a powerful unknown force.

The San Diego operation was a mess when Bernique arrived. To make matters worse, GI San Diego had just acquired Compression Labs (CLI), based in Silicon Valley, mainly for its DVB product line and international customer base. But CLI was even more distressed than GI San Diego, causing a huge management distraction. Into this fragile environment strode Bernique, a strong leader with an explosive personality who took command of any room he was in. He was like the proverbial bull in a china shop. It was difficult not to cringe with empathy when an unfortunate employee ended up on the wrong side of one of his outbursts.

But at the same time, Bernique was intelligent and articulate, a savvy business executive with a broad worldview, combining a ruthless competitive instinct with a customer-first sales mentality. He and his wife, Diana, hosted extravagant parties for his staff and their spouses at their home in La Jolla, high up on Mount Soledad with expansive views of the Pacific Coast.

This was also the time when GI began receiving more formal recognition for its contributions to the communications and entertainment fields, receiving two separate Emmy Awards in 1996. The first one was given to the company for its DigiCipher television security and encryption system. Keith Kelley and Paul Moroney accepted the award on behalf of GI, with Carolyn Bell, Annie Chen, Mark Eyer, Bob Gilberg, Eric Sprunk, Allen Shumate, and me in attendance. This award represented a dramatic comeback for GI and strong vindication of our position during the piracy wars of the late 1980s. It underscored the importance of security to the pay TV industry and the unique technology that had, and has, to date, never been broken.

The second Emmy awarded to GI that year was broader and more general in scope: for the creation and development of DigiCipher, the world's first multi-channel digital television system. It was awarded to the five individuals who had made up the original, full-time team in San Diego: Jerry Heller, Ed Krause, Paul Moroney, Woo Paik, and Marc Tayer. Four MIT PhDs and me.

As CEO, Rick Friedland wanted to make his imprint on the company he had helped guide from a diversified technology conglomerate to a highly focused leader in the digital television business. In July 1997, he changed the company name from General Instrument to NextLevel Systems,[2] reflecting the name of subsidiary Next Level Communications, whose switched digital video technology many believed would become the video architecture of the future. Concurrently, Frank Drendel's coaxial and fiber optic cable business, CommScope, and the power semiconductor business, General Semiconductor, were spun off as independent public companies.

Cognizant of the chain of command, Bernique was respectful and deferential to Friedland, his boss at GI's Chicago headquarters, but he was dismissive to other corporate staff members, perceiving them to be interfering with his business in San Diego. This situation reached a breaking point at a fateful meeting an hour's drive north in Irvine, at Broadcom headquarters.

Bernique and I attended this meeting, along with Bob Gilberg, a semiconductor veteran who led GI San Diego's internal Very Large Scale Integration (VLSI) chip design team, a group of more than thirty engineers at its peak. Gilberg's group had a strong track record developing custom chips for successive generations of GI products. The group had successfully designed several chips for the company's DigiCipher I digital satellite boxes and was now starting to deliver DigiCipher II chips, both for the second-generation digital satellite receivers and for the digital cable set-tops being developed in Hatboro. In fact, GI's San Diego management viewed this team as a highly strategic asset, providing a sustainable competitive advantage in cost and product features. But the entire company was undergoing a periodic belt-tightening phase to improve profitability, and Gilberg's chip design group was a ripe corporate target, being a relatively self-contained and expensive team of engineers.

With GI Hatboro as its new customer, Broadcom was off to a strong start with its QAM/FEC digital cable transmission chip business. But its two co-founders, Henry Nicholas and Henry Samueli, knew they needed to gobble up more of the set-top box's functionality if they were to realize their full IPO dreams. The division leaders in Hatboro had taken the position that, with the advent of technical standards such as MPEG-2, the internal San Diego chip design group was becoming redundant, as the ability to buy cost-effective set-top chips from merchant semiconductor companies would expand and proliferate. From the San Diego team's perspective, the advent of standards in the digital TV business meant that set-top box competition would become increasingly stiff, and the company needed its competitive advantages more than ever. In fact,

Gilberg's group had recently finalized development of the world's first integrated chip combining MPEG-2 video and Dolby Digital audio on a single device, ahead of leading merchant semiconductor companies such as C-Cube and SGS Thomson.

The corporate office in Chicago smelled a financial opportunity and supported Hatboro's position by entering into negotiations with Broadcom without San Diego's involvement. The basic outline of the deal was that the technology blueprint for San Diego's new MPEG-2 video/audio chip would be traded to Broadcom. The company's invaluable encryption/security chip and its supporting team would remain with GI. GI would also commit to purchasing most of its future chips from Broadcom. In exchange, GI would receive a sizable chunk of Broadcom's pre-IPO equity. While there was no explicit arrangement to transfer Gilberg's chip designers from GI to Broadcom, after the deal Broadcom would start poaching some of the key engineers, knowing that their future was not secure at GI.

As Bernique, Gilberg, and I arrived at Broadcom's headquarters, we knew extensive dealings between the rest of the company and Broadcom had already transpired, but we didn't quite realize the extent to which the cake had already been baked. The meeting started out fine, with each of the Broadcom product managers giving a summary of their existing businesses along with projections of market size, growth, and the competitive landscape. But at some point it became apparent that Broadcom was assuming the deal was a given; GI would trade away its chip design and commit to a big order for Broadcom chips in exchange for an equity stake in Broadcom.

At first Broadcom seemed to think that if they had successfully navigated around the powerful forces in Chicago and Hatboro, the San Diego group would be a breeze. Nicholas was a formidable executive in his own right, but he didn't know Michael Bernique. Bernique, quickly sensing that he had been set up, had no intention of handing over one of his prized possessions, the VLSI chip design group, to satisfy some broader corporate agenda. Bernique's patience and diplomacy were pushed beyond their limits and the meeting quickly degenerated into an escalating war of words. Nicholas was smart enough to retreat, finding a way to end the meeting without a massive blow-up.

Soon thereafter, in September 1997, Bernique left the company. Friedland had hired him hoping he would help bridge the unhealthy gap between San Diego and Hatboro, but instead the coastal divide had deteriorated. Bernique's strong pushback during the Broadcom deal, during which San Diego licensed away its prized chip design technology for "the corporate greater good," was surely a factor contributing to his departure. He had instilled some much-needed discipline into a disjointed San Diego organization—perhaps too much. Now the place was shell-shocked and leaderless once again, apprehensive about what would happen next.

38 THE MEGADEAL

A few weeks after Bernique's dismissal, GI chairman and CEO Rick Friedland also left the company. Sales were flat and profits were suppressed due to high R&D expenditures, preceding the imminent high-volume ramp-up of digital cable set-top box production in Taiwan. Worse yet, 1998 financial projections had been "called down" to Wall Street, reflecting the fact that GI needed a major cost reduction on the digital cable box in order to improve product gross margins. The stock price wasn't moving fast enough for Forstmann Little, which had already made a killing by selling shares earlier but still retained a big equity stake in the company. It had been over seven years since they had acquired GI, and they were anxious to cash out and move on.

Friedland had tirelessly dedicated his professional life to GI, rising from accounting in 1978 to director of corporate financial planning in 1985, to Treasurer, then CFO, then president and COO, and finally chairman and CEO. In his ultimate role, he was more active and engaged with the operating divisions than Rumsfeld, and far more than Akerson, running the company with a longer-term perspective, perhaps ironic for a financial guy but nonetheless severely underappreciated by Wall Street. By spinning off CommScope and General Semiconductor as separate public companies, it was Friedland who ultimately crystallized GI into a pure-play broadband communications equipment leader. The digital cable box business was about to explode into a multibillion-dollar bonanza, and the company was poised for action on an even bigger stage.

Ed Breen was named chairman and CEO of NextLevel Systems (GI) on December 17, 1997. He had successfully made the leap from head of sales to president of the cable business in Hatboro. With Bernique gone, Breen oversaw all of the company's business units in Hatboro and San Diego. Now, with Friedland also out of the way, it was Breen's time to shine, and he started off with a big bang and a flurry of activity.

First, in October, as Acting CEO, Breen placed trusted Hatboro executive Tom Lynch in San Diego as general manager of the digital satellite TV and cable modem business units. Second, the day he was elected chairman and CEO by the board, he announced that the company name would revert back to General Instrument Corporation. Breen's biggest customers, the cable operators, had never understood or appreciated the change to the NextLevel name. In fact, they thought the telcos were clueless about video, and they wanted "their" GI back. Third, Breen moved the company headquarters from Chicago to a new, modern facility in Horsham, Pennsylvania, just fifteen minutes from the long-standing Hatboro location.

Finally, and most important of all, Breen announced his "Megadeal." Using his mentor John Malone as a financial engineering role model, Breen structured the Megadeal brilliantly. GI's digital cable boxes had been rolling out to multiple cable operators throughout 1997, but Scientific Atlanta had won the Time Warner digital contract, a huge win for SA, who was expected to start shipping in 1998.

Breen accomplished two objectives with the Megadeal. First, he locked in the majority of the cable industry for future digital equipment purchases with GI, just when SA was getting closer to market with a competing digital platform. His second goal was to accelerate the pace at which the cable operators rolled out digital TV to their subscribers, driving sales and profits. Cable operators were infamous for their unwillingness "to spend a dime before its time," and Breen wanted to speed up the timetable by which GI's digital boxes were deployed within the 65 million cable homes throughout America.

Inked the week before Christmas 1997, the Megadeal was structured as a massive purchase order for GI digital cable set-tops, crowned with a warrant deal under which nine major cable operators, including TCI, Time Warner, Cox, and Comcast, could acquire up to 16 percent of GI's equity. The aggregate purchase order for 15 million digital boxes, to be delivered over the following three years, valued the deal at $4.5 billion. The warrants were priced at $15 each, equal to 85 percent of the $17.6875 closing stock price on December 17, 1997. Wall Street loved the deal and GI's stock price started to move immediately. Multiple constituencies stood to make hefty profits: GI, through increased equipment sales; GI's management, through stock options; GI's cable operator customers, through the warrants; and GI's investors, through a rising stock price. Ed Breen was an instant superstar CEO on top of GI, Wall Street's latest tech darling, and he was just getting warmed up.

Over fifteen years later, in a 2013 interview with Michael Useem, director of The Wharton School's Center for Leadership and Change Management, Breen was asked about "bold, big decisions," prompting him to reflect on the Megadeal.

> **Breen**: Well, let's take GI. By the way, in my whole thirty-four-year career, I've probably made ten big decisions that really, really mattered, that moved the needle in a big way. One was at GI when we developed the first digital technology for the whole industry, and it was too expensive for anyone to want to buy. Everyone was trying to take our position away from us: Microsoft, Cisco, Samsung, Sony. We decided to sell warrants in our company to our customers, or give them the warrants, if they would buy our digital set-top boxes from us. We locked up two-thirds of the industry within a couple weeks. The industry ended up owning 15 percent of the company. If you go back and look at GI's history, that's what made the company take off. We won the digital war, and a company that was valued at $1.6 billion to $1.7 billion, we sold to Motorola for $18 billion. So that's a situation when, if you worry about every other issue besides creating long-term shareholder value, a lot of people wouldn't do that kind of deal. It was absolutely the right deal for us.[1]

In January 1998, Breen placed the telco equipment subsidiary, Next Level Communications, into a limited partnership, getting its large operating losses off of GI's books. Outside investors were the general partner, with GI retaining a majority equity position as a limited partner, in case things turned around with respect to the telcos' switched digital video rollouts.

That same month, Breen announced a strategic alliance with Sony to jointly develop future digital TV technologies and products. As part of the deal, Sony purchased 5 percent of GI for $25 a share, a 38 percent premium over the prior day's closing price. Sony had beaten out Thomson for the deal, and GI contemplated eventually using Sony branding and retailing for its products. The two companies also planned to collaborate on HDTV products, as well as incorporating new features like Sony's home networking architecture into GI's product line.

A lifetime Pennsylvanian, Ed Breen had joined GI in 1978 at age twenty-two after graduating from Grove City College, north of Pittsburgh. Rising to the top through a spectacular career in sales, the Megadeal had been by far his biggest transaction to date. But as magnificent as it was, the stage was now set again for his grandest deal of all, the sale of the entire company.

And although the digital SDTV markets for satellite and cable TV were in high gear, still to come from the digital revolution were HDTV, on-demand video, and the Internet.

■ ■ ■

From left to right, the DigiCipher team, **Marc Tayer, Jerry Heller, Woo Paik, Ed Krause, and Paul Moroney.**

DIGICIPHER: ON THE LEADING EDGE
OF U.S. TECHNOLOGICAL ADVANCEMENTS

General Instrument's original DigiCipher team, spring 1990.

GI video compression expert Ed Krause, 1991.

Bob Rast and Woo Paik with GI's digital HDTV prototype
for FCC testing, 1991.

Donald Rumsfeld, GI's chairman and CEO in the early 1990s.

GENERAL INSTRUMENT
VIDEOCIPHER DIVISION

December 15, 1992

TO: All VideoCipher Employees

FROM: Jim Bunker

SUBJECT: Congratulations!

DEC 1 6 1992

All VideoCipher employees should personally accept a "congratulations" and a "job well done" from Don Rumsfeld's attached memo.

The entire division pulled together in support of the TCI deal, and whether you played a major or a minor role in the development, engineering, operations, marketing or administrative effort required to close the deal, you should feel a deep sense of pride in our accomplishment.

Jim

****

December 3, 1992

TO: Jim Bunker

FROM: Donald Rumsfeld

My congratulations to you and the rest of your team at VideoCipher on the TCI deal. You had the baton, and you brought it across the finish line.

Congratulations!

DR/nla
12392.36

Donald Rumsfeld's congratulatory memo to GI San Diego team
upon completion of digital cable deal with TCI, 1992.

Author skiing at Val D'Isere, France, after chairing crucial MPEG-2 intellectual property rights meeting in Paris, 1994.

Author (second from right) with CCTV-affiliated joint venture partners for China's digital TV villages project, 1999.

Viacom owner/chairman Sumner Redstone at JFK Library
public service event, October 1999. With Caroline Kennedy,
Ted Kennedy, and Colin Powell.

Motorola (GI) event celebrating the industry pioneers on the ten-year
anniversary of digital TV, June 2000. San Diego division head
Tom Lynch congratulating Marc Tayer, Bob Rast, Paul Moroney,
Woo Paik, and Jerry Heller.

Ed Breen, president of Motorola Broadband (GI), June 2000.

Frank Drendel, CEO of CommScope, June 2000.

Marc Tayer and Dario Santana of broadband streaming video start-up
Aerocast at Globosat, Rio de Janeiro, 2001.

Bob Zitter, Barbara Jaffe, and Craig Cuttner,
HBO's longtime technology triumvirate.

Liberty Media chairman John Malone; dedication of the
John Malone Theater at The Cable Center, Denver, 2012.

Digital satellite TV at cave house in Cappadocia, Turkey, 2013.

Eric Sprunk, VP of security engineering, at Arris San Diego (the business
unit previously owned by GI, Motorola, and Google), 2014.

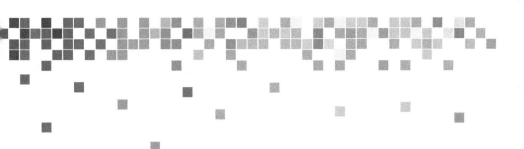

PART THREE
THE INTERNET AND HDTV

39 REJUVENATING SAN DIEGO

Tom Lynch knew he had a tremendous challenge on his hands when he arrived in San Diego in the fall of 1997. He had been dispatched by General Instrument's new CEO, Ed Breen, to rescue the distressed operation that had ignited the digital television revolution eight years prior.

Gregarious and with a wholesome attitude, Lynch had lived his entire life on the East Coast. Going to California was a novel adventure, an opportunity he embraced with unbridled enthusiasm. During his fifteen years at GI, Lynch had blossomed from a division controller into a seasoned, well-balanced general manager with outstanding people skills. A classic delegator, he surrounded himself with competent hard workers, encouraging them to succeed in their jobs while he focused on the big picture.

CEO Ed Breen knew that the company's underlying value would skyrocket when the digital cable boxes started shipping in much higher volumes. But he needed to start showing stronger corporate profits immediately, initially through painful cost reductions, and gave Lynch his initial marching orders. In November, Lynch cut 20 percent of the San Diego workforce, shedding 225 of the 1,110 domestic employees. Then he shut down the operation's factory in Barceloneta, Puerto Rico, severing an additional 1,100 workers and moving production to a contract manufacturer.

Although most employees understood Lynch was just doing what needed to be done, the sentiment in San Diego reverted to a state of shock. Lynch knew he had to take immediate and positive action on two fronts: first, by assembling his own loyal management team; second, by convincing the survivors that they were valued and critical to the company's future. Lynch, whom I'd known for over ten years, took me for a walk outside, and said: "I've been thinking about what Marc Tayer's biggest contribution to the company would be going forward, and I think it's for you to lead our business development activities—doing deals with content providers, expanding our international business, and developing new areas like cable modems and HDTV. Would you want to do that?" I was a bit puzzled at first, thinking, "Isn't that the job I already have?" But then I realized he was resetting his team, seeking fresh commitments, and I replied affirmatively.

Then Lynch called an all-employee meeting at an off-site location. His message centered around three key points: "First, this is where digital started; you should all be very proud of what you've accomplished for this company and for the entire industry. Second, last week's downsizing was painful but necessary; we will be going through a very difficult healing period, and I completely understand that. Third, we'll get through this together and have a thriving business again." As he presented his talking points, he paced back and forth across the auditorium stage, gesticulating energetically and connecting with the hundreds of employees. It was a masterful performance.

While skeptical and still nursing its wounds, the San Diego workforce was starting to feel like it might have a brighter future. PrimeStar was purchasing large quantities of digital satellite receivers; the Star Choice satellite TV business in Canada, owned by Shaw Communications, was taking off; and another promising new product, a cable modem, was under development in anticipation of the broadband Internet explosion. Many of the San Diego engineers were also supporting GI on the East Coast, with a renewed spirit of collaboration, as the cable operators continued rolling out digital cable TV service. And the HDTV market was finally showing signs of becoming a real business opportunity.

One of our most promising new projects was a joint venture across the Pacific. China Central Television (CCTV), China's state-owned broadcaster, was already a GI customer for digital satellite delivery to cable headends and local TV stations. A company affiliated with CCTV, Huaguang, had been granted an exclusive license to deliver digital satellite programming to the villages throughout China. Capitalism was just starting to take hold in Beijing and Shanghai in the late 1990s. But the country's massive urban migration was at an early stage, with 900 million of China's 1.3 billion people still living in rural villages.

The basic idea of "The Villages Project" was that CCTV would use GI's technology to deliver many new digital TV channels to the rural villagers, many of whom had never seen television. We knew it would involve carefully controlled content. After all, this was China, whose ruling elite, the top government bureaucrats and the leaders of the Communist Party, were deeply paranoid about Western media and entertainment corrupting its populace. Nonetheless, we perceived it as a big step forward culturally and an exciting business opportunity.

My immediate task was to negotiate the joint venture agreements with Huaguang and CCTV. Working with me were Ron Kurth, Director of International Business Development, and Stephen Eng, our well-connected consultant. The three of us traveled regularly to Beijing, where we would sit through endless, smoke-filled negotiating sessions, discuss the Chinese market, and be entertained by our hosts at banquets and during excursions to the Great Wall and the Forbidden City.

On one memorable trip, in early September 1998, I attended a performance of *Turandot*, Puccini's opera about the beautiful Chinese ice princess, Liu, who has her suitors beheaded, one after the other, before ultimately succumbing to love. This extravagant production was staged in an ancient Ming Dynasty temple within the Forbidden City, a venue seemingly handpicked by Puccini from his grave. It featured star Western performers, an orchestra from Florence conducted by Zubin Mehta, and a cast of several hundred Chinese extras dressed in lavish costumes. In effect, it represented China's cultural embrace of the Western world in parallel with its incipient economic transformation. It struck me that this awakening was occurring just as our digital television technology was being rolled out in a country whose vast majority had still not seen TV.

The China joint venture negotiations proved to be a lengthy process. Our primary goal was to secure a long-term business opportunity while protecting our core intellectual property. We finally signed the contracts and a new company, Huaguang General Instrument (HGI), was formed. Tom Lynch and I were appointed to its board of directors. In China, Ms. Liu, HGI's energetic and assertive marketing director, was hopscotching around the countryside, signing up villages to receive the eight new digital channels of CCTV content.

40 THREE'S A CROWD

By the middle of 1997, competition was heating up in the US small-dish satellite TV market. Hughes's DirecTV was in the lead with over 2.5 million digital satellite subscribers. PrimeStar was approaching the 2 million mark. And Charlie Ergen's Dish Network had just passed the half-million customer milestone. Even the big-dish, C-band business was still vibrant with over 2 million subscribers, mostly still analog, as GI introduced its digital TV technology to this legacy market. Similar digital satellite TV services were launching in Canada, Latin America, Europe, and Asia.

With the US direct broadcast satellite (DBS) market finally booming, one person determined not to be left behind was Rupert Murdoch. He had inherited his father's Australian newspaper business in Adelaide in the early 1950s, which he then expanded throughout his native country and also to New Zealand and the United Kingdom. In 1967, Murdoch divorced his first wife and married Anna Torv, an employee at one of his Australian newspapers. The couple had three children—Lachlan, James, and Elisabeth—all of whom had major executive roles at News Corporation at one time or another. In 1981 he bought the *London Times*. But his appetite was growing beyond publishing.

Murdoch's earliest US satellite TV enterprise was his 1983 Skyband venture, which never got off the ground. Skyband signed a five-year, $75 million lease for medium-power Ku-band transponders, and Murdoch intended to beat General Instrument's United Satellite Communications Inc. (USCI) venture and Comsat's Satellite Television Corp. (STC) subsidiary to market with a five-channel, analog national service. However, he encountered difficulty procuring sufficient content and equipment, which he attempted to partially cure by offering to acquire Showtime for $160 million. In the same time frame, he purchased nearly 7 percent of Warner Communications in an apparent step toward acquiring the company but was rebuffed by Warner CEO Steve Ross. The stars were clearly not aligned, and Murdoch soon pulled the plug on Skyband.

After temporarily abandoning his satellite TV dream, Murdoch turned his attention to the movie and broadcasting business. He acquired 20th Century Fox in 1985 for less than $600 million and then bought six local television stations from Metromedia for under $2 billion. This TV station group became the foundation for his 1986 launch of the Fox Broadcasting network. He successfully persuaded the Federal Communications Commission to overlook its restrictions on foreign ownership of broadcast networks in order to create more competition for the Big Three: ABC, CBS, and NBC. Murdoch continued expanding his US television empire for the next decade, hiring political and media power broker Roger Ailes in 1996 to launch and build Fox News. Murdoch also acquired numerous regional sports networks and created new cable channels such as FX.

In the United Kingdom, his Sky Television medium-power satellite TV service had a head start over the high-power British Satellite Broadcasting (BSB) platform, allowing Murdoch to force a merger in 1990. In 1993, he acquired the pan-Asian Star TV satellite service from Hong Kong billionaire Richard Li. Yet despite owning these valuable international assets, Murdoch still had a glaring hole in his global media empire—a US DBS business—and MCI was going to be his ticket.

In January 1996, MCI successfully bid $682.5 million in an FCC auction for 28 DBS frequencies at the highly desirable 110 degree west orbital location. This spectrum acquisition became the impetus for an incredible sequence of shifting alliances and one-upmanship, involving not only MCI and Rupert Murdoch, but also John Malone, Charlie Ergen, Time Warner, PrimeStar, and the US Department of Justice.

That spring Murdoch formed ASkyB, a DBS joint venture between News Corporation and MCI. In parallel, Murdoch and Malone were discussing a DBS venture. But Malone was stepping out of bounds from his PrimeStar cable partners, causing Time Warner to block the deal using its contractual veto rights.

At this point, the ever-opportunistic Charlie Ergen entered the picture. By February 1997, Murdoch and Ergen agreed to a billion-dollar deal combining Ergen's existing Dish Network operation with the MCI/Murdoch ASkyB assets in a 50-50 partnership. The ASkyB forecast called for signing up 8 million DBS subscribers in less than five years.

From the cable industry's perspective, ASkyB was the new "Deathstar." As if DirecTV wasn't a big enough problem, the cable guys would be facing the formidable combination of Murdoch's financial muscle and media savvy, MCI's prime orbital slot, and Ergen's rapidly growing Dish Network. Ted Turner, now at Time Warner due to its 1995 acquisition of Turner Broadcasting, declared war on Murdoch, a personal nemesis and the latest persona non grata in the cable industry. Just as the cable cabal had stared down HBO's Crimson satellite TV plans in 1988, it was now threatening to blacklist Murdoch and thwart cable carriage of Fox News.

John Malone sensed a renewed opportunity to be a major player in the high-power DBS business. He reopened discussions with Murdoch, along with TCI president Leo Hindery and News Corporation COO Chase Carey. By June 1997, PrimeStar had a deal in place to acquire ASkyB's DBS slot, with News Corporation and MCI retaining a 20 percent interest and a convertible note allowing the purchase of an additional 11 percent. PrimeStar would also obtain the two high-power satellites under construction by MCI. Finally, Murdoch and MCI agreed to a ten-year non-compete clause against Malone and PrimeStar for the US market.

In one fell swoop, it appeared that Malone had neutralized Murdoch as a threat to cable while also achieving his goal of participating in the high-power DBS business. But less than a year later, in May 1998, the US Justice Department sued PrimeStar, TCI, Time Warner, MediaOne, Comcast, Cox, GE Americom, Newhouse, News Corporation, MCI, and Rupert Murdoch to prevent PrimeStar from entering the US DBS business through the deal with Murdoch and MCI. In the civil antitrust suit, the Justice Department claimed the cable group "recognized the magnitude of the competitive threat and sought to 'nip it in the bud' to protect their dominance and monopoly profits for years to come."

Needless to say, this turn of events sent the PrimeStar partners into a tailspin, causing cancellation of a $400 million bond offering and the installation of Carl Vogel as PrimeStar's new chairman and CEO. Some excerpts from the Justice Department's lawsuit illustrate the government's state of mind:

> The United States of America, acting under the direction of the Attorney General of the United States, brings this civil action to enjoin the acquisition by the largest cable companies in the United States of control of the only remaining high-power orbital satellite slot capable of distributing a nationwide package of video programming competitive with that offered by cable. Completion of this acquisition would effectively foreclose the use of this scarce and valuable asset to challenge defendants' monopoly power.

> Cable firms are in large part unregulated monopolists...the Commission reaffirms the conclusion that is apparent to American consumers: cable firms continue to dominate the multi-channel video programming distributor ("MVPD") marketplace.

> Direct broadcast satellite ("DBS") has emerged as the first real challenge to cable's dominance and the best hope for consumers who seek alternatives to their local cable company. DBS transmits video signals from an orbiting satellite directly to a dish antenna

located at the customer's residence. The customer either rents or buys the dish and pays the DBS firm a monthly fee for the programming... increasing numbers of DBS subscribers are former cable subscribers.

If permitted, the proposed asset acquisition would result in a lessening of competition and an enhancement of monopoly power in local MVPD markets in much of the United States, and would therefore harm a broad sector of the American public. Moreover, the transaction constitutes an agreement that would unreasonably restrain trade and would allow PrimeStar's cable owners to maintain their market power in local markets throughout the country, thereby depriving millions of American consumers of the benefits of competition, including lower prices, higher quality, greater choice, and increased innovation.

Reacting to the ASkyB announcement at the National Cable Television Association ("NCTA") meetings in March 1997, senior Time Warner executive Ted Turner proclaimed that "we're going to make it as tough [for Murdoch] as we possibly can. Kind of like the Russian Army did with the German army... either Murdoch is going to go hungry or we are."

Leo Hindery, president of TCI, the country's largest cable system operator, recently testified before a Senate subcommittee that "more than any other non-cable MVPD, DBS has fundamentally changed the video distribution landscape and the competitive dynamics of the marketplace. It has altered the way that cable operators package and price their services and the way that we serve our customers."

The United States requests:

1. That the proposed acquisition be adjudged to violate Section 7

of the Clayton Act…and Sections 1 and 2 of the Sherman Act;

2. That the defendants be permanently enjoined and restrained from carrying out the Asset Acquisition Agreement, dated June 11, 1997, or from entering into or carrying out any agreement, understanding, or plan, the effect of which would be to transfer the DBS assets of News Corporation/MCI to PrimeStar; or, in the alternative, that the PrimeStar cable owners be required to divest their ownership interests in PrimeStar, Inc.[1]

Malone, undaunted by the lawsuit, sought to buy his way out of PrimeStar and proceed independently. But Time Warner blocked him once again, causing PrimeStar to bail out of the Murdoch/MCI deal. The next year, in 1999, PrimeStar sold its 2.3 million satellite TV subscribers and assets to DirecTV, representing another setback in John Malone's and Rupert Murdoch's independent aspirations for a piece of the US DBS business.

With the cable partners stymied by the government, exacerbated by internal dissension between TCI and Time Warner, the stage was set for Charlie Ergen. It took him only a few more months to step firmly into the void. By the end of 1998 he closed a deal with Murdoch, securing for Dish Network the invaluable 110 degree west DBS slot, giving him the ability to blanket the United States with additional high-power digital satellite TV signals.

As for John Malone, he started navigating a Rubik's Cube of three parallel worlds: the telephone companies desiring to enter the video business, the increasingly valuable television content business, and satellite TV. In June 1998, AT&T announced a $48 billion agreement to acquire Malone's TCI in a stock-for-stock transaction, including $16 billion of assumed debt. AT&T completed the acquisition in March 1999 after regulatory approval, creating AT&T Broadband and appointing Leo Hindery as CEO. AT&T followed the TCI acquisition by acquiring

MediaOne (formerly Continental Cable) in 2000. Malone formed Liberty Media Group as a publicly traded tracking stock of AT&T. A couple of years later, Liberty Media was split off from AT&T, becoming Malone's content fountainhead. But his satellite TV ambitions would remain unfulfilled, at least for the time being.

The importance of this entire episode cannot be overstated. The US government had successfully blocked the high-power DBS dreams of John Malone and Rupert Murdoch. As a result, there would be two, not three, satellite TV companies in the United States. DirecTV would own the 101 degree west orbital position, with Ergen's Dish Network owning the two slots at 110 and 119 degrees. There were five additional DBS orbital slots authorized by the FCC, but they represented far less valuable assets since, unlike the three prime locations, they didn't cover the entire continental United States.

In addition, a big telephone company, AT&T, had finally gotten itself squarely into the home entertainment business. Rupert Murdoch secured his cable carriage deals for Fox News and his growing collection of TV channels. And John Malone, while temporarily cashed out of the domestic cable operator business, was in firm control of his own valuable content assets through Liberty Media.

41 LET'S DO IT AGAIN!

As the twentieth century faded, Tom Lynch's contagious optimism and relentless focus were permeating General Instrument's San Diego organization. PrimeStar had vaporized as a customer as a result of the US government antitrust suit, a huge loss for GI. But the Canadian satellite TV market was thriving, and Star Choice was ordering large quantities of our digital satellite TV boxes. We also had a strong business selling digital TV encoding systems to content providers around the world.

And the exciting new markets for HDTV and broadband Internet equipment were finally starting to take shape. Even so, it was time for GI San Diego to come up with another major innovation.

Television and the Internet had evolved along two independent paths. The former emerged from its black-and-white roots to color; from over-the-air broadcast to cable, satellite, and fiber optics; from analog waves to digital bit streams; from the digital SDTV content explosion to the spectacular pictures of HDTV; and from one-way broadcast to the convenience of on-demand video and time-shifted viewing.

The Internet grew out of its 1960s US government and research university origins. It morphed from the ARPANET and packet switching to internetworking and the World Wide Web; from supercomputers and telecom switches to IP routers, personal computers, and search engines; from dial-up narrowband copper phone wires to broadband over cable and DSL (digital subscriber line); and from fixed, wired locations to the freedom of wireless.

As television migrated to digital and as the Internet moved toward broadband, it was inevitable that the two distinct worlds would collide, with digital video as the common thread. The two markets would continue evolving separately while also beginning to intersect, a fertile and synergistic double-helix of content and distribution.

The Internet was becoming ubiquitous by the late 1990s and the cable industry knew it had a gigantic new opportunity providing high-speed Internet connections to homes and businesses. Several technology companies were already shipping proprietary cable modems including Bay Networks (through its acquisition of LANcity), Motorola, Com21, GI, Zenith, and Terayon. These disparate activities represented an untenable situation for the cable industry. There were half a dozen companies with unique, proprietary solutions vying for control of the nascent market. This free-for-all of incompatible technologies would inhibit the growth of a promising new business, limiting cable's broadband Internet platform against its emerging telco DSL competitors.

DOCSIS[1] became the cable operators' rallying cry, both to herd the feuding vendors and to consolidate the industry's competitive position versus the telcos. The DOCSIS cable modem standard became extremely successful, creating a booming new data business for cable operators. It also became the technical foundation for digital telephony, cable's third leg in its "triple play" of video, data, and voice services. A future version of DOCSIS would become the cable industry's platform for Internet video services.

By 1999, the first DOCSIS cable modems were certified by Cable-Labs. Motorola and Terayon avoided jumping on the standardization bandwagon, thinking they could prevail against the DOCSIS tide. But GI's cable modem team in San Diego clearly saw the writing on the wall, informed in large part by the company's prior experience trying to resist the MPEG-2 video standard. So GI shelved its proprietary cable modem roadmap, wholeheartedly shifting its product strategy toward the CableLabs DOCSIS standard. In fact, the DOCSIS standard consisted of intellectual property contributed by GI and Bay Networks.

At this time, my business development responsibilities encompassed cable modems in addition to digital satellite TV. It was therefore my job to negotiate the company's first cable modem deal with AT&T Broadband (formerly TCI). This was the exciting beginning of another leading market position for the company. But Tom Lynch soon agreed to transfer internal ownership of the new product line to GI's cable group in Horsham, Pennsylvania, where it fit better with the company's sales structure. Most of the cable modem engineering team, however, remained in San Diego.

Lynch fully understood that the transfer of this new business to Horsham, just when it was finally taking off after three long years of

R&D and market development, would be a huge blow to the GI San Diego workforce. But he also knew it was a political battle he could not win. He called me and Paul Moroney into his office, and kicked off the meeting by saying, "You know why we had to give up the cable modem business to Horsham. You guys helped start our digital TV business, which is now a home run for the company. How did you come up with that? We need to figure out a major new business and do it again, right here in San Diego."

We brainstormed and drew furiously on Lynch's whiteboard, retracing the genesis of the digital TV concept a decade earlier. We drew parallels to what might happen in the Internet market, searching for areas we could capitalize on. After a few hours, we thought we were onto something big.

Digital television had first launched over satellite, then over cable, and most recently through over-the-air broadcast spectrum. Fundamentally, the Internet was just another distribution avenue. The Internet was inherently two-way and interactive. Moreover, the Internet was a global phenomenon, an interconnected network of networks.

It was almost too obvious. The Internet was going broadband and we were the leading broadband technology company. We were bemused by how the computer and Internet community had co-opted the term "broadband" as if it were something new. At GI, way back in the pre-digital, pre-Internet 1980s, we described ourselves as the leading broadband communications equipment company. Video required broadband. Video was broadband. It seemed clear that the more broadband the Internet became, the more video would be pumped through it. Video was our sweet spot, especially secure video, and the Internet would be its next big pipe.

42 AEROCAST: THE IDEA

With the advent of the DOCSIS cable modem and telco DSL standards, a few of us at General Instrument in San Diego believed there would eventually be an entirely new market for video. There were only about 1 million broadband cable modem subscribers in 1999, but the numbers were surely going to increase dramatically. Sometime in the future there would be 20 million high-speed Internet subscribers. At that point, Internet video would become a real business, with advertisers and consumers paying the bills.

The primary reason GI had been so successful in the digital TV market, other than being first, was that the company brought an entire communications system to the table. We didn't just develop a single piece of the puzzle, an isolated product or component. Instead, we created and integrated a complete system. The distributed hardware and software elements comprised digital video compression, digital transmission, security and conditional access, and interactive program guides. Our products were connected touch points in the end-to-end content delivery chain, reaching all the way from content origination to content distribution and consumer reception.

There were already some attempts at streaming video over the Internet, using technology from RealNetworks, Apple, and Microsoft. InterVU, a San Diego start-up, was facilitating content providers delivering video over the Internet. Broadcast.com, a Dallas-based Internet radio company, was also starting to get into Internet video. But the moving images resulting from these early solutions only occupied a fraction of the computer screen. It was ridiculed as "postage stamp" video due to the tiny pictures and poor video quality. The images would stop, stutter, and freeze up, often requiring a computer reboot. Still, it was a novelty for consumers to get any motion video at all on their computer screens.

The three of us at GI San Diego—Tom Lynch, Paul Moroney, and I—sketched out a straw man on the whiteboard. The basic premise was that Internet video was a logical and inevitable extension of both digital television and of the Internet. We agreed that over time, as broadband proliferated, Internet video would embark on an unstoppable path. It would get better every day, forever. The Internet was poised to be the next big step for digital video. Someday, we speculated, the Internet might even bring video to the living room, the entertainment center of the home. And the entire scenario was in the range of our core competencies.

Reminiscent of what people had initially said about GI's digital TV project nine years earlier, our leap of faith soon became a controversial subject. Many people inside and outside the company said it would never really happen. The Internet was simply not built for video. The cost of delivery was too high and the video quality would remain inferior. But we pushed ahead.

We had internal expertise in the areas of digital video and content security, but we knew we were deficient when it came to understanding the inner workings of the Internet. Our cable modem product experience had been focused on the "edges" of the Internet, from the cable headend to the subscriber, not on its inner core. But if we could develop a complete system—with video compression, digital transmission, and content security—just like we had done with digital TV, we might have something sustainable.

It also seemed like a good time to get started. In a few years there could be 10 million cable modem subscribers. A few years later there would be 20 million, our somewhat arbitrary threshold for breakout business potential. At this point we believed the major content providers, our pre-existing customer base from the pay TV market, would start participating in a much bigger way.

Over the next few months we refined our ideas with help from

Ed Zylka. Zylka had been the company's point man in San Diego on the early cable modem activity and had become well connected with some Internet gurus. Soon we were meeting with Nathan Raciborski, a visionary Internet serial entrepreneur who had been seeding various companies in the space. He helped expand our thinking into a staged, evolutionary plan of becoming a major player in the Internet video content distribution market. It would start with more video content being delivered, at a much better quality level, to personal computers. But at some point the Internet would connect to digital cable boxes and TVs. We needed to own this space before someone else did.

That was the origin of Aerocast. We formalized a business plan to focus our thoughts and help sell the concept internally. Just as Woo Paik and his team had done a decade earlier with digital TV, Raciborski and his Internet warriors worked furiously to put together a demo system. We flew to Dallas and met with Broadcast.com, co-founded by Mark Cuban and Todd Wagner. They had created the radio streaming category and were starting to get into video as well. We talked about doing something together. But then in April 1999, the discussion suddenly stopped when Yahoo bought their company for $5.7 billion.

Through many fits and starts, it became clear that Aerocast needed to be a separate start-up or it would never get off the ground. GI, intensely focused on its bottom line for Wall Street, didn't have the budget or appetite for risk to hire new engineers in San Diego. Venture capital was plentiful and start-up valuations were sky high. CEO Ed Breen agreed that we could split off Aerocast as a start-up. The only caveat was that we had to get a friendly strategic partner to invest, like Microsoft co-founder Paul Allen, owner of Charter Communications, or John Malone's Liberty Media.

We started selling the Aerocast concept in Seattle to Paul Allen and his Vulcan Ventures. Initially we intended to launch an open, self-publishing video platform. Eventually we would use our content security technology to bring in the traditional content providers and movie studios. The Aerocast vision was YouTube going to Netflix, before those companies existed as streaming video sites. Paul Allen seemed to like what he heard, and after a few meetings Vulcan Ventures verbally agreed to invest. This deal never materialized, however, as Allen became completely absorbed by the initial public offering of Charter, and his venture capital firm stopped returning our phone calls.

We quickly shifted gears to Denver and opened discussions with Liberty. Our pitch was "Malone's 500 digital TV channels was a good start. But with the Internet there will be a million channels. There will be infinite streams of every type of video imaginable. Aerocast will be in the middle of it all, providing servers, software, and security to enable higher-quality video content, an Internet version of what GI had done with digital TV. Except this time we'll be a content aggregator as well, at least to get the market primed." John Orr, Gary Howard, and the other Liberty executives listened intently to our vision and saw our lab demonstration.

When they asked what we were looking for in terms of a deal, I said, "$20 million for 40 percent of Aerocast." They agreed almost immediately, not even pushing back on price. GI would receive an equivalent equity stake in Aerocast for seeding the concept internally, with Aerocast founders and employees sharing the remaining 20 percent.

Tom Lynch, Ed Zylka, Nathan Raciborski, and I were ecstatic. But we were also concerned about being a start-up captive to two big companies. Moreover, Motorola had recently acquired GI, so a big company had just become much bigger. We traveled to Silicon Valley to talk to a few traditional venture capital firms, seeking some balance away from the strategic corporate interests of Motorola and Liberty Media. Two of the top-tier firms, Benchmark and Kleiner Perkins, turned us down for different reasons. Benchmark was turned off by the fact that Aerocast was spinning out of Motorola. Even worse, Lynch and I were still Motorola employees, making them skeptical of the entire situation.

Kleiner Perkins honed in on the issue of @Home, the broadband Internet service provider they had funded. Before it crashed, @Home had become the dominant force connecting the Internet with US cable systems. But @Home had a contractual limitation with its cable partners, handicapping its ability to get into the video business. A maximum time limit of ten minutes per session had been imposed on any @Home streaming video activity. Kleiner Perkins's position with us was, "Until you explain how we solve the @Home problem, we're not interested."

Zylka and I met with a few other venture firms that indicated a willingness to invest. But when we brought their overtures back to Liberty and Motorola, the response was, "No, they don't bring any value. We have all the money and time and industry contacts you need. This is going to be our long-term venture to win the emerging Internet video market. We want to own it ourselves." They even rejected the participation by Waterview Advisors, a venture fund run by Frank Biondi, Viacom's former CEO. Later, they did agree to let in one of the George Soros/Stanley Druckenmiller funds for a small equity stake with no board seat.

Tom Lynch had been in San Diego for two eventful years. He had turned around the GI division, helped transition it into Motorola, and played a key role in getting Aerocast started. He was trying hard to revive the entrepreneurial juices in San Diego, but he also knew that the culture of innovation had been progressively damaged. A majority of the employees were relatively new to the company, lacking the institutional memory and continuity essential to an organization's pride and morale.

Lynch asked his assistant Cheryl Kates to orchestrate a major ceremonial dinner in San Diego, celebrating the ten-year anniversary of digital TV. The idea was to honor the original GI team and to boost morale in the process. Various customers including HBO and PBS attended the event, held at the Hilton La Jolla Torrey Pines. Dick Wiley, the former FCC Chairman and head of the FCC's advisory committee on advanced television, gave a congratulatory speech via satellite. The company's top executives from the East Coast also attended, including Ed Breen, Frank Drendel, Geoff Roman, and Dave Robinson.

It was a spirited and uplifting experience for the San Diego workforce, just what Lynch wanted. But it was impossible not to notice one thing. Of the seven people being honored for creating digital TV at GI—Jerry Heller, Woo Paik, Paul Moroney, Ed Krause, Larry Dunham, Bob Rast, and Marc Tayer—only two were still at the company. And I was preparing to leave with Aerocast, making Paul Moroney the sole survivor.

43 CRACKING THE HDTV EGG

The turn of the century arrived a decade after General Instrument's breakthrough in digital TV technology. The first HDTV sets were on display in retail outlets and high-end home theater stores, but they cost several thousand dollars each and there was almost no HD content to watch. It was a complicated chicken-and-egg situation. Consumers wouldn't buy HDTV sets without lower prices and a critical mass of HD content. Programmers and service providers wouldn't invest to create and distribute HDTV channels until there were many more viewers. And consumer electronics companies needed high volumes in order to slash manufacturing costs and prices.

Under Chairman Reed Hundt, the FCC had issued an April 1997 Report and Order mandating that TV stations in the top 30 markets, covering half of US television households, must start broadcasting digital signals by November 1999. There was no requirement, however, for the content to be in the high definition format. But the signal had to be digital with at least standard definition (SDTV) resolution. The FCC also required that, by 2005, digital TV tuners had to be in at least half of the TV sets sold larger than 25 inches in diameter. By March 2007, all new TVs in the United States had to incorporate digital tuners. And by June 12, 2009, full-power broadcast TV stations could transmit only digital signals. Analog over-the-air television broadcasts would then be shut down, and the vacated spectrum would be auctioned by the government.[1]

The vision of Joe Flaherty, CBS's HDTV champion who had pushed GI to submit its all-digital solution into the FCC process in 1990, was alive but off to a very slow start. A typical TV station would transmit a minimal amount of HDTV programming during prime time, and deliver one or more "multicast" digital SDTV signals the rest of the day through the same 6 MHz channel. The HD broadcasts were initially reserved for prominent special events. On October 29, 1998, astronaut and US Senator John Glenn became the oldest person to fly in space aboard the space shuttle *Discovery*. Eight CBS affiliates carried the network broadcast in high definition. The next month, Disney's ABC network delivered the movie *101 Dalmatians* in high definition. ABC upstaged itself on January 30, 2000, by broadcasting Super Bowl XXXIV in HD, showcasing the St. Louis Rams beating the Tennessee Titans, 23–16.

HBO prided itself on its technological firsts. It had been the first US cable television programmer to deliver TV signals via satellite; the first satellite TV programmer to encrypt its signals; the first domestic content provider to launch a digital SDTV multiplex to cable headends; and the first to provide a large content library to cable operators for video-on-demand. But when it came to HDTV, HBO's unbroken chain of industry leadership appeared to be coming to an end.

For the prior two years, I had been trying to persuade Bob Zitter at HBO that they should be GI's initial, flagship HDTV customer. His response was consistent. HBO's digital SDTV signals looked so good that he didn't see the benefit in going first with HDTV. This time, HBO would take a wait-and-see approach. With high upfront production costs, new operational expenses, large bandwidth requirements, unknown consumer adoption, and a questionable financial payback, HDTV just didn't make a lot of sense for HBO.

But the broadcasters, led by CBS, were slowly moving in the direction of HD. And there were rumors of DirecTV planning an HDTV movie service. One day in late 1998 our phone rang in San Diego. It was HBO's Bob Zitter asking how quickly we could deliver an HDTV system. This was exciting news. HBO was going to launch in the full glory of high definition and wanted a proposal from us immediately.

We later found out what had swayed HBO and Zitter, turning them from follower to leader in the HDTV market. Ted Turner, Time Warner's vice chairman and largest individual shareholder, had been talking to his cable industry peers. They decided that cable needed an HDTV service to equalize what the broadcasters were doing. They further agreed that HBO, a sister company of Time Warner Cable, was the strongest and most recognizable brand. ESPN was the other logical choice, but it was owned by Disney, a pure content provider not under cable's control.

Bob Zitter reported to HBO CEO Jeff Bewkes, and Bewkes reported directly to Ted Turner. So when Turner called Bewkes to say the company was going to announce an HBO HD channel the following week, Bewkes quickly passed the ball to Zitter, who called us. If we could meet HBO's price and delivery goals, they needed our new HDTV products urgently. A negotiation quickly ensued between Zitter's right-hand businessperson, Barbara Jaffe, and me, supported by GI attorney Matt Gettinger and HBO technologist Craig Cuttner. We signed the deal in San Diego, with HBO executives present, at a Dom Perignon–infused ceremony.

HBO started converting its film library to the 1080i HD format as quickly as possible. It also made a clear distinction between "upconverted" SDTV content versus the actual HD programs it wanted to distribute.[2]

When HBO HD launched in March 1999, there were still two big problems inhibiting the market. First, HDTV sets remained expensive. Retail prices averaged over $2,000. The second issue, bandwidth, was even more problematic. HDTV was a huge bandwidth hog, even with GI's digital video compression technology. Each local TV station had a free, additional 6 MHz channel, courtesy of the FCC. But where would the satellite and cable TV service providers find the enormous bandwidth needed to deliver more than a handful of HD signals to their subscribers? Regardless, GI had high hopes that other leading content providers would follow HBO's lead, putting pressure on service providers to expand their bandwidth capacity.

The next big shoe to drop was Viacom. In the fall of 1999, Viacom asked GI if it would purchase a table at a major event being hosted by Sumner Redstone in his hometown of Boston. Tom Lynch, head of GI San Diego, readily agreed. His time on the West Coast had informed him of the content providers' strategic importance to the company. I arrived in Boston early since I had been in New York the prior week on business, meeting with Viacom CTO Paul Heimbach on GI's HDTV products.

The big event was a fundraising dinner marking the twentieth anniversary of the JFK Library and Museum. Colin Powell started the evening off with an inspiring keynote speech about public service. Caroline Kennedy then delivered a speech about the importance of public service to the Kennedy family and to her brother John, who had been killed in a plane crash earlier that year. After dinner there was some social time and I was able to speak briefly with Sumner Redstone. He thanked us for attending and knew we were in discussions regarding providing the equipment for Viacom's upcoming launch of Showtime HD.

In May 2000, federal regulators approved Redstone's $45 billion merger of Viacom and CBS. CBS had first achieved greatness under William S. Paley, surviving through some difficult years under Laurence Tisch and then Westinghouse. Viacom had been spun off from CBS in 1971. Now CBS was in the hands of Sumner Redstone and Viacom, a corporate offspring buying its one-time parent. Viacom/CBS would become an HDTV content powerhouse, for the time being under a single corporate umbrella.

By the end of 2001, only 2.2 million HDTV sets had been shipped,[3] representing less than 2 percent of US households. But there were already 32 million digital SDTV subscribers in the country, split almost evenly between satellite and cable homes. Nearly a third of the television homes in America were receiving digital TV signals. The video digitization of America was well on its way. But digital HDTV was just getting out of the starting gate, fueled by the powerful triumvirate of HBO, CBS, and Showtime.

44 SEAMLESS MOBILITY

Motorola was one of the true pioneers of communications technology. The company dates back to 1930, when founder Paul Galvin introduced one of the first successful car radios. The once-iconic brand was an amalgam of "motor," as in the automobile, and "Victrola," the phonographic music machines masquerading as furniture in the 1910s and 1920s.

Motorola's initial foray into the TV business, in 1947, was as a television set manufacturer. This unit, including the Quasar brand, was sold to Matsushita in 1974.

The prior year, in 1973, Motorola introduced the world's first portable handheld phone. A decade later the FCC approved Motorola's DynaTAC, the world's first commercial cell phone. In 1991, the company demonstrated the world's first digital cell phone, based on the GSM standard, which had been developed in Europe for mobile telephony. Motorola remained the global market share leader in mobile phones until 1998, when it was displaced by Nokia.

Another lasting innovation was Six Sigma, Motorola's manufacturing quality improvement process. It was initiated in 1986 and adopted by many other companies, including General Electric.

One of Motorola's biggest failures, however, was its Iridium satellite communications venture, using sixty-six low-earth orbiting satellites to cover the entire planet. Expensive and late to market, the Iridium entity went bankrupt in 1999. It was recapitalized in 2001 with private investors and is operational today with many customers, including the US Department of Defense.

Motorola had observed General Instrument closely over the years, selling it various semiconductor devices and impressed by how GI dominated its chosen market segments. Motorola had been trying for years to break into the cable equipment business, finally achieving some success with its proprietary CyberSURFR cable modem. But the life of this product ended with the DOCSIS cable modem standard, an industry movement that Motorola was reluctant to embrace.

Motorola desperately needed to diversify and expand. During the Internet boom of the late 1990s, broadband and digital were the buzzwords of the future, and size and scale were viewed as the keys to market dominance. Motorola needed to move from data and voice into video, and from wireless communications into the wired world of broadband. The notion of acquiring GI bubbled up in Motorola's Illinois offices.

Jeff Huppertz, a business development executive in Motorola's Multimedia Group, had been advocating an acquisition of either Scientific Atlanta or General Instrument since 1995. Each time, his idea was rebuffed by higher-ups, convinced they could successfully enter the cable video market independently. But Huppertz knew better. He understood the cable business well, having cut his teeth at Scientific Atlanta, where he worked with Time Warner Cable on the Full Service Network project in Orlando. He was convinced that GI's and SA's stranglehold on the set-top box business, using their conditional access and content security technologies as the ultimate barrier to entry, made it nearly impossible for a new entrant to succeed. He believed that if Motorola acquired GI or SA, it would instantly become the broadband technology company of the future, a powerful enterprise uniquely able to bridge the gap between wireless and wired, across data, voice, and video.

In 1998 Huppertz made a third and final attempt to convince Motorola's senior management to proceed. At first they approached Scientific Atlanta. Huppertz was more familiar with SA and felt it would be a better cultural fit with Motorola. But SA was standoffish, prompting Motorola management to direct Huppertz to test the waters with GI. So in late 1998, Huppertz contacted his friend Ed Zylka, then in GI's corporate development group, which was headed by Dick Smith. When Huppertz arrived in Horsham, Pennsylvania, Zylka ushered him into a boardroom filled with GI's executive management team, including CEO Ed Breen, Geoff Roman, Dave Robinson, and Dan Moloney.

At GI, Ed Breen had been pondering a follow-up act to his digital cable megadeal. He was considering how to operate more efficiently on a global scale, critical for international expansion. He also coveted enhanced credibility with the giant telcos, which with their deep pockets were poised to get into the video business once and for all.

When Motorola proposed an equity investment of up to 20 percent, Breen was immediately receptive. He had become disillusioned, however, by how Sony's 5 percent investment in GI had not led to anything meaningful. He liked the fact that Motorola was an American company.

He also believed the digital set-top box market might finally go retail, in which case Motorola's brand name would be invaluable. So Breen upped the ante, proposing that Motorola buy GI in its entirety, a full acquisition. The idea was approved by Merle Gilmore, president of Motorola's Communications Enterprise unit. It was also supported by CEO Chris Galvin, scion of Motorola's founding family.[1]

A stock-for-stock deal was crafted. Upon closure in January 2000, Motorola acquired General Instrument for $17 billion, more than a tenfold increase in value from the $1.6 billion price paid by Forstmann Little for GI in 1990. Overnight, Motorola was the world leader in broadband communications systems, a large market segment it knew would hold the future.

Digital TV had been kind to GI over the years. Sales had grown from around $1 billion annually in the late 1980s to $1.5 billion in 1995 and nearly $3.5 billion in 2000. But Motorola had $37 billion in annual revenue, over half of which consisted of its cell phone and wireless infrastructure units.

For GI, the acquisition represented an enormous payoff for its shareholders and an enhanced ability to operate with a global footprint. Wall Street loved the story. The wired and wireless worlds were converging, and Motorola was the only company with a strong position on both sides. It had the unique ability to create "seamless mobility" for voice, data, and video services. The possibilities were limitless.

Soon Ed Breen became the president and COO of Motorola Inc., with company patriarch Chris Galvin the only barrier between him and the top post. Breen appointed Dave Robinson as president of the GI business, renamed Motorola Broadband Communications Systems. When Robinson later departed after a dispute with Motorola's bureaucracy, Dan Moloney took over that side of the business. Tom Lynch left the San Diego operation, first becoming head of Motorola's automotive electronics unit and then president of its cell phone business. To keen observers it seemed like GI had taken over Motorola, but perhaps without realizing what it had bitten off.

Amid these GI/Motorola management changes and moves toward business integration, a few of us in San Diego were busy establishing Aerocast, Inc. as an independent start-up to focus on Internet video. After more than fifteen years with a big company, which had just become much bigger, I was ready for new challenges. The clincher for me occurred while attending Motorola's annual corporate officers' meeting in Chicago. It was formal and well orchestrated, but I was not impressed. The corporate culture felt stale. The many "lifer" Motorolans seemed competent but complacent in their careers. They were waiting around for comfortable retirements with cushy pensions, defending their fiefdoms and cautious about moving the company in new directions. I knew I didn't want to be one of these guys. It was time to get into start-ups.

45 AEROCAST: THE LAUNCH

Once Aerocast's venture funding from Liberty Media was secure, I resigned from Motorola and jumped into the new company as co-founder and SVP of Business Development. We hired Dario Santana as Aerocast president. A Purdue-educated engineer and Harvard Business School graduate, he had done a stellar job as head of investor relations for GI, supporting Breen's high profile with Wall Street and thus contributing to the meteoric rise of GI's stock price. Before that he had been in charge of product management for the analog cable set-top business. We also hired Marc Kauffman as VP of Engineering. Kauffman had been one of the top engineers at GI in Pennsylvania but was attracted by the frontier of Internet video and curious about life on the West Coast. Nathan Raciborski, Aerocast co-founder and CTO, brought in some of his Internet software buddies, complementing the more formally trained engineers working under Kauffman. We also hired a couple of Internet product marketing experts, Mike Sawyer and Peter Coppola.

We found a start-up space in the Sorrento Mesa business park of San Diego, just a few blocks from GI's original Building 1, where the digital TV revolution had begun a decade earlier. Motorola's Ed Breen and Tom Lynch were on our board of directors along with Carl Vogel and John Orr from Liberty Media. We assembled an influential advisory board including Leo Hindery, former CEO of AT&T Broadband, and Mark Schneider, CEO of UPC, Europe's largest cable operator. There was a buzz in the industry that Aerocast was on to something big.

Aerocast's vision was that anyone could be a video publisher in the Internet age. We believed this chaotic free-for-all would coexist with the eventual streaming video activities of established content providers. The streaming video market would start with the PC, fed by ever increasing numbers of cable and DSL modem high-speed Internet connections, and would eventually move to the TV.

A core founding principle of Aerocast was that protection of content would be a critical concern. To that end we structured a deal to work with Paul Moroney's R&D group nearby at Motorola San Diego. Aerocast committed to fund Motorola's development of an Internet video digital rights management (DRM) security solution, coupled with MPEG-4 video. MPEG-4 was starting to emerge as the new video compression standard, the successor to MPEG-2, with twice the bandwidth efficiency. In return, Aerocast received a limited period of exclusivity for the DRM/MPEG-4 solution in the Internet field of use.

The fiftieth annual National Cable & Telecommunications Association (NCTA) show was held in Chicago in June 2001. I published a document in the *NCTA Technical Papers* book titled "The Future of Streaming Media" and presented it during a panel discussion of upcoming technologies and markets. Internet video was a new concept to the cable industry. Cable modems were ramping up quickly but were only in about 2.5 million homes, representing less than 4 percent of US cable subscribers.

Aerocast had a tiny section inside Motorola's expansive booth but we attracted a disproportionate share of attention. When Comcast's Brian Roberts and Julian Brodsky came by at the end of the exhibition hours, they saw the video quality enabled by Aerocast, streaming live into the show over the Internet. Roberts summed it up in two words: "That's amazing."

Our big break came soon after in a dinner meeting with ESPN and Disney at Donovan's Steak and Chop House on La Jolla Village Drive. Motorola was hosting its two prominent customers to discuss new products and find out about their future digital TV plans. ESPN executives Chuck Pagano and Manish Jha were there, along with Disney's Vince Roberts. I was invited to tell them about Aerocast, in part because of my long-standing relationship with Pagano and Roberts. Still, it was humbling to be in the room with my former customers and former employer, representing an unknown start-up in the presence of three global brands.

At Aerocast, we had been making the case with cable operators that they should start using Internet video to help "upsell" their cable modem subscribers to a higher speed tier for a higher monthly fee. The dinner discussion with ESPN and Disney caused a lightbulb to go off with Manish Jha, ESPN's new media strategist. When he returned to the East Coast, he began evangelizing a new broadband Internet concept to ESPN management, based on Aerocast technology. It was called ESPN Broadband, and it would later evolve into ESPN360 and ESPN3.

After a flurry of product development, Aerocast had an initial platform consisting of a subscriber management system, easy-to-use video publishing software, and a content delivery system. We placed our video servers at the "edges" of the Internet, adjacent to the cable headends and close to the cable modem subscribers of Comcast and AT&T Broadband, both of which had agreed to participate. The DRM/MPEG-4 piece was still under development with Paul Moroney's group at Motorola San Diego.

Suddenly we were an operational business, working closely not only with ESPN but also with Charlie Cerino and Debbie Brodsky at Comcast's broadband Internet group. Each night ESPN provided us with various video highlights from sports events that day. We would then position the files on our edge servers, and the next morning Comcast and AT&T Broadband cable modem subscribers could go to the ESPN Broadband website and stream entertainment-quality video clips to their PCs at full screen. The word was spreading. Cable modem subscribers could get entertainment-quality sports content on their computers.

Because the videos were being served from the edges of the Internet over cable's managed pipes, rather than over the long-haul Internet, the delivery cost was economical. Furthermore, by streaming from the edge, the video clips were not subjected to the performance vagaries of the Internet, which was not yet equipped to handle smooth streaming at the bit rates we were using. At the time, other companies were streaming video at about 200 kbps, limiting the quality and image size to a very small area. But Aerocast was able to stream ESPN Broadband at four times that rate, allowing full-screen PC viewing of good-quality video.

The X Games became a pivotal event showcasing video over the Internet. ESPN decided to supplement its TV coverage of the X Games with daily video highlights on the ESPN Broadband website. Aerocast provided ESPN's video publishing and delivery platform for the 2001 Summer X Games in Philadelphia and the 2002 Winter X Games in Aspen.

ESPN Broadband was a trailblazing product that became popular with early cable modem subscribers, underscoring the fact that cable's Internet pipe was destined to be much more than a data conduit. It would become a video delivery platform in its own right, a parallel universe to the pre-existing digital cable TV infrastructure.

With any start-up, the market timing of its technology is absolutely critical for success. In our case, even with the ESPN deal, we were too early. The business models were not there yet. Streaming video was still in its infancy, with advertising and subscriptions not yet viable.

Content Delivery Network (CDN) companies like Akamai were emerging, placing edge servers in Internet data centers and then charging websites for speeding up delivery of their graphics, text, and content over the Internet. But we didn't want to get pigeonholed as a CDN business because we perceived that it would become commoditized over time. We were starting to get some early revenue from another new company, Limelight Networks, which was utilizing Aerocast's Internet video technology for its own CDN business.

ESPN was trying to charge Comcast a small carriage fee for ESPN Broadband, consistent with the cable TV model. However, Comcast refused to pay, not wanting to establish a precedent for Internet video.

But being ahead of the market was not even our biggest problem. In fact, Liberty and Motorola's previous rationale for excluding traditional venture capital firms from investing in Aerocast was that we didn't need their money. Liberty and Motorola, as strategic investors, intended to provide sufficient funding and were ostensibly committed for the long haul. They claimed to have the patience to wait out the market so Aerocast would be in place when Internet video reached its heyday.

Unfortunately for us, in 2002 Ed Breen resigned from Motorola to become Tyco International's new CEO. He was recruited to clean up the malfeasance mess left by Dennis Kozlowski. Breen soon hired

Tom Lynch and several other former GI executives. At Aerocast, we were suddenly left without our two biggest champions within Motorola. Since Liberty had led the Series A round investment, it was Motorola's turn to lead the Series B round. But with Breen and Lynch gone, the remaining Motorola management seemed to view Aerocast more as a threat than an opportunity. It was becoming clearer to Motorola that the Internet would grow into an important new market for video content, and they didn't want Aerocast in their way.

So Motorola stalled as long as possible. When it finally produced an investment term sheet, it limited Aerocast's business potential by carving up the market potential, changing the deal with Liberty. Liberty was livid and demanded to be bought out by Motorola, resulting in Motorola acquiring Aerocast. At first Motorola was going to hire Aerocast's two dozen or so engineers and proceed with the business, including the ESPN and Comcast operation. But Motorola was experiencing some tough times financially and didn't have the patience or focus. In the end, it defaulted to a losing scenario of just maintaining the Aerocast software source code, effectively shutting down the entire business and the opportunity.

At Motorola's cell phone business unit, a similar missed opportunity was taking shape. Motorola had acquired a Seattle start-up called 4thpass, one of the early leaders in content delivery software for wireless data networks. Ringtones and games were the main content types being downloaded at the time, indicative of the limited bandwidth of the emerging 3G networks. But as with the wired Internet, the wireless world was also going to evolve with more bandwidth and the ability to deliver additional types of content.

Ed Zylka had moved from the Motorola cable group in Pennsylvania to Chicago, where the cell phone group was headquartered, and the 4thpass subsidiary was reporting to him. Zylka hired me as a consultant and we put together a business plan and presentation for Motorola management. We made the case that the cell phone would become much more than a device merely able to download ringtones and games. It would become a mobile entertainment device, capable of handling music and even video at some point. Importantly, as with pay TV and Internet video, security would become an essential element for protecting the content. 4thpass was in an ideal position to capitalize on this evolution. Or so our argument went.

Motorola management heard our pitch, and some of the executives agreed with the strategy to make 4thpass an important strategic growth opportunity for the company. But they seemed incapable of making any bold, substantive decisions. The 4thpass acquisition was squandered, much like what happened to Aerocast. Perhaps part of it was a bad hangover from the failed Iridium mobile satellite communications initiative, but it went much deeper than that.

Motorola also became frustrated and impatient with the near-term business prospects for its digital satellite TV business in China. HGI, Motorola's 50/50 joint venture with state-owned broadcaster CCTV, was continuing to order products delivering digital TV to cable headends and to the rural villages throughout China. But the market wasn't ramping up as quickly as expected, so Motorola's San Diego unit decided to shut down the joint venture.

"Seamless mobility" was a prescient and powerful vision, and it had justified Motorola's acquisition of GI. Courageous product development and market execution, however, trump clever marketing slogans every time. Motorola was still the leader in digital set-top boxes and was still number two in cell phones after Nokia. But other companies would capitalize on the promising future of Internet video, mobile content delivery, and digital TV in China. When it came to bold new ventures and initiatives, Moto had lost its mojo.

46 THE NEW KING OF CABLE

The passage of power from Ralph Roberts, Comcast founder and CEO, to Brian Roberts stands out as a remarkably successful father-to-son corporate leadership transition. It reflected the senior Roberts's careful study of other family businesses, assessing why some worked while many others failed. It also resulted from the younger Roberts's self-initiative and business acumen. He rose through the ranks with certitude, humility, and a sense of destiny, absent pressure from his dad.

Ralph Roberts was born after World War I into a well-to-do family in Westchester County, New York. But his dad died during the Depression and the Roberts family lost everything. His mother moved to a shared apartment in Philadelphia, where Ralph attended the University of Pennsylvania's Wharton School. He later owned a local belt-manufacturing business where he met a fellow Wharton graduate, Julian Brodsky, assigned by his accounting firm to help Roberts sell the belt company.[1] The two men co-founded Comcast in 1963 along with Daniel Aaron, purchasing their first cable system for $500,000: a 1,200-subscriber system in Tupelo, Mississippi.[2]

Brian Roberts graduated from Wharton in 1981, forty years after his father. Emblematic of a quiet, competitive spirit, he was an All-American squash player at Penn and subsequently won gold and silver medals at the Maccabiah Games. He started at the bottom of Comcast's ladder, which he scaled rapidly. When the cable industry bailed out Ted Turner and Turner Broadcasting in 1986, it was Brian, not Ralph, who joined Turner's board. At age thirty, in 1990, he was appointed president of Comcast. During the 1990s, he became an effective business partner with his dad on some important deals: acquiring QVC (with TCI) in 1994; bringing in a $1 billion investment from Bill Gates's Microsoft in 1997 for 11.5 percent of the company; and acquiring a stake in E! Entertainment from Time Warner, with funding provided by Disney.

But these deals were just warm-ups for two vastly larger and more transformative transactions: the acquisitions of AT&T Broadband and NBCUniversal. In November 2002, Comcast became the nation's largest video service provider, acquiring AT&T Broadband for $29.2 billion. The AT&T deal catapulted Comcast overnight from 8.5 million to nearly 22 million cable subscribers. Brian Roberts was the putative new king of cable, becoming CEO in 2002 and chairman in 2004.

As part of its purchase of AT&T Broadband, Comcast obtained the National Digital Television Center south of Denver, built by AT&T Broadband executives David Beddow and Gary Traver and arising from the original TCI/GI digital cable deal. This massive state-of-the-art facility, renamed the Comcast Media Center and more recently Comcast Wholesale, is among the world's largest content ingestion and distribution facilities. It securely delivers hundreds of digital SDTV and HDTV channels via fiber optics and the Headend in the Sky (HITS) digital satellite platform, along with video-on-demand files, digital ads for program insertion at cable headends, and various interactive TV applications.

Comcast's acquisition of AT&T Broadband was monumental. But being the largest content distributor was far from the endgame for Brian Roberts. He was intrigued by the rapid march of technology, and he deeply understood the intrinsic value of content. By wrapping together content, distribution, and technology, the Comcast of the future would be a new type of company: a full-service communications powerhouse built for the twenty-first century.

47 I Want My HDTV

The national launch of HBO's initial HDTV channel in the spring of 1999, followed by the debut of Showtime HD in 2000, marked a turning point for content providers. Among the broadcast networks, CBS was the HDTV front-runner. Mark Cuban's HDNet went live via satellite in late 2001, delivering exclusive HD coverage of the US invasion of Afghanistan. Discovery HD Theater launched in June 2002. It was a slow but steady march.

CBS executive Martin Franks asserted: "HDTV gives us the ability to differentiate ourselves. As good as *CSI* is in standard (definition) television, it's a different experience in HDTV… Four years ago, HDTV was a hobby and an experiment for CBS. On an operating basis, thanks to advertising, HDTV is now a profitable business for us. We're past the point of saying, 'HDTV will fail.'" Other industry leaders would also elevate the tone toward HDTV. "Because we position ourselves as a premium service," said Bob Zitter, HBO's senior vice president for technology operations, "it's essential that we offer subscribers the highest quality picture and sound."[1]

A key factor pacing HDTV market adoption was the retail price of the digital TV sets. Prices dropped by more than 50 percent in four years, declining from an average selling price of $3,500 at the beginning of 1999 to roughly $1,500 by early 2003. There were even entry-level sets under the magic number of $1,000.

Another breakthrough occurred at the end of March 2003, when ESPN HD debuted with the Major League Baseball season opener between the Texas Rangers and the Anaheim Angels. ESPN also announced plans to deliver 100 professional baseball, basketball, hockey, and football games live in HD. But much of the initial content on the ESPN HD channel was "upconverted" from standard definition, an inferior video quality relative to true HDTV.

Still, Gary Shapiro, president of the Consumer Electronics Association, declared: "ESPN HD will be a tipping point in the transition to digital television. When consumers see a Randy Johnson fastball coming straight at them, or feel the reverberations of a power dunk by Shaq, they'll know what is so magical about high definition TV." In Bristol, Connecticut, at ESPN headquarters, chief technologist Chuck Pagano and his team were busy building a new 120,000-square-foot digital TV production facility, intended to be the largest HD-capable facility in the world. George Bodenheimer, ESPN's president, confidently stated: "HDTV is the next great wave in technology. This will give our fans the best sports television experience yet."[2]

By 2003, there was clearly some momentum on the content side of the HD equation, with a handful of channels launched. But it was a painfully slow process. Fewer than 700 local commercial TV stations were broadcasting digital signals, and the majority of the content was digital SDTV, not HDTV. The other half of the country's broadcast stations were still sitting on the sidelines, having been granted waivers by the FCC.[3] A critical mass of HD content was desperately needed in order to transform HDTV from an object of desire for early adopters to mainstream status.

One day in late 2002, after Motorola acquired my first start-up, Aerocast, my cell phone rang. It was Ben Griffin, HBO's outside counsel. Griffin knew me from his role representing HBO on GI/Motorola's previous deals for our digital television content delivery products. He was representing a new client, Cablevision Systems, and HBO's Barbara Jaffe had suggested to him that I could help Cablevision with a new project.

Wilt Hildenbrand, Cablevision's technology leader, needed an independent industry person to write a document for the FCC in conjunction with an application by Rainbow, Cablevision's content subsidiary, for a new high-power direct broadcast satellite (DBS) service. Cablevision had formed a subsidiary, Rainbow DBS, to hold its DBS license from the FCC.[4] Cablevision had a major problem, however. Rainbow only had the rights to use thirteen DBS frequencies.

If Hildenbrand didn't find a much smarter way to use that limited satellite bandwidth relative to the vastly greater spectrum already owned by its entrenched competitors, DirecTV and Dish Network, the new Rainbow DBS venture wouldn't have a chance.

Chuck Dolan, at the ripe age of seventy-six, was still in control of Cablevision and preparing to launch another new business. More than three decades after starting HBO at Time Inc., and then building Cablevision from scratch into a valuable, diversified media company, his entrepreneurial spirit was as strong and passionate as ever. Five years after the US government effectively shut down PrimeStar, leaving DirecTV and Dish Network as the only two domestic DBS companies, Dolan was nonetheless confident that there was room for a third player.

His hook was to use HDTV content as the differentiator. His industry peers were still dragging their feet on HDTV, and he sensed a huge opening to become the leader in HDTV content and distribution. Rainbow DBS, branded as the Voom HD satellite TV service, would be his platform to get there. No temporary limitation on his satellite bandwidth capacity was going to hold back Chuck Dolan, and Wilt Hildenbrand had the unenviable task of finding a way to achieve the near-impossible.

With only thirteen DBS frequencies, Hildenbrand needed someone outside Cablevision to make an independent case with the FCC that MPEG-4 video technology would soon become available, doubling the bandwidth efficiency compared to MPEG-2 compression. Furthermore, he needed to claim that a more advanced type of digital modulation technology called "8PSK" would also soon be available. He knew me from the early digital TV days and just needed a credible, independent document to supplement Rainbow's FCC filing.

The essence of my argument in the FCC filing was that these next-generation technologies, MPEG-4 video compression and 8PSK modulation, would become available in the near future. They would allow Rainbow to send 50 Mbps of digital HDTV content through each DBS satellite transponder, nearly double the throughput relative to the existing MPEG-2 technology used by DirecTV and Dish Network. The combined effect of these two new technologies was that at least 8 HDTV signals could be sent through each satellite transponder, a phenomenal advance that could make Voom a viable service provider and the leader in HDTV. The goal was to be the first to get to 15 HD channels, then 50, and finally the magic number of 100 HDTV channels and beyond.

48 VOOM

One thing led to another and soon I was working for Wilt Hildenbrand and Steve Pontillo, Rainbow's chief technologist, helping to get Voom launched. My role was to be Voom's guy on the West Coast, managing an ecosystem of technology vendors: Motorola in San Diego; NDS and Broadcom in Orange County; Harmonic, Equator, and Intel in Silicon Valley; and Microsoft in Seattle. I also managed Rainbow's vendor-selection process for encoders, digital satellite receivers, and the outdoor dish and related equipment. After being on the "sell" side of the technology business at GI/Motorola for so many years, it gave me a very different and refreshing perspective to be on the "buy" side, the customer side of the fence. Suddenly the technology vendors were wooing me, hoping Cablevision would buy their products.

I commuted from San Diego to the Rainbow facility in Jericho, Long Island, every few weeks. The situation was hectic beyond belief. The Voom satellite had not even been launched yet, but there were virtually unlimited tasks to accomplish beforehand. Chuck Dolan was fully engaged with a strong staff including DBS pioneer Mickey Alpert, former HBO and Viacom technology chief Ed Horowitz, TVN founder Stu

Levin, DirecTV's former head of marketing Bill Casamo, content executive Sandy McGovern, Rainbow chief technology officer Steve Pontillo, and many more. Josh Sapan, Rainbow's CEO, had the gargantuan task of creating 21 new HD programming services for exclusive distribution by Voom.

The Rainbow 1 DBS satellite launched flawlessly from Cape Canaveral, Florida, on July 17, 2003.[1] By the end of the year, Voom was on the air with Motorola's digital TV system. Voom had no choice but to launch with MPEG-2 video since MPEG-4 technology was still at least a year away. Keith Kelley and his team of Motorola engineers therefore had to design the initial receivers with a hardware upgrade slot, allowing future MPEG-4 circuit cards to be installed.

During its too-short lifespan, Voom became a primary catalyst for the HDTV market. By 2004, the company was delivering 36 HDTV satellite channels: the 21 unique Voom networks plus the entire third-party universe of 15 HD channels licensed from HBO, Showtime, ESPN, and others. At the time, Voom's competitors—DirecTV, Dish Network, and the cable operators—were only carrying 5 to 10 HD signals each.

As soon as the new service launched, consumer demand spiked through the roof. Subscriber churn was also high, however, due to inadequate pre-launch field testing and software instability of the Motorola digital satellite receivers.

A raging debate within Voom was whether it should focus purely on HDTV content or instead compete head-to-head against the other DBS and cable companies, offering both HDTV and SDTV channels. The fundamental issue was whether an HD-only business model could be sustained, since Voom in this case would be merely an "add on" to a pre-existing pay TV service. How much more would subscribers pay for an HD-only service, when they were already paying over $50 per month for DirecTV, Dish Network, or cable TV?

Going head-to-head seemed ambitious, but that's what Voom decided to do, believing it was the only way to develop a long-term sustainable business model. So Voom embarked on a content licensing buying spree. Before long, Voom was transmitting not only its industry-leading 36 HDTV channels, but also 80 SDTV channels and 18 digital music channels, all squeezed into 13 satellite transponders. Bandwidth was unquestionably a major short-term problem for Voom. But in addition to the planned MPEG-4 upgrade, Chuck Dolan had a master plan to alleviate the issue, procuring dozens of additional high-power Ku-band DBS transponders to be available over the next few years. Rainbow also obtained licenses for five Ka-band orbital positions.[2]

Chuck Dolan and his Voom team were going big, intent on becoming the top HDTV content platform, whatever it took and for however long. But Dolan's son, Jim, didn't see it that way. His dad had made him the CEO in 1995, and Jim Dolan was trying to establish independent credibility with Wall Street. The analysts and investment bankers didn't like Cablevision's stagnant stock price, believing it would rise dramatically if Chuck's Voom venture was not weighing down the company's earnings. Jim was listening intently, and agreeing, as were several of Chuck's board members.

It didn't matter that Chuck Dolan had been the founder of HBO. It didn't matter that he'd built Cablevision into a media powerhouse. Wall Street didn't want Cablevision's financial resources poured into a high-risk DBS venture, especially with DirecTV and Dish Network already up and running with millions of subscribers each. They didn't care that none of the other satellite or cable service providers was focused yet on HDTV. And it didn't register with them that Chuck Dolan was absolutely convinced he could end up a huge winner once again in only a few years, owning the industry's leading HDTV content platform. A few years was an eternity to the Wall Street mind-set. Its time horizon was the next quarter, or at most the next year. Plus, it would cost over $1 billion before Chuck Dolan's high-flying HD dream might start turning a profit. Wall Street wanted the company's stock price to increase now, and that meant killing Voom to improve quarterly earnings. "Shut down Voom!" was The Street's collective cry.

The big showdown occurred at an impromptu Cablevision board meeting in January 2005. The majority of the board sided with Jim Dolan. Those of us inside the Voom venture could hardly believe the drama as it played out before our eyes. Chuck made a valiant last-ditch effort to buy the business himself, but Voom's fate was sealed. The Rainbow 1 DBS satellite, the most advanced high-power Ku-band satellite built to date, was sold to Charlie Ergen and his Dish Network for a bargain price of $200 million. Richard Greenfield, an analyst with Fulcrum Global Partners, said: "This is an important step in Jim's credibility with investors since it shows that he is focused on driving Cablevision's stock price."[3]

Once again Charlie Ergen had come out ahead. A shrewd businessman, he seemed to always have fortune on his side as well. He had been lucky a decade earlier when he launched EchoStar's first DBS satellite on the cheap with the low-cost but risky Chinese Long March vehicle. When PrimeStar's high-power DBS ambitions were shut down by the US Justice Department, Ergen jumped in as the opportunistic beneficiary of Rupert Murdoch's and MCI's invaluable orbital position. This time he had simultaneously eliminated a new competitor, Voom, and acquired a precious in-orbit satellite at a deep discount, just when an entirely new bandwidth war, for HDTV leadership, was about to begin.

Chuck Dolan had lost this battle, but he had nothing to prove. He had already built a dynasty, making a fortune for himself and his investors. In addition, his controversial Voom venture had proven something very important to the world: consumers were absolutely starved for HDTV content. HBO, Showtime, Discovery, and a few others were doing their part, but Voom underscored the glaring imbalance between the supply of HD content and demand for it. Once consumers experienced the brilliant new high definition pictures in their living rooms, whether it was a movie on HBO, a football game on ESPN, or a fashion event on Voom's Ultra HD channel, they would never go back. SDTV had become an annoying anachronism to these TV viewers, as distasteful as a retrograde dial-up phone line connection was to early broadband Internet users.

With Voom vanishing from the landscape in April 2005, there was a deep HDTV content vacuum to fill. Ergen's Dish Network was still only carrying 10 HD channels. DirecTV carried a similar number, and cable operators provided even fewer. None of them had the spare bandwidth for a massive HD expansion, and even if they did, the HD content, absent Voom, was sparse. By this time, over 1,400 TV stations in more than 200 markets, serving over 99 percent of the country, were transmitting digital signals in some form. But the proportion of the digital TV content in true HD format remained negligible.

49 HDTV REACHES CRITICAL MASS

As Voom wound itself down in 2005, another seminal event was occurring in the digital television industry: the giant telephone companies were finally building video networks and entering the TV business. Bell Atlantic and the other Baby Bells had played around with digital video in the mid-1990s, only to walk away after weak and unsuccessful attempts. AT&T had acquired TCI in 1999 and MediaOne in 2000, only to sell the combined AT&T Broadband cable unit to Comcast in 2002. But this time was different. This time the telcos were going all-in.

Verizon was committing $20 billion to build its own advanced fiber optic cable systems. It planned to string fiber optics all the way to the outside of the residence, and then use coaxial cable to bring digital TV signals into the home. In this sense, it was like a cable system except the fiber went much deeper. Verizon FiOS launched in 2005, and was soon lauded for the quality of its service and user experience. FiOS used a Motorola MPEG-2 digital system to drive its TV service, a next-generation version of what Motorola had built for its cable customers.

Also in 2005, SBC acquired its former parent AT&T, mainly for its wireless service. SBC then changed its name to AT&T, still a powerful brand, and started making plans for an entirely new type of video infrastructure. AT&T intended to build a digital TV system based on the Internet Protocol (IP), using a new switched architecture called "IPTV" with souped-up twisted pair copper wire and advanced DSL technology. AT&T's U-Verse service got off to a very rocky start when it launched in 2006. U-Verse employed a Microsoft software infrastructure, with Motorola and Cisco MPEG-4 IPTV set-top boxes and encoders. There were many problems with the Microsoft software, and it appeared for a while that U-Verse might not survive as a service. But Microsoft finally got the crippling bugs out of the system and stabilized the technology.

There was no doubt that HDTV was going to be the next battleground for video service providers. The only question, in the aftermath of Voom's demise, was who would go first and take the lead. Predictably, the high ground was seized by DirecTV. In January 2007, the digital satellite TV company announced it would be the first to offer 100 HD channels. It was inconceivable how all that content could come into existence so quickly. But before long the roadmap was in sight, with virtually all of the premium and basic cable channels, plus some new ones, finally stepping up to the plate.

DirecTV and Dish Network achieved the 100 HD channel milestone first, followed by Verizon FiOS and AT&T U-Verse. The cable operators were lagging, trying to figure out how to create the necessary bandwidth to carry such a burdensome load of HDTV content. They had collectively invested $80 billion during the previous decade building out their Hybrid Fiber Coax two-way cable infrastructure, capable of carrying the triple play of video, high-speed Internet, and digital voice. But they didn't have the bandwidth necessary to broadcast 100 HD channels. Not even close. Since millions of their subscribers were still using analog set-top boxes, they had to carry dozens of old-style analog NTSC signals, sucking up the majority of their systems' capacity. But there were plenty of ways for cable operators to create more bandwidth; it just took time and money.

Following my Cablevision/Rainbow adventure with Voom, I had been introduced by a San Diego venture capital firm and a local businessman, Fred Cary, to two Israeli engineers, Ron Gutman and Doron Segev. They were trying to start a new company based on a clever invention in the digital video field. They had devised a brilliant method of gaining more bandwidth efficiency from the digital television communications spectrum. Impressed by their concept and liking them personally, I agreed to join them as US founder and head of marketing and business development.

The venture capital industry was still reeling from the dot-com bubble, demanding nearly immediate revenues in exchange for investing, despite the fact that we were nowhere near having an initial product. But by October 2005, we finally raised an initial round of venture capital, allowing us to establish a start-up headquarters in Cardiff-by-the-Sea, just north of San Diego, with R&D remaining in Israel. We named the company Imagine Communications. Our initial focus on enabling greater bandwidth efficiency and better video quality later evolved into the vision of delivering personalized TV to every screen.

To increase its HD channel offering, Comcast needed to find a way to squeeze three MPEG-2 HDTV signals into a single 6 MHz cable channel, providing 50 percent more capacity than the current limit of two HDTV signals per cable channel. In theory, anybody could do this simply by compressing the signal more, but video quality would suffer horribly as a result. That was the catch. Comcast had to be able to accomplish this large capacity increase without sacrificing HD video quality to its subscribers. It sounded like an impossible task, since MPEG-2 was already a mature technology.

But we had some secret sauce at Imagine. Gutman and Segev had devised novel video algorithms that, amazingly, no one had yet thought of in the ten-year history of MPEG-2 digital video encoding. We developed our initial product, leading to a $30 million contract with Comcast, nirvana for a start-up. Armed with Imagine's technology, Comcast was marching toward 100 HD channels, hot on the heels of its satellite and telco TV competitors.

Seventeen years after General Instrument announced its digital TV technology breakthrough, more than a decade after the FCC adopted the Grand Alliance system, HDTV was finally achieving its mass market potential.

50 POWER TO THE CONSUMER

The initial phases of digital television enabled more channels, new competitors, and the rise of HDTV, all within the confines of scheduled broadcasting. But once the signals existed in a digital format, radically different consumer viewing behavior became possible. The technical seeds and legal underpinnings of this transformation date back to the analog television era and a crucial precedent established by the Supreme Court.

Jack Valenti cut his teeth as President Lyndon B. Johnson's special assistant and public relations mastermind in the aftermath of JFK's assassination. He became president of the Motion Picture Association of America in 1966. When Sony Corporation introduced its Betamax videocassette recorder in the mid-1970s, the reaction by the Hollywood studios was laced with vitriolic hyperbole. Led by Universal and Disney, the studios decided to sue Sony, thereby drawing a copyright line in the sand. After winding its way up from a California District Court to the Ninth Circuit Federal Appeals Court, the case landed in Chief Justice Warren Burger's US Supreme Court. *Sony Corp. of America v. Universal City Studios, Inc.*, the so-called Sony Betamax case, was first argued in January 1983, reargued in October 1983, and then ultimately decided in Sony's favor in January 1984.

Fiercely protective of the studios' control over copyright ownership, Valenti had declared to a 1982 Congressional panel:

> But now we are facing a very new and a very troubling assault on our fiscal security, on our very economic life and we are facing it from a thing called the video cassette recorder and its necessary companion called the blank tape. And it is like a great tidal wave just off the shore. This video cassette recorder and the blank tape threaten profoundly the life-sustaining protection, I guess you would call it, on which copyright owners depend, on which film people depend, on which television people depend and it is called copyright…It is a piece of sardonic irony that this asset, which unlike steel or silicon chips or motor cars or electronics of all kinds—a piece of sardonic irony that while the Japanese are unable to duplicate the American films by a flank assault, they can destroy it by this video cassette recorder…Here is Sony that tells you that you can record one channel while watching another. You can program to record a variety of shows on four different channels for up to fourteen days in advance if you like…I say to you that the VCR is to the American film producer and the American public as the Boston strangler is to the woman home alone.[1]

In 1984, the Supreme Court initially appeared to be moving toward agreeing with the Ninth Circuit's ruling that Sony was liable for contributory copyright infringement, suggesting damages and injunctive relief. But after Justices William Brennan and Sandra Day O'Connor changed their opinions, the Supreme Court ruled 5–4 in Sony's favor, reversing the Appeals Court's ruling. The majority opinion, written by Justice John Paul Stevens, determined that a home copy of a TV program for the purpose of time-shifting was not copyright infringement because it constituted "fair use" of the content. Time shifting, facilitated by the Betamax machine, was deemed a "significant non-infringing use."

Counter to Jack Valenti's alarmist rhetoric, consumers, studios, and content distributors all benefited immensely from this landmark Supreme Court case. Cleared by the judicial system, Sony did well until it made the enormous strategic mistake of failing to license its Betamax technology broadly to other consumer electronics companies. As a result, the competing, more open video cassette recorder (VCR) format came to dominate the analog TV and video market. Then, in the mid-1990s, with the standardization of MPEG-2 digital video technology, digital versatile discs (DVDs) began to supersede the ubiquitous VCR, offering digital standard definition playback and storage.

51 VOD, THE DVR, AND EVERYTHING ON DEMAND

The advent of digital TV technology had already stimulated competition among service providers, expanded content genres, and improved video quality. Now digital television was promising to revolutionize consumer viewing behavior. This sea change started at the turn of the century, with early video-on-demand (VOD) offerings from Time Warner Cable and others. In parallel, it was driven by the development of the digital video recorder (DVR) by two Silicon Valley start-ups: TiVo and ReplayTV.

Since its inception, the television business had revolved around the broadcasters' schedule of programming. "Prime time," the block of viewing hours between 8:00 p.m. and 11:00 p.m., generated the highest ratings and advertising revenue due to having the largest number of consumers tuning in. The television advertising business centered itself around the broadcast schedule, using audience-measurement techniques based on paper diaries and electronic meters in samples of homes.

The introduction of VOD and the DVR triggered a transformation away from the traditional television-viewing paradigm and toward the concept of "time shifting." With the important exceptions of live sports and news, consumers are now empowered with their own viewing schedules, able to record programs on their DVRs and watch content on-demand from the network cloud. The advertising community has been reacting, striving to devise new ways to track viewership and generate more revenue in this dynamic environment.

With cable VOD, digital content (SD and HD) is stored on servers at remote locations in the cable infrastructure. Subscribers with digital set-top boxes can access vast libraries of content on-demand: movies, premium channel series, sports, prime-time TV shows, special interest programs, and local content.

VOD comes in three general flavors:

- Free VOD: TV series episodes from networks and basic cable channels are available at no charge to digital cable subscribers. In most cases, ads are inserted into free VOD programming.

- Subscription VOD (SVOD): A growing volume of content is viewable on an SVOD basis, with no additional charge for pre-existing subscribers. SVOD includes premium services such as HBO, Showtime, and Starz. These companies provide access to SVOD libraries as a way to add value to their monthly subscriptions.

- Transactional VOD: Movies and special events are made available on a pay-per-view basis, typically with multiple views allowed within a twenty-four-hour period.

VOD got off to a slow and rocky start, a big strategic mistake by the cable industry because it allowed DirecTV and Dish Network to become more entrenched. A more aggressive and effective VOD rollout not only could have slowed the rapid growth of satellite programming, but it also would have placed cable in a much stronger position relative to the onset of Internet video services such as Netflix.

It was almost as if cable didn't want VOD to succeed. Two major hindrances were the clumsy VOD user interface and limited content availability. The VOD content library has long been partitioned from the linear cable channels, setting up an awkward process by which consumers find and access specific VOD titles. As for content availability, the cable operators were especially delinquent in placing a critical mass of HD VOD titles on their servers. Perhaps this was due to the expensive bandwidth implications: every VOD stream occupied its own chunk of precious cable spectrum, and HD streams were particularly bandwidth intensive.

Comcast strove to be an exception, positioning VOD as central to its service offering. But even its efforts were inadequate to preempt the overwhelming onslaught from the Internet. Cable operators allowed Internet content aggregators such as Vudu (acquired by Walmart) and Netflix to steal their thunder with high-definition streaming video. Another impediment was Redbox, filling the void left by Blockbuster's bankruptcy, offering convenient and cheap movies on Blu-ray and DVD, accessible at supermarkets, where consumers were already flocking.

The cable operators finally started coming around, recognizing VOD as not only a strong revenue generator but also a potent weapon against competitors. But VOD content availability, while improving, remained relatively sparse, especially in an age when consumers want to catch up on entire previous seasons of shows. The other big flaw was the user interface and program guide, the portal by which content is searched, discovered, and accessed by the subscriber. Comcast, Time Warner Cable, and Charter began introducing cloud-based Internet guides to overcome this limitation.

By putting even more control over viewing of content into the hands of consumers, the DVR was even more transformative. As with VOD, the DVR fundamentally altered the television viewing experience, bringing video storage inside consumers' homes. This capability gave subscribers unprecedented convenience, allowing them to become masters of their own viewing destiny.

TiVo and ReplayTV launched the DVR revolution in 1999. A DVR is a consumer device, often integrated with a digital cable or satellite box, containing navigational software and a hard disk drive for recording video programs in a digitally compressed format. According to Nielsen Media Research, the leader in tracking North American TV viewing habits, 49 percent of US households had at least one DVR as of 2013.

We also now have Network DVRs, a hybrid of VOD and the DVR. As with VOD, the digital video content is stored in the service provider's network cloud, accessible on-demand by the subscriber. Time Warner Cable offers two complementary Network DVR services: "Start Over" and "Look Back." With Start Over, certain programs are tagged so that digital cable subscribers can tune in after the program has begun, but while it is still being broadcast, and start the program from the beginning. With Look Back, the subscriber can watch previous episodes of the same show within a seventy-two-hour prior time window. Time Warner also ties some of these shows to its VOD library, allowing generic VOD access typically for a month after the live airing.

Cablevision pioneered a Network DVR service called "Multi-Room DVR" in the New York metropolitan area. For a monthly fee, subscribers can simultaneously record many shows, with storage occurring in Cablevision's headend servers. To view the content, the subscriber doesn't even need a home DVR, just an authorized digital cable TV box.

Cablevision's Multi-Room DVR grew out of the company's Remote Storage-DVR (RS-DVR) project, an activity with an important legal history. In 2006, a large group of content providers—20th Century Fox, Universal Studios, Paramount Pictures, Disney, CBS, ABC, and NBC—sued Cablevision, seeking an injunction to stop the RS-DVR service dead in its tracks. The plaintiffs asserted that the RS-DVR service was more like VOD than a home DVR, and therefore Cablevision needed to obtain a copyright license for each piece of content.[1]

In March 2007, a New York District Court ruled that Cablevision's RS-DVR service was violating federal copyright laws. But in August 2008, the Second Circuit Federal Appeals Court reversed the District Court's decision, ruling for Cablevision on three legal grounds. First, the copy of the content in the server was "transitory" and therefore did not meet the "duration" test for copyright infringement. Second, the playback copy was generated by the subscriber, not by Cablevision. Third, the digital transmission from Cablevision's server was to a single home, and therefore did not constitute a "public performance."

Stunned by the decision, the content providers appealed to the US Supreme Court. In January 2009, the Supreme Court asked the Office of the Solicitor General, then led by Elena Kagan, to issue a brief regarding whether Supreme Court review was merited.[2] Kagan's legal brief, recommending that the Supreme Court refuse to hear the case on appeal, was filed in May 2009. A month later, on June 29, 2009, the Supreme Court declined to take the case, effectively green-lighting Cablevision's RS-DVR service.

Dish Network's Charlie Ergen pushed the legal and technology limits to another level. In May 2012, CBS, Fox, and NBC sued Dish Network over the "AutoHop" capability enabled by its Hopper HD-DVR. AutoHop automatically records the prime-time content of the four main broadcast networks and then makes it easy for subscribers to skip the ads. Federal District Court Judge Dolly Gee denied the broadcasters' attempted injunction against the Hopper but did rule that Dish Network may be in contractual infringement of copyrights. In July 2013, the Ninth Circuit Court of Appeals declined to hear an appeal of this decision. Dish Network was not totally insensitive to the broadcasters' concerns. As part of a 2014 contract renewal agreement with Disney, Dish Network agreed to disable AutoHop access to ABC programs for three days following a show's initial broadcast.

Fox sued Dish Network again in 2013, this time because of "place shifting" as opposed to ad skipping. Its "Dish Anywhere, Hopper with Sling" technology transmits the recorded content over the Internet, allowing Dish Network subscribers to watch live and recorded TV on multiple screens, both inside and outside the home. Ergen had moved the copyright boundary even further.

As VOD, the DVR, and the Network DVR revolutionized consumer viewing behavior, these digital TV derivatives also shook up the advertising business. In 2007, Nielsen introduced its C3 system, which tabulates time-delayed viewing for three days beginning with a show's live airing.[3] C3 enlarged the measured audience, allowing broadcasters to charge for ad viewership over time. However, delayed viewing soon extended beyond the three-day window for which advertisers were paying. The next step was to measure viewing data in the four-to-seven-day window following the live broadcast. As this trend continues, content providers will eventually be compensated for advertising based on a full week of viewing (C7) and perhaps even longer.

Ad-supported content providers greatly favor cable VOD over home DVRs. With VOD (and Network DVR), the subscribers' fast-forwarding capability is typically disabled, making it more likely that the ads are being viewed. In contrast, ad skipping is straightforward with a home DVR, although a surprisingly high percentage of consumers still watch the ads.

After many years of R&D, cable operators also introduced dynamic ad insertion technology for VOD content. Instead of the same ad being seen by every viewer of a given VOD title, dynamic ad insertion enables more personalized ad placement and an incremental revenue stream. For consumer eyeballs to count in the Nielsen C3 ratings, however, the same ad must occur within the VOD stream as that which aired during the live broadcast. But after the three-day period, the cable operators and content providers can switch to a more targeted commercial via dynamic ad insertion.

Even more far-reaching than C3 and C7, Nielsen announced in 2013 its Cross-Platform Campaign Ratings solution, designed to measure viewing across the multiscreen universe. Nielsen will also measure television households that have cut the cord with their cable or satellite providers and instead watch only Internet TV. Finally, Nielsen will measure viewership on mobile devices such as tablets and smartphones, which, after all, can function as mobile HDTV sets.

Digital TV technology paved the way for VOD and the DVR, allowing a major disruption in consumer viewing behavior. But even as the legal system and the advertising business struggle to catch up, the Internet, wireless mobility, and multiscreen video are extending the boundaries to new places.

52 MotoGoogle

The strong growth of the HDTV market was a welcome boon for Motorola's digital TV equipment business in the 2000s, allowing higher prices and strong product margins for the HD-DVR boxes that were in such great demand by cable operators and their subscribers. But Motorola's cell phone business was in financial quicksand, bleeding money and losing market share with no coherent strategy to pull out of it.

Smartphones were the tech industry's new engine, sitting at the nexus of computing, consumer electronics, and mobile communications. Apple and Samsung emerged as the two dominant leaders, blindsiding and supplanting Nokia and Motorola from the prior era. Ed Zander, former president and COO of Sun Microsystems, was recruited to be CEO of Motorola in 2004, followed in 2008 by Sanjay Jha, Qualcomm's former COO. But neither of them could lift the company from its deep hole.

It was not just Apple and Samsung, but also LG, HTC, Nokia, and RIM (Blackberry) that were all fighting for market share, with Motorola hanging in the balance. There had been a brief window when Nokia and Motorola together could have created a winning applications platform based on the Symbian operating system. But the two companies were vicious competitors, and when Nokia took over the Symbian OS in 2008, Apple and Google stepped into the vacuum and seized control of the market.

Motorola's cable, satellite, and telco TV business units continued to deliver respectable financial results, although they were still subject to the whipsaws of the service providers' capital expenditure cycles. In 2006, Cisco acquired Scientific Atlanta for $6.9 billion. Thus the long-standing GI/SA duopoly had morphed into Motorola versus Cisco. Other competitors were finding success entering the market as well, including Pace, which had dusted off its old DigiCipher technology license and gained significant digital cable set-top market share.

Strategically, Motorola had become trapped inside its own set-top box, a product category with declining margins on a clear path toward commoditization. The industry's value (and profits) was shifting to software, services, and semiconductor chips. But Motorola was moving too slowly toward software and services. In addition, Motorola had exited the chip business years earlier, spinning off ON Semiconductor in 1999 and Freescale in 2003, echoing GI's previous sale of its own three semiconductor businesses.

A seminal event then occurred in 2005. Motorola's last bastion of proprietary technology, its prized conditional access, encryption, and security system, was placed into a joint venture with Comcast called CCAD (Combined Conditional Access Development). This deal gave Comcast, and by proxy the US cable industry, unprecedented control over the direction of Motorola's crown jewel, its pay TV security technology.

In January 2011, Motorola split into two separate public companies: Motorola Solutions and Motorola Mobility. Motorola Solutions contained the profitable but more mundane electronics businesses in the government and public safety sectors, such as two-way radios for police departments. Motorola Mobility, ostensibly the higher growth and more exciting company, contained the smartphone division and Motorola Home (the former GI), which focused on cable, telco, and satellite TV.[1]

The Motorola Home group, still largely driven by the GI culture, was disillusioned with the new corporate structure. Its business remained strong and reasonably profitable but was being dragged down by the cell phone unit of Motorola Mobility. A previous attempt had been made to sell the mobile phone business. But with a plummeting market share and heavy operating losses, the highest offer was embarrassingly low. Instead of shutting it down to stop the bleeding, management bundled it with

Motorola Home. The cable and satellite business was stuck with the cell phone group, weighing down the entire entity. Then, a market shock in the smartphone industry shook everything up once again.

Apple, Google, Samsung, Microsoft, and Motorola were in the midst of a wireless patent war. Steve Jobs's twin obsessions—that Samsung had stolen the iPhone design and that Google had created Android by ripping off Apple's iOS operating system—survived him. Google freely licensed Android to all comers, resulting in the Android operating system quickly gaining a much higher market share than Apple's iOS. But Google had a weak intellectual property position in this area, leaving the company and its many licensees vulnerable.

Nortel, the Canadian telco and wireless equipment giant, had filed for Chapter 11 bankruptcy in 2009 and was auctioning off its assets. In April 2011, Google bid $900 million for Nortel's wireless patent portfolio, confident it would win. But in July, a consortium of Apple, Microsoft, RIM, Sony, and Ericsson stepped in with a $4.5 billion cash offer, blowing Google's bid out of the water. Google was left empty-handed, more exposed than ever to Apple and the others.

In shopping for another patent portfolio, a logical candidate for Google was InterDigital, a pure-play wireless intellectual property powerhouse. But Google had grander ideas. Google saw, and envied, how the Apple of Steve Jobs, Jony Ive, and Tim Cook had become the world's most valuable company by tightly controlling the entire ecosystem of hardware, software, content delivery, and applications. Microsoft was also tilting more toward designing hardware devices combined with its software. Its Xbox was already a huge success, and now Microsoft was pushing forward with smartphones and was entering the tablet space with Surface. And Amazon was buttressing its dominant online retail presence with the Kindle.

Although the search advertising business was an invaluable franchise, Google thought it needed to be in the hardware business too, like its peers. In May 2012, Google closed a $12.5 billion acquisition of Motorola Mobility, getting Motorola's 17,000 patents but also swallowing its ailing smartphone business along with the healthier Motorola Home division. While the patent portfolio was the main prize, Google also believed it could emulate Apple's highly successful model of tightly bundling software and hardware.

With its $40 per share cash acquisition, Google paid a huge premium, 63 percent above Motorola Mobility's publicly traded stock price at the time of the deal. Some analysts felt Google had overpaid, but what's a few billion dollars to Google? In desperate need of a wireless patent arsenal, Google had unintentionally bailed out Motorola Mobility from its untenable situation, a high-tech deus ex machina. The perception from some at Motorola was that CEO Sanjay Jha had run circles around Google during the negotiations, convincing them that if they didn't buy the whole company, including the patents and equipment businesses, a big rival such as Microsoft would beat them to the punch.

Google had no real interest in Motorola Home, the broadband communications equipment business formerly known as GI. To the extent that Motorola had been a dysfunctional home for GI, Google was an even worse fit. Google's open Internet "information wants to be free" philosophy was diametrically opposed to Motorola Home's proud and ingrained culture of protecting content on behalf of its customers. The Motorola security engineering team in San Diego tried to offer Google help with its Google TV initiative, especially with respect to winning the trust and confidence of the content community. But the overture was dismissed. Google strove to disrupt the status quo. It would continue going "over the top" with its video strategy, effectively fighting against the gatekeepers and their walled gardens.

In July 2012, Google brought in cable operator technology executive Marwan Fawaz to position Motorola Home for sale, and thirty-year GI/Motorola veterans Dan Moloney, president of Motorola Mobility, and Geoff Roman, CTO, left the company.

53 THE WHITE KNIGHT

The ascension of Arris to the top tier of the cable equipment business is a story of ambition, persistence, and acquisitions. Arris traces its heritage to two early cable equipment companies: Anixter Brothers and Antec. Anixter Brothers emerged in 1957 as an electrical wire and cable distributor. Its president, John Egan, formed Antec in 1991 as a cable equipment distributor, reselling GI products to the cable operators.

After Egan took Antec public in 1993, the company went on an acquisitions spree, transforming itself from distributor to manufacturer. Egan also entered into a partnership with AT&T's equipment business, where a unit led by Bob Stanzione had developed an analog AM fiber optic system for cable operators, a precursor to today's Hybrid Fiber Coax cable architecture.

In 1995, Antec and Nortel, the now-bankrupt Canadian telecom equipment giant, created a joint venture called Arris Interactive to develop voice and data products for the cable industry. Bob Stanzione was recruited from AT&T to be the CEO of the joint venture, owned 75 percent by Nortel and 25 percent by Antec. A few years later, Stanzione became Antec's president and COO.

Separately, Nortel acquired data networking company Bay Networks in 1998 for $9 billion. A couple of years earlier, Bay Networks had purchased LANcity, a cable modem pioneer, for $59 million. Nortel then traded its LANcity cable modem division to Arris Interactive, increasing Nortel's ownership of the joint venture to 81 percent.

Three years later, in 2001, a new company called Arris Group was formed, serving as a vehicle for Antec to acquire the majority interest of Arris Interactive from Nortel. The surviving company was called Arris, and Stanzione succeeded Egan as CEO. Foreshadowing bigger deals ahead, in 2007 Arris paid $730 million to acquire C-Cor, a cable equipment company focused on distribution electronics and nCUBE VOD servers.[1]

Earlier in 2007, Arris had been outbid by Ericsson in a $1.2 billion attempt to buy Tandberg Television. Tandberg, along with Harmonic and Motorola, was a market leader in developing digital video encoders sold to content companies and service providers, driving their digital television services. Tandberg also had a strong position in VOD infrastructure software.

Arris was stung by the loss of Tandberg to Ericsson, and it stuck in Arris's mind as it developed its digital TV product strategy. During the next few years, Arris bought a series of small digital video companies at bargain prices.[2] Even with this string of video-related acquisitions, Arris's strength remained in the data and voice segments of the cable equipment market. It was still a minor player in the digital TV domain compared to Motorola and Cisco.

To complete its triple play of data, voice, and video, to really make it to the big leagues of the cable equipment business, Arris knew it still had a huge gap to fill. So when Google quietly started shopping Motorola Home to potential buyers, it was time for Arris to make its big move.

This time, if Arris was going to succeed in buying the biggest fish of all, the former GI, still the market leader in digital set-tops, digital video infrastructure equipment, and cable modems, it had to bid to win. Pace, Technicolor, and Huawei were also interested in Motorola Home. But in December 2012, Arris emerged as the winner, agreeing to a $2.3 billion price consisting of $2 billion in cash and the rest in stock. Comcast, anxious to ensure that Motorola, its top equipment supplier, landed in friendly hands, played the role of background facilitator and agreed to invest $150 million for nearly 8 percent of Arris. In April 2013, the Justice Department approved the transaction, tripling Arris's size overnight.

It was clearly a transformative acquisition for Arris. But from the perspective of Motorola Home, it was an anti-climactic escape from a dysfunctional situation with Google. Fifteen years earlier, in December 1997, GI's New York Stock Exchange market capitalization was $2.2 billion. The company's value skyrocketed to $17 billion upon the January 2000 acquisition by Motorola. With the Arris deal, the value had fallen all the way back down to the pre-megadeal level in nominal dollars, and significantly lower after factoring in fifteen years of inflation. It was an outcome far removed from Hal Krisbergh's vision of leveraging GI's central position in the digital television revolution into becoming one of the world's most important companies. And it was a distant cry from former CEO Dan Akerson's goal of growing GI to be as big as Microsoft.

Such a dramatic rise and fall in value is not uncommon in the dynamic and volatile technology business, and Motorola's acquisition of GI did occur during the height of the Internet bubble. But blaming the bubble doesn't tell the underlying story.

Using digital TV as its growth engine, GI successfully reinvented itself from being a diversified 1980s technology conglomerate to becoming the broadband communications juggernaut of the 1990s. But when the digital TV and broadband Internet markets splintered into various segments, the company failed to reinvent itself anew. A fundamental value transfer occurred in the industry, shifting away from set-top boxes toward chips, software, and services. It's analogous to what happened in the PC industry, with Microsoft software and Intel chips capturing value from the PC hardware companies. The digital set-top box just took a much longer and slower path toward commoditization.

Semiconductor company Broadcom received its first big break with the GI digital cable set-top deal in 1996, when GI's internal VLSI chip design group was traded away to Broadcom for a chunk of Broadcom's pre-IPO shares. Now Broadcom is worth far more than the combination of Arris/Motorola. GI's earlier semiconductor spin-off, Microchip Technology, is even valued much more highly than Arris. Qualcomm, which grew out of the same Linkabit digital communications heritage as GI San Diego, has a market cap well in excess of $100 billion. It got there by continuous leadership and innovation in communications technology, with a business model focused on intellectual property and chips. Another company that climbed the ecosystem value chain quite successfully was NDS, GI's historic rival in pay TV security systems. Cisco acquired NDS for $5 billion in July 2012, enhancing the former's video business with the latter's leadership in content security and set-top software.

GI's precipitous descent, however, was more complex and insidious than simply missing the value transfer to software, chips, and services. Dating back to its 1990 leveraged buyout by Forstmann Little, GI management was driven heavily by Wall Street. Decision making tilted toward transactions and management cash-outs at the expense of building a coherent strategy and long-term value. The digital television breakthrough was a colossal innovation, guided by a strategic and comprehensive systems approach to the market. But after capturing the market, GI's corporate sales culture prevailed and its San Diego innovation legacy became subjugated. Moreover, after becoming part of Motorola in 2000, GI became stranded inside a much bigger company that lost its way. Management discontinuity was yet another debilitating factor, especially in San Diego. Finally, while being captive to Comcast, Verizon, and a few other big customers was profitable, it was not a recipe for reinventing the company.

The cable duopoly had shifted over the years: from GI/SA to Motorola/Cisco and finally to Arris/Cisco. At the same time, the cable industry is more wide open than ever, with a range of other companies —Pace, Technicolor, Harmonic, SeaChange, Rovi, NDS, CommScope, RGB, ActiveVideo, BlackArrow, Imagine,[3] Elemental, and others—all vying for a piece of the action.

Perhaps Arris got another bargain with its purchase of Motorola Home. The business Arris acquired was essentially General Instrument as it had evolved during its thirteen years of ownership by Motorola and, briefly, Google. With its laser focus on the broadband communication business, Arris is certainly a better strategic fit for GI.

Cisco appears to be de-emphasizing its consumer video products business, and Arris stands to gain market share as the cable operators migrate toward an Internet-based video system, with sophisticated home video gateways feeding simple IP set-tops throughout the home. Arris may also gain share in the cable headend Internet infrastructure business, and it has obtained a strong foothold in the telco TV market, attributable to Motorola's success with Verizon FiOS, AT&T U-Verse, and many international telco TV providers.

By acquiring Motorola Home, Arris finally arrived at the epicenter of the broadband communications business. The company will play a pivotal role as its customer base of service providers shifts from managing independent silos of video, data, and voice toward providing integrated bundles of Internet-based services.

But inside the home, incumbent service providers and independent Internet video companies will compete for subscriber control by continuously addressing new technological dynamics and consumer behavior. Technology firms with rapid product innovation cycles and aggressive pricing will challenge Arris to break out of its historic role as a captive supplier to cable operators and to discover its innovative soul.

PART FOUR

WHERE ARE WE AND WHERE ARE WE GOING?

54 DIGITAL PLANET

Digital television has migrated from satellite to cable and from over-the-air terrestrial broadcast to the Internet. It is ubiquitous throughout North America and the world. Globally, more than 400 million homes receive digital TV signals via cable, satellite, or telco landline (IPTV), and over 1 billion mobile devices are capable of receiving video from wireless data networks. To be more specific:

- Over 100 million US homes now receive digital TV signals. At the end of September 2014, there were approximately 50 million digital cable homes, 34 million digital satellite homes, 12 million digital telco TV homes, and 7 million free digital over-the-air homes in the United States. There are also still about 4 million analog cable homes. Nearly 90 percent of US television households have at least one digital HDTV set and half the country's TV households have a digital video recorder.

- Canada transitioned most of its terrestrial broadcast infrastructure to digital by 2011. Canadian digital satellite and cable service providers Rogers, Shaw, Videotron, and Bell Canada battle it out for subscription TV market share.

- Digital TV is prevalent in Asian countries such as Indonesia, South Korea, Taiwan, Vietnam, and Thailand. Japan's leaders are Sky PerfecTV and Wowow (digital satellite), NHK (digital satellite and terrestrial broadcast), and J:Com (digital cable). Digital satellite is the rage in India, with several competitors including Dish TV, Tata Sky, and Sun Direct, and the country's urban cable infrastructure is also switching over from analog to digital. China reported over 140 million digital cable subscribers in 2013 and numerous digital satellite TV services are also delivered.

- Digital satellite TV is widespread in Russia, which also has digital cable and digital terrestrial broadcast infrastructure.

- Australia has Austar Digital satellite and Optus Digital cable, and Foxtel offers digital TV services over both satellite and cable. Aussies can also receive Freeview digital terrestrial signals and free VAST digital satellite service in remote, rural areas. Consumers in New Zealand have Sky digital satellite, Vodafone digital cable, and Freeview digital terrestrial service.

- DigiTurk and two competitors offer digital satellite TV in Turkey, and the country's entire terrestrial broadcast infrastructure is switching over to digital by 2015.

- Each country in Europe has its own mix of satellite, cable, IPTV, and free-to-air digital "bouquets," and HDTV is in full bloom with several dozen channels in many countries. According to pan-

European media company RTL Group, 87 percent of the households in European Union countries received digital signals in 2013. Direct-to-home satellite was the most popular method, followed by digital terrestrial broadcast, digital cable, and telco IPTV. Moreover, Europe is finally catching up to the United States in HDTV penetration, with 77 percent of homes having HDTV sets.

- DirecTV Latin America reported 12.3 million digital satellite subscribers as of September 30, 2014. Sky Mexico, of which DirecTV Latin America owns 41 percent, had an additional 6.5 million subscribers. There are also more than 10 million digital cable subscribers in the region, and most Latin American countries are broadcasting multiple, free digital terrestrial TV signals.

- In Sub-Saharan Africa, there are more than 25 million digital satellite and digital terrestrial (over-the-air) TV homes in 10 countries, and the total is expected to approach 70 million by 2020.[1]

- For a sure sign that digital television has indeed circled the planet, consider that in September 2014, Afghanistan commenced digital terrestrial TV broadcasting.

Digital TV, in its various formats and delivery methodologies, has moved front and center throughout the United States and most of the world. It will expand even more rapidly with the development of Internet video. Cisco's 2013 Visual Networking Index, which annually projects statistical trends in global Internet traffic, includes some astounding data. Worldwide, out of a global population exceeding 7 billion, there will be nearly 2 billion Internet video users (excluding mobile-only) by 2017, up from 1 billion in 2012. In addition, video traffic will be 69 percent of total worldwide consumer Internet traffic in 2017, up from 57 percent in 2012.

So how are consumers benefiting from this extensive digitization of the video communications spectrum?

- Market forces in most regions have ushered in a wide variety of digital technology and services. The initial effect was an increase in content choice, driven in part by digital SDTV's efficient use of bandwidth.

- New video service providers entered the market, unleashing greater competition.

- Digital HDTV brought dramatically enhanced picture quality.

- Video-on-demand and DVRs revolutionized viewing convenience and behavior.

- The broadband Internet, the most topsy-turvy agent of all, threatens to disrupt pre-existing business models and spur changes throughout society: from entertainment to education, the arts, medicine, and law enforcement and security.

Chuck Dolan articulated the consumer benefits of digital TV technology back in 2000:

> The limitless capacity of digital technology should lead to the development of even greater and more robust competition among program and service providers—competition not for access but for customer enthusiasm... Digital technology helps us to enable customers to take what they choose and reject that which they do not want. Finally, customers will be the selectors—not the cable company, not the program suppliers, and not the government.[2]

55   DIGITAL DIVIDENDS: MORE CONTENT, BETTER QUALITY, AND GREATER COMPETITION

Despite the growing pains, video choices in North America and elsewhere are indeed expanding exponentially, covering every imaginable genre and niche. We have unprecedented access to sports, movies, news, and entertainment. Digital technology has enabled content to be sliced and diced with topics focusing on food, history, travel, science, children, women, men, religion, ethnicity, military, horror, shopping, music, and reality TV. There's even DogTV, a channel for dogs created by pet experts, available on DirecTV and via Internet streaming. And in an age where literally anyone with a smartphone or tablet can be a digital video publisher, there is an infinite variety of impromptu user-generated videos, some of which spread across the planet like electronic wildfire.

The trend toward more targeted programming is also occurring in the free, over-the-air digital broadcast market. Bounce TV, whose founders include Martin Luther King III and former U.N. Ambassador Andrew Young, delivers content oriented toward the African-American audience. The service is delivered by embedding its SDTV signal into the multichannel digital transmissions of over-the-air TV stations owned by local stations and station groups such as Gannett, Nextstar, and Raycom. In Los Angeles, Spanish-language broadcaster KJLA delivers eight additional digital SDTV over-the-air Vietnamese channels and one in Mandarin.

Fortunately, it's not just content quantity but also programming quality that has become nothing short of astonishing. A larger market and enhanced competition led to a bigger investment pool. The increased funding feeds enormous television production budgets, attracting unprecedented talent and inspiring unbridled creativity. This virtuous circle has brought us to a new golden age of television. We have content for the masses and content for the smallest of groups. We have enjoyed the creations of David Chase (*The Sopranos*), Ken Burns (*Baseball, Jazz,*

The Roosevelts), David Simon (*The Wire, Treme*), Matthew Weiner (*Mad Men*), Vince Gilligan (*Breaking Bad*), David Fincher (*House of Cards*), Jenji Kohan (*Weeds, Orange Is the New Black*), and Julian Fellowes (*Downton Abbey*). And that's just the tip of the iceberg.

Many top actors have embraced the medium of television, often rotating adeptly among film, theater, and TV. Halle Berry, Kenneth Branagh, Glenn Close, Bryan Cranston, Alan Cumming, Jeff Daniels, Robert DeNiro, Michelle Dockery, Jane Fonda, James Gandolfini, Maggie Gyllenhaal, Jon Hamm, Woody Harrelson, Jeremy Irons, Derek Jacobi, Jessica Lange, John Lithgow, William H. Macy, John Malkovich, Matthew McConaughey, Frances McDormand, Ian McKellen, Helen Mirren, Al Pacino, Mary-Louise Parker, Mandy Patinkin, Julia Roberts, Liev Schreiber, Maggie Smith, Kevin Spacey, Billy Bob Thornton, Lily Tomlin, Jon Voight, Kerry Washington, Robin Wright, and many more are gracing our TV sets.

John Malone's 500-channel metaphor has become a reality—and then some. There are thousands of on-demand titles on cable VOD plus billions of streams across the Internet.

Not only has digital TV expanded content variety and quality, but it has also enabled the emergence of more video service providers. Competition in the domestic subscription TV industry was virtually non-existent until the mid-1990s, when digital technology made possible the small-dish satellite TV market, ending the North American cable monopoly. Today, most US households have a choice of three or four multi-channel video service providers.

Nielsen estimates 116.3 million television households in the United States for the 2014/2015 season. Of this total, there are roughly 100 million multi-channel video subscribers. In 1993, before the consumer digital TV transformation began, cable had 95 percent US market share. Twenty years later, by September 30, 2014, the market share split for pay

TV subscribers had changed dramatically: 54 percent cable, 34 percent DBS satellite, and 12 percent telco TV.

The following table shows the top ten US multi-channel video service providers and the number of their subscribers as of September 30, 2014. Data is from public company reports; for privately held companies (Cox and Bright House), estimates are adjusted from SNL Kagan research.

Service Provider	US Video Subscribers (as of September 30, 2014)
Comcast	22.4 million
DirecTV	20.2 million
Dish Network	14.0 million
Time Warner Cable	10.8 million
AT&T	6.0 million
Verizon	5.5 million
Cox	4.3 million
Charter	4.2 million
Cablevision	2.7 million
Bright House	2.0 million
Total Top Ten	92.1 million

Note that two of the top ten in 2014 did not exist until the mid-1990s (DirecTV and Dish Network) and another two did not emerge until the mid-2000s (Verizon FiOS and AT&T U-Verse). These later entrants owe their very existence to digital TV technology,[1] as do virtually all new video service providers around the globe, whether they deliver over satellite, cable, or the Internet.

The meteoric rise of DirecTV and Dish Network, from 0 to 34 million subscribers in less than 20 years, is far beyond what market analysts predicted back in the 1980s and 1990s. Their phenomenal success can be attributed to consumers' thirst for an alternative to cable, better customer service, and product differentiation. For example, Dish Network has combined its price leadership with a broad offering of ethnic programming. DirecTV has moved beyond its stranglehold on the "NFL Sunday Ticket" package, offering its subscribers unique content such as the critically acclaimed series *Damages*, starring Glenn Close, *Friday Night Lights*, which aired first on DirecTV before showing on NBC and ESPN, and the crime drama *Rogue*.

The competitive scene is complicated by industry consolidation, which is an important recurring trend. Comcast, Verizon, and AT&T are nearly certain to survive intact due to their diverse revenue base and overall size and scale. Comcast is planning to buy Time Warner Cable and AT&T is purchasing Dish Network, while John Malone is using Charter as a cable acquisitions vehicle. Whether Cox, Cablevision, and Bright House remain independent will depend ultimately on private family decisions. Assuming Comcast acquires Time Warner Cable and AT&T acquires DirecTV, new Comcast spin-off GreatLand Connections would become number eight with 2.5 million subscribers ("subs") and Suddenlink would move up to number ten with its 1.1 million subs.

The broadband Internet has now emerged as the fifth platform for digital video, following distribution over satellite, cable, broadcast, and telco facilities. It promises to be the biggest of all, with explosive growth and global connectivity.

Especially with the rise of the broadband Internet, the situation has become something of a free-for-all, creating opportunities for those who can provide good service, differentiate their products, and create order from chaos. This heightened competition will act as a check-and-balance against even higher prices, partially offsetting the escalation of content licensing fees. It will also allow greater differentiation in content and program packaging. As much as we like to complain, there is nothing like competition to drive improvements in customer service.

56 Today's Media Kingpins

It's been more than a quarter-century since GI formalized its original digital TV project in the fall of 1989. We're over twenty years into the consumer digital television age, marked by the 1994 launches of Prime-Star and DirecTV. Our media titans have capitalized on an array of technologies, building their empires into global forces. Yet while some of these corporations continually expand, others split apart and refocus in a dynamic, perpetual accordion of content and distribution.

The global TV/video service market exceeded $220 billion revenue in 2013 according to Infonetics Research, which projects an increase to $260 billion by 2017. In the United States, by far the largest single market, Infonetics estimated 2013 revenue to be $158 billion, roughly half from subscription fees and the other half from advertising. Of this total, 95 percent came from traditional TV with the remaining 5 percent coming from online video.[1] But the landscape and revenue mix is tilting gradually and inexorably toward the Internet.

A brave new generation of entrepreneurs and video service providers is vying against the mainstay incumbents in a quest to capture a larger slice of a growing pie, even as the media establishment itself embraces the Internet. Each incumbent has charted its own course, driven by a unique combination of passion, instinct, and shareholder value.

56.1 COMCAST

Brian Roberts has transformed Comcast into a $68 billion (2014 revenue) behemoth, building his dad's Philadelphia-based company into the modern, massive-scale model for ownership of content, distribution, and technology.

Comcast became the largest cable operator in 2002 by acquiring AT&T Broadband. In 2004, unfulfilled by Comcast's content portfolio of E!, The Golf Channel, and a smattering of sports assets, Roberts made a $54 billion hostile bid for Disney. Disney's board rejected the offer, however, and Comcast's stock price declined, forcing an end to the deal.

But Roberts remained steadfast in his pursuit of quality content. Seven years later, in 2011, Comcast purchased a 51 percent controlling interest in NBCUniversal from GE for $13.5 billion. Then, in 2013, Comcast acquired GE's remaining 49 percent interest for $16.7 billion, installing Steve Burke as CEO of wholly owned subsidiary NBCUniversal. The king of cable had married a queen of content.

By absorbing NBCUniversal, Comcast gained sole control of 15 national cable networks (including USA, CNBC, MSNBC, Syfy, E!, Bravo, The Golf Channel, and NBC Sports Network), 11 regional sports and news channels, and various international channels. The company also owns the NBC broadcast network, along with 10 local NBC affiliate TV stations, plus the Telemundo Spanish-language network and 15 TV stations. Universal Pictures, and the Universal theme parks in Orlando and Hollywood, round out an astonishing portfolio.

In February 2014, Comcast made a $45 billion offer for Time Warner Cable, blindsiding rival Charter's initial offer of $37 billion just as Charter, with John Malone behind the scenes, was proposing to replace Time Warner Cable's board with thirteen of its own directors.[2] Time Warner Cable, with 2014 revenue of nearly $23 billion, had become vulnerable by losing more than 800,000 video subscribers the prior year, in part due to its acrimonious summer standoff with CBS over retransmission fees. Assuming regulatory approval of its deal, anticipated in 2015, Comcast will end up with nearly 30 million domestic video subscribers, and a similar number of broadband Internet subscribers. Comcast will also be taking possession of Time Warner Cable's various local news and sports channels, including SportsNet LA (also known as The Dodgers Channel).

Since Comcast's and Time Warner's cable footprints don't overlap, the FCC and the Justice Department are more likely to impose strict conditions on Comcast than to block the deal outright. The quid pro quo will focus on fair and reasonable carriage of other companies' content over Comcast's TV and Internet pipes.

Comcast intends to sell 1.4 million of the Time Warner subscribers to Charter and spin off another 2.5 million subscribers in a new public company, GreatLand Connections, to be run by Michael Willner, Insight Communications' former CEO. These transactions would bring the combined entity's market share of multi-channel TV subscribers below 30 percent and its share of broadband Internet subscribers (including DSL) to around 35 percent. This gesture is clearly intended to smooth the government approval process, as a previous federal court case rejected the FCC rule imposing the 30 percent cap.[3]

Whether this acquisition will benefit consumers remains an open question. Operating on an even bigger national scale could accelerate advanced technology rollouts and mitigate higher content prices due to increased negotiating leverage. But smaller TV channels will be at the mercy of Comcast more than ever before. While the combination should be very good for a select number of equipment suppliers, especially Arris, new tech companies won't have much of a chance in the domestic cable industry without Comcast's endorsement. Most importantly, Comcast's market share of broadband Internet service is a factor the FCC will zero in on with respect to its goal of maintaining an open Internet.

Central to Comcast's corporate strategy is a strong emphasis on technology. Chief Technology Officer Tony Werner and Chief Network Officer John Schanz are charged with powering a suite of digital services into subscribers' homes. The result is a highly successful "triple play" of video, data, and voice services, with 55 million monthly revenue-generating subscription units from more than 26 million US households. Virtually all of the company's TV subscribers are digital, and well over half of these homes have HD and/or DVR capability.

Comcast Wholesale (formerly the Comcast Media Center), near Denver, provides national delivery of high definition (and standard definition) content, enabling local Comcast systems to provide over 100 HD channels. The company has rolled out DOCSIS 3.0 technology nationwide, enabling some of the industry's fastest Internet speeds, even as CableLabs issued the DOCSIS 3.1 specs in late 2013, allowing the future possibility of 10 Gbps downstream and 1 Gbps upstream. It is important to keep in mind, however, that the DOCSIS cable architecture is a shared Internet pipe, so individual household speeds depend on how many homes are in a service group or node.

Comcast has been the most aggressive and successful cable operator with video-on-demand, providing tens of thousands of VOD choices to its digital cable subscribers while also offering a large content library for Internet streaming to computers and mobile devices. Subscribers can download the Xfinity TV Go app from iTunes or Google Play, enabling viewing of content both inside and outside the home through WiFi and 4G networks. This app supports streaming video and downloads, and allows dozens of live TV channels including many of the most popular cable brands.

Comcast's Streampix Internet video service, designed to compete against Netflix and Amazon, offers movies and TV shows to subscribers for viewing on smart TVs, PCs, tablets, and smartphones.

X1 is Comcast's most forward-looking digital TV consumer platform, a new class of service with a cloud-based guide and a modern user interface linking to social media and other customized apps. With new software releases, the guide is becoming more personalized, featuring a remote with voice control, an advanced content search and recommendation engine, multiscreen access, and cloud-based storage. Comcast's "Cloud DVR" is a Network DVR service allowing subscribers to store content in data centers, while also enabling in-home streaming of the company's entire line-up of linear (scheduled) subscription channels. Comcast X1 subscribers can tap into the Cloud DVR platform to watch content on their mobile devices.

Comcast is also leading a next-generation technology architecture activity for set-top boxes and home gateways using open-source software and a reference design kit for product developers. Comcast, Time Warner Cable, and Liberty Global formed a joint venture company (RDK Management LLC) to co-manage this activity. Other participating cable operators include J:Com (Japan) and Kabel Deutschland (Germany), giving the cable industry a potential opportunity to create a vibrant, global, multiscreen TV apps environment.

56.2 TIME WARNER

Jeff Bewkes, previously the head of HBO, became Time Warner's CEO in 2008. In striking contrast to Comcast, Bewkes moved Time Warner in the other direction, effectively dismantling its corporate marriage of content and distribution. This leaves unanswered the question of whether it makes economic sense to have both categories under one umbrella.

In March 2009, Time Warner completed its spin-off of Time Warner Cable into a separately traded public company, followed by the AOL spin-off in December 2009. Its venerable magazine business, Time Inc. (including *Time* magazine, *People*, and *Sports Illustrated*) was spun off in June 2014 into another public company. The new Time Inc. purchased an equity stake in 120 Sports, an upstart Internet video network featuring highlights of professional and college sports. Major League Baseball Advanced Media and the National Hockey League are also equity investors.

These spin-offs leave Time Warner Inc. as a pure-play content company holding the crown jewels of Home Box Office, Turner Broadcasting, and Warner Brothers. Home Box Office comprises both HBO and Cinemax, while channel brands falling under Turner Broadcasting include TNT,

TBS, CNN, HLN, Cartoon Network, Turner Classic Movies, Adult Swim, and truTV.

More than any other single channel, HBO has elevated the home entertainment experience. The company has set a very high bar for TV content, lifting production quality at its premium service competitors, on basic cable channels, and even on network television. Highly profitable and often the first to embrace new technology, HBO pushes the boundaries of television. Its immeasurable contribution to the pay TV business is captured in its pithy tag line: "It's not TV. It's HBO."

From *The Sopranos*, *The Wire*, and *Six Feet Under* to *The Newsroom*, *Boardwalk Empire*, and *Game of Thrones*, HBO's multi-season series continue to captivate audiences. Its comedies—*Curb Your Enthusiasm*, *Entourage*, *Veep*, *Real Time with Bill Maher*, and *Silicon Valley*—capture our zeitgeist and keep us laughing. *Sex and the City* and *Girls* coincided with, and perhaps even influenced, new waves of feminism. HBO's miniseries—*Angels in America*, *Band of Brothers*, *The Pacific*, and *John Adams*—have incisively portrayed our history and culture. *HBO Sports* is essential to the sport of boxing, and HBO's documentaries often rival those of PBS.

HBO was late to the Internet TV party, but its HBO Go (TV Everywhere) service has become quite popular as a no-charge addition to an HBO subscription. Sister company Warner Brothers offers an online service, Warner Archive Instant, for a monthly fee. Classic movie and TV shows are available to computers from Warner's own website and to TV sets as a Roku channel.

In a manic merger environment, Time Warner's focus on content leaves it vulnerable to acquisition. Murdoch's 21st Century Fox tried to buy Time Warner for $80 billion in July 2014. Time Warner rebuffed the overture, claiming the price was much too low, and Murdoch withdrew his offer the next month. At some point, Time Warner must decide whether it wants to get bigger again or get bought.

56.3 DISNEY

The Walt Disney Company has mostly stayed true to its content roots, along with its signature theme parks and consumer products businesses. Bob Iger became CEO in 2005, succeeding Michael Eisner. Iger came to the Disney family through the company's 1996 acquisition of Capital Cities/ABC, where he was president. Iger built upon The Walt Disney Studios' movie heritage by acquiring Pixar for $7.4 billion in 2006 (making Steve Jobs Disney's largest individual shareholder), Marvel Entertainment for $4.6 billion in 2009, and Lucasfilm for $4 billion in 2012.

ESPN and Disney/ABC Television Group are the two major entities rolling into Disney Media Networks. The ESPN unit includes 8 domestic channels, 5 of which are HD, plus nearly 50 international networks. The Disney/ABC unit comprises the ABC Television studios, network, and stations; ABC Family; Disney Channels Worldwide; and the company's equity stake in A&E Television Networks (including A&E, Lifetime, History, LMN, and FYI). Disney Channels Worldwide is a global portfolio of more than 100 kid-oriented channels.

As with its peers, digital technology has been fundamental to the growth of ESPN and Disney. Chuck Pagano has been ESPN's executive vice president of operations and chief technology officer (although he will be retiring in 2015). Vince Roberts has the equivalent title and role at Disney.

In 2004, the year after the launch of ESPN HD, Pagano opened the ESPN Digital Center in Bristol, Connecticut, one of the industry's most advanced television production facilities, with four digital HD studios. A decade later, ESPN opened Digital Center 2, the futuristic new home for its flagship program, SportsCenter. Pagano also spearheaded the 2009 opening of ESPN's Los Angeles Digital Production Center. For these accomplishments and many others, Pagano was inducted into the Broadcasting & Cable Hall of Fame in 2012 and to the Sports Broadcasting Hall of Fame in 2013.

The company has numerous TV Everywhere multiscreen applications, including the hugely successful WatchESPN app. Disney further accelerated its move toward the Internet by purchasing Maker Studios in 2014 for $500 million, a price that could increase to $950 million if certain performance targets are achieved. This acquisition places Disney at the center of the short-form online video business, as Maker Studios is one of the largest content suppliers to YouTube.

The company also launched Disney Movies Anywhere in 2014. From this Internet portal, consumers can purchase movies from the Disney, Pixar, or Marvel studios. The titles then populate iTunes or Google Play for perpetual access from Internet-connected devices.

56.4 VIACOM AND CBS

Sumner Redstone burnished his media crown once again in 2006 when Viacom subsidiary Paramount Pictures spent $1.6 billion to acquire DreamWorks SKG from Steven Spielberg, Jeffrey Katzenberg, and David Geffen. In the same time frame, Redstone spun off CBS into a separately traded public company. He remains as chairman and controlling shareholder of both Viacom Inc. and the new CBS Corporation.

With Redstone now in his nineties, Viacom is run day-to-day by his longtime confidant Philippe Dauman. Viacom's portfolio includes Paramount Pictures, MTV, Nickelodeon, Comedy Central, VH1, and BET. It owns over 160 channels globally. In a further shift toward international markets, in 2014 Viacom announced the $757 million acquisition of Channel 5 Broadcasting, the fifth of five British public broadcasters. "Five," as it is known in England, has an equity stake in Top Up TV, a digital terrestrial broadcast pay TV service offered on top of Freeview; Freeview, a joint venture between the BBC, ITV, Channel 4, BSkyB, and Arqiva, is the aggregation of 50 SDTV and 12 HDTV free-to-air digital terrestrial broadcast TV services in the United Kingdom. Five also owns digital TV channels 5* and 5USA, both carried by BSkyB and Virgin Media.

Les Moonves is the CEO of CBS Corporation. Its holdings include Showtime, The Movie Channel, Flix, CBS Sports, CBS Television Network, and The CW network (in a joint venture with Warner Brothers).

Matt Blank, chairman and CEO of Showtime Networks, was originally hired into HBO by Jerry Levin in 1976. Blank departed twelve years later for Showtime, where he has greatly enhanced its branding and content portfolio, along with subscription revenues, closing the gap with long-time rival HBO. Like HBO, Showtime offers series, movies, documentaries, comedy, and boxing events. The Showtime brand has become synonymous with subversive, edgy shows such as *Homeland, Dexter, Weeds, Californication, Shameless, Ray Donovan*, and *Masters of Sex*.[4]

56.5 21ST CENTURY FOX AND NEWS CORPORATION

Rupert Murdoch has ventured thousands of miles and billions of dollars from his father's Australian newspaper business. His long-time dream of owning a US DBS satellite TV service was finally attained in December 2003 when News Corporation bought a controlling interest in Hughes Electronics from General Motors for $6.6 billion. GM had originally acquired Hughes in 1985, nearly a decade before the launch of DirecTV. After divesting Hughes to News Corporation, the new company was named The DirecTV Group.

But Murdoch's US DBS dream was short-lived. Only three years later, in December 2006, Murdoch announced his intent to exchange News Corporation's 38.5 percent controlling interest in The DirecTV Group, along with three regional Fox Sports channels plus cash, to John Malone's Liberty Media in exchange for most of Liberty's 19 percent ownership in News Corporation. Murdoch wanted Malone out of his family business and was willing to relinquish his DirecTV stake to make it happen.

While Murdoch and Malone had done many deals together over

the years, the circumstances precipitating the DirecTV transaction is a convoluted story in and of itself. It traces back to each man's involvement in the TV program guide business. In 1988, Murdoch acquired Walter Annenberg's Triangle Publications, owner of *TV Guide* magazine, for nearly $3 billion. Nine years later, Gemstar, a California-based VCR software company, purchased electronic program guide pioneer StarSight Telecast for $255 million. But GI's digital cable boxes contained the competing Prevue Interactive program guide, developed by TCI subsidiary United Video Satellite Group. In 1999, TCI's United Video acquired TV Guide from Murdoch for $2 billion, and rebranded its digital TV navigation software as TV Guide On Screen. Later that year, Gemstar purchased United Video/TV Guide, resulting in both Malone and Murdoch owning stakes in the combined company, Gemstar-TV Guide International.

The following year the two structured a transaction whereby Malone traded his shares in Gemstar-TV Guide to Murdoch for an equity stake in News Corporation. Murdoch then installed Fox cable programming president Jeff Shell as Gemstar's CEO.[5] The end result was that Murdoch became the largest shareholder in Gemstar-TV Guide, while Malone became the largest shareholder, outside the Murdoch family, in News Corporation. These News Corporation shares are the ones Malone used to his benefit several years later; in 2008, following FCC approval, Malone exchanged most of these shares for Murdoch's controlling interest in DirecTV.

News Corporation split into two companies in 2013, in the aftermath of the phone hacking scandal in England that led to the demise of Murdoch's News of the World. The entertainment business was renamed 21st Century Fox. The newspaper publishing business was spun off into a new News Corporation.

Numerous news, sports, and entertainment TV channels in the

United States are owned by 21st Century Fox, including Fox News, Fox Sports, and FX; the 20th Century Fox Film and Television arms; and the Fox Broadcasting network, plus 27 local TV stations in various markets.

It took many years for Roger Ailes to build Fox News into the market share leader in domestic cable news. Now Murdoch is preparing to make the final push in a head-to-head confrontation with ESPN in national sports programming. Over the years, Fox accumulated a portfolio of more than 20 regional sports networks, many of which were joint ventures with Chuck Dolan's Rainbow Media. Given ESPN's market dominance, a truly competitive national sports network has been elusive. But Murdoch will not give up. In August 2013 he launched Fox Sports 1, superseding Speed, his motorsports channel. At the same time, he replaced Fuel TV, his extreme sports channel, with Fox Sports 2.

Starting with raw police drama *The Shield*, the FX channel has become a mainstay of basic cable, assembling a diverse repertoire of critically acclaimed productions. *Fargo*, based on the Coen Brothers' dark comedy film, is an outrageously quirky, twisted series starring a sociopathic Billy Bob Thornton on the icy edge of the Midwest. *The Americans* is a taut, polished spy thriller, featuring a KGB couple embedded as an American family in the suburban shadows of Washington DC during the final years of the Cold War. *Sons of Anarchy* brings Shakespearean dimensions to a California motorcycle gang plagued by brutal violence and a bizarre code of honor. Anthology series *American Horror Story*, starring Jessica Lange, consistently gets high ratings. On the lighter side is *Louie*, created by and starring comedian extraordinaire Louis C.K.

With FX targeted at 18-to-49-year-olds, and the FXM movie channel catering to the 25-to-54 demographic, Murdoch launched a third channel, FXX. All three channels fall under the FX Networks umbrella. The comedy-oriented FXX, designed for young adults, received its initial boost in November 2013 when it acquired exclusive broadcast syndication, video-on-demand, and Internet rights to the 25 seasons (552 episodes) of *The Simpsons*.

In Europe, 21st Century Fox owns many channels of content pumped through a powerful distribution network to approximately 20 million digital satellite TV subscribers in the United Kingdom, Italy, and Germany. In 2014, Murdoch created Sky Europe by selling 21st Century Fox's full ownership of Sky Italia and its 57 percent stake in Sky Deutschland to BSkyB, the UK satellite TV powerhouse already under his control. The result is a pan-European force rivaled only by Malone's Liberty Global. Murdoch pulled more than $7 billion out of the transaction, and retained a controlling 39 percent interest in the new Sky Europe.

The company also has an interest in the Star TV group of companies, which have numerous digital TV services distributed across Asia. In India, digital satellite service Tata Sky, a joint venture between Tata Sons and 21st Century Fox, had 11.5 million subscribers by year-end 2013. The service offers 200+ SD channels and a couple dozen HD channels.

News Corporation remains Murdoch's global force in newspapers and book publishing. In 2007, Murdoch acquired Dow Jones, owner of the *Wall Street Journal*, from the Bancroft family for $5 billion. Additional assets include HarperCollins, the *Times* (of London), the *New York Post*, and the *Australian* and the *Daily Telegraph* in Australia, where the company is still by far the largest newspaper publisher. The Australian Foxtel pay TV services, delivering digital TV via cable, satellite, and the Internet, also reside within News Corporation.

Rupert Murdoch even engaged personally with Steve Jobs in the waning years of the consumer product guru's life. They were strange bedfellows, considering Murdoch's political leanings and Jobs's counterculturalism, but the two men openly discussed many topics, including food, politics, and technology's role in the future of publishing and education.[6]

Jobs must be rolling in his grave, however, given that Google's Android technology was subsequently selected by Amplify, Murdoch's new educational endeavor. Amplify, a News Corporation subsidiary, is aiming to transform K–12 public education. Its CEO, Joel Klein, former chancellor of the New York City Department of Education, has a mission of enabling personalized education in the classroom via a custom Android-based educational tablet under each teacher's control.

Another News Corporation division, Storyful, was acquired for $25 million in December 2013, underscoring Murdoch's belief in the confluence of news, video, and social media. Based in Dublin, Ireland, Storyful positions itself as the first news agency of the social media era. It discovers videos and news on various websites and social networks, verifies the content for accuracy, and then distributes the aggregated results to its newsroom clients.

As he enters his mid-eighties, Rupert Murdoch is clearly thinking of succession planning for his far-flung family business. In March 2014 he elevated his oldest son, Lachlan, to non-executive co-chairman of both 21st Century Fox and News Corporation, and promoted his second son, James, to co-chief operating officer of 21st Century Fox alongside president and COO Chase Carey. His daughter Elisabeth Murdoch, married to Sigmund Freud's great-grandson, Matthew Freud, has charted her own entrepreneurial path. She was the founder and CEO of Shine TV, a successful British TV production company that is now part of Shine Group, which she chairs.

Murdoch made an unsuccessful $80 billion bid for Time Warner in the summer of 2014. He was especially attracted by his target's HBO franchise and by the sports rights owned by Turner Broadcasting. After being rejected, he and his team at 21st Century Fox are redoubling the focus on their global content assets, at least for now.

56.6 LIBERTY MEDIA AND LIBERTY GLOBAL

Trying to follow John Malone's ever-changing composition of tracking stocks, spin-offs, and acquisitions will make anyone's head spin. Liberty Media did very well over the years with its ownership of Starz, Discovery, and many other TV-related assets. In parallel, Malone transitioned from running TCI, the largest domestic cable operator, to building Liberty Global, the largest international cable operator.

By the end of February 2008, the FCC and the Justice Department approved the $11 billion transfer of Rupert Murdoch's controlling interest in DirecTV to Malone's Liberty Media. It had been almost ten years since Malone was shut out of the US high-power DBS business by the Justice Department, after which he sold TCI to AT&T. Now it was Malone's turn to own the preeminent US satellite TV service. But his hard-earned tenure was short-lived.

In 2009, Malone announced a complex transaction that would reduce his company's ownership in DirecTV and terminate his management role. First, he split off subsidiary Liberty Entertainment, the entity which owned three regional sports channels and a majority interest in the Game Show Network, into a new company. Simultaneously, The DirecTV Group was merged into a new entity, and then both Liberty Entertainment and The DirecTV Group became subsidiaries of a new public company, DirecTV. As a result, Malone's stake in DirecTV declined to 24 percent. In 2010, Malone stepped down as chairman of DirecTV after exchanging his preferred stock for common shares, reducing Liberty's voting interest to less than 5 percent.

In January 2013, Liberty completed its spin-off of Starz Entertainment as a separate public company. Starz is generally considered the number three premium TV subscription service in the United States, after HBO and Showtime. Traditionally known more for movies, Starz is starting to hold its own with original series such as *Da Vinci's Demons*, *Black Sails*, and *Outlander*.

Malone maintains a 29 percent voting stake in Discovery Communications. In a classic Malone maneuver, he first spun off Liberty Media's 50 percent interest in Discovery Communications into Discovery Holding Company in 2005. Then, in 2008, he merged and consolidated his interest into a new public company, Discovery Communications, Inc. Today, Discovery owns a global footprint of television channels reaching 2.7 billion cumulative subscribers in more than 220 countries and territories.[7] The company has 13 domestic channels focused on science, technology, and history. In 2014, Discovery gained majority ownership of Eurosport, a collection of international sports channels, some of which reach more than 50 countries in various languages.

While these content-related transactions were generating wealth, Malone was busily building an international cable giant with a European epicenter. In June 2005, Malone created Liberty Global with CEO Mike Fries by merging Liberty Media International and UnitedGlobalCom, the parent company of UPC, Europe's largest cable operator.

In June 2013, Liberty Global acquired Virgin Media in a $24 billion deal for stock and cash. Virgin Media, formed by the 2006 merger of NTL, Telewest, and Richard Branson's Virgin Mobile, is the largest cable operator in the United Kingdom. We will now see Malone's Virgin Media, Murdoch's Sky, and BT's IPTV service (BT TV) battling it out in the United Kingdom for years to come.

Malone also acquired a minority interest in Ziggo, Holland's largest cable operator, and then agreed to purchase the remaining shares in 2014 for $6.7 billion. Consolidating Ziggo will give Liberty Global more than 24 million video subscribers (70 percent of which are digital), spread throughout a dozen European countries, plus Chile and Puerto Rico. Liberty Global's other European assets include Unitymedia KabelBW in Germany, Telenet in Belgium, and UPC in various countries.

Also in 2014, Liberty Global and Discovery Communications agreed to pay $930 million for All3Media, one of the largest television production houses in the United Kingdom. Clearly, Malone wants to supplement his powerful European cable distribution arm with content, even as Discovery continues enhancing its own international presence.

Liberty Global also acquired a minority stake in British commercial broadcaster ITV, the original broadcaster of *Downton Abbey* in the United Kingdom and Ireland. ITV has its own Internet video player in competition with the BBC's iPlayer.

In 2013, Malone re-entered the US cable business when Liberty Media acquired a 27 percent interest in Charter Communications for $2.6 billion. The deal limits Liberty's ownership to less than 40 percent while giving Liberty four seats on Charter's board. With Comcast outbidding Charter for Time Warner Cable, Malone and Tom Rutledge,[8] Charter's CEO, will seek alternative ways to increase their domestic cable position. For starters, Charter is poised to acquire 1.4 million subscribers from the pending combination of Comcast and Time Warner Cable.

Malone is also chairman, and Greg Maffei is CEO, of Liberty Interactive Corporation, a holding company with interests in numerous e-commerce businesses including Evite, QVC, HSN, Expedia, and TripAdvisor. The various assets of Liberty Interactive Corporation are partitioned into two separate tracking stocks: QVC Group and Liberty Ventures Group.

Liberty Media is a constantly changing conglomerate. Together with CEO Greg Maffei, Malone continues to spin off and swap assets while increasing value and minimizing taxes. In November 2014, Liberty Media spun off Liberty Broadband as a separate public company. Liberty Media owns or has stakes in the digital music service SiriusXM; the Atlanta Braves baseball franchise; concert/ticket company Live Nation Entertainment; and minority shares in Time Warner and Viacom. Liberty

Broadband holds the equity positions in Charter, Time Warner Cable, and geolocation specialist TruePosition.

As John Malone enters his mid-seventies, his sprawling empire of media assets is well positioned for the next generation of broadband television. The big question is whether he supplements Liberty's dominant position in European cable with a major accumulation of cable assets in the United States. The answer lies within one man's hands.

56.7 CABLEVISION, AMC NETWORKS, AND THE MADISON SQUARE GARDEN COMPANY

Chuck Dolan remains strategically active in his late eighties as chairman of Cablevision, where his son Jim is CEO. Cablevision is the leading triple-play (video, data, and voice) service provider in the New York metropolitan area. Chuck is also chairman of AMC Networks, led day-to-day by Josh Sapan.

Cablevision provides its own version of TV Everywhere inside the home and throughout its extensive WiFi network in the tri-state area of New York, New Jersey, and Connecticut. Roaming cable subscribers can watch "TV to GO" on laptops and mobile devices in coffee shops, train stations, and many other locations.

Jim Dolan is executive chairman at The Madison Square Garden Company. Spun off to shareholders in February 2010, the company's iconic assets include the Madison Square Garden arena, the MSG Networks TV channels, Radio City Music Hall, the Beacon Theater, the Chicago Theater, the New York Knicks, the New York Rangers, and various regional sports channels.

The Dolans' content subsidiary, Rainbow Media, was spun off in 2011 as AMC Networks. The brand equity and value of AMC (the channel) have climbed impressively as it morphed from showing classic movies to debuting critically acclaimed and wildly popular hit series. From the gripping crime drama vibe of *The Killing* to the bittersweet nostalgia of *Mad Men*, and from the gut-wrenching immorality of *Breaking Bad* to the addictive zombiedom of *The Walking Dead*, Josh Sapan and his team have done a remarkable job with this transformation.

SundanceTV is also on the rise with outstanding spy thriller miniseries *The Honorable Woman*, the well-received *Rectify*, and movies carefully curated for the channel's target audience. On the uber-creative side of the spectrum, consider Isabella Rossellini's performance art series, available on the Sundance.tv website. In Rossellini's two-minute films, she takes viewers on visual adventures in the realm of animal behavior. The themes range from reproduction in the "Green Porno" episodes to seduction in "Seduce Me" and to motherhood in "Mammas."

IFC provides movie and TV classics as well as comedy series such as *Portlandia*. WE tv is oriented toward women while also carrying syndicated classics with a broader appeal.

In an international twist, AMC Networks paid $1 billion in 2014 for Chellomedia, the international content arm of Liberty Global. This acquisition expands the company's global footprint into more than 100 countries. Also in 2014, AMC Networks invested $200 million for a 49.9 percent interest in BBC America.

The Dolans' three companies—Cablevision, AMC Networks, and Madison Square Garden—hold a treasure chest of assets. But where this impressive assortment of content, distribution, sports teams, and entertainment venues lands in the future is anybody's guess.

56.8 DISH NETWORK AND ECHOSTAR CORPORATION

Charlie Ergen's Dish Network is another wild card. Ergen, now in his early sixties, has accumulated substantial wireless spectrum over the years, giving him some important bargaining chips. Still, if he is to execute a credible broadband wireless plan, he will need to engage with a major partner. Ergen lost the bidding wars for Sprint and Clearwire to Japan's Softbank. But he could still team up with Sprint longer-term to create a formidable fixed mobile broadband service. Another possible ally is T-Mobile.

Like his peers, Ergen thoroughly understands the synergy between content and technology. In 2008, he carved out EchoStar Corporation as a separate vehicle for his technology assets. EchoStar, Ergen's original C-band satellite TV company, included Dish Network as well as his various technology assets until then. EchoStar's assets includes the internal digital set-top box business, the Sling Media "TV anywhere" technology, the Move Networks adaptive video streaming technology, and the Hughes Network Systems satellite-based Internet access business, acquired in 2011 for $1.3 billion.

Dish Network acquired Blockbuster Inc. out of Chapter 11 bankruptcy in 2011 for $228 million, closing down its retail stores but retaining the Blockbuster On Demand Internet streaming service. Dish is broadening this position in 2015 with Sling TV, an over-the-top Internet TV service, starting at $20 per month, targeted toward millennials and cord cutters. The initial few dozen linear channels[9] are licensed from Disney/ESPN, Turner, AMC Networks, Scripps Networks, and others, and the service also includes on-demand content.

Ergen has had a spectacular run with Dish Network. But he knows its future growth as a pure satellite TV service is limited. Given the potential for fusing 14 million satellite TV subscribers with the broadband Internet and wireless mobility, we surely have not heard the last from Charlie Ergen.

56.9 DIRECTV, AT&T, AND VERIZON

It would be remiss not to mention DirecTV, AT&T, and Verizon in a chapter about today's most prominent US television companies. These three aren't run by self-made billionaires or charismatic media titans. But their size and staying power in the digital TV and broadband Internet markets make them critically important long-term players.

Although they don't own much content yet, they seem to be leaning in that direction. DirecTV retains exclusivity for NFL Sunday Ticket and also owns Roots Sports, a group of four regional sports channels in the DirecTV Sports Networks unit. These channels remained with DirecTV after Malone and Liberty relinquished control of DirecTV. The company also owns 42 percent of Game Show Network (GSN), in a joint venture with Sony Pictures Television, also resulting from the Malone/Liberty transaction.

AT&T also appears to be tiptoeing into the content game. In September 2014, Otter Media, a joint venture between AT&T and the Chernin Group, took control of Fullscreen, one of the most successful and popular networks on the YouTube platform.

What makes DirectTV and AT&T most threatening to their competitors are their merger plans. In May 2014, just a few months after Comcast's agreement to acquire Time Warner Cable, AT&T announced the purchase of DirecTV for $48.5 billion in cash and stock.

DirecTV has a long history of operating under expansive corporate wings. It came to life in the 1990s as a start-up within Hughes Communications, which General Motors had acquired in 1985. In 2003, it fell under the control of Rupert Murdoch and News Corporation. Finally, in 2008, John Malone's Liberty Media took over. Malone's reign was short-lived, however, as DirecTV's Board of Directors gained managerial and voting control, cashing Malone out.

The logic behind a major telco acquiring a national satellite TV operator has always been compelling. It's much easier to buy than to build a 20-million-home subscriber base. AT&T will likely allow DirecTV to continue operating autonomously, but there is also strong synergy with respect to service bundling. AT&T instantly obtains a national video footprint while DirecTV finally gets a strong broadband Internet outlet, in both the wired and wireless domains.

The combined entity will be a much more formidable competitor against Comcast, increasing the likelihood that both deals receive regulatory approval from the Justice Department and the FCC. It is almost inconceivable that regulators will allow one deal and not the other. The biggest concern with Comcast buying Time Warner Cable is that the largest video provider and the largest Internet provider will be under one roof. In contrast, the major competitive issue with AT&T acquiring DirecTV is that the two are direct video competitors in many major markets. In these regions, representing roughly a quarter of the country's television households, most subscribers would have a choice of three independent video service providers (Dish, DirecTV/AT&T, and the local cable operator) rather than four. But if the deal is approved, AT&T is promising to bring broadband Internet to 15 million new homes by 2019, including many in underserved, rural areas. AT&T is also dangling the possible expansion of its 1 Gbps GigaPower fiber footprint to at least 2 million additional homes.

If both deals close, more than half of the country's video subscribers and over half of the country's broadband wireline (cable or DSL) Internet subscribers will be served by Comcast and AT&T. But these two service providers have both agreed to abide by the FCC's 2010 Open Internet Order for certain periods, even though a federal court has vacated these network neutrality rules as being beyond the FCC's authority.[10]

The transactions also raise the question of what Verizon will do in response. Verizon FiOS, for digital TV and high-speed Internet, receives industry-leading customer service ratings. But it is unavailable to most US households due to the exorbitant capital required for Verizon to expand it nationally. Verizon Wireless is also developing LTE Multicast, allowing higher-quality broadcast video over its 4G network. And Verizon Wireless is brewing a separate Internet mobile TV venture for launch in 2015, which includes deals with Viacom and others for content.

Clearly Verizon would love to get its hands on Dish Network's wireless spectrum. But one should not rule out the likelihood of Verizon eventually acquiring Dish Network in its entirety. Then there would be three national-scale giants in both video and high-speed Internet service: Comcast, AT&T, and Verizon.

57 TV EVERYWHERE

With ubiquitous broadband Internet and proliferation of connected devices, the era of digital video anytime and anywhere was inevitable. HDTV sets light up our living rooms while tablets and smartphones are tethered to our bodies. We're living in a multiscreen, hyperconnected world. Convenient and instantaneous access to enormous libraries of content is the new norm. Appointment TV (for programs broadcast at specific times) is hotter than ever for live sports, breaking news, and first airings of popular TV shows. But for the rest of video consumption, it's all about personal choice, instant gratification, and the erosion of physical boundaries.

An epic battle is taking shape between the traditional content distribution model and an over-the-top Internet future in which video content is delivered directly to consumers via the Internet, without a middleman serving as content distributor. Against the surging popularity of over-the-top content providers like Netflix and YouTube, the video incumbents are pushing TV Everywhere as extensions to their pre-existing channels and subscription packages.

TV Everywhere is the video incumbents' marketing umbrella for content delivered to their subscribers' multiple screens inside and outside the home. Originally introduced by Time Warner Cable, TV Everywhere boasts a rapidly increasing volume of content designed to engender subscriber loyalty by adding value to the pay TV subscription. With TV Everywhere, authenticated[1] multi-channel subscribers can receive branded video content on their computers, smartphones, and tablets for no additional charge. The free over-the-air networks—PBS, CBS, NBC, ABC, and Fox—have also entered the TV Everywhere community, in some cases not requiring subscriber authentication.

Premium channels are also making use of the TV Everywhere branding. For instance, all major video service providers offer HBO Go to their subscribers for computer and mobile viewing. It follows HBO's proven, value-added marketing model of giving subscribers more content and more viewing options—digital multiplex channels, HD channels, VOD content—without increasing the monthly price. Similarly, Showtime offers Showtime Anytime and Starz provides Starz Play, Encore Play, and MoviePlex Play, all marketed under the cable industry's TV Everywhere umbrella.

Disney is pursuing TV Everywhere with its own branded Internet and mobile applications.

- WatchESPN provides live Internet streams of several ESPN linear TV channels including ESPN and ESPN2. It is also used by TV and broadband Internet subscribers for access to ESPN3, an Internet-only streaming video service. Notably, ESPN3 delivered all sixty-four matches of the 2014 World Cup live to connected devices.

- The Watch Disney Channel app allows multiscreen access to full episodes of Disney shows over the Internet.

- Through Watch Disney Junior, kids were able to watch *Sheriff Callie's Wild West* on mobile devices before the episodes aired on the company's TV channels.

- Watch ABC is the first broadcast television network derivative allowing live streaming for the entire lineup of ABC network content. It is available in each of the eight local markets where ABC owns a TV station, as well as in certain other markets where ABC's affiliates own and operate local stations.

- Watch ABC Family allows access to full episodes of many ABC Family shows on various mobile devices.

Turner Broadcasting is another active TV Everywhere participant. It streams the complete programming lineups of TBS and TNT live on these channels' websites, as well as to mobile devices through the Watch TBS and Watch TNT apps. Turner even includes the NBA and MLB games for which it has broadcast rights. Live Internet streaming feeds of CNN and HLN are also available to authenticated subscribers. CNNgo, launched in 2014, combines the linear news feed with on-demand content as well as other interactive and personalized features.

NBC Sports Live Extra enables a broad array of live sporting events including National Hockey League and Major League Soccer games. Content is streamed to the computers and mobile devices of participating service providers' subscribers. The same app was used for live and on-demand streaming of virtually all the events during the February 2014 Sochi Winter Olympics.

FXNOW is 21st Century Fox's TV Everywhere multiscreen app for the FX, FXX, and FXM networks. Super Bowl XLVIII, between the Denver Broncos and Seattle Seahawks, was streamed live over the Internet on February 2, 2014, using Fox Sports GO. Separate English and Spanish language streams were made available to computers and iPads, but not to smartphones, a segment controlled by Verizon Wireless through a separate deal with the NFL.

Highlighting the ongoing importance of live events, Fox's Super Bowl network TV broadcast reached the largest audience in US television history, an average of 112.2 million viewers.[2] The live Internet multicast broke the streaming record for a sports event with an average of 528,000 viewers per minute; and on Twitter, a new record was set for the most tweets (24.9 million) associated with a live TV event.[3]

USA Network, Cartoon Network, Comedy Central, NBC, Syfy, Discovery, National Geographic, the Big Ten Network, Pac-12 Networks, the Tennis Channel—just about every cable channel has joined the TV Everywhere party.

The major video service providers also aggregate multiscreen content into their own branded versions of TV Everywhere. For example, Comcast's TV Go app allows subscribers with smartphones or tablets to download or stream on-demand content and dozens of live linear channels over domestic WiFi and 3G/4G wireless networks. Time Warner Cable's TWC TV, Cablevision's Optimum TV to GO, and DirecTV Everywhere each have their own activity, enabling subscribers to watch content inside and outside the home on various devices.

Internationally, the BBC has been at the vanguard of Internet TV. Its iPlayer supports on-demand video streaming across various television platform brands, game consoles, and mobile devices, also connecting to social media networks such as Facebook and Twitter. BBC's science fiction television cult classic, *Doctor Who*, celebrated its fiftieth anniversary on November 23, 2013, with a "global simulcast" at 2:50 p.m. ET. Just as the show's good-versus-evil plot involves space and time travel, the event itself cut across technological and national boundaries. It was simulcast to ninety-four countries, including availability to Internet-connected mobile devices and 3D theaters.

Murdoch's BSkyB created the Sky Go app, allowing millions of UK subscribers to watch their content on laptops and mobile devices.

Adobe's US Digital Video Benchmark claims authenticated streaming via TV Everywhere grew even faster in 2014 than online-only Internet services, with more than one in five subscription TV households participating in TV Everywhere.[4] But some refinements are needed for this success to continue. A more coherent marketing framework would help, along with a continually updated content directory, enabling subscribers to determine what is available through their service providers. Also, the technical authentication process can be a nuisance and is inconsistent across content and service providers, underscoring the need for a simpler, more streamlined approach.

In the United States, TV Everywhere is an ambitious, industry-wide extension of the bundled subscription model. Its objective is to leverage the Internet and its multiscreen environment to add value for consumers, thereby creating subscriber stickiness. Despite some technical and marketing hurdles, it appears to be working quite effectively in sustaining the subscriber cord. But in the long run, will TV Everywhere be enough to stem the over-the-top Internet tide?

58 NEW KIDS ON THE BLOCK

As traditional content and service providers extend the bundled subscription model with TV Everywhere, independent Internet video activities abound. The connected world is bubbling up all around the entrenched incumbents. Fresh content, new program packagers, and innovative consumer devices are combining forces to make over-the-top Internet TV a growth business. We have pure-play Internet video sites, independent media companies, giant retailers that happen to sell digital video and electronic gadgets, and gadget makers with ecosystems that aggregate content. In recognition of the importance of these new content creators and distributors, the National Cable Telecommunications Association is rebranding The Cable Show, its annual trade show, to the Internet and Television Expo, with a Chicago debut in May 2015.

Internet video would have eventually occurred irrespectively of the digital television revolution once Internet bandwidth attained its broadband destiny. But digital TV occurred first (over satellite, cable, and broadcast), reflecting earlier readiness both from a technology and a business perspective. It paved the way for Internet video. Now, with digital video dominating Internet traffic and content providers of all stripes on board, the two markets are developing together, even as they continue to evolve separately.

There is a new breed of content aggregator—led by Netflix, You-Tube, Hulu, and Amazon—supported by rapidly evolving categories of consumer electronics: Samsung and Sony smart TVs; LG and Panasonic Blu-ray players; Roku and Apple TV boxes; Xbox and PlayStation game consoles doubling as broadband connectivity devices; and mobile devices based on software from Apple, Google, and Microsoft.

A clear sign of Internet video's coming of age is the Interactive Advertising Bureau's Digital Content NewFronts. This forum serves as Internet video's counterpart to the TV industry's long-standing "upfront" market, during which advertisers are enticed to commit dollars in advance of the upcoming season. The NewFronts' second annual event occurred in April 2013. Presenters included Microsoft, Yahoo, AOL, Hulu, CBS Interactive, YouTube, the *Wall Street Journal*, Univision, Vevo, Disney Interactive, Sony Crackle, and Condé Nast. These companies showcased their upcoming plans for new video content unique to the Web. The event expanded in April 2014, from 5 days to 8 days, and with over 20 presentations, including the *New York Times'* "Times Video," PBS Digital Studios introducing dozens of web series, and Condé Nast's debut of various new branded video channels.[1]

In conjunction with the 2014 NewFronts event, the Interactive Advertising Bureau issued its "2014 Original Digital Video Study." The report claimed that 52 million US adults, more than one in five, view original, professionally produced Internet video content each month, up from 45 million in 2013. The study distinguished this type of video from network TV shows viewed online and from "amateur online video," making the case that now is the time for advertisers to step up their Internet video budgets.

58.1 NETFLIX

Netflix is the gold standard for over-the-top Internet TV, having master-fully transitioned away from mail-order DVDs of movies. An ad-free, on-demand streaming video service, Netflix had nearly 55 million pay-ing subscribers as of December 31, 2014, 38 million of which were in the United States.[2] Its 17 million international subscribers were spread throughout nearly 50 nations, including Canada, Latin America, and many countries in Europe.

Netflix has emulated HBO in certain respects, evolving from a movie reseller to a diversified content distributor. It has placed an increasing emphasis on original TV series such as *House of Cards* and *Orange Is the New Black*. Netflix sells directly to consumers, while HBO is distributed through cable, satellite, and telco TV service providers in the United States and in most of its overseas markets.[3] Netflix's top-line revenue approached HBO's in 2014, but HBO retains a commanding lead in prestige and profitability: HBO won nineteen Primetime Emmy Awards in 2014, the most of any TV network for the thirteenth consecutive year. Netflix did not receive any Primetime Emmy Awards that year, although it did receive seven in the less-prestigious Creative Arts session. Also, HBO produces and owns a substantial portion of its content, giving it much higher profit margins than Netflix.

Netflix offers a deep library of films and TV shows but has many content gaps. Recent movies and current season TV shows are often missing, and the service doesn't carry live events or sports. For this reason, Netflix is primarily an add-on service, like HBO and Showtime, rather than a substitute for a multi-channel content package.

Netflix's ongoing challenge is to continue growing its Internet subscriber base by providing more unique and original content, an expensive proposition. However, Netflix is finding new ways to capitalize on subscriber loyalty and in the process is introducing new viewing habits as well as new content.

Just as *The Sopranos* transformed HBO, *House of Cards* catapulted Netflix to a new level of prestige. Starring Kevin Spacey and Robin Wright, it quickly became the definitive Machiavellian political thriller. By simultaneously releasing all 13 episodes of the first season in February 2013, Netflix popularized the "binge-watching" phenomenon, contravening a nearly seventy-year history of TV channels steadily pacing the release of episodes. A year later, in February 2014, Netflix repeated the act, releasing all 13 episodes of Season 2.

The company clearly recognizes the importance of possessing a rolling stable of unique shows in various genres. Seven years after Fox ended a three-year run of the cult comedy series *Arrested Development*, Netflix gave it new life in 2013, providing 15 new episodes available all at once. Sensual crime show *Spiral* premiered in France in 2005 on the Canal Plus pay channel, then moved to Britain, and finally to Netflix in 2012. Jenji Kohan's *Orange Is the New Black* exudes the edgy, adult-oriented, graphic qualities associated with similar shows on Showtime and HBO, both of which passed on the women's prison drama before it was snapped up by Netflix. In December 2014, all 10 episodes of *Marco Polo* Season 1 were placed online. *Grace and Frankie*, a new comedy series starring Jane Fonda and Lily Tomlin, is coming to Netflix in 2015. The company also signed a deal with Chelsea Handler. The former E! star will host periodic Netflix comedy shows during 2015, leading up to a new talk show beginning in 2016. The genre of documentaries is also in Netflix's sights for original content, especially those concerning humanitarian or environmental themes.

Netflix is aggressively targeting the younger demographic, with its "Just for Kids" section. It has licensed animated films from Disney studios Pixar, Marvel Studios, and Disney Animation, as well as from

Sony Animation. In 2013, DreamWorks Animation licensed over 300 hours of new, original television content to Netflix in a multi-year deal starting with *Turbo FAST*, followed by a 2014 agreement for three new original series: *King Julien*, *Puss in Boots*, and *Veggie Tales in the House*.

Also in 2013, Netflix struck a broader, multi-year agreement with Disney, gaining rights to many Disney Junior channel shows oriented toward kids in the three-to-nine-year age group, as well as some Disney XD shows, aimed at slightly older children. Toward the end of the year, Disney's Marvel Television unit agreed to produce a "serialized epic" for Netflix comprising four separate live-action shows starting in 2015, culminating in a mini-series of *The Defenders*.

Beyond expanding its deep library of films and series, the company is also trying to differentiate itself in the first-release movie business. Netflix has an exclusive agreement to show four new movies produced by and starring Adam Sandler. In August 2015, Netflix and The Weinstein Company will stream *Crouching Tiger, Hidden Dragon: The Green Legend* the same day it opens in certain IMAX cinemas. Major theater chains are rebelling, however, with AMC, Cinemark, Regal, and others boycotting exhibition of the movie. Most Hollywood studios and theater chains will hang on as long as possible to their traditional release window, which typically gives cinemas a three-month exclusive period before new movies are offered through additional outlets such as hotels, pay-per-view, and subscription TV.

Netflix captures extensive data on its subscribers' viewing habits, factoring the information into its decision criteria for acquiring new content. The company has received much praise for its consumer-friendly user interface and its content-recommendation engine. A single household account is partitioned into multiple profiles, allowing content personalization for individual family members.

To increase profitability, however, Netflix must not only keep growing its subscriber base, but also continue carefully shifting away from its "all-you-can-watch, one-size-fits-all" monthly pricing model. Initial steps taken in this regard include charging more for a larger number of simultaneous streams allowed per household account and also differentiating by video quality (SD versus HD versus Ultra HD). In spring 2014, the company raised its basic price to $9 per month for new members, allowing two simultaneous HD streams per account. Netflix's platinum plan, which includes some Ultra HD (4K) content and allows up to four simultaneous streams, is $12 per month. Netflix's future tiered pricing structure could also reflect differentiated pools of content.

The addition of the Internet not only allows new financing options for video content but also incremental windows of distribution. For example, in 2013 Netflix collaborated with the AMC channel to bring crime thriller *The Killing* back from the dead. AMC first broadcast the new Season 3 episodes through its traditional cable and satellite distributors. The day after each AMC episode aired live, Netflix subscribers in the United Kingdom and Ireland were able to stream the shows over the Internet. A few months later, Netflix's US subscribers were able to binge on the full season. Netflix then renewed the series for a fourth and final season, independently of AMC, for exclusive streaming on Netflix starting in August 2014.

The public visibility of Netflix has been so pronounced that a social media action undertaken by its CEO, Reed Hastings, forced the Securities and Exchange Commission to update its disclosure rules for public corporations. The SEC's Regulation Fair Disclosure (Reg FD) was adopted in 2000, requiring companies with publicly traded stock to simultaneously publish all material information to all investors, thereby attempting to prevent one investor from gaining an unfair advantage in the market. But in late 2012, Hastings posted a congratulatory Facebook message to his employees regarding Netflix breaking the billion-hour streaming video barrier in a single month. The SEC regulations were obviously outdated. Although no penalties were assessed on Netflix, the event forced the SEC to update its policies. Companies can now designate certain social media sites as legitimate methods of corporate communications, consistent with Reg FD.

Netflix competitors are popping up around the world. In Canada, Rogers and Shaw created Showmi, a $9 per month over-the-top Internet service, and Bell Media debuted CraveTV for $4 per month. Elsewhere, subscription services Fandor and Mubi launched for film buffs; Viddsee and Viki emerged with an Asian content emphasis; and Singapore-based Spuul provides Indian content to subscribers worldwide.

If Netflix can continue serving a growing subscriber base with a broader pool of unique content for reasonable prices, it will have a bright future. But higher profitability and reliable access to sufficient bandwidth all the way to consumers' homes, especially for HD and Ultra HD, are significant stumbling blocks.

58.2 YOUTUBE

YouTube was acquired by Google in 2006 for $1.7 billion. More than 1 billion unique users visit the site each month, watching over 6 billion hours of video. The quantity and breadth of content accessible is overwhelming. The company claims that more than 100 hours of video are uploaded to YouTube every minute. Primarily known for its user-generated short-form content, YouTube remains the mecca of video democracy even as it moves up the food chain with an aggressive, carefully contrived strategy. In 2015, YouTube Music Key will become the latest subscription music service, featuring videos and music for $10 per month ($8 per month for beta participants).

The YouTube.com website is cluttered but is better organized than the haphazard free-for-all that it once was. Content partners can create their own "channels" of video, and users can search for channels across every conceivable genre. The partner program includes over 1 million content creators from more than 30 countries, with thousands of channels making six figures per year.[4]

YouTube's biggest content partners, such as AwesomenessTV, Maker Studios, and Fullscreen, have created multi-channel networks, each comprising tens of thousands of individual content channels. CNN and BuzzFeed, the viral real-time media website, teamed up to create "CNN BuzzFeed," a YouTube channel targeted to the youth news audience. MOCAtv is a contemporary art video channel introduced in 2012 by LA's Museum of Contemporary Art. Awesomeness TV, the collection of popular teen-oriented YouTube channels, was acquired by Dream-Works Animation in 2013. A year later, the company launched Dream-WorksTV, a family destination on YouTube, including original shows targeted toward young children.

YouTube's primary business model to date has been advertising driven. The company typically retains 45 percent of the ad revenue generated from its content partners. In May 2013, YouTube entered the subscription video business, debuting various partners' channels for as low as $1 per month. YouTube itself is a channel on Internet TV devices such as Roku, a one-click portal into YouTube's universe of videos.

To facilitate content production, the company has built state-of-the-art studios, called YouTube Spaces, in Los Angeles, London, Tokyo, and New York City. These free facilities and their camera equipment are made available to content creators, who are enticed not only by the low entry price but also by the ability to maintain creative control over their ideas.

With its vast quantity of Internet music videos, YouTube has almost singlehandedly transformed the way in which a song can become a hit. *Billboard,* founded in 1894 as one of the world's oldest trade magazines, started publishing the Billboard Hot 100 music singles popularity chart in 1958. To make the list, a song originally had to achieve a certain level of radio airplay and sales data, starting with physical copies of records and later CDs. In the Internet era, Billboard added Internet downloads (iTunes) and streaming (Spotify), as measured by Nielsen Soundscan. Finally, in February 2013, the Billboard Hot 100 started factoring in streaming video on ad-supported websites such as YouTube.

The most popular version of the video "Gangnam Style," by South Korean pop rapper Psy, surpassed 2 billion cumulative views in May 2014. But the most dramatic example of Billboard's revised formula was "Harlem Shake," a hip-hop tune by Baauer, an electronic dance music master. After a slow start, it suddenly went viral on YouTube, with fans uploading thousands of different versions of themselves and of cartoon characters dancing crazily to the song. As a result, "Harlem Shake" went straight from obscurity to number one on the Billboard Hot 100 due to Nielsen's new measurement technique incorporating YouTube streams.[5]

Nearly a half-century after Jerry Heller's groundbreaking digital communications work on deep space probes at Jet Propulsion Laboratory, years before he brought his digital television vision to General Instrument, the situation has come full circle. When retired Canadian astronaut Chris Hadfield lived and worked aboard the International Space Station in 2013, he used a broadband Internet connection to deliver YouTube videos back to earth. He was not only striving to convey what it's really like to be in outer space but also why it matters. Hadfield's digital videos relayed from space included one of peanuts defying gravity, and a "selfie" of him performing a cover version of David Bowie's "Space Oddity."

Google, YouTube's owner, has a small equity stake in—and an ad revenue sharing partnership with—Vevo, a music video website owned by Sony Music, Universal Music/EMI, and Abu Dhabi Media. One of the most popular channels on YouTube, Vevo is the record industry's attempt to put the genie back in the bottle and regain a measure of control over the music business. Warner Music has its own competing venture with Viacom's MTV. The Vevo consortium also launched Vevo TV in 2013, a

24/7 ad-supported music channel streamed to tablets, smartphones, and Internet TV boxes in North America.

Barry Diller's IAC owns Vimeo, a YouTube competitor. YouTube has a much wider reach and enables video for the masses. But Vimeo's user base is passionate and many videophiles prefer Vimeo due to generally higher quality standards and more professional-looking videos. The Vimeo on Demand platform allows content creators to maintain complete control of the pricing, distribution, and quality of their videos. The company is also developing original content, and is planning a subscription service for 2015.

Google's acquisition of YouTube was a brilliant move. While operating as an independent business unit, it will remain central to Google's overall video strategy. During Christmas 2014, Sony Pictures' release of *The Interview* was derailed by the major theater chains' refusal to exhibit the film, following the cyberthreat allegedly by North Korea. Google, along with Microsoft, came to the rescue, offering the movie on Google Play, YouTube Movies, and Xbox Video. YouTube's new Music Key service is destined to play a significant role in the mobile subscription and social media landscape. YouTube wins the award for being the most disruptive and most democratic video platform, hands down.

58.3 HULU

Hulu is owned by Disney-ABC Television Group, Fox Entertainment Group, and NBCUniversal. In 2012, Providence Equity Partners sold its 10 percent share of Hulu to the other three partners for $200 million, privately valuing the company at $2 billion. Hulu Plus, the company's subscription service, had more than 6 million subscribers paying $8 per month in 2014, and total company revenue exceeded $1 billion annually, including advertising.

Hulu is hindered by the differing agendas of its owners: Disney favors the advertising model, Fox prefers the subscription model, and Comcast remains silent due to regulatory constraints imposed upon its acquisition of NBCUniversal. Hulu's board has explored selling the company twice, in mid-2011 and then again in the summer of 2013. In the latter case, DirecTV was apparently prepared to pay close to $1 billion. But Hulu's owners decided to stay the course and instead committed $750 million, primarily for new content acquisition and development.

Hulu is the leading online provider of current season shows from the TV broadcast networks, not a surprise considering its ownership structure. For cinephiles, Hulu Plus includes more than 800 classic and foreign films from the Criterion Collection. It also aggregates many foreign TV shows. Hulu is also funding an array of original content to further differentiate itself.

In 2013, the service introduced *The Awesomes*, an original animated series featuring Seth Meyers. It contained traditional ads as well as integrated product placements and episode extensions with brand partners. Other Hulu originals include sports mascot documentary series *Behind the Mask*, supernatural comedy *Deadbeat*, inner-city Latino teen drama *East Los High*, reality TV parody *The Hotwives of Orlando*, and Scandinavian crime drama *The Bridge*. In 2014, Hulu gained exclusive Internet rights to the *South Park* back catalog, as well as non-exclusive rights to current episodes which will also be broadcast on Viacom's Comedy Central channel.

Hulu has much to offer, but without an ownership change it is best viewed as a hedge and placeholder for Disney, Fox, and NBC. Nonetheless, it is carving out a solid position in the Internet TV space and will continue to grow with the market.

58.4 AMAZON INSTANT VIDEO

Amazon will get its fair share of the Internet video market due to price leadership, staying power, and its dominant position as a retailer. The company also appears committed to producing a steady stream of original content.

Amazon Instant Video is bundled for no additional charge with Amazon Prime, the $99 per year two-day, free-shipping, web shopping membership. Consumers can also stream or download certain movies and TV shows on a per transaction basis. The content is accessible through many third-party electronic devices.

Amazon sells its own set-top box, Fire TV, similar to how it uses the Kindle tablet to work hand-in-glove with its book, music, and general retailing business. Fire TV has voice-activated search capability and a personalized recommendation engine, accessing content not only from Amazon Instant Video but also from Netflix, Hulu Plus, Showtime Anytime, WatchESPN, MLB.TV, and many others. Amazon also introduced its Fire TV Stick, a tiny, inexpensive device that plugs into the HDMI port of a smart TV, competing directly against Google's Chromecast.

In 2013, Amazon entered into a multi-year agreement with Viacom for exclusive rights to children's programming from Nickelodeon. The deal also includes rights to certain shows from Viacom's MTV and Comedy Central channels. For example, after the 2014 first-season finale of hit show *Broad City*, it was only available on Amazon Instant Video and on Comedy Central's TV Everywhere website. Sumner Redstone's other company, CBS, is also working with Amazon. *Under the Dome*, based on a Stephen King novel, is monetized not only through traditional advertising and CBS's retransmission agreements with its cable and satellite distributors, but also by licensing exclusive online rights to Amazon.

In 2014, Amazon licensed a major package of outstanding legacy content from HBO including *The Sopranos*, *The Wire*, *Oz*, *Six Feet Under*, *Band of Brothers*, *Angels in America*, *Parade's End*, and *Boardwalk Empire*. Amazon is also the online home for the vaunted PBS series *Downton Abbey* and *Mr. Selfridge*.

In a sign of the future, Amazon and Mattel created an alliance linking kids' video content with online shopping. The company is offering cartoon episodes of *Fireman Sam*, owned by Mattel's Hit Entertainment unit, alongside the convenient ability to purchase related retail merchandise.[6]

Amazon has entered the original content game in a significant way. Garry Trudeau's *Alpha House* is a political satire starring John Goodman with cameo appearances from the likes of Bill Murray, Wanda Sykes, and Amy Sedaris. Other originals from Amazon Studios include crime drama *Bosch*, classical music comedy *Mozart in the Jungle*, dysfunctional family comedy *Transparent*, and a series written and directed by Woody Allen planned for 2016.

Amazon places trailers, full-length test movies, and original pilots on its website. User feedback then helps determine whether a series or movie will be produced. For example, Whit Stillman's *The Cosmopolitans* is a romantic heartbreak comedy about expatriates living in Paris. Positive feedback could lead to a six-episode first season.

Amazon released its Fire Phone in 2014. Featuring product- and object-recognition technology, it is essentially a mobile cash register in the guise of a high-end smartphone. It also continues Amazon's outstanding customer service with a smartphone button enabling live 24/7/365 customer service through a digital video link. Despite all this, initial sales are apparently low.

Also in 2014, Amazon acquired Twitch for $1.1 billion. The Twitch network enables amateur and professional video game players to broadcast their gaming sessions live over the broadband Internet. By aggregating huge audiences for certain events, Twitch.tv gives Amazon a millennial demographic with consumers as likely to be watching video games as TV.

Amazon will remain a significant force in the Internet video business, especially if it continues its aggressive content acquisition strategy. Its corporate culture is to play the long game, forgoing short-term profits, and it has an outstanding customer service reputation. Furthermore, Amazon has become a master at integrating technology, content, and distribution into a unified ecosystem that includes the Amazon Web Services (AWS) cloud computing platform, Kindle, Fire TV, Fire TV Stick, Fire Phone, and the company's best-in-class online retail catalog, shipping logistics, and customer service.

58.5 WALMART/VUDU

Walmart, the world's largest bricks-and-mortar retailer, would like to close the gap with Amazon in online commerce, and video is an important component of its strategy. Walmart placed itself squarely in the Internet video business by acquiring Vudu in 2010 for about $100 million.[7]

Vudu started life in 2004 as a set-top box and Internet video start-up in Silicon Valley. Today its software application is embedded in many third-party connected HDTV sets, game consoles, and Blu-ray players, as well as Roku boxes, Google Chromecast, iPads, and certain Android devices.

Vudu is not a subscription service. Instead it offers thousands of movies and TV shows rentable on-demand (typically for twenty-four-hour viewing) or downloaded to own. The service is known for its high-quality "HDX" digital video encoding in the MPEG-4 1080P HD format. Content is distributed through a proprietary peer-to-peer content delivery network. Vudu is an active participant in the UltraViolet ecosystem, allowing purchasers of movies and TV shows to have persistent access to their content via the Internet cloud and various connected devices. Members can share their content collections with a limited number of family and friends. Vudu is also linking its user base to Disney Movies Anywhere, Disney's Internet movie service that uses a technology different from UltraViolet.

The combination of Walmart's retail prowess and Vudu's technology ensures a reasonable share of the Internet video business. Vudu's strong embrace of UltraViolet (and Disney's alternative method) is a differentiator that could become attractive to more consumers if marketed effectively. Without original content, however, the service will be confined to one of mass market reseller.

58.6 YAHOO

Yahoo lost its way in the Internet video space following its high-profile $5.7 billion acquisition of Mark Cuban's Broadcast.com in 1999 near the peak of the Internet bubble. But this video drift was obscured by Yahoo's broader failure to keep pace in the rapidly growing Internet advertising business.

Now, under CEO Marissa Mayer, Yahoo is intent on competing against the major Internet video content players. The company desperately needs to offset a declining share of web display ads, its historic bread-and-butter, with the higher-growth market for online video ads. The rekindling of Yahoo's video strategy was punctuated by its 2013 deal to stream *Saturday Night Live* clips, along with an increasing amount of content in multiple categories, on the Yahoo Screen website.

Yahoo is clearly trying to make its mark in the comedy genre, featuring *Saturday Night Live*, *The Colbert Report*, *The Daily Show with Jon Stewart*, and *The Onion*. Yahoo is also funding production of two original comedy series to air on Yahoo's website in 2015. *Outer Space* is a galactic adventure set in the early twenty-second century, and *Sin City Saints* portrays a Las Vegas professional basketball expansion team owned by a Silicon Valley billionaire.

Yahoo also hosts Vevo music videos and a broad spectrum of sports clips and news channels. Katie Couric came on board in 2014 as the "global anchor" of Yahoo News, including two new weekly shows: "World 3.0" and "Now I Get It."

The Yahoo Screen website is cleanly organized with a youthful skew. Yahoo is competing directly against YouTube in part by offering content creators a higher split of ad revenue. The company is also trying to crack the code on live Internet streaming, another potential differentiator from its peers. In partnership with entertainment giant Live Nation, Yahoo Live plans to stream a live concert every day, 365 days a year.

Yahoo's valuation has been dominated by its equity stake in Alibaba, the immense Chinese e-commerce company that went public in September 2014.[8] By monetizing its Alibaba position, Yahoo has a real shot at reinventing itself. The Yahoo Screen video site is a crucial element in that difficult endeavor. Internet video advertising is a booming market, and Yahoo has no intention of ceding that growth to Google and Facebook. Flush with cash from Alibaba's initial public offering, Yahoo agreed in November 2014 to acquire BrightRoll, a leading online video advertising company, for $640 million. Another potential bright spot for Yahoo is its Tumblr social media platform, increasingly being used for promotions and community-based discussions on TV content.

As for Alibaba, it has become China's dominant Internet company, an Asian amalgamation of eBay, Amazon, and possibly Netflix. In July 2014, Alibaba entered into a strategic relationship with Lionsgate. Lionsgate Entertainment World, a subscription Internet video service for mainland China, has an initial content library including TV shows such as *Nashville*, *Mad Men*, and *Weeds*, and a film library containing the *Hunger Games* and *Twilight* franchises.

58.7 OPPER SPORTS AND VICE MEDIA

Before the broadband Internet, an independent digital TV content provider needed to beg, often unsuccessfully, for precious shelf space and distribution deals with cable and satellite operators. Now, content providers can create their own distribution over the Internet, completely bypassing these middlemen.

A case in point is Ira Opper and Opper Sports. Thanks to the rise of digital video and the broadband Internet, Opper was able to transform his lifetime passion for surfing into a successful media distribution business.

Growing up in the Southern California of the 1960s, Opper and his surfing buddies hung out at their local beach shack in Malibu with Kathy Kohner (the actress who played Gidget). Her father's fictional book and screenplay based on Gidget and her friends launched the popular explosion of surf culture in America. "Surfin' U.S.A," the Beach Boys' 1963 hit, became the sport's founding anthem. And when *The Endless Summer* premiered in 1966, hard-core surfers finally had their own serious movie, a documentary depicting a lifestyle of traveling the world in search of the perfect wave. As a teen, Opper saw *The Endless Summer* premiere at the Santa Monica Civic Auditorium, narrated live by director Bruce Brown. This singular event provided the inspiration for his career, traveling the world making surf movies and accumulating a growing content library.

As a youth, Opper borrowed his grandfather's 8mm Kodak movie camera to pursue his hobby. Hoping to distract him from his surfing addiction, his parents sent him away to Arizona State University, where he studied broadcast journalism and television production. Over the next few decades, he filmed and licensed his way into possession of the world's largest surf video library.

In the early days of digital TV, he was blocked from traditional cable and satellite distribution. Instead he sold DVDs and produced surf videos for branded channels like ESPN, Fox Sports, and National Geographic.

His breakthrough came in 2005, when Apple added video capability to iTunes. After Apple rejected his request to be part of the iTunes ecosystem, Dustin Hood, Opper's chief technology officer, devised a clever software maneuver. Consumers could purchase and download movies on Opper's surf website, with the content subsequently appearing in their personalized iTunes libraries. Opper and Hood also achieved compatibility with third-party Android devices. Then they added streaming capability using Amazon's cloud-based service platform, AWS, and created a dedicated surf channel for the Roku box.

Today, Opper's online video platform includes theSURFnetwork, theSNOWnetwork, and theMOTOnetwork, as well as a fitness channel. Consumers can download to own individual titles, rent content for seventy-two hours, or subscribe to premium services. In 2014, the company launched VaporVue, an extreme sports streaming aggregation site containing more than 1,000 titles accessible for $10 per month. It also features a content-recommendation engine and social media links. The business is growing steadily, with half of its sales outside North America.

Another independent outlier is Shane Smith's Vice Media. Vice started as a free magazine but then grew into a diversified media company, including online video and TV. The company's ambitious goal is to continuously capture and curate the best current stories from around the world. It positions itself as the online CNN and MTV for the millennial generation. Tom Freston, former CEO of MTV Networks and Viacom, is an investor and strategic advisor.

Vice has an evolving relationship with established media outlets. Its newsmagazine show on HBO depicts conflicts around the world and "the absurdity of the modern condition." In 2013, Rupert Murdoch's 21st Century Fox purchased a 5 percent stake in Vice Media for $70 million. In 2014, A&E Networks agreed to invest $250 million for around 10 percent of Vice, seeking to tap into its youthful demographic niche. Technology Crossover Ventures also ponied up $250 million.

Still, Vice remains apart from the establishment. The Vice Network is a popular destination on YouTube, with various channels showing sports, news, and special interest videos. It was Shane Smith and Vice that originally arranged for Dennis Rodman and three Harlem Globetrotters to visit North Korea in 2013, knowing supreme leader Kim Jong-un's obsession with basketball and the Chicago Bulls. It was Vice News, an online news channel, that embedded reporters with the self-proclaimed Islamic State (ISIS) in 2014. The chilling video footage depicted the ISIS jihadis on their brutal mission: implementing Sharia law, establishing their version of a caliphate, and directly challenging the United States with taunting messages.

59 TECH JOCKEYS IN THE LIVING ROOM

GI (Motorola) and Scientific Atlanta (Cisco) historically dominated the cable set-top box business. The box was the terminal of their end-to-end broadband communications systems. Consumer electronics companies were mostly relegated to making low-margin TV sets and standalone DVD and Blu-ray players.

But the Internet has opened up a whole new ball game. Apple, Google, Roku, Sony, Microsoft, TiVo, Samsung, and Amazon are all vying for primacy in the living room. Many are both developing consumer hardware and aggregating content, with a long view toward providing more services. By aligning squarely with over-the-top Internet TV, these companies' products initially supplement, but eventually strive to displace, the cable box duopoly of Arris and Cisco.

- *Apple* is the early US market share leader but its solution is getting dated. Over 20 million Apple TV boxes were sold through the middle of 2014, typically for $99 each. While Apple TV brings many Internet video services to the living room screen, its strength lies within Apple's loyal customer base and the iTunes ecosystem.

  It would be surprising if the Apple of CEO Tim Cook doesn't attempt a far more transformative technological shift in the consumer television experience. Apple has a ripe opportunity to combine elegant product design, user-friendly software, and an intuitive grasp of consumer behavior. Who would be better than Apple to gracefully and transparently bridge the Internet and the traditional television domain? A deal with a major service provider would go a long way toward realizing this vision, but one is unlikely to be struck until the thorny issue is resolved of who has primary control of the subscriber.

- *Google* acquired YouTube in 2006 for $1.7 billion, an incredible bargain in retrospect. Since then, Google's foray into the Internet TV space has been clumsy. Its sporadic launches of Google TV in 2010 and 2012 were premature and ill-conceived. The strategy was partially vindicated by the successful debut of Chromecast in 2013. But the big question is whether Google will finally get it right with Android TV.

Chromecast is a tiny $35 WiFi device that plugs into the HDMI port of a smart TV. It brings Internet video content from mobile devices to the living room screen, using a smartphone or tablet in lieu of a dedicated remote control. With a growing number of content apps and an exceptionally low price point, Chromecast is giving Apple TV and Roku a run for their money.

Android TV, the third incarnation of Google TV, is a much bigger play, going head-to-head against Apple, Roku, and Amazon. The streamlined user interface will be integrated into various smart TVs and Internet set-tops, including Google's own Nexus Player, with dedicated remotes. It makes extensive use of Google's search algorithms for access to video, music, apps, and gaming content from the Google Play store. As with Chromecast, Android TV allows consumers to Google-cast (mirror) their content from computers and mobile devices to the big screen.

Google's hardware strategy has been erratic. The Google Nexus mobile devices are well-designed but don't sell well. The company jumped into the hardware deep end with its $12.5 billion acquisition of Motorola Mobility in 2013. It sold the Motorola Home (GI) business to Arris in 2013 for $2.3 billion. In 2014, it announced the $2.9 billion sale of the Motorola smartphone unit to Lenovo, the Chinese company that acquired IBM's ThinkPad PC business in 2005. These divestitures leave Google with Motorola's valuable wireless patent portfolio, the primary reason it bought Motorola in the first place.

Perhaps Google's other hardware endeavors will be more sustainable. Chromecast was a good start. In 2014, Google paid $3.2 billion for Nest Labs, a Silicon Valley "Internet of Things" start-up focused on user-friendly home appliances such as thermostats and smoke alarms. And the $99 Nexus Player, positioned directly against similar boxes from Apple TV, Roku, and Amazon, will gain some share.

Google's Internet TV strategy has been plagued by fits and starts. But with an extravagant abundance of money and talent, Google will likely figure it out and play a significant role above and beyond YouTube and Chromecast.

- **Roku** is a well-regarded consumer brand providing access to the widest variety of Internet content. While its market share lags that of Apple TV, it has carved out a strong and credible position by embracing the broadest possible range of content providers. Roku provides a window to over 1,000 Internet channels, including Netflix, Amazon, Hulu, HBO Go, Showtime Anytime, WatchESPN, Yahoo Screen, YouTube, MLB.TV, Crackle, Vudu, and M-GO.

The Roku box has become a mainstay, a consumer-friendly conduit for Internet video. The company is also licensing its software for integration into smart TVs, starting with inexpensive models from

Chinese companies TCL and Hisense. It introduced a $50 WiFi-enabled Roku Stick that, like Google Chromecast, plugs into the HDMI port of a digital TV. This combination of capabilities could make Roku an attractive acquisition candidate for a larger electronics company.

- **Sony** was once the shining star of consumer electronics. In the 1970s through the 1990s, Trinitron TVs commanded premium prices and Walkman music players were the iPods of their time. The company is striving to recapture its living room glory by assembling an Internet TV service, PlayStation Vue, planned for 2015. The ambitious endeavor will initially include around 75 linear TV channels from Viacom, CBS, NBCUniversal, Scripps Networks, 21st Century Fox, and Discovery, as well as on-demand content, all seamlessly integrated with an advanced user interface.

In July 2014, Sony Visual Products was incorporated as a subsidiary for the company's TV set business. The unit is an early leader in the Ultra HD (4K) market, and this could become a bright spot for Sony if the 4K market takes off.

Sony's installed base of 35 million connected PlayStations will serve as the initial target market for the PlayStation Vue Internet TV service. In late 2014, Sony launched PlayStation TV, a $99 device that attaches to the TV. It enables both gaming from the PlayStation ecosystem and Internet video from various services such as Netflix and Hulu.

By virtue of its $3.4 billion acquisition of Columbia Pictures in 1989, Sony is as much a content creator as a technology company.[1] Sony Pictures' Crackle subsidiary is a free, ad-supported Internet video service providing movies, TV shows, and some original content such as "Comedians in Cars Getting Coffee," hosted by

Jerry Seinfeld, and weekly game show "Sports Jeopardy!" Crackle is accessible from most modern Internet set-tops, game consoles, Blu-ray players, and mobile devices.

In 2014, Sony announced the acquisition of CSC Media Group, a substantial force in the UK television business with sixteen digital TV channels delivered over various platforms such as Murdoch's BSkyB and Malone's Virgin Media.

Sony's anticipated Internet TV service could finally achieve the company's vision of fusing content with consumer electronics. The Viacom deal is a strong foundation, but Sony needs a critical mass of more third-party TV programming if it is to succeed with this new venture. Some major content providers may refuse to license content to a Sony-controlled enterprise, however, and Sony Corporation continues to struggle financially.

- *Microsoft* also has the potential to play a unifying role in the Internet video market, balancing its interests in software, services, and hardware. Technologically, its Smooth Streaming solution and its PlayReady digital rights management (DRM) system rival the equivalent Internet video products from Apple and Adobe. In addition, Microsoft's Xbox franchise rivals that of Sony PlayStation. The Surface tablet is elegantly designed, although it hasn't achieved significant market share. Microsoft instantly became a major player in the smartphone business with its $7.2 billion acquisition of Nokia's cell phone business in April 2014. But gaining share against Apple, Samsung, and a new cadre of aggressive Chinese competitors, such as Huawei, ZTE, and Xiaomi, will be a major challenge.

The successful introduction of Xbox One during Christmas 2013 builds on Microsoft's huge installed base of connected game consoles, including nearly 50 million Xbox Live members in over forty countries who are playing interactive games and streaming video content. Microsoft originally positioned the Xbox One as an all-in-one "dream box" for the living room. It features an optional advanced version of the Kinect sensor, capable of being controlled by voice and by multiple hand gestures. It also incorporates a 1080P digital video camera for Skype video chats. The Xbox SmartGlass app links Xbox 360 and Xbox One consoles with PCs and various Microsoft, Apple, and Android-based tablets and smartphones. Despite these capabilities, Microsoft has decided to emphasize the Xbox One's primary utility for games.

Microsoft's content partners include Netflix, Hulu, HBO, MLB, the NBA, the NHL, ESPN, Nickelodeon, and Paramount Pictures. Microsoft was also developing original Internet TV content through Xbox Entertainment Studios, available exclusively to users of Microsoft devices. But the company shut down this activity as part of a July 2014 corporate restructuring. In November 2014, Microsoft paid $2.5 billion to acquire Swedish company Mojang, owner of Minecraft, the most popular online Xbox game.

Microsoft is going head-to-head against Apple, Samsung, Sony, Google, and Amazon. Given the intense competitive landscape, Microsoft remains an underdog when it comes to true leadership in the Internet TV business. But perhaps CEO Satya Nadella will figure out how to break away from the pack.

- *TiVo*, a digital video recorder (DVR) pioneer, continues to reinvent itself, most recently with new DVR products and a cloud-based software-as-a-service business model. TiVo is renowned for its consumer-friendly software and user interface. The company's DVR-related patents have been a lucrative source of revenue. For instance, through its "time warp" patent, TiVo has long claimed ownership of the fundamental intellectual property for time-shifting of TV programs. It has collected hundreds of millions of dollars in royalty settlements from set-top manufacturers and service providers—but usually only after litigation.

TiVo's DVRs should have been much more successful in the market, but the products were severely limited by the major video service providers and their captive set-top box suppliers. Although TiVo was once a favored supplier of DVR set-tops to DirecTV, it was squeezed out after Murdoch acquired DirecTV, which instead started procuring boxes from NDS, a company Murdoch also owned at the time.

Even so, TiVo's Roamio DVR product line continues to enchant high-end videophiles. And the TiVo Mega DVR, containing 6 digital tuners and a monstrous 24 terabytes of storage, can hold up to 2,000 HD movies.

More than just a box maker, TiVo has nearly 5 million subscribers, mostly through service providers such as Virgin Media in the United Kingdom and ONO in Spain. TiVo is trying again to break into the US cable market, incorporating a Netflix app into its boxes. The solution offers cable operators a clean integration of the linear TV world with the parallel universe of over-the-top Internet video, but so far mostly small to mid-sized operators are biting.

In 2014 TiVo acquired Digitalsmiths for $135 million. This leader in cloud-based search and recommendation software uses data analysis to drive the personalized video market.

From a technology standpoint, TiVo is in an ideal position to help consumers unify the traditional television world with Internet video. But its lack of market power is a major handicap, making an acquisition by a bigger company a more likely path.

- *Intel* is desperate to reduce its dependence on the PC and server microprocessor markets. The company has been trying for years to diversify into other devices. Yet it remains a secondary player in providing low-power, less-expensive chips to smartphones, tablets, and set-top boxes. In the early digital TV days of the 1990s, GI announced digital set-top box partnerships a couple different times with Intel and Microsoft, but none of these efforts materialized.

  In its biggest video venture to date, Intel Media was planning its own Internet TV service, OnCue. But Intel sold the operation to Verizon after having difficulty procuring top-tier content. Verizon plans to use the OnCue technology, including its highly touted user interface and advanced search and navigation software, for the future Internet video services of both Verizon FiOS and Verizon Wireless.[2]

  Like Microsoft and Motorola, Intel is a classic case of a large company with a dominant market position struggling to reinvent itself. Nonetheless, Intel remains the world's largest semiconductor company. It has reduced its product development cycles and is finally creating significant buzz for its new, low-power chips for tablets and smartphones.

- *China* is a market where homegrown Internet leaders are mirroring the frenzied activity occurring in the United States. Internet TV leader Youku—with a name that translates into "excellent and cool"—has its own Content Delivery Network and claims more than 200 million unique monthly online video users. Baidu, China's search engine giant, has assembled a streaming video website, iQiyi, coupled with its PPS.tv online content aggregation service. Smartphone leader Xiaomi has developed an Internet TV operating system, along with a set-top box and the MiTV smart TV, and plans to invest $1 billion in content.[3] Tencent Video will distribute HBO content over the Internet in China, although each program requires approval by China's government censors. And e-commerce behemoth Alibaba is keeping pace with its own Internet TV hardware, software, and content ventures.

- *ActiveVideo*, unlike the companies discussed above, which are competing for a direct role in the living room, is seeking to increase the functionality of consumer equipment by adding technological capability to the Internet cloud. Service providers use ActiveVideo's headend products, such as its CloudTV platform, to bring online content, interactive and personalized ads, cloud-based guides, and advanced user interfaces to their pre-existing digital TV subscribers without placing additional hardware in the home.

Backed by venture capitalist Gary Lauder, ActiveVideo started life as ICTV in the 1990s. In its early years, the company developed intellectual property related to interactive television, offering interactive services to skeptical cable operators. The company acquired Switched Media in 2006 and Avinity Systems in 2009.

ActiveVideo's CloudTV platform is used by Cablevision in New York, Ziggo in the Netherlands, Charter Communications, and others. Liberty Global's cable operation in Hungary uses CloudTV to deliver YouTube Internet videos through legacy digital cable boxes to the TV set. Similarly, HBO Europe teamed up with ActiveVideo and its CloudTV solution to allow European cable operators to deliver HBO Go content to digital cable subscribers via the traditional set-top box.

ActiveVideo was ahead of its time as a pioneer in interactive TV but has struggled over the years to find a profitable business model. With the increasing importance of the Internet to the digital TV environment, however, the company is finally gaining significant traction with multiple service providers.

60 THROUGH THE ELECTRONIC PORTALS OF OUR HOMES

It is exhausting to absorb the hyperactivity of this diverse group of Internet video content and technology companies. Pondering the implications is even more daunting.

We are being bombarded by limitless content options and the endless proliferation of connected devices. An inevitable consequence of this fertile environment is the chaotic Balkanization of the living room. But unlike Yugoslavia, glued together until 1980 by the dominant presence of Tito, the Internet video market is evolving without a benevolent dictator holding it all together.

The power is shifting inexorably toward the consumer through a democratic and decentralized process. Some consumers, especially of the younger demographic, enjoy the freewheeling structure. They thrive as creators and masters of their own video destiny. But most others will gravitate toward simplification, relying on a primary service provider to help maintain a semblance of order.

Apple, Google, and Roku will become the choice for many consumers to access content, while most service providers continue to work through Arris and Cisco. The home architecture is migrating toward a centralized and sophisticated home gateway, a super-router for all things digital. Digital TV, VOD, online video, website access, music, telephony, and residential security will all be filtered throughout the home via high-speed wires and WiFi.

With such an unwieldy array of technologies and services, the consumer interface becomes critical. Personalized content search and recommendation, in a simple and intuitive manner, is the Holy Grail. The remote control is ripe for disruption, incorporating modern technologies such as touch screen, voice recognition, and motion control.

Successful solutions must remain cognizant of the distinction between television and the Internet. Television, especially on the big screen, remains a "lean back, watch TV" experience. For an apps platform to succeed on the television platform, it needs to be positioned as an option, not a takeover. And the TV apps universe must be more closely controlled than that of the smartphone and tablet. AT&T U-Verse has been at the forefront of enabling TV apps for its subscribers. They have learned that the best apps are those which enhance, and don't distract from, the primary viewing experience.

At the same time, the living room has become a multiscreen arena. The big display remains a shared centerpiece, a visual vortex for family and friends. It is especially conducive to the relaxed, lean-back form of entertainment. In parallel, the room's individual viewers click away on tablets and smartphones, multi-tasking and supplementing their big-screen TV experience with social media interaction, ancillary viewing, and unrelated activities.

The quid pro quo of the Internet is consumers' implicit willingness to sacrifice privacy and security for convenience and efficiency. The living room is one of the last bastions of our untainted privacy. Yet consumers are installing smart TVs and Internet video boxes like there's no tomorrow, apparently oblivious to the implications of electronically opening up their homes. Ironically, even as we rage at the NSA's overzealous data collection and surveillance, under the cloak of protecting us from terrorism, we barely blink when it comes to intrusion by the masters of the Internet, their electronic wands following our every move and squeezing more money out of our wallets.

61 SPORTS, THE GREAT DIVIDE

In the brewing battle between the established service providers and the

Internet newcomers, sports content is the great divide. Distribution rights to the most popular sports events are owned by five major media companies: ESPN (Disney), Fox Sports (21st Century Fox), NBC Sports (Comcast), CBS Sports (CBS), and Turner Sports (Time Warner). Many of these events can also be watched on the Internet, but only by multi-channel subscribers via these same five companies' TV Everywhere platforms, not on Netflix, Hulu, or Amazon.

The role of sports programming in television is integral to pricing, packaging, customer satisfaction, and cord cutting. Sports content serves as a primary differentiator between competing platforms, while also exerting upward pricing pressure on the bundled package. And the rising importance of live, scheduled broadcasts of major sporting events is a salient paradox in an age of on-demand video.

Even as the five dominant sports programmers outbid one another for national sports rights, the professional leagues and the collegiate conferences launch their own dedicated channels. Consulting services firm PricewaterhouseCoopers estimated North American media rights for sports to cost $12.4 billion in 2013, rising to $17.1 billion in 2017.

Yet it's the consumer, the 100 million US multi-channel TV house-holds, who pays the ultimate bill in the form of pricey, bloated subscriptions. Continually escalating sports rights fees may become the straw that breaks the camel's back, driving a wedge through the broadly bundled content package.

ESPN is the most aggressive player in these bidding wars, helping it to become the leading sports television franchise. It is by far the most expensive basic cable programmer, collecting $6 per subscriber per month from its cable and satellite distributors. Assuming a reasonable retail markup, consumers are effectively paying as much for ESPN as they are for Netflix, creating a growing chorus of multi-channel subscribers who don't watch sports to question the value. ESPN3, the company's

Internet-only streaming video service, is available to subscribers of multi-channel packages from affiliated ISPs.

Fox Sports 1 launched in 2013 at less than $0.25 per subscriber per month, and the fee rose to $0.68 by 2014. Murdoch is in it for the long haul. We will surely see his new sports channel continue to climb the two-pronged revenue ladder over time, boosting ad revenue and demanding higher monthly fees from distributors, much like what he and Roger Ailes accomplished with Fox News.

In the United States, football sits at the top of the food chain. As the National Football League's revenue approaches $10 billion per year, an expanding pile of money spreads through the economy. The price of a thirty-second ad for Super Bowl XLIX, broadcast live by NBC on February 1, 2015, was around $4.5 million, more than twice the price in 2000 and four times the tab in 1995. Clearly this represents a startling burst of spending. But where else can an advertiser find more than 114 million people tuned in at the same time, many of whom are actually eagerly anticipating the ads? In this context, the Super Bowl ad price of about $39 per CPM[1] is not so exorbitant, similar to what advertisers pay for ordinary prime-time TV access to the consumer.[2]

Skyrocketing sports rights fees show no signs of abating. Consider the deals being made by professional sports organizations:

- *Football.* In 2011, the National Football League cut a record-setting $40 billion broadcast deal with NBCUniversal, CBS, Fox, and ESPN. The agreements cover nine years, from 2014 through 2022, for a fee of $4.4 billion per year, on average. In addition to broadcast rights, the contracts encompass TV Everywhere; the networks can simulcast games to computers and tablets, but not to smartphones, a niche the NFL carved out separately.

  Starting in 2014, the NFL entered into an exclusive four-year, $1 billion agreement with Verizon Wireless, allowing it to stream live regular-season and post-season games to smartphones. This superseded Verizon's $720 million NFL smartphone deal for the four years ending in 2013.

For another $300 million, the NFL separately licensed eight Thursday night games to CBS for the 2015 season, even though the NFL Network will carry all Thursday games on its own channel.

DirecTV has long offered out-of-market "NFL Sunday Ticket" games to its subscribers by virtue of a deal worth $1 billion per year to the NFL through 2014. DirecTV also offers these games on JetBlue flights and over Sony's PlayStation network, and to computer, tablet, and smartphone subscribers via its NFL Sunday Ticket app. Roughly 10 percent of DirecTV's 20 million subscribers pay extra for NFL Sunday Ticket.

NFL Sunday Ticket is such an important differentiator in the multi-channel pay TV business that the deal's renewal was a contractual contingency of AT&T's $48.5 billion acquisition of DirecTV. In October 2014, DirecTV reached agreement with the NFL for another eight years of NFL Sunday Ticket, reportedly for around $1.5 billion per year.

- **Basketball.** David Stern, a lawyer by training, was the commissioner of the National Basketball Association for thirty years, retiring in February 2014. He was also one of the early visitors to see GI's first digital television prototype in San Diego. He evidently took the technology to heart. During the David Stern era, basketball became the second most popular sport in the world, after soccer, and the NBA established itself as a global brand.

The league brings in $930 million per year through the 2015/2016 season for licensing television rights to ESPN and TNT. In this eight-year deal, ESPN and TNT also have VOD and streaming rights to PCs and mobile devices. The NBA now broadcasts into more than 200 countries, and along with multiscreen mobile rights, the next NBA television deal was destined to be far more lucrative.

Sure enough, in 2014, Disney (ESPN and ABC) and Turner Broadcasting (TNT) extended their TV rights through the 2024/2025 season, together agreeing to pay the NBA an average of over $2.6 billion per year for the nine-year extension. An important part of the deal is that ESPN will create an a la carte Internet streaming channel, which the NBA will have an equity stake in.

- **Baseball.** Major League Baseball inked a blockbuster $12.4 billion deal in 2012 with ESPN, Fox, and Turner Broadcasting. The new contracts cover the eight seasons from 2014 through 2021, with average annual payments of $700 million (ESPN), $500 million (Fox), and $300 million (TBS). In addition, the MLB Network, the league's own TV channel, retains broadcast rights for certain games to the more than 70 million US homes it now reaches.

Major League Baseball has been at the forefront of streaming sports over the Internet through MLB Advanced Media (known as "BAM"), a profitable company owned by the league's thirty professional teams. For the 2014 season, the basic subscription to MLB.TV, costing $110, included every regular season out-of-market game in HD (live and on-demand). The premium subscription, MLB.TV Premium, was $130 and included additional features plus viewing on over 400 different Internet-connected devices. BAM also has an official mobile app, MLB.com At Bat, allowing subscribers to watch instant replay videos on their mobile devices.

Beyond streaming professional baseball games over the Internet, BAM's Internet video technology infrastructure serves other franchises such as ESPN3.[3] The online video platform is also used by the National Collegiate Athletic Association's NCAA March Madness basketball tournament, and by the WWE (World Wrestling Entertainment) Network, a 24/7 Internet video subscription service producing live pay-per-view events and TV shows. BAM is even expanding outside the sports domain, distributing concerts and licensing its Internet streaming capabilities to entities as diverse as media commentator Glenn Beck and Southwest Airlines.[4]

Regional sports channels are yet another factor. During the 2014 baseball season, Time Warner Cable launched SportsNet LA (the Dodgers Channel), after reportedly committing $8.3 billion over twenty-five years to the Dodgers' new owners. As it attempted to start recouping this massive investment, Time Warner Cable once again found itself embroiled in controversy. It apparently demanded over $4 per subscriber per month from major unaffiliated service providers such as DirecTV, Dish Network, AT&T U-Verse, Cox, Charter, and Verizon FiOS. Time Warner Cable insisted that SportsNet LA be carried on these companies' basic cable tier, as opposed to being offered a la carte. And consumers in the Los Angeles area could not stream the games on MLB.TV due to the league's local blackout rules. At the end of the season, Time Warner Cable tried to redeem itself by letting KDOC-TV, an independent TV station serving LA, broadcast the first-place Dodgers' last six games.

- **Hockey.** During the early years of HDTV, a funny but true justification for the new technology was that viewers could finally see a hockey puck skimming across the ice in a televised game. In a ten-year $2 billion deal, lasting through the 2020/2021 season, Comcast's NBC Sports unit is producing and broadcasting National Hockey League games. The NHL Stanley Cup Playoffs are broadcast live on the NBC, NBCSN, and CNBC channels, as well as on computers and mobile devices through the NBC Sports

Live Extra app. Certain games are also carried on the hockey league's own NHL Network channel.

In hockey-crazed Canada, Rogers cemented a $5.2 billion deal with the NHL for twelve years starting in 2014, including television, Internet, and wireless rights.

- **Other sports.** Farther down the US sports food chain are soccer, tennis, auto racing, and golf. In anticipation of a growing domestic television audience, ESPN, Fox, and Univision committed over $700 million ($90 million per year) to Major League Soccer for the eight years spanning from 2015 to 2022. Fox and Spanish-language network Telemundo, owned by Comcast/NBC, agreed to pay a total of $1 billion, outbidding ESPN and Univision, for the rights to broadcast men's World Cup soccer in 2018 and 2022, and the women's World Cup games in 2015 and 2019.

  In the tennis arena, ESPN is paying $825 million over eleven years, starting in 2015, for exclusive rights to the US Open, ending CBS's franchise. In 2011, ESPN snapped up the rights to Wimbledon, superseding NBC, by paying $500 million for twelve years.

  NBC Sports secured NASCAR auto racing coverage through 2024, replacing ESPN by committing to a ten-year deal for $420 million to $450 million per year.

  And Rupert Murdoch shocked the golf world in 2013 when Fox Sports outbid NBC and ESPN for rights to the US Open. Fox reportedly paid more than $1 billion ($93 million per year for the twelve-year period ending in 2026) to the United States Golf Association to help kick-start his new Fox Sports 1 channel.5 Various PGA Tour events are divvied up between CBS Sports, NBC Sports, and Golf Channel through 2021.

Where does all this money go? One of the primary beneficiaries is the athletes' pockets. Superstar athletes, expected to "move the needle" for a team, in terms of both game scores and team revenues, will continue to command enormous premiums, and average salaries will continue to rise as well. The NFL, the NBA, and the NHL have instituted team salary caps as a check and balance and as an equalizer between teams. Major League Baseball has a "luxury tax," whereby teams exceeding an aggregate salary threshold pay a financial penalty, which goes back into the league's development fund. But as the television deals get bigger and bigger, the team salary caps grow as a result, a cycle with no end in sight.

While football salaries are not guaranteed, top NFL quarterbacks such as Drew Brees of the New Orleans Saints and Joe Flacco of the Baltimore Ravens are making around $20 million per year. In basketball, Kobe Bryant's salary, paid by the Los Angeles Lakers, scaled from $1 million in 1996/1997 to an NBA league record of $30 million in 2013/2014. LeBron James limited his deal to return to the Cleveland Cavaliers to 2 years and $42.1 million, betting he will be able to negotiate for much more starting in 2016 when a new NBA television rights deal kicks in. The New York Yankees' 2007 deal with an aging Alex Rodriguez, $275 million for 10 years, handcuffed the team financially. The Detroit Tigers signed an 8-year contract in 2008 with MVP and Triple Crown winner Miguel Cabrera for $152 million. Dodgers southpaw pitcher Clayton Kershaw signed up in January 2014, at age 25, for a 7-year, $215 million deal, an astonishing $30 million per year.

Sports rights fever has also caught on overseas. In February 2013, BT, operating its BT Vision IPTV (Internet Protocol Television) service, acquired ESPN's UK and Irish TV channels, which were loaded with soccer games as well as American sports content including NCAA college football, NCAA college basketball, and NASCAR racing. In

November 2013, BT paid $1.4 billion for three-year exclusive UK rights to Champions League and Europa League soccer matches, outbidding Murdoch's BSkyB, the previous holder of these rights.

On the talent side, according to *Forbes* magazine, Argentine soccer legend Lionel Messi took in $41.7 million in salary and winnings from FC Barcelona in 2014, while Cristiano Ronaldo was paid $52 million by Real Madrid.[6]

The professional leagues dominate sports TV inflation, but other sports contribute as well:

- *Olympics.* Comcast's NBCUniversal retained its hold on the Olympic Games with a winning bid of $4.4 billion for the four Olympics through 2020: the 2014 Winter Games in Sochi, Russia; the 2016 Summer Olympics in Rio de Janeiro; the 2018 Winter Olympics in Pyeongchang, South Korea; and the 2020 Summer Games in Tokyo. Subsequently, in May 2014, NBC extended its franchise through 2032 in a $7.75 billion deal with the International Olympic Committee. Every two years we will see Olympic events saturating not only NBC's affiliate TV stations, but also on NBCSN, USA, MSNBC, and CNBC.

  During the 2014 Sochi Games, NBC offered live Internet streaming of virtually every Olympic event, except the Opening Ceremony, on a TV Everywhere basis (for no additional charge to authenticated multi-channel subscribers). In the men's semifinal hockey game, in which Canada beat the United States in a 1–0 shutout, 2.1 million unique viewers streamed the event live to their Internet devices, believed to be the largest authenticated Internet streaming audience to date.[7] By the end of the Games, 61.8 million unique users had streamed one or more live events from NBCOlympics.com.[8]

  From the same website, NBC also provided access to every event on-demand. And parent company Comcast provided live Internet streaming to the living room screens of its X1 cable subscribers, even offering "start over" capability of certain events in several test markets.

The Olympics will, forever on, be a multiscreen panoply of live and on-demand choices for consumers.

- **College Sports.** The college sports category has also entered the pay TV picture in a big way. ESPN invested over $15 billion in college sports television rights, extending through the middle of next decade in some cases. For example, it paid $7.3 billion for college football playoff rights from 2014 through 2026.[9]

Jim Delany, commissioner of the Big Ten Conference for the last twenty-five years, recognized that digital TV technology could drive the Big Ten into a much bigger league financially. In 2006, Delany struck a ten-year, $1 billion television rights deal with Disney's ABC and ESPN. The next year, he created the Big Ten Network in a joint venture with Murdoch's Fox Entertainment Group.

The Big Ten Network, owned 51 percent by Fox and 49 percent by the Big Ten Conference, generated an estimated $270 million in 2013 for the conference and its colleges.[10] Based in Delany's hometown of Chicago, the Big Ten Network delivers over 1,000 HD events per year and is available to more than 60 million multichannel subscribers in the United States and Canada. With the 2014 addition of Rutgers University and the University of Maryland, the fourteen schools in the Big Ten have nearly 5 million alumni nationwide and a fan base of about 20 million.[11]

Not to be outdone, the Pacific-12 Conference consummated a twelve-year, $3 billion television deal in 2011 with ESPN and Fox. It also created the Pac-12 Networks, including one national channel and six regional college sports networks.

In partnership with ESPN, the Southeastern Conference launched the SEC Network in August 2014, utilizing ESPN's Charlotte, North Carolina, production facility.

Together, the three major college conferences generated over $760 million in revenue in 2012, with the Big Ten Conference garnering the most, $315.5 million.[12] Filling yet another gap, ESPN is creating fifteen Internet channels of college sports content from the smaller conferences, accessible through its WatchESPN app.

In 2010, Turner Broadcasting and CBS signed a fourteen-year, $10.8 billion deal for the NCAA March Madness men's basketball tournament ($770 million per year). Separate from these cash infusions, the NCAA learned from its professional-league counterparts the financial benefits of retaining some other assets for itself. The NCAA also operates an ad-supported website for March Madness, allowing viewing of live games over the Internet as well as on-demand viewing of prior games' highlights.

The sports TV business is an embarrassment of riches for many Division I universities. It's no wonder that the regional National Labor Relations Board in Chicago ruled in March 2014 that Northwestern University football players are employees of the university and therefore have the right to form a labor union. It's no wonder that a federal judge in California ruled in August 2014 that certain NCAA rules banning payments to college athletes violate antitrust law, and therefore some Division I athletes can be paid up to $5,000 per year for the use of their images in broadcasts and video games.

It should also be no surprise that the pricing of multi-channel TV packages containing sports programming—whether professional, Olympian, or collegiate—continues to rise.

62 CONTENT PRICE INFLATION

Inflation in the price of sports rights is demand driven, with consumers' insatiable viewing habits fueling the cycle. TV channels like ESPN and CBS Sports bid up the rights. Then they negotiate for steeper carriage fees from their cable and satellite distributors and higher rates from their advertisers. The service providers pass on what they can to their subscribers. But at the end of the chain, the TV households pick up the tab.

In addition to sports, another notable source of content price inflation is the retransmission fees charged by commercial broadcast stations. According to the 1992 Cable Act, every three years each commercial broadcast station can either elect "must carry," thereby forcing cable and satellite TV companies to distribute the broadcaster's signal with no fee paid to the TV station by the distributor, or "retransmission consent," whereby distribution fees are negotiated. Most of the popular network stations, the affiliates of CBS, NBC, ABC, Fox, and The CW, select retransmission consent. They know subscribers will demand their content, so they may as well get paid by their distributors. The parent companies of the broadcast networks typically bundle in their other cable channels as well, further inflating the prices paid by cable and satellite subscribers.

Janney Capital Markets estimates that retransmission fees for broadcast TV stations will grow from $3.5 billion in 2013 to nearly $6 billion in 2017. The networks typically receive over $1 per cable or satellite subscriber per month for their major market stations, with CBS reportedly getting in the $2 range as part of its acrimonious 2013 settlement with Time Warner Cable.[1]

Aereo, an Internet TV subscription service founded by Chet Kanojia, attempted to use new technology and the Internet to avoid retransmission fees for broadcast TV signals. The venture was backed by Barry Diller, chairman of Internet conglomerate IAC/InterActiveCorp and former head of Paramount Pictures, Fox Broadcasting, and Home Shopping Network. But Aereo ceased operations after a crucial Supreme Court decision in June 2014, and filed for Chapter 11 bankruptcy in November 2014.

Aereo's technology threatened to blow a hole in broadcast copyright law and reduce the fees received by the TV stations. The company used many remote, miniature antennas, along with cloud servers, to receive and store local over-the-air HD broadcast signals. It then streamed the channels over the Internet to connected devices, offering consumers monthly plans starting at $8 per month.

A group of broadcasters—CBS, NBC, Fox, ABC, and PBS—sued Aereo for copyright infringement, claiming it should pay retransmission carriage fees just like the cable operators. Relying on the Sony Betamax and Cablevision RS-DVR legal precedents, Aereo's defense invoked the fair use argument, asserting it was merely providing remote antennas and storage facilities for free over-the-air television programming. Because it assigned an antenna to each viewer, it claimed it was not making "public performances" and therefore did not infringe on the broadcasters' copyrights.

Starting in 2012, various federal courts ruled alternatively for and against Aereo. In January 2014 the US Supreme Court agreed to hear the case, *ABC Inc. v. Aereo*. In a 6–3 decision written by Justice Stephen Breyer in June 2014, the court ruled that Aereo was infringing the broadcasters' copyrights by conducting public performances, acting too much like a cable operator even though it used different technology. Justice Antonin Scalia authored the dissent, joined by Justices Samuel Alito and Clarence Thomas, which said the plaintiffs failed to prove Aereo was making public performances.

This landmark case provided a huge boost to the over-the-air broadcasters, solidifying their long-standing practice of collecting retransmission fees from service providers delivering their TV signals to consumers.

In a best case scenario for Aereo, the FCC may decide to classify certain Internet TV platforms offering broadcast stations and other linear channels as Multichannel Video Programming Distributors (MVPDs). If this occurs, Internet-based MVPDs would have equivalent program acquisition rights as cable and satellite TV operators, but they would similarly have to negotiate carriage fees with content providers.

The Supreme Court decision on the Aereo case means business as usual for the broadcasters. Content price inflation from popular TV stations will persist; thus retail pricing for multi-channel packages will continue to rise as well. Although the FCC and local municipalities regulate consumer pricing for multi-channel TV packages offered by cable and satellite distributors, and the increased competition among service providers helps keep a lid on prices, higher programming costs and large capital investments will continue the upward cost trends. SNL Kagan estimates that basic cable TV service, priced at an average of around $55 per month in 2014, will rise to nearly $62 by 2018. This equates to an annual increase of about 3 percent.

The retail rates, however, do not rise commensurately with the service providers' costs. The net result is that cable operators' video profit margins are being squeezed. SNL Kagan estimates that Comcast's video profit margins declined to 27 percent in 2013, while Charter's fell below 15 percent. In contrast, their high-speed Internet profit margins were in the 55–60 percent range, reflecting both less competition in this segment and a lack of rising cost pressure. The broadband ISPs continue to invest in their Internet infrastructures, but they don't have to pay for the content flowing through these pipes.

To alleviate some of this upward cost pressure, cable operators are implementing diverse strategies. In September 2014, mid-sized cable operator Cable One instituted a $2.94 monthly sports surcharge for all of its 730,000 subscribers, regardless of whether they watch sports.[2] For

$9 extra per month, Time Warner Cable offers Sports Pass, a package of more than a dozen sports channels including NFL RedZone, NHL Network, Fox Soccer Plus, CBS Sports Network, and Tennis Channel. Starting in January 2015, Time Warner Cable instituted a $2.75 per month sports surcharge on its subscribers' bills, on top of a similar "broadcast TV" surcharge, which several other operators also assess.

Fortunately for the cable operators, their conversion of subscribers to the triple play of video, data, and voice nearly doubled in the five years between 2008 and 2013, from 21 percent to over 40 percent. This diversification not only increases monthly revenue per subscriber but also lifts the average profit margins across the three product lines.[3]

The standoffs between content providers and distributors have also become more frequent, with consumers caught in the middle as channel blackout victims. These self-inflicted crises, whereby neither side is willing to concede until the situation reaches a breaking point, cause lasting breaches in consumer satisfaction.

CBS's summer 2013 retransmission fee dispute with Time Warner Cable, during which CBS, Showtime, and other channels were blacked out for millions of subscribers, was a watershed event for popular TV networks gaining the upper hand over distributors. Time Warner lost 300,000 video subscribers during that quarter (primarily to competing service providers), and CBS achieved its goal of getting higher retransmission fees for its broadcast network. But at some point the fee increases will exceed the tolerance of the subscriber. That is where cord cutting and content repackaging come into play.

63 CORD CUTTING

The reports of TV's death have been greatly exaggerated.[1] However, the days of receiving your television content bundled in a nice, neat package from a single service provider, delivered to a solitary, stationary screen in the living room, are certainly numbered. The blossoming of the broadband Internet brings forth the ability to procure content from multiple sources. But that doesn't mean that the entrenched multi-channel video providers are in trouble. On the contrary, their businesses are thriving and their Internet-based TV Everywhere offerings are growing in both reach and popularity. What will undoubtedly change is the increasing proportion of content that consumers view over the Internet, both to smart TVs and to mobile devices.

So what does this mean for the future? Will subscribers ditch their service providers and instead order content a la carte over the Internet?

In a single week in October 2014, HBO, CBS, and Univision separately announced a la carte Internet TV services that will be sold directly to US consumers. Yet these content leaders must position their new over-the-top services in a way that doesn't cannibalize their lucrative pre-existing business model of selling through service providers. Most consumers will continue to demand packages of content for the simple reason that it gives them more content for less money. At the same time, market forces will necessitate smaller, less expensive, and more personalized offerings.

Traditional television viewing is alive and well. Nielsen reported that in the second quarter of 2014, US adults (18 and over) spent an average of roughly 4.5 hours per day watching live TV plus another half-hour per day viewing time-shifted TV (DVR or VOD). The combined total of just over 5 hours per day had declined 8 minutes from the second quarter of 2013. This slight decline was more than offset by Internet video viewed on computers and mobile devices, which increased during the same period across all demographics, even for the 50–64-year demographic. Adults in the 18–34-year group increased their computer/mobile digital video consumption from an average of 23 minutes per day in the second quarter of 2013 to 35 minutes per day in the second quarter of 2014.[2]

Digital TV multiplied subscribers' choices, viewing options, and video quality. But the freedom of the Internet gives consumers more control over what content they pay for and from whom it is obtained. So far, the incumbent video service providers barely have chinks in their armor. The number of US multi-channel TV subscribers is hovering around 100 million, equal to 86 percent of the 116.3 million television households estimated by Nielsen. But in the fullness of time, their powerful legacy will come under increasing assault from over-the-top Internet video services.

Some TV consumers are already abandoning video service providers and "cutting the cord," or terminating their monthly cable, satellite, or telco TV subscriptions and instead relying on some combination of Internet video and free over-the-air broadcast television. The potential for consumers to cut the cord will continue to be the subject of heated debate.

The term "cord cutter" is a bit of a misnomer, however. Perhaps cord swapping would be more accurate; those who cancel their cable TV subscription generally switch to or retain a broadband Internet cord, typically provided by the same company.

Experian Marketing Services separately identifies "cord nevers," broadband Internet subscribers who never signed up for multi-channel pay TV subscriptions in the first place. Experian estimated the total number of "cord nevers" to be 7.6 million US households in 2013, up from 5.1 million in 2010.[3]

Nielsen estimates a slightly smaller "Zero TV" group, comprising about 5 million US households in 2013, up from about 2 million in 2007.[4] These consumers still watch plenty of video, but they are a new breed apart from Nielsen's legacy definition of TV Households. They obtain their content solely from non-traditional viewing devices, such as Roku and Sony PlayStation boxes connected via the Internet to their TVs, or from computers and mobile devices. In 2014, Nielsen added broadband-only homes (with at least one operable TV/monitor) to the definition of TV Household, leading to its estimate of 116.3 million TV homes in the United States for 2014/2015.

For the last several years, most cable operators have continued to experience video subscriber losses each quarter but mostly to competing telco TV and satellite providers. In other words, a disgruntled Time Warner Cable subscriber might switch to Verizon FiOS or DirecTV. Yet the total number of US multi-channel TV households remains around 100 million, and the number of true cord cutters is only several million so far.

The next wave of cord cutters will come from the younger demographic group, consumers who grew up using the Internet and believe that service providers charge excessive fees for content packages containing many channels they don't want. Consumers uninterested in live sports and live news are also susceptible to the cord-cutting bug, as are those who choose to get free over-the-air content by installing DTV antennas to receive digital terrestrial broadcast signals.

The video incumbents are highly resilient, however, and the vast majority of households will retain the advantages of having a primary provider of multiple services, so long as it is a reasonable value proposition. The established service providers will continue to adapt to the market, leveraging and modifying their service-bundling strategies and breadth of content, to sustain the subscription cord. The industry's video-on-demand and TV Everywhere initiatives are designed to further lock in the cable model, and so far this strategy appears to be working rather effectively. Nonetheless, they will ultimately need to offer more flexible video packages and prices, including lower cost options, or risk losing substantially greater numbers of video subscribers.

Netflix aspires not only to be a popular add-on to existing multi-channel packages, but also to become the primary alternative for consumers who have become disenchanted with their incumbent service providers. It has established itself as a competitor to HBO and

Showtime using aggressive pricing, effective marketing, an outstanding user interface, a deep library of movies and TV shows, technology leadership, innovative customer service, broad reach onto Internet-connected devices, and a content strategy increasingly inclusive of original content. But Netflix has too many gaps, especially in sports, news, and current TV episodes, to become a full replacement for multi-channel packages. So far it is primarily a supplement to a traditional multi-channel subscription rather than a threatening base layer of an Internet do-it-yourself package.

But as the Internet options continue to expand, one can envision a growing pool of cable and satellite subscribers taking only a basic package from their service providers and supplementing it with Netflix and other Internet options, or completely switching to the Internet. Anticipating these potential trends, Comcast and Time Warner Cable are experimenting with lower priced, smaller content packages that include HBO and around twenty other channels.

Whether cord cutting remains a dribble or becomes a drove, growing from today's single-digit percent of TV households to tomorrow's 20 percent and beyond, will depend on multiple factors:

- the extent to which a critical mass of high-quality original and unique content can be assembled from an assortment of Internet providers

- the addition of more live sports events to the repertoire of Internet content

- whether the cable TV incumbents dramatically improve their customer service

- more flexible and cost-effective content packaging options offered by the incumbents

- potential government regulation and litigation

The unpredictable behavior of the consumer is another big factor. In particular, as more households are formed by the millennial generation,[5] Internet-only viewing will become a badge of pride, and cord retention will face its most formidable challenge. The millennials and their successors perceive multi-tasking, the Internet, and freedom of choice as innate birth rights—not exactly the best fit for the traditional television content-packaging model. They also thrive on an eclectic viewing paradigm: binging on multiple episodes from Netflix or HBO; snacking on brief clips from YouTube or Vine; and seamlessly switching between the screens of the living room and their mobile devices.

If cord cutting were to take hold in the broader consumer market, one can envision three broad, overlapping phases during which people will progressively migrate to the Internet for their video consumption:

- **2005 through 2015:** The Internet starts to become an attractive video platform, with continuously improving content offerings from MLB.TV, ESPN, Netflix, Amazon, YouTube, and many others. These Internet video services are primarily supplemental to traditional pay TV packages.

- **2016 through 2025:** Smaller, independent cable operators either get acquired or begin abandoning their legacy subscription TV business in favor of higher-margin broadband Internet service. Following HBO, CBS, and Univision, Internet versions of the most popular linear TV channels are made available a la carte. In response, leaner and more personalized content packages are offered by the incumbent service providers.

- **2026 through 2035:** Major wireline service providers (Comcast, Verizon) continue migrating away from their legacy TV architectures to the Internet. They still provide content packages to subscribers, although mini-packages and a la carte options become widely available. Sports content becomes less of a divide between traditional TV and the Internet. Over-the-top video providers continue to have equal competitive access to subscribers through ISPs' broadband pipes. Wireless broadband becomes a competitive factor in the video business.

Cord cutting is a real trend, but the multi-channel incumbents are too strong and too smart to sit idly by awaiting a mass exodus. By owning the "last-mile" pipes into homes, they will continue finding ways to make money within the boundaries of the open Internet. "The times they are a-changin'," but the change is gradual. In the meantime, consumers are benefiting from more video suppliers, more content, and more viewing options.

64 CONTENT PRICING AND PACKAGING

The Internet is a powerful agent of change. The monthly TV bill, and the corresponding value accruing to consumers, will become increasingly sensitive as less expensive alternatives proliferate over the Internet. The very threat of cord cutting is causing the content community and traditional video service providers to experiment and rethink their business strategies related to content packaging and pricing. But we should not underestimate the inertia weighing in favor of the entrenched service providers.

The most minimalist package of cable TV service is typically in the $20–25 per month range, including local TV channels plus some others. "Expanded basic," a broad-based assortment of digital SDTV and HDTV content, is priced at $55–60 per month. Premium services such as HBO or Showtime (including their digital multiplex HD and SD linear channels, VOD, and TV Everywhere offerings) are around $15 per month, sometimes less with promotions or if purchased as part of a triple-play bundle. The average US cable subscriber pays approximately $75–80 per month for video service, including set-top box rental fees. At the high end, in the third quarter of 2014, Cablevision received $97 on average for video service, and the average DirecTV monthly bill was $107. Relative to the expenses associated with taking a family out to the movies, or for monthly smartphone service, these numbers are not unreasonable.

In contrast, a cord cutter might pay $40 per month for high-speed Internet, plus $9 per month for Netflix and $8 per month for Hulu Plus. Free Internet content, such as YouTube or Crackle, is also available, and the consumer may be able to receive free over-the-air local digital HD channels with a TV antenna. That $57 sum is similar to the price of an expanded basic digital cable package. However, in the Internet-only package, there is substantial content missing from what certain members of a typical family might want, especially with respect to live sports and current episodes of many TV shows. Live news is less of an issue, as many promising video news sites are popping up on the Internet, including HuffPost Live, Reuters.TV, Al Jazeera's AJ+, and CNNgo.

If one considers the most popular expanded basic channels—USA, TNT, ESPN, ESPN2, Disney, A&E, AMC, FX, Comedy Central, TBS, Fox News, CNN, MSNBC, CNBC, Discovery, E!, BET, HGTV, ABC Family, Food Network, Lifetime, Syfy, History, Bravo, Nickelodeon, MTV, SundanceTV, Cartoon Network, and a number of others—a wide variety of content is still only available with a cable or satellite subscription. On the other hand, some consumers don't mind waiting for their favorite content to find its way onto the Internet.

There is also the stubborn presence of the Internet pirate market, filling the content gap for less scrupulous consumers. These website directories and video sources come and go depending on law enforcement activities. Movies and TV shows, including the most recent episodes, are found from websites like Project Free TV, vast content directories that link Internet users to servers located in various countries. File downloads are facilitated by BitTorrent technology and its derivatives or by content-specific "magnet" links, through websites such as The Pirate Bay, KickassTorrents, and YTS (formerly called YIFI Torrents).

BitTorrent, Inc., the company that originated the Internet file delivery technology, is attempting to succeed as a legitimate Internet technology company. It is even trying to use crowdfunding to help develop original Internet video content. *Children of the Machine* is set in Malibu, California, in 2025. A free trailer depicts a fourteen-year-old girl ruminating about the coolest new teen trend, a chip embedded under the skin that induces "jolting," a fresh state of augmented reality. If BitTorrent is able to raise enough money, it will finish producing its first season of episodes.[1]

Some pundits believe that the success of Internet video will force the cable and satellite TV providers to fully unbundle their content packages and offer channels on an a la carte basis, meaning the ability to buy individual channels rather than an entire package. But alas, content pricing is far more complicated than that, and implementing new packaging strategies to retain subscribers is a much more likely scenario than moving to a true a la carte model. For example, Comcast, Time Warner Cable, and AT&T are experimenting with smaller packages of content and a lower "buy through" hurdle in order to get HBO, even as HBO moves toward an a la carte Internet option in 2015.

The stronger content providers will increasingly offer over-the-top, a la carte services as an adjunct to their traditional bundled distribution. But the great paradox of a pure a la carte model is that it would not necessarily reduce monthly fees for most consumers, especially families that collectively demand a broad variety of content. Furthermore, a complete shift to a la carte would force many special interest channels out of business, a

Darwinian win for the survivors but a utilitarian and macroeconomic loss. The deep packaging of content—by content providers and then, in turn, by distributors—enables niche channels to survive.

Content companies and service providers must move very carefully toward offering a la carte channels. Viacom, Time Warner, Fox, Disney, and NBCUniversal typically negotiate all-or-nothing multi-channel carriage agreements with their distributors. For example, in 2012, Comcast and Disney announced an unusually comprehensive agreement allowing Comcast to distribute seventy Disney services for a ten-year period, encompassing broadcast, video-on-demand, and multiscreen TV Everywhere rights. However, the result of deals like this one is that the distributors end up paying rather handsomely for channels their subscribers may not watch. Then the distributors, in turn, offer even broader packages of content to their subscribers.

Bundled packages of content will likely continue to prevail, absent litigation or legislation to stop the practice. Quite simply, linear TV channels are addicted to their dual revenue streams of advertising and carriage fees. For example, in addition to ad revenue, ESPN collects around $6 per subscriber per month in carriage fees from its cable and satellite distributors, generating $6–7 billion in annual revenue. Some regional sports networks command over $2 per subscriber per month. TNT and Disney Channel each receive well over $1 per subscriber per month, and most other channels generate between $0.10 and $1 on the same basis, depending on the number of subscribers managed by the distributor. These channels negotiate for higher carriage fees with their distributors every chance they get. Of course they are also distributing content over the Internet. But this TV Everywhere activity is primarily a strategic addition to their mainstream arrangement.

For many years, Senator John McCain has been pushing unsuccessfully for a la carte pricing. Most recently, in May 2013, McCain introduced legislation called the Television Consumer Freedom Act of 2013, with the following introduction: "For over 15 years I have supported giving consumers the ability to buy cable channels individually, also known as 'a la carte'—to provide consumers more control over viewing options in their home and, as a result, their monthly cable bill."[2]

If a la carte content does come to fruition, however, the service providers and the surviving content providers will find ways to maintain their revenues, and aggregate monthly bills to consumers will not necessarily decline. Pricing for individual services would increase relative to the imputed pricing of the same channels within a bundle.

One can imagine a scenario in which service providers offer subscribers a choice between packages of content or a la carte channels. Hypothetically, consider subscribing to ESPN at $15 per month; USA, Fox News, CNN, Disney, and FX at $3–5 each per month; and Comedy Central, Food Network, and Nickelodeon at $1–2 each per month. Some single people might opt for just a handful of channels and save some money. Families would select a bigger list of individual channels, satisfying the different ages and interests of their members. Most would find it more cost-effective to purchase a content package.

A la carte sounds good in theory. But a full transition to a la carte content seems impractical given the complex and established dynamics of the subscription television business. It makes infinite sense for service providers to continue experimenting with new, more flexible packages, including lower-cost options. More sports packages; more economical mini-bundles of content; HBO, Showtime, and Starz a la carte: These trends will continue given the nature of the beast. The broadband Internet is an incredibly disruptive and motivating force.

65 SPEED AND COMPETITION IN THE BROADBAND FUTURE

We should remind ourselves that most major service providers have separate pipes for TV content and Internet content. Digital cable TV architecture is based on digital video compression using the MPEG-2 or MPEG-4 video standards, 256 QAM transmission, and MPEG-2 transport stream packets. The DOCSIS broadband Internet cable modem platform also uses QAM for modulation. But unlike the digital cable TV pipe, DOCSIS employs Internet protocols and passes through whichever video compression technique the content provider happens to be using.

If the Internet becomes the ultimate destination for all content, major video service providers will facilitate a long-term migration to Internet architecture. As a result, they will need to adapt their pricing and business models. Data caps and pricing tiers will become more commonplace, especially on heavy users.

As of 2014, the United States had broadband Internet penetration greater than 75 percent (more than 92 million households), feeding connected devices throughout the home.[1] These figures exclude wireless Internet usage. The choices for broadband Internet Service Provider (ISP) are more limited than for subscription TV service, however, with only one or two high-speed competitors in most markets. Cable modems remain the US market leader for wired broadband Internet access, followed by DSL and fiber-to-the-home. Also, average data speeds in the United States lag behind such places as Hong Kong, South Korea, Japan, the Netherlands, and even Latvia, while pricing remains stubbornly higher than in these other countries. Outside North America, DSL and fiber optics are generally more prevalent than cable modems, and the higher Internet speeds in many markets are the result of national industrial policies and smaller populations (fewer homes to connect).

There are hopeful signs, however, that broadband speeds in the United States, spurred by competition, are on the rise. Cable operators have adopted the DOCSIS 3.0 standard for cable modems, and they will move toward the multi-gigabit per second DOCSIS 3.1 architecture starting in late 2015. Verizon's FiOS fiber optic service is available in 20 percent of the country, while AT&T U-Verse is available to about a quarter of US homes, using advanced, high-speed DSL. AT&T is building 1 Gbps networks ("GigaPower") in Austin and Dallas, with additional plans in parts of North Carolina and many other metropolitan areas.

Google is the biggest wild card. Google Fiber in Kansas City, Provo, Utah, and Austin, Texas, advertises speeds up to 1 Gbps, although actual speeds are slower. But it is still exponentially faster than a typical cable modem home. The company is planning similar networks in many other cities. Google's pricing for its blazing-speed Internet service alone is $70 per month. It charges $120–130 per month for both Internet and basic digital TV service, with optional pay packages for sports, HBO, Cinemax, Showtime, Starz, and Hispanic content. Other than the Internet speed, none of this is earth-shattering. But once Google's technology and service infrastructure is embedded and widespread, the company could start turning business models upside down. Google Fiber has the potential to be a game changer. On the other hand, if the company can't finesse the leap from search advertising leader to broadband service provider, Google Fiber could end up as an expensive experiment.

If nothing else, these aggressive initiatives are upping the ante and forcing Comcast, AT&T, and Verizon to keep pace, to continue investing, and to build faster and more advanced Internet pipes that will carry the content of the future. In Austin, three companies are vying for leadership with 1 Gbps service: AT&T U-Verse, Google Fiber, and Grande Communications. Time Warner Cable is also in the mix with its 300 Mbps service. Other companies announcing 1 Gbps speed in limited areas include Bright House Networks, Cox, Atlantic Broadband, and Cincinnati Bell. Some municipalities and other organizations have also built these high-speed fiber networks in places such as Chattanooga, Tennessee; Lafayette, Louisiana; Bristol, Virginia; Wilson, North Carolina; Seattle, Washington; Springfield, Vermont; and Hollis, New Hampshire.

Then there are the Internet alternatives, great for convenience and general access but insufficiently robust and impractical for mainstream video. New generation satellites from WildBlue (owned by Viasat) and HughesNet (owned by EchoStar) have improved their data speeds. And once again there's Google, which intends to invest over $1 billion for a global satellite Internet platform.[2]

WiFi outside the home is increasingly widespread, but coverage can be spotty and unreliable.[3] The CableWiFi Alliance—Comcast, Time Warner Cable, Cox, Cablevision, and Bright House—announced over 250,000 WiFi roaming hotspots nationwide in 2014. Comcast alone is scaling up its WiFi ambitions to 8 million US hotspots and is teaming up with Liberty Global on an international WiFi roaming deal potentially covering up to 45 million roaming subscribers between the United States and Europe.

In the wireless telco domain, 4G LTE is a dramatic improvement over 3G. Digital video over 4G networks can look surprisingly good, but only in less populated areas with uncrowded cells; 4G doesn't have the intrinsic bandwidth to support video services on a mass scale. In South Korea, wireless carriers SK Telecom and LG's U+ are taking the lead in "LTE Advanced," combining three different wireless bands of spectrum to allow data speeds up to 300 Mbps and beyond. Someday 5G and 6G wireless standards will arrive, using additional spectrum and new technologies to enable much higher speeds.

The sum of these new activities and advanced technologies will eventually turn high-speed Internet into a very competitive business. It may take five to ten more years, but when this finally happens, the battle between cable and telcos, and between wired and wireless services, will reach a crescendo—and consumers will benefit with more choices and lower prices.

66 NETWORK NEUTRALITY AND THE OPEN INTERNET

The US Department of Defense funded the origins of the Internet, and the US government's laissez-faire approach allowed the Internet to grow in utility and popularity in the United States and around the world. But it was private enterprise that transformed the Internet into a commercial success. AT&T and Level 3 built fiber optic backbones; Cisco and Juniper developed routers and switches; Akamai and Limelight designed content delivery networks (CDNs); and Comcast and Verizon invested in last-mile broadband pipes for residential and business access.

A basic tenet of the Internet, as it evolved, is that it should be "open," adhering to an unwritten constitution stipulating universal access and freedom of expression. A related goal was to ensure that no gatekeepers were established. Participants should not be inhibited or precluded from delivering or accessing whatever legal content they desire. The Internet has remained remarkably true to these principles, along with a broad consensus that it should remain open, with fair and equal access to all comers.

But in a commercial context, we should not confuse "open" with "free." We should not confuse freedom of access with a free ride. As long as there is sufficient competition and consumer choice, we should not presume that the definition of "open" precludes content companies and service providers from charging reasonable prices for their products and services. Consumers pay Internet Service Providers (ISPs) and subscription services for monthly access; CDNs charge content providers for faster delivery; and backbone networks settle up financially when there are substantial traffic imbalances. This framework evolved through tough negotiations, by trial and error, and in the presence of competitive forces.

So with consumers watching an increasing volume of video over the Internet, and with video occupying a rapidly growing share of the Internet's traffic and bandwidth, what should be the new rules of the road? Who should be able to charge whom, and for what? Is there sufficient competition? Who should even decide these big questions: The Federal Communications Commission? Congress? The Supreme Court? The open marketplace? All of the above?

A fateful decision occurred in March 2002. With Michael Powell as chairman, the FCC declared Internet access via cable modems to be an "information service" rather than a tightly regulated "telecommunications service." The Telecommunications Act of 1996 distinguishes between the two, with the latter category remaining heavily regulated under the "Title II" common carriers provision of the Communications Act of 1934.[1] The FCC's rationale in classifying high-speed data over cable as an information service was based on a belief that its premier objectives— stimulating investment in broadband communications infrastructure, encouraging innovation, and promoting universal availability—would be best served by market evolution rather than government regulation.

As the Internet continued to progress toward its enormous commercial success, concerns escalated regarding the potential for censorship and favoritism, and the term "network neutrality" entered the public discourse. The phrase originated in a 2002 memo entitled "A Proposal for Network Neutrality," written by legal scholar Tim Wu.[2] The philosophy of net neutrality is that all legal content, services, and applications, and their associated data packets, should be treated equally with regard to delivery over the Internet; and that consumers should have unfettered access to such content.

In June 2005, the Supreme Court, in a 6–3 decision, affirmed the FCC's classification of residential broadband service as a lightly regulated information service. This ruling occurred in the "Brand X" case, in which a small California ISP sought to force cable operators to share their broadband infrastructure with competitors. Justice Clarence Thomas delivered the majority opinion, while Justice Antonin Scalia issued a vigorous dissent arguing that cable ISPs are providing telecommunications services subject to Title II. Five weeks later, the FCC also classified DSL service as an information service, placing telcos and cable ISPs on equivalent regulatory footing.

In September 2005, the FCC issued a broad, non-enforceable statement of principles related to encouraging broadband deployment and to promoting and preserving an open Internet. The features of an open Internet, however, were not easily defined. And with a limited number of broadband ISPs controlling the last-mile pipes into consumers' homes, a debate erupted over whether anyone should be allowed to prioritize content over the Internet and how scarce bandwidth should be allocated fairly. The controversy intensified with the surging popularity of bandwidth-intensive Internet video.

In 2010, the FCC issued its Open Internet Order under Chairman Julius Genachowski. This set of rules, intended to instantiate network neutrality, focused on three general aspects of broadband Internet service:

- The "transparency" rule was designed to ensure that broadband ISPs publicly disclose the performance, pricing, and network management aspects of their services.

- The "no blocking" rule asserted that ISPs could not prevent legal content, services, applications, or devices from gaining access to their networks.

- The "no unreasonable discrimination" rule stated that service providers' traffic policies should not "harm innovation, investment, competition, end users, and free expression." Notably, this third rule allowed "reasonable discrimination" in the context of "reasonable network management."

Verizon sued the FCC, however, claiming the rules exceeded the agency's regulatory authority and could inhibit market growth. In January 2014, the US Court of Appeals for the DC Circuit ruled in Verizon's favor, dealing a major blow to the FCC's role with respect to network neutrality. The court decided that since the FCC had long classified broadband Internet as an information service, rather than as a telecommunications service, the agency lacked the authority to implement its own network neutrality rules. In essence, the transparency rule was upheld, but the antiblocking and antidiscrimination rules were denied.

FCC Chairman Tom Wheeler, a former CEO of the National Cable Television Association, took a glass-half-full approach, interpreting the court ruling as affirming his agency's authority over both ISPs (such as Comcast) and Internet content providers (such as Netflix).[3] By April 2014, the FCC announced a forthcoming new set of rules subject to a notice of proposed rulemaking and public comment. A record-shattering deluge of 3.7 million comments was submitted to the FCC by September 15, when the public comment period officially ended. The FCC is now in a difficult position, testing its own power while navigating a complex concoction fraught with political, economic, legal, and regulatory issues.

At minimum, the new FCC rules, expected in 2015, will contain broad measures seeking to protect consumers and smaller content providers, and to maintain competitive markets. The wireless Internet, exempted from the previous rules, will also officially become part of the framework. A separate network neutrality debate is occurring in the European Parliament and in the European Union, with a political attempt being made to orchestrate a pan-European set of rules.

Some open Internet advocates, including President Obama, are urging the FCC to reclassify broadband ISPs as Title II telecommunications service providers. In this scenario, they would become tightly regulated as common carriers, considered to be providing a basic utility like telephony. But such an approach would face tremendous opposition, an uphill battle with severe legal and political hurdles. There is a legitimate fear that such a heavy-handed approach would inhibit private investment at a time when our broadband infrastructure is still evolving. For Internet video to reach its ultimate destination, we need broadband service providers to invest billions more in DOCSIS 3.1 and 1 Gbps networks.

What all of this means for Comcast, Netflix, and their industry peers is up in the air. Comcast, as part of its original purchase of NBCUniversal, agreed to abide by the 2010 network neutrality rules until at least January 2018. The company has broadened this commitment to any additional homes it obtains as part of the proposed Time Warner Cable acquisition. But the January 2014 federal appeals court decision, along with a divided FCC, softens the network neutrality bite of the FCC, putting into play once again the rules of the road.

In late February 2014, a month after the federal court vacated the FCC network neutrality rules, Netflix and Comcast announced an Internet "peering" agreement. Netflix is now paying Comcast to directly connect Netflix's video servers to Comcast's broadband Internet pipes, rather than continuing to go through an intermediary. Netflix has also struck broadband ISP peering agreements with AT&T, Verizon, and Time Warner Cable.[4] Peering arrangements have long been customary in the Internet business when there is a substantial traffic imbalance between two parties. But these precedents were generally between similarly situated long-haul Internet carriers, not between content providers and residential broadband ISPs. Furthermore, this agreement doesn't guarantee Netflix a specific quality of service, or a minimum sustained bit rate, for moving traffic down Comcast's last-mile broadband pipes into homes.

Netflix's video occupies up to a third of Comcast's total Internet traffic during prime-time hours.[5] The more successful Netflix becomes, the more contention will occur during peak hours for Comcast's finite Internet bandwidth. The average bit rate for Netflix streams delivered to Comcast's cable modem subscribers had been above 2 Mbps from November 2012 until November 2013. But then it started to decline, hitting a low of 1.5 Mbps in January 2014. By March, shortly after signing the Comcast peering deal, Netflix's average rate to Comcast subscribers spiked up to 2.5 Mbps, and then rose to 3.1 Mbps in November 2014.[6] Note that even these higher rates, on average, are insufficient to sustain a high-quality HDTV picture for certain content, although Netflix has done an impressive job with its adaptive streaming and video encoding technologies.

So should Comcast be allowed to charge Netflix for an "express" lane that would allow Netflix's subscribers to receive high-quality video over Comcast's Internet pipes? The rubber will meet the road with Ultra HD (4K), which offers four times the video resolution of the current generation of HDTV technology. Along with the promise of beautiful new pictures comes the infrastructure price tag associated with this colossal new bandwidth hog. It will be fascinating to watch the future industry machinations as Netflix, Amazon, YouTube, and others start trying to deliver more Ultra HD content to broadband Internet subscribers. Netflix is recommending consumer access speeds of 25 Mbps for Ultra HD, eight times its current average rate over Comcast's broadband Internet pipes.

The basic problem with the FCC explicitly allowing Comcast to charge Netflix for an express lane is that, in practice, everyone else would be relegated to the regular information highway. Assuming that Comcast has a fixed amount of bandwidth at any given time, more bandwidth allocated to a limited number of leading content providers for Internet TV implies fewer bits, and potentially slower speeds, for everyone else. Several important over-the-top Internet video companies—Netflix, Amazon, Hulu, MLB.TV, Yahoo, Microsoft, Sony, and Google/YouTube—have sufficiently deep pockets to be able to pay broadband ISPs reasonable fees for faster access to consumers. But what about smaller content providers that are struggling to survive? And how would Comcast's own Internet video content services (Streampix, NBC Sports Live Extra) be treated in this context?

On the other hand, cable's broadband Internet pipes were built not only with private investment dollars but also with an expectation of differentiated quality of service—in other words, the ability to provide prioritized services for the benefit of consumers, rather than the "best efforts" delivery intrinsic to the general public Internet. If subscribers are paying $12 per month for the Netflix tier that includes Ultra HD content, or watching the Olympics on NBC Sports Live Extra, shouldn't they expect a better quality of service than for free YouTube music videos or pirate movies from a BitTorrent-enabled site?

Competition and innovation are the twin pillars essential for Internet video to ultimately attain equivalence with traditional digital television. Comcast and Netflix are both thriving in the current environment, as is the Internet in general. Innovation is raging, and ISPs are continually expanding bandwidth and capacity. But competition for high-speed Internet service to the home remains limited, and competition is the biggest lever for ensuring network neutrality. Ideas like investment tax credits for new broadband infrastructure and relaxing restrictions on municipalities' ability to build fiber networks should be considered. The FCC should hold the heavy hammer of reclassifying broadband ISPs under Title II in reserve as a last-ditch option, a future backstop against blatant, egregious behavior.

Assuming Comcast purchases Time Warner Cable and AT&T swallows up DirecTV, around half of the broadband subscribers in the United States are all but guaranteed to continue experiencing net neutrality, as the two companies have already committed to its preservation for the next few years. In exchange for approving these acquisitions, government regulators will likely impose some additional quid pro quo requirements focused on establishing a level playing field and encouraging more competition. And if either company were to begin reneging on its commitment after the mandatory periods expire, the FCC and Congress would surely take action.

There are few clear answers regarding net neutrality as the FCC wades through a morass of diverse opinions and conflicting information. In this unpredictable environment, the agency would be wise to tread lightly while maintaining a keen eye for trends as well as mischief. By and large, the marketplace is working. Neither the regulatory straightjacket of Title II nor the radical greenlighting of a paid express lane is appropriate or justified at this time. Before adding new rules and regulations, we should see how the Internet video market continues to develop, including with respect to Ultra HD. Consumers will benefit most from increased competition along with reasonable FCC vigilance focused on consumer protection and anti-competitive behavior. This is the best way forward for now.

67 Ultra HD (4K)

A powerful synergy exists between content and technology, a phenomenon the media titans grasped better than anyone. Content and service providers leverage new technology to gain a competitive advantage. Conversely, technology companies develop new platforms and products in anticipation of new content delivery trends. This continuous circle of innovation will persist indefinitely, enabling many successes but also creating some failures.

3DTV in the home fizzled out as quickly as it arrived, 1080P HD is a welcome but incremental improvement, and Internet TV is clearly here to stay. But the next great leap forward for high-quality home entertainment is Ultra HD, also called 4K.[1]

Ultra HD is to HDTV what HDTV was to SDTV. Just as today's HDTV gave consumers a fourfold improvement in video resolution over standard definition TV, Ultra HD provides another quadrupling of picture clarity. When viewed on large screens, these 4K pictures offer a truly immersive visual experience, the equivalent of better than 20/20 vision with extravagantly brilliant colors, exquisite detail, and elaborate surround sound. When Ultra HD takes hold, homes will be filled with entire panels and curved walls of video, displaying images so stunningly clear and realistic that they will look and feel like wide windows to the world.

From technical standardization of HDTV to mass market adoption took a full decade, but today's HDTV is now so widespread that it has become passé. Also, in order to save bandwidth, most service providers unfortunately over-compress the content, and the visual flaws of today's HD quality have become apparent.

If Ultra HD is to become mainstream, it will take considerable market development time and require much more bandwidth. But when consumers see the difference on reasonably priced large screens of at least 60 inches and above, Ultra HD will be in great demand.

Sony deserves credit for leading the initial charge. It started the ball rolling with its "Mastered in 4K" Blu-ray movie titles from Sony Pictures. A first wave of more than ten titles, including *The Amazing Spider-Man*, *Taxi Driver*, and *Total Recall*, arrived in spring 2013 for display on existing 1080P HDTV sets. Next, Sony delivered 4K Ultra HD sets, with 55-inch screens as the entry-level size, along with an Ultra HD Media Player pre-loaded with 4K video clips. Finally, through

Sony's "Video Unlimited 4K" online store, consumers with the Sony Media Player can download from a growing library of 4K movies and TV content, including every episode of *Breaking Bad*.

But it will take a lot more than Sony's laudable efforts for this market to develop, and help is on the way. At the 2014 Consumer Electronics Show, sixteen years after digital HDTV sets had their debut, Ultra HD was front and center. Consumer electronics companies are all hoping for 4K Ultra HD to revive their fortunes in the large-screen TV business, introducing sets up to ten feet diagonally.

During 2014, a smattering of Ultra HD activities grew into a flurry, and the momentum is clearly growing. Comcast and NBC experimented with Ultra HD at the February 2014 Sochi Winter Olympic Games. In May, the Vienna State Opera used Elemental's new HEVC encoder to stream Verdi's *Nabucco*, starring Placido Domingo, live over the Internet in the Ultra HD format.[2] The same month, French Open tennis matches were delivered in Ultra HD over digital terrestrial television by French broadcast services TDF and TNT, using Envivio encoders. TDF subsequently began testing Ultra HD for its NRJ Hits music channel, also delivered over it digital terrestrial broadcast channel. In July 2014, Globosat, the leader in Brazilian pay TV, delivered the final three World Cup matches in Ultra HD via digital satellite in Brazil. There will surely be a major Ultra HD splash in Rio during the 2016 Summer Olympics.

First out of the gates with a linearly programmed Ultra HD channel was Homechoice in South Korea. In April 2014, it launched its UMAX Ultra HD channel in collaboration with LG, Samsung, a few South Korean cable operators, and Ateme, a French encoder company. Netflix was the first mover for on-demand streaming in the Ultra HD format, delivering *House of Cards* Season 2 episodes in May 2014, followed by all five seasons of *Breaking Bad*. Some Vimeo and YouTube videos claim

Ultra HD resolution, and Netflix, Amazon, and Hulu all plan to start shooting some original series in the new format.

By December 2014, DirectTV and Comcast both announced upcoming plans for offering Ultra HD content. Vodafone Germany announced an Ultra HD service for launch in 2015 using a Broadcom super-chip inside a Cisco box capable of receiving digital satellite, digital cable, IPTV and over-the-top Internet video streams. SkyPerfecTV! is planning an Ultra HD satellite service in Japan, while state-owned broadcaster NHK is already pushing beyond 4K, focusing on the 8K resolution version of Ultra HD. In Taiwan, Chunghwa Telecom is conducting a VOD trial using 4K content.

The market development hurdles for Ultra HD are substantial, however, a déjà vu scenario of what it took for HDTV to finally succeed commercially. The barriers include:

- Consumer equipment cost and replacement cycle

- Content availability

- Likely over-compression of 4K content by content and service providers, making it difficult for consumers to see the radical quality improvement relative to regular HDTV[3]

- Bandwidth, bandwidth, bandwidth—a commodity for which there never seems to be sufficient supply

Netflix recommends a 25 Mbps connection speed for Ultra HD, five times its recommendation of 5 Mbps for regular HD. The company has also talked about a 16 Mbps required bit rate for Ultra HD. The discrepancy between Netflix's 25 Mbps recommended connection speed for Ultra HD and its 16 Mbps encoded bit rate can be explained by consumer video buffering requirements to ensure smooth streaming, as well as leaving some bandwidth available for other members of the household. Regardless, the extremely high bit rates required for Ultra

HD are a sure recipe for heightened tension with Netflix's broadband distributors.

There is also the issue of High Dynamic Range (HDR), a technology separate and apart from pixel resolution.[4] HDR threatens to cloud consumer adoption of Ultra HD, although some people believe it could instead accelerate demand by giving consumers an additional reason to purchase a new TV set. HDR widens the gap between the brightest whites and the darkest blacks, enabling a deepened contrast between brightness and darkness. Advocates like Dolby and Technicolor argue that HDR is equally as if not more important than the enhancements stemming from Ultra HD alone. If HDR's attributes of brightness and contrast are combined with the quadrupled resolution and expanded color palette of Ultra HD, the resulting images would be even more lifelike and representative of the reality perceived by our eyes. But it will take more time to reach an industry consensus on the technical specs of HDR and how best to match it with Ultra HD.

This is a realistic scenario for the evolution of the Ultra HD market:

1. Early adopter market over the next couple of years

2. Strong market growth phase starting around 2017

3. Widespread adoption (over 50 percent of US households) in the 2025 time frame

The catalyst for Ultra HD in the US market could be a major commitment by some combination of Netflix and Google, perhaps along with AT&T U-Verse and the select other companies building 1 Gbps residential Internet pipes. They will leverage their formidable bandwidth advantages to accomplish what their competitors would rather postpone: realization of the widespread availability and scaling of Ultra HD content. DirecTV, Verizon, and Comcast will be certain not to get left behind. Competition is the most powerful motivating force, and

Google's potentially aggressive actions would instigate a chain reaction, incentivizing the cable and satellite incumbents to invest in a capital-intensive new cycle of bandwidth creation.

68 THE PERPETUAL DRUMBEAT OF TECHNOLOGY

Ultra HD will grab most of the headlines. But behind the scenes there are many other less-sexy technologies crucial to the future of digital video. Some relate to video compression while others involve streaming protocols, wireless and wired communications techniques, and advances in high-speed home networking.

Moore's Law holds that semiconductor processors double in performance every couple of years, benefiting the cost, size, power, and functionality of devices. A derivative of Moore's Law has emerged in the video compression area: video coding bit rate efficiency seems to be doubling roughly every ten years, allowing new services to emerge. But just as a fundamental breakthrough will need to occur in chip technology for Moore's Law to continue indefinitely (as silicon approaches its theoretical limit of transistor density), a radical change in compression methodology must take place for video coding to maintain its rate of improvement.

MPEG's long-standing motion-compensated Discrete Cosine Transform mathematical technique is finally running out of gas. The MPEG-1 and MPEG-2 standards date back to the early 1990s, while the MPEG-4 Advanced Video Coding (AVC) standard (also called H.264) was finalized in 2003. MPEG-4 AVC was jointly developed by the Video Coding Experts Group of the International Telecommunications Union (ITU) and the International Standards Organization (ISO) MPEG group, with co-chairs Gary Sullivan of Microsoft and Ajay Luthra of Motorola (now Arris). In a subsequent joint effort by MPEG and the ITU, the High Efficiency Video Coding (HEVC) standard (also called H.265) was finalized in 2013. Google has developed its own proprietary video codec, VP9, competing against HEVC by providing VP9 on a royalty-free basis.

To illustrate the progression in video coding efficiency, consider the example of a regular HDTV program (1080i or 720P). Assuming equivalent video quality, a service provider can deliver this program at 10 Mbps using MPEG-2, send the same content at 5 Mbps with MPEG-4 AVC, or transmit it at 3 Mbps using the HEVC standard. In practice, these rates can vary depending on the desired video quality level, the technical proficiency of the encoder design, and the type of content (for example, live sports programming is more difficult to compress than movies).

Whether one desires to fill up mobile device screens with motion video or to move us into the future world of 4K Ultra HDTV, every last bit of this new compression efficiency is needed. The HEVC standard is critical to allowing Ultra HD content to be transmitted at reasonable bit rates (under 20 Mbps). Using the older MPEG-4 or MPEG-2 standards for Ultra HD would be a non-starter.

There are several other digital video and related technologies to watch as they develop further:

- **Glasses-free 3D**. 3D technology has received considerable success in the movie theater, especially with titles like James Cameron's *Avatar*, Martin Scorsese's *Hugo*, Ang Li's *Life of Pi*, and Alfonso Cuarón's *Gravity*. 3D theatrical movies have enabled the studios and exhibitors to charge higher ticket prices, although the market seems to have already peaked.

  3D has been notably unsuccessful in the home. Millions of 3D-capable HDTV sets have been sold, but very few subscribers have made use of them. As a result, ESPN shut down its ESPN 3D channel in 2013. Another 3D channel, 3net, owned by Discovery, Sony, and IMAX, stopped broadcasting in 2014. For 3D to succeed in the home, a new type of glasses-free technology will be required.

- **MPEG-DASH.** The "DASH" acronym in the MPEG-DASH standard stands for Dynamic Adaptive Streaming over HTTP (Hypertext Transfer Protocol).[1] The key feature of adaptive streaming, also called adaptive bit rate streaming, is its ability to automatically adjust the incoming video bit rate to the consumer's instantaneous network bandwidth conditions. It allows smoother, more continuous video over the Internet.

  MPEG-DASH is an open standard competing against the separate, proprietary adaptive streaming methods used by Microsoft, Apple, and Adobe. Netflix uses its own adaptive bit rate technique for its Internet video service, based in part on Microsoft's technology.

- **HTML5.** HyperText Markup Language, version 5, is the latest language of the Internet. It has an important relationship to digital video in that, for the first time, it incorporates video as an integral component. This higher level of integration may eventually preclude the necessity of downloading individual video players, such as Adobe Flash, to consumer devices. HTML5 still lacks some key features, however, such as the ability to support live streaming, adaptive streaming, and Digital Rights Management (DRM) for content security. As the World Wide Web Consortium works on adding these capabilities to HTML5, the traditional video player plug-ins like Adobe Flash and Apple QuickTime are still widely used for enhanced functionality.

  Vimeo, the video sharing website, revamped its video player in 2014 and made HTML5 its default technology, a strategic shift away from Flash. YouTube has also selected HTML5 as a core video technology. Netflix plans to replace Microsoft's Silverlight video framework with HTML5. And Microsoft itself appears to be designing Silverlight out of future products in favor of HTML5.

  Even Adobe, the owner of Flash, sees the writing on the wall. In

2014, Adobe added HTML5 support to its Primetime DRM system, starting with the Mozilla Firefox browser. This development potentially signals a long-term strategic move away from the Adobe Flash player. Netflix is the flagship account for Adobe's HTML5-based DRM solution, an important addition to Adobe's impressive list of Internet video customers, which also includes HBO, Comcast, Turner Broadcasting, and the BBC.

- **UltraViolet.** This evolving technology is an industry initiative supported by most movie studios and technology companies. It is a free, cloud-based digital content rights solution with a "buy once, play anywhere" philosophy, giving consumers greater flexibility in viewing the movies and TV shows they purchase. When a consumer buys content from a participating retailer, such as Walmart's Vudu or Best Buy's CinemaNow, the content is added to that person's "UltraViolet Collection." Thereafter, the consumer can watch it on compatible electronic devices including computers, smart TVs, game consoles, and mobile devices.

UltraViolet seems to be gaining market momentum, with more than 19 million registered accounts reported in 2014.[2] There is an open question, however, of how active many of these accounts are.

There is also the issue of Disney, a major exception remaining outside the UltraViolet ecosystem. Disney developed a competing cloud-based digital rights locker, KeyChest, in conjunction with iTunes. In 2014, the company announced Disney Movies Anywhere, an Internet video service allowing consumers to buy Disney, Pixar, and Marvel movies once—from the iTunes or Google Play stores—and watch them "forever" on computers or mobile devices.

- **Miracast, AirPlay, and DIAL.** Miracast is a wireless video "screencasting" standard allowing mobile devices to "fling" video content to an HDTV set, and vice versa. It was developed as an open and more generalized version of Apple's AirPlay, which works only within the Apple ecosystem of iPhones, iPads, and Apple TVs.

The consumer electronics industry, however, has been inconsistent with its support of Miracast, allowing another technology, DIAL (the Discovery and Launch protocol), to come to the fore. Developed by Netflix and YouTube, DIAL works differently from Miracast and AirPlay. Instead of literally flinging content from a mobile device to a smart TV, DIAL initiates a command from the mobile device instructing the smart TV to launch the same app or video.

Google is using DIAL for its Chromecast device, and Roku is using it for the Roku 3 box and the Roku Streaming Stick. Apple's AirPlay also has a DIAL-like smart streaming aspect whereby an iPhone can control the video streaming to an Apple TV box connected to an HDTV set.

- **MoCA 2.0 and 5G WiFi.** HDTV sets, computers, smartphones, and tablets are populating our homes, and we are being bombarded by bits from all directions. High-speed home networking has therefore become an essential capability.

  Service providers are moving toward a next-generation architecture, using "home gateways" as master storage and processing servers, transporting video, data, and voice to various connected devices throughout the home. Keeping pace in the home networking domain are the MoCA (Multimedia over Coax Alliance) and WiFi standards, both of which continue to evolve. The latest versions of each standard, MoCA 2.0 and 5G WiFi (802.11ac), enable theoretical speeds in the hundreds of megabits per second. Comcast is offering a Cisco wireless gateway containing both MoCA 2.0 and 802.11ac that provides throughput up to 700 Mbps.

The need for speed never seems to end. The successor to 802.11ac, called 802.11ax, has potential speeds in the gigabits per second range.

• *Gigasphere.* The cable industry has been successfully using the DOCSIS set of standards to enable data, voice, and video services over its Internet cable pipes. Gigasphere is the consumer-facing brand name for the next-generation DOCSIS 3.1 standard. CableLabs released the DOCSIS 3.1 specs in 2013, and cable operators plan to start deploying Gigasphere by the end of 2015.

Gigasphere uses a combination of technologies to achieve much higher speeds: channel bonding, narrowband Orthogonal Frequency Division Multiplexing carriers with higher-order QAM modulation (up to 4096 QAM versus today's 256 QAM), and an advanced forward error correction technique called Low Density Parity Check codes. Gigasphere will eventually enable downstream data rates of 10 Gbps and upstream rates exceeding 1 Gbps (shared by subscribers in a node or service group), allowing cable to compete effectively against the 1 Gbps speeds marketed by Google Fiber and AT&T U-Verse GigaPower.

Amid this proliferation of new digital video and broadband communications technologies, the average American consumer is still watching five hours of TV per day. But the younger generation is not just sitting back on a couch watching the big screen. A mind-boggling degree of activity is occurring in the areas of mobile devices and social media, fueling a multiscreen, multitasking frenzy of consumer behavior. And many other technologies will come into play in support of tomorrow's media environment, including voice, speech, and facial recognition; personalized and adaptive content menus; motion sensing, holography, and virtual reality; and neural networks infused with artificial intelligence.

69 EVERYTHING CONNECTS

As the multiscreen media world spins, digital video technology is reaching far beyond the home and mobile entertainment domains, impacting many other aspects of our society in far-reaching ways. It is subconsciously interwoven through the fabric of our daily lives, whether it's watching TV, Skyping with people in distant places, or capturing and sharing video from an iPhone. Digital video is connecting us visually, anywhere and everywhere, penetrating myriad diverse fields:

- *Movies*. Digital cinema has transformed the movie theater industry. Previously, the movie exhibition business was burdened by high recurring costs for replication and distribution of film prints to thousands of theaters. The economics of digital distribution was simply too compelling to ignore. Converting theaters to digital capability entailed high initial fixed costs, but it enabled low recurring costs and a rapid payback on capital investment.

  There were some serious early attempts to capture the market by Qualcomm and Technicolor, but neither of these independent ventures had a real chance of success. If digital cinema was going to materialize, the major studios demanded complete control. Disney, MGM, Paramount Pictures, Sony Pictures, 20th Century Fox, Universal Studios, and Warner Brothers created a joint venture in 2005 called the Digital Cinema Initiatives, which started releasing technical specifications for images, sound, and theater projectors, as well as security features such as encryption and key management. The digital files, or "digital cinema packages," can be delivered physically on computer hard drives, or by satellite or fiber optic transmission, to a storage device at the theater.[1]

  Over 80 percent of the world's cinema screens are now digital, and over 90 percent are digital in the United States and Canada. Nearly half of these digital screens are 3D capable.[2]

- *The Arts*. Funding for the arts—opera, ballet, symphony, theater, and museums—is famously challenging. A laudable goal of our cultural institutions' leadership is expanding the audience and bringing culture to the masses. Now, with digital video distribution, there is both an incremental source of funding and a powerful new mechanism to broaden the exposure.

Peter Gelb, general manager of New York's Metropolitan Opera, decided to tap into the digital movie theater market and enable live Met operas to be experienced beyond the confines of Lincoln Center. The Met's "Live in HD" initiative kicked off in 2006 with Mozart's *The Magic Flute*. Now, in addition to the 3,800 patrons seated at the Met, tens of thousands or even hundreds of thousands of people can simultaneously watch live performances in over 2,000 theaters in 66 countries.

The Met broadcasts at least 10 live operas per season, plus encore (delayed) presentations. A dedicated production crew optimizes the opera's video and sound capture for remote theatrical viewing, transmitting the performances in real time to digital cinemas via satellite in the 1080i HDTV format. The Met also provides computer access and an iPad app, "Met Opera On Demand," with annual subscriptions, monthly subscriptions, and one-time rentals.

Not only does Gelb's signature innovation allow a global audience to virtually "go to the Met," but the financial benefits have also enabled him to take more risks and add diversity to the Met's repertoire. Revenue from digital distribution was $35 million for the year ending July 2013, relative to box office (and tours) revenue of $90 million. Gelb has been able to bring more than 50 new productions to the Met since his tenure began in 2006, an impressive number considering the cost of a new Met production can range from $1.5 million to $4 million.[3]

Other cultural institutions have followed suit. The Vienna State Opera broadcasts many live performances over the Internet to smart TVs and mobile devices. The Berlin Philharmonic sells live Internet HD subscriptions from its Digital Concert Hall website as well as VOD streaming from its video archive.

London's Royal Opera House delivers operas and ballets from Covent Garden to more than 1,000 digital cinemas in over thirty countries. In addition, London's National Theater Live brings top-notch theatrical productions to digital cinemas around the world. *King Lear, Medea, A Streetcar Named Desire*, and *Of Mice and Men* were among the headline events of 2014.

BroadwayHD is striving to bring Broadway plays to digital movie theaters around the world, starting in 2014 with *Romeo and Juliet*. Another company, Broadway Worldwide, has distributed several musicals to US digital cinemas through its Direct From Broadway service, including *Memphis, Jekyll & Hyde*, and Stephen Sondheim's *Putting it Together*. In 2014, Broadway Worldwide struck a joint venture agreement with China's Sun New Light Culture Development to deliver between two and four Broadway musicals per year to digital theaters in various countries.

Fathom Events, owned by the three largest US movie theater chains, is the leading distributor of HD events to domestic digital theaters. Fathom delivers live opera, comedy, concerts, and sports events to several hundred digital theaters nationwide.

- *Education*. The field of education is undergoing a major upheaval as a result of digital video technology and the Internet. The distance-learning business has evolved greatly from the 1990s. At that time, General Instrument's digital TV customers led the way, especially Jones Intercable's Mind Extension University and Red Edusat, created by the Ministry of Public Education in Mexico. Today, many prestigious universities are using the broadband Internet for Massive Open Online Courses (MOOCs), bringing higher education to a vast, global constituency. Traditional higher education—the multiyear, structured experience with students learning on physical campuses along with peers and teachers—will continue to be in high demand. But for billions of people, this experience remains logistically impractical and financially unaffordable.

Coursera, edX, and Udacity are the three most prominent MOOCs. Coursera is a for-profit business funded by venture capital investors. When it launched in 2012, its initial educational partners were Stanford University, the University of Michigan, Princeton University, and the University of Pennsylvania. There are now several hundred online courses offered by more than 100 institutions around the world. Coursera students can watch lectures on demand, take quizzes, receive assessments and grades from peers, and interact with their classmates and teachers.[4] In 2013, Coursera announced a major expansion to the public university systems of ten states, including those of New York, West Virginia, and Colorado. Over 1 million potential students at these state universities are able to earn credit toward graduation, with the schools paying Coursera a modest monthly fee. With public educational funding under persistent pressure, this deal has potential to increase the four-year graduation rate cost-effectively and on a large scale.

MIT and Harvard University are the founding institutions behind edX, a nonprofit that licenses its MOOC courses to other universities. A variety of online classes from more than thirty universities and colleges are now offered. Led by San Jose State University, a number of California State Universities agreed to pay license fees to edX for access to its online classes.

Udacity is a MOOC company funded by Charles River Ventures and Andreessen Horowitz, with a focus on math and computer science. In 2013, the Georgia Institute of Technology shook up the academic world by announcing an alliance with Udacity to offer an actual degree, a master's in computer science, for $6,600 online versus $45,000 for the traditional degree. Georgia Tech and Udacity agreed to share the revenue.

There are many controversial issues regarding MOOCs: how to maintain students' attention, how to charge for the courses, how to handle cheating, what types of degrees or certificates to award, and how a MOOC experience fits in with the traditional classroom. But the MOOC revolution is here to stay. For the global masses, MOOCs will become a primary opportunity to gain an otherwise unobtainable, cost-effective education. For many others, they will serve as a method of continuing education, enriching and even transforming lives.

Other types of new educational experiences have also been enabled by digital video technology. Khan Academy, a nonprofit organization founded by former hedge fund analyst Salman Khan, provides thousands of free, short videos hosted by YouTube. Math is the primary area of focus but the company offers courses in various subjects, including science, economics, and history. By 2014, Khan Academy had 10 million users per month in about 200 countries.

VGo Communications, a robotic telepresence company, enables a completely different type of educational experience. VGo sells a $6,000 robot that allows severely handicapped children who can't attend school in person to actively participate from home. The homebound student controls the movements of the robot, which is physically in the classroom as the child's proxy, while a broadband Internet connection maintains the two-way digital video telepresence. The company's video-enabled robots also have applications in healthcare and in the workplace.

- **_Videoconferencing_**. Videoconferencing was the sole digital video application predating the digital television revolution. AT&T introduced the "picturephone" to the public in 1964, showcasing an experimental system connecting video phone calls between the New York World's Fair and Disneyland in California. For decades, however, the market for videoconferencing remained small; the equipment was too expensive and the video quality was poor. In the 2000s, with better video quality, inexpensive equipment, and pervasive broadband connectivity, videoconferencing (and the video phone) finally hit its stride.

  Skype, acquired by Microsoft for $8.5 billion in 2011, is a videoconferencing provider used on such a global, pervasive basis that it has become a verb, as in "Let's Skype." Apple introduced FaceTime in 2011 as a video telephony application for its user base. Cisco's TelePresence solution occupies the high end of videoconferencing, providing an audiovisual experience so immersive that participants feel like they're in the same room.

  Videoconferencing technology has also extended into the medical field. With telemedicine, high-resolution images can be transmitted from remote locations to a site with specialists, helping to diagnose or treat patients in critical situations.

- **_Video Surveillance_**. Pricey high definition video cameras were one of several factors inhibiting the HDTV market from developing at the turn of the twenty-first century. For example, General Instrument's initial HDTV encoders were priced at over $100,000 per channel. Consumers can now purchase HD video home security systems, with multiple cameras, for under $1,000. Some HD camcorders, containing built-in encoders, are priced at less than $200.

Digital video and the Internet have also opened up the video surveillance field, using digital cameras and hard drives to create "security DVRs." Corporations, municipalities, and private residences are all using digital video surveillance. In Manhattan's Times Square; London, England; and Camden, New Jersey, criminals beware: your actions will likely be caught on digital video. Faisal Shahzad, the Pakistani-American terrorist who attempted to blow up his vehicle in Times Square in 2010, was identified by digital video surveillance cameras in the area. The 2013 Boston Marathon bombers, the Tsarnaev brothers, were discovered by digital video cameras and then hunted down by law enforcement, preventing them from driving to New York to potentially carry out another attack. Newark Airport has installed Sensity Systems' LED-based light fixtures combined with digital video surveillance cameras.[5]

Hundreds of police departments are now equipping officers with miniature video cameras, "cop cams," made by companies like Taser International. This effort is intended to reduce violence, with the videos uploaded to centralized servers in the event they are needed for future case evidence. The US government is conducting R&D into crowd scanning, in which digital video cameras are used in conjunction with facial recognition and remote computer databases to identify individuals.

In northwest Africa, General Atomics' MQ-9 Reapers are used as a critical tool in America's increasingly targeted global counterterrorism strategy. These unmanned, unarmed aerial drones fly surveillance missions over northern Mali and elsewhere, streaming live digital video to intelligence analysts who use the data to help local allies identify Islamic militants.[6]

- **Action Sports.** GoPro was founded by Nick Woodman, who received his degree in visual arts from the University of California, San Diego. During a five-month Australian and Indonesian surf trip in 2002, Woodman experimented with the idea of attaching a small film camera to his wrist while surfing. After later attaching his camera to a racecar, Woodman's start-up evolved into developing compact, ruggedized HD video cameras that could be mounted on surfboards, ski helmets, and just about anything attached to people wanting to capture and share their experiences. The company's latest high-end device, the $500 GoPro Hero4 Black, features 4K video resolution (Ultra HD) at 30 frames per second. It also captures 1080P video at 120 frames per second, enabling incredible slow-motion effects.

Much more than a stellar video camera, GoPro has become a cultural touchstone. With its popular YouTube channel, the company is repositioning for growth as a media business.

GoPro completed its initial public offering in 2014 with a multibillion-dollar valuation, just as two new start-ups (Hexo+ and AirDog) were developing miniature low-flying drones with GoPro cameras on board, able to track and create videos of action sports enthusiasts from an aerial perspective.

Competitors like Sony have also entered the Point-Of-View (POV) camera business, and the market is expanding and diversifying. Zeal Optics sells a 1080P HD Camera Goggle for skiers and snowboarders. Liquid Image makes a variety of HD-enabled goggles and mountable action cameras for the snow, underwater, and motocross markets. Pivothead offers sunglasses with unobtrusive HD cameras.

- ***Webcams and Video Everywhere***. Webcams, digital video cameras fixed on a scene and connected to the Internet, have now been around for many years. They have many applications. For example, the website surfline.com monitors surf breaks all over the world in real time, allowing surfers to get a live sense of conditions before they head out to the water. In China, webcams have enabled karaoke singers and comedians to develop large audiences for live Internet broadcasts. The content is aggregated on video websites such as YY.com and 6.cn, where viewers reward the performers with virtual gifts that can be converted into cash.

Discovery's Animal Planet division has taken webcams to the next level, with intimate monitoring of animals streamed over twenty different live channels accessible through the company's apl.tv website. It started with the Kitten Cam in 2012, but then coverage expanded to other animals including penguins, wild birds, bunnies, sharks, puppies, and even cockroaches. The footage is available to various connected devices.

At the 2014 Consumer Electronics Show, navigation company Garmin introduced its Dash Cam, a $250 GPS-enabled high definition video camera that can be mounted on a car's windshield. It can be used to store evidence in the event of an accident as well as to capture anything else of interest within the wide-angle lens view.

Google had high hopes for Google Glass, a wearable computer with camera and video recording capability, mounted on the edge of an eyeglass-like frame. This device raised eyebrows as much for privacy and safety concerns as for its futuristic apps potential. The company halted its Google Glass activity in 2015, although one should not rule out a more viable future adaptation. Medicine was a promising Google Glass application, with surgeons wearing the device to receive consultations from outside the operating room, and with great potential in medical training and education.

Skybox Imaging, a venture capital-backed Silicon Valley company, plans to launch a constellation of tiny satellites capable of transmitting HD video of the entire planet back to earth. Skybox's target markets and applications including agriculture, energy, maritime shipping, disaster response, security, and humanitarian aid. In 2014, Google acquired the company for $500 million.

And the product innovations keep coming. China-based DJI Innovations sells a $1,000 "flying camera." The remote-controlled, 2.6-pound, lunchbox-sized Phantom 2 Vision camera drone can shoot 1080P digital HD video from 1,000 feet high. It can fly for up to 25 minutes, downloading video footage via WiFi directly to a smartphone running the DJI Vision app, which can be immediately shared on social media networks.

Similar drones are under consideration for commercial applications, which have been mostly precluded to date by the Federal Aviation Administration. In 2014, the FAA granted six aerial video companies exemptions to use camera drones in movie and television production during daytime hours.

- *Fashion*. The fashion industry is yet another stop in the digital landscape, creating a virtual feast for the eyes. Once again, the trailblazers were among General Instrument's digital TV customers: the Style Network (rebranded as the Esquire Network in 2013), owned by Comcast/NBCUniversal; and Ultra HD, the dazzling high-fashion channel created by Rainbow Media as one of its twenty-one exclusive Voom HD channels.[7] This upscale content niche is now being showcased on the Internet, altering the exposure and certain marketing aspects of the fashion industry in the process.

Fashion Week, the industry's flagship event held in Milan, Paris, New York, London, and other cities around the world, now features live streams from participating design houses. Belstaff, the luxury British outerwear and accessories brand, streams its fashion shows live and then analyzes the Twitter traffic—the frequency and nature of what people are saying in their tweets—to predict new buying trends for its upcoming products. Burberry conducts live streaming video tied to the ability to immediately make web purchases of new runway clothing items. Many other fashion designers, including Prada and Marc Jacobs, leverage live streaming video as a brand extension, research tool, and web sales stimulator.[8]

- **Advertising.** Digital technology is finally disrupting the resistant-to-change advertising business. Cable operators are rolling out new technology enabling dynamic ads on video-on-demand streams, the front-end of a general trend toward more personalized TV ads.

The Internet, together with social media, has laid the groundwork for an entirely new advertising category that will bring personalized video ads to a whole new level. The US market for Internet digital video ads was estimated by eMarketer, a leading Internet market research firm, to exceed $4 billion in 2013 (out of a $66 billion total TV advertising market). It is projected to grow to more than $9 billion (out of $75 billion) by 2017. YouTube, Yahoo, Facebook, and others are all vying to get a share of this rapidly growing market.

The dots of digital video are being connected horizontally, vertically, and diagonally, within and across industries, borders, and activities. Yet even in this age of hyperconnectedness, there will always be new dots to connect.

70 GOING SOCIAL

Digital TV and digital video, in their various forms, are an omnipresent source of entertainment, information, and interaction throughout society. Yet much of the action has shifted away from TV sets and personal computers and toward mobile devices and social media, where video is a central feature within a much broader context.

Twitter is the master of short-form social communications, with its 140-character limit for text messages. It acquired Vine, a mobile video app start-up, in 2012. Vine is a six-second (maximum) video sharing service, Twitter's visual counterpart to its minimalist text platform. Vine has rapidly become a force in showcasing video production creativity. The Tribeca Film Festival held its second annual #6SECFILMS competition, powered by Vine, in 2014. Over 500 entries vied for the short list of finalists in five different categories: Genre, Drama, Animation, Comedy, and AudienceAward.

Facebook's Instagram unit followed suit in 2013 with Video on Instagram, a capability designed for sharing videos with a fifteen-second maximum length. Some wrote it off as a Vine copycat. But in 2014, Instagram released Hyperlapse, a very appealing innovation in the area of consumer video production. Instagram's free Hyperlapse app allows iPhone or iPad consumers to make professional-looking time-lapse videos. Instagram's stabilization software leverages Apple's built-in gyroscope to remove jerky hand and body movements. Hyperlapse then combines this stabilization technique with an old DVR "trick mode": fast-forward capability enabled by skipping frames of video. With a one-touch slide button, consumers can then create and immediately share a new time-lapse video at one to twelve times the actual speed of the original capture.

Apart from Instagram, Facebook has been busily adding video capability to its own social media network. Facebook has the unique ability to make videos go viral by the virtue and power of its 1.3 billion monthly user base and its continuously updated, personalized News Feed.

In 2014, Facebook acquired Oculus VR, a virtual reality technology company, for $2 billion, revealing a long-term strategy of pushing beyond today's boundaries of social TV. The Oculus Rift, expected to ship in 2015, will be a wearable headset with a 3D, high-resolution display, 360-degree head tracking, and high-quality integrated audio. Samsung's Gear VR headset, powered by Oculus's technology, works in conjunction with Samsung's new Galaxy Note 4 smartphone. The Facebook/Oculus deal prompted Google to be the lead investor in a $542 million funding round in augmented-reality start-up Magic Leap.[1]

Privately held and wildly popular Snapchat also enables video sharing. The creator can program photos and videos to vanish within ten seconds after viewing.[2] In response, Facebook launched Slingshot, its version of transitory pictures and videos. And Facebook's Instagram unit introduced Bolt, a one-tap messaging app allowing videos and photos to be shared before instant vaporization.[3]

YouTube's founders, Chad Hurley and Steve Chen, started another Silicon Valley company, Avos Systems, which launched video sharing app MixBit in 2013. The next year, the company changed its name to MixBit, Inc. Using the collaborative mantra of "creating videos together," MixBit makes it easy to capture, mix, and edit digital video clips up to sixteen seconds in length, which can then be spliced with other segments into videos up to one hour long.

Mainstream media organizations are also recognizing the importance of short-form video. In 2014, Comcast's NBCUniversal News Group invested in and partnered with NowThis News, a video journalism start-up focused on mobile and social networks. This venture produces daily video news clips for distribution over Facebook, Twitter, Instagram, Vine, and Snapchat.

In China, where Twitter, Facebook, and YouTube are mostly blocked due to government control over the Internet, Sina Weibo and Tencent's WeChat rule the social media milieu, and video sharing is a growing part of their arsenal. Alibaba's Laiwang and others are trying to figure out how to catch up.

Digital TV and the Internet are intersecting in another way altogether: the category of social TV. A 2013 Nielsen study concluded that 80 percent of TV viewers who own mobile devices regularly use these devices while watching TV, potentially opening up a ripe new market for advertisers. This time the battle is not between General Instrument and Scientific Atlanta for digital TV technology platforms, or between TCI and DirecTV for digital TV services. Instead, it pits Twitter against Facebook in a land grab for what will likely become a substantial slice of the advertising business.

For major live events, millions of consumers weigh in on Twitter and Facebook with tweets, retweets, posts, and likes. For instance, the 2013 series finale of AMC's *Breaking Bad* reached a TV audience of more than 10 million domestic cable and satellite subscribers. From this TV universe, over 600,000 social media participants posted 1.2 million tweets seen by a Twitter audience of 9.2 million.

The next month, Nielsen started formally measuring social TV activity. The Nielsen Twitter TV Ratings display Daily Top Five and Weekly Top Ten lists, measuring the unique audience, the number of impressions, the unique authors, and the number of tweets associated with each TV episode.

Social media fused with digital video is once again moving us into uncharted territory. Thinking back to 1990, when General Instrument made history by formalizing its digital television project, it occurs to me how little we understood about where the technology would lead. We knew that we were embarking on an exciting and important journey. We were confident that it would open up major new business opportunities in the field of television. We sensed that it was a fundamental shift that would create new products and services beyond our imagination at the time. But we did not foresee with any specificity the radical changes in content creation, distribution, and consumer viewing behavior, or the broader societal consequences, that would ensue in less than a quarter-century.

Visual communications is a phenomenal man-made representation —and extension—of the natural world. During the upcoming decades, digital video will continue to evolve in many unforeseen directions, transforming how we understand, share, and experience the world around us. All of the tools and technologies are at our disposal. If we use them with a sense of proportion and balance, we will find ourselves more entertained, more informed, more alert, and more connected than ever before.

71 WHAT EVER HAPPENED TO...

Dan Akerson: After leaving General Instrument in 1995, Akerson became CEO of Nextel and then was hired by Craig McCaw to be CEO of XO Communications. In 2003 he joined the Carlyle Group, where he ran a large private equity fund. In July 2009, General Motors emerged from Chapter 11 bankruptcy and Akerson was appointed to its board. GM returned to profitability and completed an IPO in 2010. In September 2010, Akerson became GM's CEO, adding the role of chairman in 2011. "The car is the next great proving ground for communications technology," he said in June 2013 to the Chief Executives' Club of Boston. "The automobile will become a major platform for tech and one with far better battery life than an iPhone." He retired from GM in January 2014, a month after the US Treasury Department sold its last shares of GM, stock it had acquired as part of the government-funded bailout of the domestic automobile industry. At the Consumer Electronics Show (CES) 2014, GM announced its Performance Data Recorder, including a digital HD video camera, for the 2015 Corvette Stingray. Akerson's successor, Mary Barra, is the first woman CEO of a major US auto company.

Ed Breen: After leaving Motorola, Inc. as president and COO, Breen served as CEO and chairman of Tyco International for over ten years beginning in 2002. In 2007, Tyco spun off its health-care and electronics businesses. In September 2012, Tyco split into three separate companies: the ADT North American residential security business; flow control products (acquired by Pentair for $4.5 billion); and fire protection and security. Breen is non-executive chairman of Tyco International, the fire protection and commercial security business. In 2014, Breen was reappointed to Comcast's Board of Directors.

Chuck Dolan: Chuck Dolan is chairman of both Cablevision Systems and AMC Networks, effectively controlling those two companies and The Madison Square Garden Company through his supervoting shares. He is a donor to the Charles F. Dolan School of Business at Fairfield University in Connecticut. Together with his son Jim, he founded the Lustgarten Foundation for pancreatic cancer research, named for Marc Lustgarten, the former Rainbow CEO, vice chairman of Cablevision, and chairman of Madison Square Garden, who died of the disease at age fifty-two. In the September 2014 edition of the Forbes 400, Dolan's family fortune was estimated at $3.9 billion.

Tom Elliot: After a thirty-two-year career at TCI, including serving two years as VP of Science and Technology at CableLabs and two years as chairman of the Society of Cable Telecommunications Engineers

(SCTE), Elliot became an executive consultant and served on the boards of various tech companies.

Charlie Ergen: Ergen is chairman of the Board of Dish Network and EchoStar Corporation. His net worth was estimated at $17.2 billion in the Forbes 400 as of September 2014.

Ted Forstmann: Ted Forstmann died in 2011 with a net worth estimated at $1.6 billion, a significant portion of which came from Forstmann Little's acquisition and subsequent sale of General Instrument. His younger brother Nick, also a founding partner of Forstmann Little, died in 2001. Forstmann Little acquired the talent agency IMG in 2004 for $750 million, after which Ted Forstmann became the firm's chairman and CEO. Under his leadership, IMG expanded into a broad-based global sports, media, and marketing talent agency, handling the NCAA, the Rose Bowl, Peyton Manning, Eli Manning, Maria Sharapova, Venus Williams, and many others. In December 2013, Ari Emanuel's William Morris Endeavor talent agency acquired IMG from Forstmann Little for $2.3 billion. Ari Emanuel is the Hollywood power player whose persona was captured by Jeremy Piven, playing Ari Gold, in the HBO hit series *Entourage*.

Jerry Heller: After retiring from GI in 1993, Heller provided seed funding to Imedia, the digital video start-up founded by Ed Krause, Adam Tom, and Paul Shen, and acted as their strategic advisor. Terayon Communications acquired Imedia in 1999, and then Motorola (GI) acquired Terayon in 2007. Heller is on the board of San Diego's Mainly Mozart organization and also serves on the board of trustees of Syracuse University.

Ed Horowitz: After leaving Viacom as chairman and CEO of the Viacom Broadcast and Interactive Media Group, Horowitz joined Citigroup as EVP Advanced Development, where he founded e-citi, a unit focused on e-commerce and Internet-based financial services. From

2003 to 2005, he worked in Chuck Dolan's "office of the chairman" at Cablevision's Voom HDTV venture, and then became CEO of SES Americom. He was co-CEO of Encompass Digital Media until March 2014. Currently Horowitz serves as chairman of FairPoint Communications and chairman of EdsLink, a venture capital firm he founded in 2000.

Ed Krause: After leaving GI in 1994, Ed Krause became co-founder of Imedia, which was sold to Terayon Communications. Terayon was later acquired by Motorola, and he became co-founder of RGB Networks. Krause is now CEO of UV Networks, a Silicon Valley tech start-up in the consumer video space.

John Malone: Malone is chairman of both Liberty Media and Liberty Global. Perhaps inspired by his friend Ted Turner, and by his former mentor Bob Magness, Malone has become the biggest private landowner in the United States, with 2.2 million acres. In 2011, he purchased over 1 million acres of timberland in Maine and New Hampshire, supplementing his previous land acquisitions in Colorado, New Mexico, and Wyoming, and surpassing Ted Turner's ownership of close to 2 million acres. In 2012, Malone purchased Humewood Castle in Ireland for about $10 million. In September 2014, Forbes estimated Malone's net worth to be $7.7 billion.

Paul Moroney: Still based in San Diego, Moroney is senior vice president of advanced research and development at Arris, Inc. Since 1979, due to acquisitions, he has sequentially worked at the following corporations without having to leave his job: Linkabit, M/A-Com, General Instrument, NextLevel Systems (name change), General Instrument (name change back), Motorola Inc., Motorola Mobility, Google, and finally Arris. He is the only person in the world to have started at Linkabit and remained in the same business, through its many corporate incarnations, all the way to Arris.

Rupert Murdoch: Murdoch is chairman and CEO of 21st Century Fox and is executive chairman of News Corporation. In May 2013, he purchased the Moraga Estate, which includes a vineyard and winery, in the hills of Bel Air, California. The Murdoch family's net worth was estimated at $14.2 billion by the Forbes 400 September 2014 issue.

Woo Paik: Paik resigned from GI in 1997 and joined LG Electronics the next year, where he became chief technology officer. In 2004, he was inducted into the Consumer Electronics Hall of Fame, created "to honor the leaders whose creativity, persistence, determination and sheer personal charisma helped to shape an industry and made the consumer electronics marketplace what it is today." Apple co-founder Steve Wozniak was inducted at the same time. Paik retired from his LG CTO role in March 2011, staying on as an advisor until March 2013.

Bob Rast: After leaving GI in 1998, Rast was VP Business Development at Dolby, CEO of DemoGraFX, president at Linx Electronics, chairman of the ATSC, and also worked in business development at LG Electronics.

Sumner Redstone: Redstone remains chairman and majority owner of National Amusements, the movie theater chain company founded by his father in 1936. He is also executive chairman of the board at both Viacom and CBS Corporation. Forbes estimated his net worth at $6.5 billion in September 2014.

Donald Rumsfeld: After leaving GI in 1993, Rumsfeld was a member and then chairman of the board of pharmaceutical company Gilead Sciences until 2001. He served as George W. Bush's Secretary of Defense, the country's twenty-first, remaining in that role until December 2006. In 2011 he published his memoir, *Known and Unknown*, and in 2013 he published *Rumsfeld's Rules*, a book of his leadership lessons in business, politics, war, and life. He chairs the nonprofit Rumsfeld Foundation with his wife, Joyce. Their foundation works with organizations that benefit members of the US troops, veterans, and their families, supports microfinance projects in poor countries, provides grants to students interested in public service, and fosters closer relationships between the United States and countries in Central Asia.

Marc Tayer: See last page, "About the Author."

Bob Zitter: After thirty-two years at HBO, Zitter retired as HBO's executive vice president and chief technology officer in June 2013. He now provides advisory services to media and technology companies.

■ ■ ■

EPILOGUE

The distant future holds many possible scenarios. Video will occupy an increasingly prominent role throughout society, as bandwidth and storage capacities continue moving along their steep upward trajectories. The distinction between visual reality and perception may also begin to fade, facilitated by a confluence of advancing technologies. The following vignette is but one such scenario.

2101, A VIDEO ODYSSEY

1/1/01. It's New Year's Day, 2101. You awaken at your home in Marin County, near San Francisco. It's a holiday but you plan to go to work for a few hours, then travel to Paris to have lunch with your son. Finally, you plan to visit the great-grandfather you have never met. At forty-five years old, you feel privileged and gratified to be able to do all of this in a single day.

The ride across the Golden Gate Bridge to your office is smooth. You gaze left and see sailboats silhouetted against the sparkling allure of San Francisco Bay, the city's gleaming wind- and solar-powered towers soaring beyond. To your right are the imposing cliffs of the Marin Headlands, jutting into the mighty Pacific. You have New Year's brunch with your co-workers, wishing each other luck for the upcoming year.

Then you head south toward the airport and board your flight to Paris. As you pass the Eiffel Tower and the Seine, the City of Lights appears as lovely as ever, and at lunch it warms your heart to see how happy and successful your son is.

After bidding your son farewell, you blink your eyes three times, inducing a suspended state as you travel back a full century to the year 2001, and arrive in San Diego. Your great-grandfather is forty-one. It feels odd to be temporarily older than him and even stranger to see how primitive and quaint life was back then. He watches TV on a tiny 50-inch screen, totally separate and detached from his eyes. You try not to laugh when he describes how lifelike his new HDTV set is. The huge remote control can't even understand his voice or read his mind. He takes your visit in stride but seems puzzled when you explain that the future world of video is fully integrated with the human visual system; there is no separate display, no independence between the video and your eyes.

On this New Year's Day of 1/1/2101 you didn't physically leave your home in Marin County. You temporarily believed you were in San Francisco, Paris, and 2001 San Diego. But it was all an elaborate illusion, a simulated, technology-inspired ruse. You were taking advantage of your latest video splurge: the "100 year/10,000 mile" MindView app from Mobilla, your service provider, the company that pioneered the field of digital virtual transport (DVT) a half-century ago.

MindView opens up a five-dimensional world, incorporating the three dimensions of the human visual system plus space and time. It employs quantum computing and advanced digital video technology networked with its customers' eyes and brains. Mobilla has expanded the human visual system by integrating it with a vast global network of video indexed by people, places, objects, space, and time. It is a transcendent experience, traversing the continuum between the real and the surreal.

These fuzzy edges of the ether, where reality meets fantasy, form a visual vortex, a virtual window into the wild blue yonder.

To enter MindView's 5D visual reality, you squeeze into your pupils a couple drops of the DigitalEyes solution, which serves as the ultra-high-speed conduit between your visual system and Mobilla's network. The network contains nearly infinite storage, processing, and bandwidth resources located at data centers throughout the world, along with full-motion, HyperHD video of Earth and the entire solar system. You, and billions of other Mobilla subscribers, can go anywhere you want on Earth, anytime, and arrange meetings with a growing list of people.

It can become an expensive habit. Earth-bound travel in the present, such as your trip to Paris, can now be done at a reasonable cost. Time travel to the past costs much more, depending on how far back in time you desire to go. So far, Mobilla's video database only goes back a couple hundred years, and the Resolution Reality Factor becomes increasingly degraded the farther back you go. You can also "travel" to the moon, Mars, and other planets, but at a much higher cost. Simulated travel into the future is still in R&D.

As you "return" from San Diego that night of 1/1/2101, your sense of reality is blurring together with Mobilla's virtual world. You can still sense the difference between the two, but it's becoming more difficult to distinguish between the present and the past, between the actual and the synthesized. They're not so different anymore.

■ ■ ■

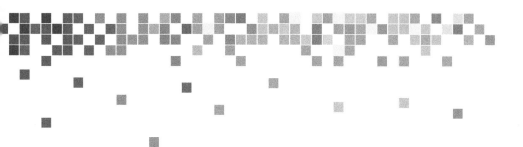

TECHNICAL GLOSSARY
AND ACRONYMS

Adaptive Bit Rate Streaming: Also called adaptive streaming, adaptive bit rate (ABR) streaming is becoming increasingly common for streaming video over the Internet. Multiple files are created for each piece of content, with each file encoded at a different bit rate and quality level. The software client then selects the appropriate file based on the consumer's instantaneous bandwidth. ABR streaming enables better and smoother overall video quality than previous Internet methods, similar to Variable Bit Rate (VBR) coding for digital television over satellite and cable.

Ad Insertion: The process of placing an advertisement into a television program such that the transitions between the program and the ad (and vice versa) appear seamlessly to the subscriber. In the digital television field, Digital Program Insertion (DPI) is the basic method of ad insertion, and there are two important Society of Cable Telecommunications Engineers (SCTE) DPI standards, SCTE 30 and SCTE 35. SCTE 35 standardizes cueing messages, while SCTE 30 standardizes the communications protocol between the ad server and splicer. With targeted ads, or addressable advertising, advertisements can reach more specific audiences, based on demographic or other subscriber-specific profiles. Ad insertion into certain VOD programs is becoming increasingly important, using dynamic ad insertion.

ADSL2+: Asymmetric Digital Subscriber Line Two Plus. An advanced DSL technique which uses more line bandwidth than its ADSL predecessor, enabling up to 25 Mbps downstream speeds over short distances (less than 3,000 feet from the DSLAM).

ATRC: The Advanced Television Research Consortium. An alliance of companies, comprising Philips, Thomson, Sarnoff, and NBC, which participated in the FCC advanced television testing process and the Grand Alliance.

ATSC: The Advanced Television Systems Committee, which adopted the Grand Alliance digital TV system to replace the original analog NTSC television standard.

Bandwidth: A quantitative measurement of signal transmission spectrum equal to the difference between the lower and upper frequencies of a frequency range. Hertz (Hz), or cycles per second, is the basic measurement unit of bandwidth. One megahertz, or 1 MHz, equals 1 million cycles per second. For example, the cable channel between 594 MHz and 600 MHz contains 6 MHz of bandwidth. In contrast to bandwidth, transmission speeds, or bit rates, are measured in bits per second (bps), kilobits per second (kbps), megabits per second (Mbps), or gigabits per second (Gbps). Depending on the modulation and forward error correction techniques used, bandwidth also represents the information-carrying capacity of a channel or frequency band. Video occupies much more bandwidth than audio or data, and HDTV video occupies four to five times the bandwidth of SDTV video.

BitTorrent: A peer-to-peer Internet protocol by which large files, such as movies or TV shows, can be downloaded from multiple simultaneous sources at efficient bit rates. The entire file must first be uploaded to one or more "seed" servers, and then can be downloaded by consumers ("clients") through various distributed "leech" or "peer" sites, each possessing only a portion of the overall file. There are legitimate and illegitimate uses of BitTorrent technology, depending on copyright infringement issues. The protocol was invented by Bram Cohen, founder of BitTorrent, Inc.

Blu-ray Disc: An HDTV optical disc format utilizing blue-violet lasers to read and write data. A single-layer Blu-ray disc can store 25 GB of data, while a dual-layer disc can store 50 GB of data. The Blu-ray format is compatible with the MPEG-2, MPEG-4 AVC, and VC-1 digital video coding standards, and handles resolutions up to 1920 x 1080 pixels.

C-band: A portion of the electromagnetic spectrum and a type of satellite and large dish which receives signals in the 4 GHz frequency range.

CBR (Constant Bit Rate): A method of digital video coding in which the bit rate stays the same over time. CBR coding is used in certain cases such as video-on-demand (VOD), Switched Digital Video (SDV), and Internet Protocol Television (IPTV).

CDN (Content Delivery Network): A managed system of Internet servers, including origin servers located in data centers and edge servers distributed closer to the end users of content. The objective of a CDN is to speed up the delivery of content relative to the public Internet. CDN companies such as Akamai and Limelight charge content providers based on peak bandwidth or quantity of data transferred per month, and they are also diversifying into related businesses such as Internet advertising.

CCAP (Converged Cable Access Platform): The new generation of cable headend Internet infrastructure products, superseding the CMTS and giving cable operators a unified Internet delivery platform for data, voice, video, and other Internet-based services.

CMTS (Cable Modem Termination System): DOCSIS-based cable headend Internet infrastructure products, comprising hardware and software, enabling cable operators to offer high-speed Internet and digital voice service to their subscribers.

Conditional Access: A system, including software and hardware, enabling content providers and content distributors to secure their signals, and allowing subscribers to have selective access to pay TV channels using encryption and key management techniques.

DBS (Direct Broadcast Satellite): A type of satellite and also a class of pay TV service operated by companies such as DirecTV and Dish Network in the United States and BSkyB in the United Kingdom. DBS satellites are high-power Ku-band satellites used to deliver television content directly to subscribers with satellite receive dishes and associated in-home electronics equipment such as set-top boxes. See also DTH.

Decryption: The decoding of a digital information stream using a cryptographic key; the opposite of encryption.

DigiCable: The brand name sometimes used for General Instrument's original digital cable system and associated products.

DigiCipher: GI/Motorola's brand name for its digital television communications system and associated products, as well as the brand used for the conditional access and encryption subsystem. DigiCipher I was GI's first-generation system, developed in the early 1990s. DigiCipher II was the company's second-generation MPEG-2 compatible system, developed in the mid-1990s. The conditional access system was later rebranded as MediaCipher.

Digital Television: A television delivery system in which video is digitized, compressed, and transported using digital transmission techniques such as modulation and forward error correction. Various other technologies are also typically incorporated such as service information, conditional access and encryption, and electronic program guides. SDTV and HDTV are two different formats of digital television involving different video resolutions. Digital Television is also used to refer to the viewing display (HDTV set) itself, along with associated internal electronics.

DOCSIS: Data Over Cable Service Interface Specification. The cable television standard for two-way data communications with subscribers using Internet Protocol (IP), QAM modulation, and forward error correction. Initially used for high-speed Internet data access, DOCSIS is now also used for digital cable telephony (Voice over Internet Protocol, or VoIP) and streaming video applications. DOCSIS 3.0 uses channel-bonding techniques to allow downstream Internet speeds of up to 100 Mbps. The DOCSIS 3.1 spec, released by CableLabs in October 2013, will eventually allow downstream speeds of 10 Gbps and upstream speeds of 1 Gbps. These high speeds will be enabled by channel bonding, Orthogonal Frequency Division Multiplexing (OFDM) of narrowband carriers used with higher-order QAM modulation (up to 4096 QAM), and Low Density Parity Check (LDPC) forward error correction coding.

DRM (Digital Rights Management): A system for determining, controlling, and managing the use or consumption of content by subscribers, such as how long or how many times consumers can view specific content, or on which and how many devices. Sometimes DRM is used interchangeably with conditional access (CA), but the distinction is that CA typically refers to a transport level of security (protection while the content is being sent), while DRM tends to have "persistent" rights qualities, which remain with the content as it is stored.

DS3: A 45 Mbps digital communications carrier, typically used for businesses.

DSL (Digital Subscriber Line): A general technology for transmitting data at high speeds over telecommunications carriers' copper wires. DSL typically uses Discrete Multi-Tone (DMT) modulation. With DSL, the transmission speed (bit rate per second) is highly dependent upon the distance of the home from the DSLAM. See ADSL2+ and VDSL2.

DSLAM (Digital Subscriber Line Access Multiplexer): A telecommunications carrier's infrastructure equipment which acts as the routing and multiplexing interface between the carrier's IP network and the individual access lines of its subscribers.

DTH (Direct to Home): A general category referring to satellite TV services providing signals directly to households equipped with dishes and receivers. DBS is a particular type of DTH service involving high-power satellites using specific frequencies.

DTV: Typically refers to over-the-air digital terrestrial broadcast signals, as distinct from television signals sent digitally over other media, such as satellite, cable, and fiber optics.

DVB (Digital Video Broadcasting): The European-based technical body which issues open, international standards for digital television applications over satellite, cable, terrestrial, and microwave media.

DVD (Digital Video Disc or Digital Versatile Disc): An optical disc storage technique which uses red lasers to read and write data. DVDs use MPEG-2 compressed video at Variable Bit Rates (VBR) for optimal storage efficiency and video quality. A DVD can store up to 4.7 GB on a single-layer disc or up to 8.5 GB on a dual-layer disc. The DVD format supports resolutions up to 720 x 576 pixels (that is, SDTV but not HDTV).

Encryption: The encoding and secure transformation of digital information, such as a digital television signal, using one or more digital keys.

The encryption key is used to transform the digital data in a specific mathematical or algorithmic manner. To decrypt the information, the user must have the correct electronic key(s).

FEC (Forward Error Correction): A digital communications technique involving adding bits to a digital signal such that a receiver can mathematically correct the errors caused by transmission.

FTTH (Fiber To The Home): Sometimes used interchangeably with FTTP (Fiber To The Premises). An advanced high-speed network architecture in which fiber optic cable extends all the way to the subscriber's home, allowing high-speed delivery of video, data, and voice.

GI (General Instrument Corporation): Leading broadband communications equipment company that developed the first digital television system, DigiCipher. In 1997, the company's name was changed to NextLevel Systems before reverting back to General Instrument several months later. After GI was acquired by Motorola in 2000, the business became known as Motorola Broadband Communications and later as Motorola Home. The unit was purchased by Google in 2012 as part of the acquisition of Motorola Mobility, and sold to Arris in 2013.

GHz: Gigahertz, or billions of cycles per second.

H.264: See MPEG-4.

H.265: See HEVC.

HDR (High Dynamic Range): Focused on brightness and contrast, HDR is the difference between the lightest and darkest tones in a video image. A higher dynamic range is more representative of the contrast between light and dark actually seen by the human visual system, but can also be used to create surreal images.

HDTV (High Definition Television): A form of digital television in which the video resolution is up to 1920 horizontal pixels by 1080 vertical pixels using interlace or progressive scanning (1080i or 1080P HDTV format), or 1280 horizontal pixels by 720 vertical pixels using progressive scanning (720P HDTV format). An HDTV signal typically occupies four times the bandwidth of an SDTV signal.

HD-VOD (High Definition Video-On-Demand): Video-on-demand in which HDTV content is digitally stored on network servers and streamed, upon request, in HDTV format to subscribers equipped with HDTV digital set-top boxes.

HEVC (High Efficiency Video Coding): The most recent international digital video compression standard, with a goal of being twice as bandwidth efficient as MPEG-4 AVC (H.264). HEVC is also called H.265. HEVC will be used for Ultra HD (4K) and other video applications.

HFC (Hybrid Fiber Coax): HFC is the predominant cable television system architecture. Fiber optic cable is used to transport signals from cable headends to local nodes, and then coaxial cable is utilized from the local nodes to individual homes. A local node typically supports 500 to 2,000 homes.

HVS (Human Visual System): A complex system involving the human brain and eyes working together to process and experience images, including synthesis of shapes, colors, orientation, motion, and depth.

IP (Internet Protocol): A communications protocol developed in the early 1980s. IP is the foundation of the Internet, a packet-based network of networks, incorporating routing and control information, for delivery of digital information (data, email, files, web pages, music, video, voice, etc.) over wired or wireless networks. IP is a layer 3 (network layer) protocol, typically used in conjunction with TCP (Transmission Control

Protocol), which is a layer 4 transport layer protocol (together, commonly referred to as TCP/IP).

IPTV (Internet Protocol Television): A type of digital television delivery system in which the digital video signals use IP transport all the way to the subscribers' set-top boxes. While typically associated with telco operators, cable operators can also provide "Cable IPTV" through their DOCSIS pipes.

ISP (Internet Service Provider): A company, such as Comcast or AT&T, which sells Internet connectivity and related services to consumers and businesses.

Ku-band: A portion of the electromagnetic spectrum and a type of satellite and dish receiving signals in the 12 GHz frequency band. There are medium-power Ku-band satellites, operating in the Fixed Service Satellite (FSS) band, and high-power satellites operating in the slightly higher frequency band of Broadcasting Satellite Services (BSS).

LTE (Long-Term Evolution): LTE, or 4G LTE, is the current standard for wireless communications to mobile devices over telecommunications carrier networks.

Mbps (Megabits per second): A digital data rate or speed measured in millions of bits per second. A typical 6 MHz digital cable channel, using 256 QAM modulation, carries 38.8 Mbps (38.8 million bits of information per second). The information can represent video, data, or voice.

MCPC (Multiple Channels Per Carrier): The predominant method of digital television delivery over satellite and cable, whereby two or more video services share a common bit stream and are modulated on a single RF carrier. See SCPC.

MHz: Megahertz, or millions of cycles per second. MHz is a unit of measurement of the bandwidth of a communications channel. For example, a US cable channel and a US terrestrial broadcast channel are both defined to contain 6 MHz of bandwidth.

MOOC (Massive Open Online Course): An educational class offered to the general population via digital video over the Internet. Also refers to a company aggregating and providing such online courses. Coursera, Udacity, and edX are the three primary MOOCs in the United States.

MPEG (Moving Picture Experts Group): A working group of the International Standards Organization (ISO) responsible for the development of standards for coded representation of digital video and audio.

MPEG-2: An International Standards Organization (ISO) audiovisual coding standard used by many digital television service providers around the world. MPEG-2 is also used on DVDs. The MPEG-2 video coding standard is independent of the MPEG-2 systems and transport stream standards.

MPEG-4: A family of International Standards Organization (ISO) audiovisual coding standards developed subsequently to the MPEG-2 standard. The most advanced MPEG-4 standard is MPEG-4 AVC (Advanced Video Coding), technically the same specification as the International Telecommunications Union (ITU) H.264 standard. MPEG-4 AVC is used by many service providers for HDTV signals, and also for much of the video traffic sent over the Internet.

MPEG-DASH: Moving Picture Experts Group, Dynamic Adaptive Streaming over HTTP (Hypertext Transport Protocol). MPEG-DASH is an international standard for streaming video over the Internet using the HTTP protocol, with the potential to replace similar proprietary methods such as Microsoft Smooth Streaming, Adobe Dynamic Streaming, and Apple HTTP Live Streaming (HLS). With MPEG-DASH, a video file is divided into short segments, each encoded at a different bit rate. The Internet client (inside a computer or Internet TV box) switches to a different segment depending on the user's instantaneous bandwidth, allowing more consistent and better quality video performance.

MUSE: Multiple sub-Nyquist Sampling Encoding. An analog HDTV system developed in the 1980s by NHK in Japan.

Network DVR: Network Digital Video Recorder. Instead of (or in addition to) a home-based DVR, a Network DVR stores digital television program files on network infrastructure servers. In one Network DVR scenario, a digital subscriber can start a program from the beginning, even if the beginning of the scheduled broadcast was missed. In another scenario, content is stored digitally in personalized network storage "lockers," with such storage based specifically on individual subscriber selection of particular programs. See also RS-DVR.

NTSC (National Television System Committee): Developed in the 1940s and 1950s, the US standard analog television waveform format incorporating composite color video, 525 lines of resolution, and interlace scanning of 60 fields per second. NTSC is also used in Canada, Japan, and other parts of the world. NTSC also refers to the original US committee that established the NTSC standard. The digital version of NTSC, containing similar video resolution, is called digital Standard Definition Television (see SDTV).

Over-The-Top (OTT) Internet: Refers to Internet video or Internet TV services which utilize the high-speed broadband data pipes of cable or telco networks. It is called "over-the-top" because the consumer receives the video service directly from the content provider, without a middleman distributor such as a cable operator reselling the content to the subscriber.

PAL (Phase Alternation by Line): An analog television standard used in many parts of Europe, Africa, and South America. The PAL standard incorporates color video, 625 lines of resolution, and interlace scanning of 50 fields per second. Another analog television standard, SECAM (Sequential Color with Memory), also has 625 lines of resolution at 50 fields per second. Variations on SECAM are used in France, Eastern Europe, and parts of Africa. The digital version of PAL, containing similar video resolution, is called digital Standard Definition Television (see SDTV).

Pixel: A picture element, the basic point or element of resolution on a video screen. More pixels per screen corresponds to higher resolution. An HDTV picture in the 1080-line format contains 1920 pixels per line, for a total of 2,073,600 pixels per frame of video.

QAM (Quadrature Amplitude Modulation): The modulation technique used for transmitting digital TV signals over cable television systems. QAM conveys digital information by continuously changing the amplitude of two out-of-phase carrier waves. For nearly error-free transmission, QAM techniques are combined with powerful forward error correction (FEC) algorithms. In a 256 QAM digital system, there are 8 bits per symbol, enabling 38.8 Mbps of information flow in a 6 MHz cable channel.

QPSK (Quadrature Phase Shift Keying): A phase modulation technique with four states, typically used for transmitting digital TV signals via communications satellites to DBS (direct broadcast satellite) subscribers or to cable or telco headends. QPSK modulation is combined with forward error correction (FEC) techniques for nearly error-free transmission. With QPSK, two information bits per symbol are transmitted. Many satellite TV broadcasters, including DirecTV, Dish Network, and HBO, now use a more advanced satellite modulation technique called 8PSK (phase modulation with eight states) for digital satellite television. Used in conjunction with turbo coding or Low Density Parity Check (LDPC) coding techniques, 8PSK has 3 bits per symbol, enabling much higher data rates through the same satellite transponder. The DVB standardized an 8PSK technique called DVB-S2.

RF (Radio Frequency): Communications over wireless or cable electromagnetic spectrum using modulation techniques. The frequency is expressed in thousands of cycles per second (kilohertz, kHz), millions per second (megahertz, MHz), or billions per second (gigahertz, GHz).

RS-DVR (Remote Storage Digital Video Recorder): The name that Cablevision Systems originally used for its Network DVR service. Each subscriber's digital video storage is located remotely in Cablevision's data centers instead of on the hard drive of the subscriber's digital cable box. Cablevision subsequently rebranded this service as Multi-Room DVR.

SA (Scientific Atlanta): A leading broadband communications equipment company acquired by Cisco in 2006.

SCPC (Single Channel Per Carrier): A type of digital television delivery in which only one video service is modulated on an RF carrier. See MCPC.

SDTV (Standard Definition Television): A form of digital television in which the resolution is up to 704 horizontal pixels by 480 vertical pixels (in NTSC countries such as the United States and Japan) or 704 horizontal pixels by 576 vertical pixels (in most PAL and SECAM countries).

SDV (Switched Digital Video): A digital TV delivery technology used by telco IPTV operators and some cable operators. With SDV, only the requested service comes into the home, as opposed to traditional cable where all linear channels are broadcast to all homes.

Statistical Multiplexing (statmux): A bandwidth-optimization technique in which digital television services sharing a common aggregate bit stream are deterministically allocated an instantaneous bit rate depending on the relative complexity of each service at any given time. With a statmux system, each underlying individual bit stream is coded at a Variable Bit Rate (VBR). Statmux increases channel efficiency farther beyond basic VBR since video complexity differs between the individual streams at any given time.

TCI (Tele-Communications, Inc.): TCI was the largest US cable operator in the 1980s and 1990s, run by John Malone, who led the cable industry into the digital television era. AT&T acquired TCI in late 1999, creating AT&T Broadband, and then Comcast acquired AT&T Broadband in 2002.

TCP (Transmission Control Protocol): Along with the Internet Protocol (IP), one of the two core communications protocols of the Internet, originally developed in the early 1980s.

3DTV: A television or video image which includes a depth-perception factor enabling viewers to see in three dimensions: horizontally, vertically, and with depth. Technologies in use today, in digital cinemas or home theaters, require the viewers to wear certain types of glasses. In the future, new "glasses-free" 3D technologies may become commercialized.

Threshold: A concept in communications technology measuring, in decibels (dB), the level at which the signal or carrier needs to exceed the noise in order for the receiver to obtain a good-quality signal. With a digital signal, the threshold is the level above which the receiver can get virtually all of the digital information bits intact, and below which the signal rapidly deteriorates to unwatchable video. This "all or nothing" effect of a digital signal is known as the digital "cliff."

TV Everywhere: The industry-wide brand name for the ability of multi-channel TV subscribers to receive content on multiple screens inside and outside the home. The subscribers are usually authenticated by technical means, enabling them to watch this growing pool of content for no additional charge on computers and mobile devices such as tablets and smartphones.

Ultra HD: The next generation of HDTV technology with much higher resolution than current HDTV. There are 4K and 8K versions of Ultra HD. The 4K resolution is 3840 horizontal pixels by 2160 vertical pixels (2160P), equal to four times the pixel count of 1080-line HDTV. The 8K version of Ultra HD has a resolution of 7680 horizontal pixels by 4320 vertical pixels (4320P), equal to sixteen times the pixel count of today's 1080-line HD.

UltraViolet: An Internet cloud-based digital content rights framework, whereby consumers can purchase a movie or TV show once and then watch it in the future on various compatible devices such as PCs, smart TVs, smartphones, tablets, and game machines.

VBR (Variable Bit Rate): A method of digital video coding in which the bit rate continuously changes over time. VBR is the optimal method of digital video coding since it represents the natural "peaks and valleys" of digital video, with scene complexity continuously changing over time. VBR allows the best video quality for any given average bit rate or storage capacity, and also ensures consistent video quality over time. Contrast with CBR.

VDSL2: Very-high-bit-rate Digital Subscriber Line Two. VDSL2 is the most recent DSL standard from the International Telecommunication Union (ITU). With VDSL2, downstream transmission speeds of up to 50 Mbps can be achieved for short distances from the DSLAM (1,000–2,000 feet). A more recent technique called VDSL2 Vectoring utilizes a method of crosstalk elimination, similar to noise cancellation, to achieve rates over 100 Mbps.

VideoCipher: The brand name of GI's original satellite TV encryption system and associated products, with scrambled analog video and encrypted digital audio. VideoCipher I, developed in 1983, was the company's first-generation system, used mainly by Major League Baseball and the CBS Television network. The second-generation VideoCipher II system, developed in the mid-1980s, was used by virtually all of the television content providers in the United States. The third-generation VideoCipher II Plus system (sometimes called VideoCipher RS, Renewable Security) was developed in the early 1990s to resolve the pervasive piracy problem with VideoCipher II.

VideoCipher Division: The name for GI's business unit in San Diego until the early 1990s.

VLSI (Very Large Scale Integration): An integrated circuit, or chip, usually made of silicon, with hundreds of thousands, or even millions or billions, of transistors. VLSI devices can be of a general-purpose nature (microprocessors), application specific, or customized. The VLSI group was also the internal name of GI's engineering group in San Diego that designed custom chips for internal products such as digital satellite and digital cable boxes.

VOD (Video-On-Demand): A digital television technology and service in which video content is stored in headend or Internet servers and then viewed on demand by consumers. Subscribers access the content whenever they want. With VOD, every stream is unique to a subscriber viewing session. HD-VOD uses roughly four times the bandwidth (per stream) of standard definition VOD. Content providers and advertisers generally prefer VOD to home DVR technology because with VOD they can prevent ad skipping.

VP9: Google's proprietary video codec designed to compete against the HEVC standard (H.265).

VSB (Vestigial Sideband): 8 VSB is the modulation method originated by Zenith. It was adopted by the Grand Alliance and the FCC for the ATSC digital terrestrial (over-the-air) broadcasting standard. Since it is an 8-level technique, 3 bits per symbol are transmitted (2^3), and the information rate, net of forward error correction, is about 19 Mbps through a 6 MHz VHF or UHF channel.

■ ■ ■

NOTES

CHAPTER 1. FROM CAMBRIDGE TO CALIFORNIA

1. Heller's MIT PhD thesis was titled "Sequential Decoding for Time Varying Phase Channels." Combining phase characteristics with error correction in a synergistic way, sequential decoding was one of the earliest channel coding techniques for achieving near-maximum transmission capacity through space while still correcting errors in the receiver of digitally transmitted information.

2. The vertical blanking interval (VBI) is the brief time required for the electron gun in an analog TV to move back up to the top of the screen. The VBI typically consists of 40 lines of the 525-line NTSC television standard.

CHAPTER 3. A NEW LIFE IN A FAST LANE

1. CableData was acquired by DST Systems in 1998.

CHAPTER 4. THE DAWN OF DIGITAL

1. Randall Sukow and Peter Lambert, "Compression: Changing the World of Television?" *Broadcasting* magazine, June 11, 1990.

CHAPTER 5. DIGICIPHER

1. Denise Gellene, "David Hubel, Nobel-Winning Scientist, Dies at 87," *New York Times*, September 25, 2013.

2. MHz stands for Megahertz, or a frequency of 1 million cycles per second.

3. Importantly, the Shannon Limit is a function of both the bandwidth (linearly) and the signal-to-noise ratio (logarithmically) of the communications channel. It is also characterized by a concept called "entropy," or the unpredictability of a random variable, and the concept of "redundancy," whereby extra bits of information can be added to the payload in order to ensure reliable transmission. The addition of these extra bits to the signal, allowing transmission errors to be mathematically corrected in the receiver, is called "forward error correction."

Chapter 7. Piracy and Cryptomania

1. Secret writing, or steganography, originally meant the hiding or concealment of written messages. In contrast, the objective of cryptography is to hide the meaning (as opposed to the existence) of a message or of information through the use of an encryption algorithm and one or more encryption keys, which are finite strings of digital data. A cipher is similar to, and often synonymous with, encryption.

2. Simon Singh, *The Code Book* (New York: Doubleday, 1999), 149–160.

Chapter 8. DBS, Still Just a Dream

1. Sarah Bartlett, "General Instrument Blindsides Comsat," *Fortune*, April 18, 1983.

2. Hughes's FCC license was at the highly desirable 101 degree west (longitude) orbital position, above the equator and directly south of the midpoint of the continental United States.

3. "A Look Back at 1990," *Satellite Business News,* November 1, 1990, http://www.satbiznews.com/90look.html.

Chapter 10. Technology LBO: Gold Mine or Oxymoron?

1. While Ted Forstmann used the word "wampum" pejoratively in the context of KKR, in early American history it derived from the Massachusett and Narragansett word for polished white beads, which the Native Americans in New England used for spiritual and romantic purposes. The European colonists used wampum as a form of currency for trade with the natives until the eighteenth century, its value established by convertibility into animal pelts.

Chapter 13. The Specter of MPEG

1. ANSI, the American National Standards Institute, is the technical body representing US companies in international standards activities. The US ANSI delegation, in turn, operates under the umbrella of MPEG and the International Standards Organization.

Chapter 14. The Mavericks of Nassau County

1. Mark Gunther, "Cablevision's New Frontier TV Maverick Chuck Dolan and His Son, Jim, Don't Get Much Respect. To Prove Their Skeptics Wrong, They Are Parting Ways," *Fortune*, June 14, 2004.

Chapter 15. Shrinking the Dish

1. An acronym for this early type of C-band elliptical satellite antenna was BUD, or "big, ugly dish."

2. Ku-band satellites utilize a 12 GHz downlink frequency range versus C-band's 4 GHz. GHz stands for gigahertz, a frequency of 1 billion cycles per second.

Chapter 16. Star Wars

1. GE acquired RCA in 1986 and then sold the RCA brand to French-owned Thomson Consumer Electronics in 1988. RCA Labs was transferred to SRI International and renamed David Sarnoff Research Center (Sarnoff Corporation). In 2000, Thomson acquired Technicolor, and in 2010 the combined entity's name was changed to Technicolor.

Chapter 17. All Roads Lead to San Diego

1. QPSK, or Quadrature Phase Shift Keying, was the method we had selected to modulate a digital satellite signal, while QAM, or Quadrature Amplitude Modulation, was the method we'd determined would be best for cable. The reason for this distinction is that the signal-to-noise ratio is much lower for satellite communications than for cable. (See Chapter 5, Note 3 on the Shannon Limit.) As a result, more bits per Hz can be transmitted over cable versus satellite. Satellite transponder bandwidths are much larger than cable and terrestrial broadcast bandwidths (24 Hz and higher versus 6 MHz), compensating for the bits/Hz imbalance.

Chapter 18. The King of Cable

1. Trgyve Myhren, *The Cable Center Interview of John Malone*, October 22, 2001, https://www.cablecenter.org/m-o-listings/john-malone.html.

2. Susan Gonzalez, "Communications Mogul John Malone Offers Advice to Students: 'Be Willing To Take Risks,'" *Yale Bulletin & Calendar*, October 18–25, 1999, http://www.yale.edu/opa/arc-ybc/v28.n9/story2.html.

3. Thomas P. Southwick, *Distant Signals: How Cable TV Changed the World of Telecommunications* (Overland Park, Kansas: Primedia Intertec, 1999), 143.

4. Twenty years later, in January 2013, Gore would receive his own share of criticism in the media business when he sold his Current TV channel for $500 million to Qatar-based Al Jazeera, personally netting $100 million.

5. Andrew Kupfer, "The No. 1 in Cable TV has Big Plans: John Malone's Tele-Communications Inc. is the World's Largest Owner of Cable TV Systems. Already a Demi-billionaire, He Now Wants to Rule the Information Highway," *Fortune*, June 28, 1993.

6. Charlie Rose, *Interview of Josh Sapan*, KPBS, July 17, 2013.

Chapter 19. TCI Takes Charge

1. After the corporate strategy meeting, over a drink at the cocktail party, I had a conversation with Rumsfeld that sticks in my mind. In 1992, the Bosnian War was raging with reports of ethnic cleansing between Muslim Bosniaks, Christian Serbs, and Catholic Croats, and there were heated political discussions occurring in Washington DC and Europe regarding whether the United States or NATO should intervene. Curious about his opinion, I asked Rumsfeld what he thought. He said, "With centuries-old ethnic conflicts, we have to be really careful what we do." When we entered the second Iraq War more than a decade later, with Rumsfeld as Secretary of Defense, I often thought back to that conversation and wondered what he might have said to George W. Bush and Dick Cheney about the likelihood of ethnic warfare between Shiites, Sunnis, and Kurds, especially given his famous saying, "It is easier to get into something than to get out of it."

Chapter 20. The Race to Market

1. Star TV was a 1991 joint venture between Li Ka-Shing and Hutchison Whampoa. Richard Li, son of Li Ka-Shing, was Star TV's founder and CEO until Murdoch acquired the business in 1993.

Chapter 21. A Healthy Competition Gets Vicious

1. General Instrument Corporation, "VideoCipher Makes History with DigiCipher HDTV," *GI VideoCipher Division Employee Newsletter*, Summer 1992.

2. Joel Brinkley, *Defining Vision: The Battle for the Future of Television* (New York: Harcourt Brace, 1997), 185–196.

Chapter 22. MPEG World Tour

1. Dan Stanzione, Bob Stanzione's older brother, would become the eighth president of Bell Labs, from 1995–1999, during which he completed the 1996 spin-off of Lucent (and most of Bell Labs) from AT&T. Arun Netravali would later succeed Dan

Stanzione as Bell Labs' ninth president, from 1999–2001, before becoming Lucent's CTO and then its chief scientist. Bob Stanzione would later become CEO of cable equipment supplier Arris, which would acquire GI (Motorola Home) from Google.

CHAPTER 23. THE BEST WESTERN SHOW

1. Mark Robichaux, "Need More TV? TCI May Offer 500 Channels," *Wall Street Journal,* December 4, 1992.

2. Ibid.

CHAPTER 24. BEHIND THE SCENES

1. "TCI's Malone on the Digital TV Age," *Satellite Business News,* January 13, 1993.

2. Peter Lambert, "Comcast Joins TCI on GI Bandwagon," *Multichannel News,* February 22, 1993.

CHAPTER 25. CONTENT IS KING

1. Gary Kim, "Star TV, Rainbow Make Move to Digital, HBO Weeks Away from Test," *Multichannel News,* July 20, 1992.

2. Peter Lambert, "Digital Revolution Sweeps the World," *Multichannel News,* March-April 1993.

3. "BBC World Service Chooses DigiCipher," *World Broadcast News,* May 1993.

4. Thomas A. Stewart, "General Instrument: How a High-Tech Bet Paid Off Big," *Fortune,* November 1, 1993.

CHAPTER 26. FROM DIGITAL TV TO HIGH-SPEED DATA

1. The Mosaic web browser predated the Netscape Navigator. Netscape co-founder Marc Andreessen was the connective tissue—he led the software development team that created Mosaic at the National Center for Supercomputing Applications, which is part of the University of Illinois at Urbana-Champaign.

CHAPTER 27. THE TROJAN HORSE OF SOUND

1. Dolby used the numbering format of "5.1" channels for its six-channel surround sound system. The six channels are left, center, and right channels adjacent to the TV set; rear left and rear right channels behind the viewer; and a sub-woofer, low-frequency channel, designating the sixth channel (after the decimal point).

2. Dolby's noise-reduction technology was adopted by the music industry in the 1960s and 1970s for analog tape machines. Movie studios selected Dolby's surround sound system in the 1970s, and Dolby developed a home theater surround sound solution in the 1980s. The theater in Hollywood, California, where the Academy Awards are presented each year, will be called the Dolby Theater through 2032. Ray Dolby died at his San Francisco home on September 12, 2013, at the age of eighty.

3. The MPEG-2 transport (systems) specification, dealing with issues like packet size, headers, and audio/video synchronization, is independent of the MPEG-2 video coding specification. They are considered two separate standards, even though they are often used together.

CHAPTER 28. THE GRAND ALLIANCE

1. Brian Santo, "FCC Urges 'Grand Alliance' for US HDTV," *EE Times*, January 1, 1993.

2. Edmund L. Andrews, "Top Rivals Agree on Unified System for Advanced TV," *New York Times*, May 25, 1993.

3. William J. Cook, "A Clear Picture for TV," *US News & World Report*, June 7, 1993.

CHAPTER 29. THE FIRST CONSUMER DIGITAL TV SERVICES

1. Johnnie L. Roberts and Mark Robichaux, "Probe of General Instrument Resulted in Large Part from Viacom, TCI Feud," *Wall Street Journal*, March 10, 1994.

2. Edmund L. Andrews, "Antitrust Inquiry on Cable Gear, General Instrument's Dominance at Issue," *New York Times*, March 9, 1994.

CHAPTER 30. BICOASTAL BICENTRICITY

1. Kevin Kelly and Peter Coy, "Infobahn Warrior, Why General Instrument Could End Up as a Highway Heavyweight," *Business Week*, August 8, 1994.

2. After Jim Bunker left the company as president of the VideoCipher Division, Hal Krisbergh became president of the two combined divisions. The Jerrold and VideoCipher names were dropped in favor of GI Communications Division, encompassing the Hatboro and San Diego operations as well as the manufacturing facilities in Taiwan, Mexico, Puerto Rico, and the United States.

CHAPTER 31. DOESN'T "OPEN" MEAN "FREE"?

1. An essential patent is one which is unavoidably infringed by implementing a technical standard or specification.

2. Leslie Ellis, "MPEG Licensing Group Starts Road Show," *Multichannel News*, July 14, 1997.

CHAPTER 32. YET ANOTHER COMPETITIVE HURDLE

1. "Competing Digital Groups Hold Meetings on the Same Day," *TVRO Dealer*, December 1994.

CHAPTER 33. YOU GO LEFT, I'LL GO RIGHT

1. Thomas P. Southwick, "Cable Television: The First 50 Years," *Cable World* magazine supplement, November 1998.

2. The predominant cable architecture, utilizing fiber optics from the cable headend to a neighborhood node, and then coaxial cable from the node to the homes, is known as Hybrid Fiber/Coax (HFC). TCI did its own share of HFC upgrades, especially in its urban and suburban systems, even though the company used its satellite-based digital Headend in the Sky for execution of its digital cable TV rollout.

3. Time Warner, "Time Warner Cable's Full Service Network Launches New Services," press release, November 29, 1995.

4. The Trellis Coded Modulation technique was invented by Gottfried Ungerboeck in the 1970s. Ungerboeck was an Austrian engineer working at IBM Zurich Research Laboratory. Frustrated by IBM's unwillingness to enter the communications chip business, he joined Broadcom in 1998.

5. With 64 QAM, 6 bits can be sent per digital "symbol" of information (2^6), while 256 QAM allows 8 bits per symbol (2^8). Combined with different symbol rates and forward error correction codes, GI devised a way for this increase in symbol density to translate into 44 percent more digital information throughput per 6 MHz digital cable channel.

6. DVB's digital cable transmission standard became known as ITU J.83 Annex A (ITU J.83A), while GI's was designated ITU J.83 Annex B (ITU J.83B). ITU stands for the International Telecommunications Union.

CHAPTER 34. TWO HENRYS AND A NEW CHIP

1. Bethany McClean, "Sex, Lies and Underground Lairs, Dr. Nicholas and Mr. Hyde," *Vanity Fair*, November 2008.

2. General Instrument Corporation, "General Instrument Announces Royalty-Free Licensing of 64/256 QAM/FEC Technology," press release, November 6, 1996.

CHAPTER 35. SITTING IN (HDTV) LIMBO

1. Edmund L. Andrews and Joel Brinkley, "The Fight for Digital TV's Future," *New York Times*, January 22, 1995.

2. Ibid.

3. Joel Brinkley, *Defining Vision: The Battle for the Future of Television* (New York: Harcourt Brace, 1997), 382.

4. Chris McConnell, "HDTV Model Station Kicks Off," *Broadcasting & Cable*, August 12, 1996.

5. Reed Hundt, "A New Paradigm for Digital Television" (white paper, September 30, 1996).

CHAPTER 36. GAMBLER HITS THE JACKPOT

1. Sam Marshall, "Biography of Charlie Ergen," *Encyclopedia for Business,* 2nd edition.

2. Peter Kafka, video interview of Charlie Ergen, "All Things Digital, D: Dive Into Media" (event, Ritz Carlton, Laguna Niguel, California, February 11, 2013).

3. "A Look Back at 1996," *Satellite Business News,* February 28, 1996, http://www.satbiznews.com/96look.html.

CHAPTER 37. TROUBLE IN PARADISE

1. Robert B. Shirley, "Ha Tien, Entrance to the Giang Thanh River, Gulf of Siam East of An Thoi," accessed February 15, 2013, http://www.pcf45.com/sealords/hatien/hatien.html.

2. To minimize confusion, the company name "GI" will continue to be used in this book instead of "NextLevel Systems." The company name reverted back to "General Instrument" in December 1997.

CHAPTER 38. THE MEGADEAL

1. "Tyco's Ed Breen: During a Crisis, 'Spend a Lot of Time on the Big Swings,'" *Wharton Leadership Digest,* interview transcript published February 13, 2013, accessed October 31, 2014, http://wlp.wharton.upenn.edu/LeadershipDigest/tyco-ed-breen.cfm.

CHAPTER 40. THREE'S A CROWD

1. United States of America, Department of Justice, Antitrust Division v. Prime-Star, Inc., et al., lawsuit filed in the United States District Court for the District of Columbia, May 12, 1998.

CHAPTER 41. LET'S DO IT AGAIN!

1. DOCSIS (pronounced "dok´ sis") is an acronym for the Data Over Cable System Interface Specifications.

CHAPTER 43. CRACKING THE HDTV EGG

1. The idea that broadcast spectrum should be licensed for small fees, on a first-come, first-served basis, to entities that met certain legal requirements, was first deemed economically illogical by Nobel Prize–winning economist Ronald Coase. In October 1959, Coase published an article titled "The Federal Communications Commission," in the *Journal of Law & Economics,* arguing that the FCC would better serve the economy by auctioning broadcast spectrum to the highest bidder, letting the winner determine the spectrum's use.

2. Standard definition (SDTV) content can be upconverted to HDTV content by methods such as pixel interpolation. A pixel, or picture element, is a physical point in an image. Pixel interpolation involves estimating a new pixel in between two actual pixels, simulating an increase in resolution but not representing actual resolution or true HDTV.

3. Rodolfo La Maestra, "HDTV Adoption—Not as High in Number of HDTV Sets," *HDTV Magazine* (using Consumer Electronics Association data), February 28, 2013.

CHAPTER 44. SEAMLESS MOBILITY

1. Chris Galvin was the grandson of Motorola founder Paul Galvin and the son of former CEO Robert Galvin.

CHAPTER 46. THE NEW KING OF CABLE

1. Bob Fernandez, "On Eve of His Departing, Comcast's Brodsky Looks Back on His Many Wins," *Philadelphia Inquirer*, May 1, 2011.

2. Meg James, "Comcast Goes All In on NBCUniversal," *Los Angeles Times*, February 13, 2013.

CHAPTER 47. I WANT MY HDTV

1. Eric A. Taub, "HDTV's Acceptance Picks Up Pace as Prices Drop and Networks Sign On," *New York Times*, March 31, 2003.

2. Ibid.

3. Ibid.

4. Cablevision acquired this license for thirteen DBS satellite transponders at the 61.5 degree west orbital position through a prior deal with Loral and Continental Satellite Corporation.

CHAPTER 48. VOOM

1. Rainbow 1 was launched by International Launch Services (ILS) and Lockheed Martin.

2. The Ka-band uses downlink frequencies in the 18 GHz range, as opposed to Ku-band, which uses the 12 GHz range. Both can use high-power satellites, enabling small receive dishes.

3. Geraldine Fabrikant and Andrew Ross Sorkin, "Cablevision's Founder Loses Voom Unit Fight to Son," *New York Times*, January 19, 2005.

CHAPTER 50. POWER TO THE CONSUMER

1. "Congressional Hearings on Home Recording of Copyrighted Works," April 12, 13, 14, June 24, August 11, September 22 and 23, 1982 (testimony of Jack Valenti, president of the MPAA).

CHAPTER 51. VOD, THE DVR, AND EVERYTHING ON DEMAND

1. The home DVR was more obviously protected by the Supreme Court's "fair use" ruling in the 1984 Sony Betamax case.

2. The Solicitor General is part of the US Department of Justice. Elena Kagan was Solicitor General prior to her 2010 Supreme Court appointment by President Barack Obama.

3. Nielsen's C3 commercial ratings measure consumers' viewing of commercials within TV programs from the original live airing of the show until three days later, including DVR playback and VOD viewing.

Chapter 52. MotoGoogle

1. From this point forward in this book, "Motorola Home" and "GI" are used interchangeably.

Chapter 53. The White Knight

1. nCUBE was an early VOD server company funded personally by Oracle's Larry Ellison. C-Cor acquired nCUBE in 2005 for $89 million.

2. In 2009, Arris acquired digital video encoder company EGT. Later that year, Arris acquired Digeo for $20 million. Digeo had been funded by Paul Allen to develop Moxi, an advanced digital set-top box. Then, in 2011, Arris acquired switched digital video company BigBand Networks for $172 million, another bargain considering BigBand was sitting on a $119 million cash position from its 2007 IPO.

3. In January 2014, Imagine Communications was acquired by Harris Broadcast. Harris Broadcast subsequently split into two companies: Imagine Communications (digital video solutions) and GatesAir (TV/radio transmitters).

Chapter 54. Digital Planet

1. Digital TV Research, "Digital TV Homes to Triple in Sub-Saharan Africa," press release, January 8, 2014.

2. Charles Dolan interview, "Memories of the Future," *Multichannel News* supplement, September 18, 2000.

Chapter 55. Digital Dividends: More Content, Better Quality, and Greater Competition

1. Note that 100 percent of DirecTV, Dish Network, Verizon FiOS, and AT&T U-Verse subscribers receive digital signals. In total, approximately 90 percent of US cable subscribers received digital signals in 2014.

Chapter 56. Today's Media Kingpins

1. Laura Martin, "Video in 2014: Catching Fire," Needham & Company (research paper, January 10, 2014).

2. In the stock-for-stock transaction, Time Warner Cable shareholders will receive 2.875 Comcast shares for each share of Time Warner Cable owned. Comcast shares closed at $55.24 on February 12, 2014 (the day the companies agreed to merge), implying a price of $158.82 per share for Time Warner Cable's 284.9 million outstanding shares, for a total of $45.2 billion. The actual purchase price, however, will depend on Comcast's stock price on the day the deal closes, assuming it receives regulatory approval, anticipated in the first half of 2015.

3. In August 2009, the U.S. Court of Appeals for the DC Circuit rejected the FCC cap of 30 percent national multichannel TV ownership as "arbitrary and capricious," given the increase in video competition from satellite and telco companies.

4. Susan Karlin, "Practically Subversive," *Pennsylvania Gazette*, May/June 2013.

5. Jeff Shell became president of Comcast's cable programming group in 2005, and is now chairman of Universal Filmed Entertainment.

6. Walter Isaacson, *Steve Jobs* (New York: Simon & Schuster, 2011), 507–509.

7. Discovery Communications, "The Hub Network to Become Discovery Family Channel on October 13," press release, September 25, 2014.

8. Prior to joining Charter as CEO in 2012, Tom Rutledge was Cablevision's chief operating officer; before that he was president of Time Warner Cable.

9. Linear channels are programming services scheduled in advance, with certain programs or events broadcast at specific times, as opposed to content that is available on-demand.

10. Comcast agreed to adhere to the FCC Open Internet Order's "no blocking" and "no unreasonable discrimination" Internet rules until January 2018 as part of its acquisition of NBCUniversal, expanded by its Time Warner Cable deal. AT&T has similarly agreed to comply for three years after the close of its acquisition of DirecTV. Net neutrality is discussed further in Chapter 66.

Chapter 57. TV Everywhere

1. Authentication is the technical process through which service providers verify that the subscribing household is legitimate. By sharing passwords with people outside

the family or household, however, it is possible for nonsubscribers to also receive TV Everywhere content.

2. Rob Golum, "Fox Says Record Super Bowl Audience Revised Up to 112.2 Million," February 4, 2014, *Bloomberg*, http://www.bloomberg.com/news/2014-02-04/fox-says-record-super-bowl-audience-revised-up-to-112-2-million.html. On February 1, 2015, the average audience for NBC's Super Bowl XLIX, during which the New England Patriots defeated the Seattle Seahawks 28–24, was estimated to be 114.4 million.

3. "Fox Breaks TV, Streaming Records with Super Bowl XLVIII," February 3, 2014, http://www.foxsports.com/nfl/story/super-bowl-xlviii-ratings-record-020314.

4. Adobe Systems, "US Digital Video Benchmark, Adobe Digital Index, Q1 2014," http://www.cmo.com/content/dam/CMO_Other/ADI/Q12014_VideoBenchmark/Q12014_VideoBenchmark.pdf.

CHAPTER 58. NEW KIDS ON THE BLOCK

1. Stuart Elliott, "PBS Seeks Web Sponsors, but Big Bird Still Won't Sing Jingles," *New York Times*, May 6, 2014.

2. Reed Hastings and David Wells, *Netflix Q4 14 Letter to Shareholders*, January 20, 2015.

3. In Scandinavia (Sweden, Finland, Denmark, and Norway), HBO Nordic is distributed over-the-top at around $10 per month. HBO has announced an over-the-top Internet service to be launched in the United States in 2015, separate from its TV Everywhere HBO Go service.

4. YouTube, "Statistics," https://www.youtube.com/yt/press/statistics.html, accessed October 24, 2014.

5. Ben Sisario, "What's Billboard's No. 1? Now YouTube Has a Say," *New York Times*, February 20, 2013.

6. Brooks Barnes, "Amazon and a Mattel Unit Plan a 'Content Hub' Focusing on Children," *New York Times*, June 2, 2014.

7. Miguel Bustillo, "Wal-Mart Re-enters Digital Downloading of Movies with Purchase of Vudu," *Wall Street Journal*, February 23, 2010.

8. Alibaba completed its initial public offering on September 18, 2014. The deal was priced at $68 per share, raising $21.8 billion in cash for Alibaba and valuing the company at $168 billion. Yahoo's stake in Alibaba was worth around $35 billion,

representing over 80 percent of Yahoo's market capitalization. On its first day of trading on the New York Stock Exchange, Alibaba's market cap quickly blew through the $200 billion barrier. The total amount raised for Alibaba (and some selling shareholders such as Yahoo) was increased the next day to $25 billion, using the underwriters' "green shoe" option of buying additional shares to satisfy high investor demand, making it the biggest IPO of all time.

CHAPTER 59. TECH JOCKEYS IN THE LIVING ROOM

1. Another corporate example of mixing electronics with content occurred with Matsushita (Panasonic) and Universal Studios. In 1990, Matsushita, Sony's Japanese consumer electronics competitor, acquired MCA/Universal Studios for $6.6 billion. Matsushita sold Universal to The Seagram Company in 1995, which sold it in 2000 to French company Vivendi. In 2004, Vivendi sold Universal to General Electric, which already owned NBC. Finally, GE sold a controlling interest in NBCUniversal to Comcast in 2011, and sold the remainder to Comcast in 2013.

2. Brian Chen and Quentin Hardy, "Verizon Plans to Buy Intel Media Division to Expand Its Television Services," *New York Times*, January 22, 2014.

3. Steven Millward, "Xiaomi to Invest $1B in Content to Make Its Smart TV More Appealing," *Tech in Asia*, November 4, 2014.

CHAPTER 61. SPORTS, THE GREAT DIVIDE

1. CPM is the acronym for Cost Per Thousand viewers. Along with Nielsen ratings, CPM is an essential metric in the TV advertising business, measuring advertisers' cost of reaching viewers in the hope of influencing their buying behavior.

2. Eric Chemi, "Super Bowl Ad Insanity Explained in Six Charts," *Bloomberg Businessweek*, January 20, 2014.

3. In 2001 and 2002, ESPN Broadband was the first customer of Aerocast, the broadband streaming video start-up funded by Liberty Media and Motorola. ESPN Broadband morphed into ESPN360 in 2005 and then evolved into ESPN3 in 2011.

4. Brian Stelter, "M.L.B. Unit Buys Rights to Broadcast Live Concert," *New York Times*, August 26, 2013.

5. Ron Sirak, "The Fox and The Peacock," *Golf Digest*, November 2013.

6. Kurt Badenhausen, "The World's 100 Highest-Paid Athletes 2014," *Forbes*, June 11, 2014.

7. NBC Sports, "Team USA-Canada Olympic Men's Hockey Semifinal Highest-Rated Hockey Ever on NBCSN & Leads Network to Record Weekday Daytime Viewership," press release, February 22, 2014.

8. NBC Sports, "NBCUniversal's Unprecedented Coverage of 2014 Sochi Games Reaches More Americans Via More Platforms Than Any Winter Olympics," press release, February 25, 2014.

9. James Andrew Miller, Steve Eder, and Richard Sandomir, "College Football's Most Dominant Player? It's ESPN," *New York Times*, August 24, 2013.

10. Ben Strauss, "The Big Ten's Bigger Footprint," *New York Times*, December 1, 2013.

11. Estimated by Nate Silver, writer, statistician, and editor-in-chief of *FiveThirtyEight* (ESPN blog).

12. Adam Gajo, "Big Ten Leads Conferences in Total Revenue in Fiscal 2012, Despite Drought in National Championships," SNL Kagan research, January 17, 2014.

CHAPTER 62. CONTENT PRICE INFLATION

1. Joe Flint, "CBS Fight with Time Warner Cable Shows Dinosaurs Are Still Scary," *Los Angeles Times*, September 3, 2013.

2. Cable One is owned by Graham Holdings Company, formerly known as The Washington Post Company. The company's name was changed in 2013 after the Graham family sold the *Washington Post* newspaper to Jeff Bezos, founder and CEO of Amazon.

3. Robin Flynn, "Rising Retransmission Fees: The Potential Impact on Cable MSO Video Margins," SNL Kagan research, November 2013.

CHAPTER 63. CORD CUTTING

1. Mark Twain's actual quote was: "The report of my death was an exaggeration." In 1897, he wrote this statement in a letter to a *New York Journal* reporter after a cousin's illness was misconstrued as his own.

2. Nielsen Holdings, *Shifts In Viewing: The Cross-Platform Report Q2 2014*, September 2014.

3. Experian Marketing Services, *Cross-Device Video Analysis*, April 21, 2014.

4. Nielsen Holdings, *The Nielsen March 2013 Cross-Platform Report: Free to Move Between Screens*, March 8, 2013.

5. The millennial generation is typically defined as people born from the early 1980s through the turn of the century. The US Census Bureau estimates this demographic will be 26 percent of the US population in 2015.

CHAPTER 64. CONTENT PRICING AND PACKAGING

1. Ross Miller, "Biohacking Meets 'The O.C.' in This Trailer for BitTorrent's Sci-Fi 'Children of the Machine,'" *The Verge*, August 19, 2014.

2. "Floor Remarks by Senator John McCain Introducing New A La Carte Cable Bill," May 9, 2013, http://www.mccain.senate.gov/public/index.cfm/floor-statements?ID=8a43ba62-920c-475e-b15e-f15273e5d466.

CHAPTER 65. SPEED AND COMPETITION IN THE BROADBAND FUTURE

1. The seventeen largest US broadband ISPs had more than 51 million cable modem subscribers and more than 35 million telco (DSL or fiber) Internet subscribers as of September 30, 2014. Another 6 million broadband subscribers were connected to smaller cable or telco ISPs. Source: Leichtman Research Group, "About 700,000 Add Broadband in the Third Quarter of 2014," press release, November 18, 2014.

2. Alistair Barr and Andy Pasztor, "Google Invests in Satellites to Spread Internet Access," *Wall Street Journal*, June 1, 2014.

3. The FCC is authorizing more unlicensed WiFi spectrum in the newer 5 GHz frequency band.

CHAPTER 66. NETWORK NEUTRALITY AND THE OPEN INTERNET

1. The FCC's regulatory authority over common carriers comes from Title II of the Communications Act of 1934. This law, enacted by President Franklin D. Roosevelt, also created the FCC.

2. Jeff Sommer, "Defending the Open Internet," *New York Times*, May 11, 2014.

3. The FCC is relying on its presumed authority under Section 706 of the Telecommunications Act of 1996.

4. Netflix also has its own video Content Distribution Network (CDN), called Open Connect, which provides direct connectivity and settlement-free peering at various Internet exchange hubs. But Comcast and most other major ISPs have not agreed to use this method of interfacing to Netflix.

5. Sandvine, *Global Internet Phenomena Report, 2H 2014*, https://www.sandvine.com/downloads/general/global-internet-phenomena/2014/2h-2014-global-internet-phenomena-report.pdf, accessed December 24, 2014.

6. Netflix, Inc., *Netflix ISP Speed Index*, November 2014, http://ispspeedindex.netflix.com/usa.

CHAPTER 67. ULTRA HD (4K)

1. "4K" refers to the nearly 4,000 horizontal pixels, or picture elements, per line on a display (the actual number is 3,840). This is twice as many pixels per line as the 1,920 horizontal pixels in the 1080i (interlace) or 1080P (progressive) versions of HDTV. There is also an 8K version of Ultra HD with 7,680 (nearly 8,000) horizontal pixels.

2. The new High Efficiency Video Coding (HEVC) standard is generally matched with the Ultra HD 4K format in order to produce Ultra HD files or signals at a reasonable bit rate. Compressing Ultra HD with the older MPEG-2 or MPEG-4 AVC standards would be too inefficient from a bandwidth perspective.

3. A similar phenomenon has occurred with 1080P (1080 lines progressively scanned), which is twice the video resolution of 1080i (interlace scanning). Most 1080P content on Blu-ray discs has superior video quality relative to the 1080P content streamed by Netflix or YouTube. Blu-ray discs have the luxury of immense storage capacity, so the studios don't have to compress the video as much and can therefore use high bit rates and maintain excellent quality. In contrast, Internet content providers such as Netflix are constrained by the communications bandwidth of their broadband ISPs, so they compress the 1080P content to a much greater extent than Blu-ray does.

4. The field of High Dynamic Range (HDR) for computer graphics and computer-generated imagery (CGI) originated in the early 2000s with the pioneering work of Greg Ward, software consultant, and Paul Debevec of the USC Institute for Creative Technologies.

CHAPTER 68. THE PERPETUAL DRUMBEAT OF TECHNOLOGY

1. HTTP is a basic method by which information is exchanged or transferred over the Internet. It is used for adaptive bit rate video streaming in lieu of other Internet streaming protocols such as the Real-time Transport Protocol (RTP) and the Real Time Streaming Protocol (RTSP).

2. Erik Gruenwedel, "UltraViolet Accounts Top 19 Million," *Home Media Magazine,* September 12, 2014.

Chapter 69. Everything Connects

1. The Digital Cinema Initiatives specifications include two resolutions: 2K or 4K. The 2K resolution (2048 horizontal pixels × 1080 vertical pixels) is similar to today's highest home HDTV resolution (1920 × 1080), while 4K is about four times higher in resolution (4096 × 2160 pixels), similar to the new Ultra HD format.

2. Motion Picture Association of America, Inc., *Theatrical Market Statistics 2013*, http://www.mpaa.org/wp-content/uploads/2014/03/MPAA-Theatrical-Market-Statistics-2013_032514-v2.pdf, accessed November 9, 2014.

3. Chip Brown, "The Operatic Reign of Peter Gelb," *New York Times Magazine*, March 24, 2013.

4. Trey Popp, "MOOC U.," *Pennsylvania Gazette*, April 2013.

5. Diane Cardwell, "At Newark Airport, the Lights Are On, and They're Watching You," *New York Times*, February 17, 2014.

6. Eric Schmitt, "Drones in Niger Reflect New US Tack on Terrorism," *New York Times*, July 11, 2013.

7. In 2004 and 2005, Voom's Ultra HD fashion channel was delivered in the 1080i high definition format using GI/Motorola encoders, and had no relationship to the technology called Ultra HD (4K), which didn't exist at the time.

8. Stephanie Clifford, "Via Video, Front-Row Seat," *New York Times*, February 21, 2013.

Chapter 70. Going Social

1. Liz Gannes and Peter Kafka, "Look Who Else Is Joining Google to Back Magic Leap, the Secret 'Augmented Reality' Startup (Updated)," *Re/code*, October 20, 2014.

2. In 2014, Snapchat settled charges with the Federal Trade Commission related to the company's deceptive promises to users that its images truly disappear. In fact, there were instances and methods by which these pictures could be captured and stored indefinitely. The FTC complaint alleged other privacy violations as well, and Snapchat agreed to be audited by an independent company for the next twenty years, an attempt to ensure that its privacy commitments are honored.

3. Ellis Hamburger, "This Is Bolt, Instagram's New Messaging App," *The Verge*, July 29, 2014.

INDEX

ABOUT THE AUTHOR

Marc Tayer joined General Instrument's New York corporate headquarters in 1985 and transferred to its San Diego–based VideoCipher Division in 1987. Two years later, he was appointed core team leader and product manager for GI's new digital television project, a role for which he received an Emmy Award. Tayer served as vice president of global marketing upon GI's acquisition by Motorola  in 2000. He then co-founded two digital video start-ups, while working for Cablevision's Voom HDTV venture along the way. He received his BA from Williams College and his MBA from The Wharton School of the University of Pennsylvania.